JOHANN CORNIES, THE MENNONITES, AND RUSSIAN COLONIALISM IN SOUTHERN UKRAINE

Johann Cornies, the Mennonites, and Russian Colonialism in Southern Ukraine

JOHN R. STAPLES

UNIVERSITY OF TORONTO PRESS
Toronto Buffalo London

© University of Toronto Press 2024
Toronto Buffalo London
utorontopress.com

ISBN 978-1-4875-4916-9 (cloth)   ISBN 978-1-4875-4917-6 (EPUB)
                                 ISBN 978-1-4875-4918-3 (PDF)

Tsarist and Soviet Mennonite Studies

Library and Archives Canada Cataloguing in Publication

Title: Johann Cornies, the Mennonites, and Russian colonialism in southern
    Ukraine / John R. Staples.
Names: Staples, John Roy, 1961– author.
Series: Tsarist and Soviet Mennonite studies.
Description: Series statement: Tsarist and Soviet Mennonite studies |
    Includes bibliographical references and index.
Identifiers: Canadiana (print) 2023046775X | Canadiana (ebook) 20230467857 |
    ISBN 9781487549169 (cloth) | ISBN 9781487549183 (PDF) |
    ISBN 9781487549176 (EPUB)
Subjects: LCSH: Cornies, Johann, 1789–1848. | LCSH: Mennonites – Ukraine,
    Southern – History – 19th century. | LCSH: Germans – Ukraine, Southern –
    History – 19th century. | LCSH: Agricultural colonies – Ukraine, Southern –
    History – 19th century. | LCSH: Russification – Ukraine, Southern – History –
    19th century. | LCSH: Ukraine, Southern – Ethnic relations – History –
    19th century. | LCSH: Ukraine – Colonization – History – 19th century.
Classification: LCC DK508.425.G47 S73 2024 | DDC 947.7/3 – dc23

Cover design: Heng Wee Tan
Cover image: Daniel Schlatter, *Bruchstücke aus einigen Reisen nach dem südlichen
Russland, in den Jahren 1822–1828: mit besonderer Rücksicht auf die Nogayen-Tataren am
Asowschen Meere* (St. Gallen: Huber und Comp., 1830), pl. "Tatarische Wirthschaft."
Zentralbibliothek Zürich, NR 714, https://doi.org/10.3931/e-rara-25089.

We wish to acknowledge the land on which the University of Toronto Press
operates. This land is the traditional territory of the Wendat, the Anishnaabeg, the
Haudenosaunee, the Métis, and the Mississaugas of the Credit First Nation.

University of Toronto Press acknowledges the financial support of the Government
of Canada, the Canada Council for the Arts, and the Ontario Arts Council, an agency
of the Government of Ontario, for its publishing activities.

For Harvey Dyck, teacher, mentor, and friend

Contents

List of Illustrations   ix
Acknowledgments   xi
Abbreviations and Maps   xiii

1 Introduction   3
2 Land of Opportunity, 1804–1817   23
3 A Public Life, 1818–1824   48
4 Awakening, 1824–1828   77
5 Imposing Order, 1828–1834   107
6 Mennonites and the Era of Small Reforms, 1834–1838   137
7 "A Useful Man," 1838–1842   163
8 The Warkentin Affair, 1841–1842   187
9 An Agent of the State, 1842–1847   217
10 Conclusion: "Something for the Future," 1847–1848   245

Notes   255
Bibliography   297
Index   311

Illustrations

Maps

1 Mennonite settlements in New Russia, ca. 1880   xiv
2 The Molochnaia Mennonite settlement   xv

Photograph

1 The gravestone of David Cornies   27

Acknowledgments

As I write the final words of this manuscript it is January 2023 and the Molochnaia region is occupied by Russian troops while the cities that administered the area are daily targeted by Russian missiles. I offer my profound thanks to the people in the cities, towns, and villages of southern Ukraine who welcomed me and helped me understand their homeland. Their well-being is constantly in my thoughts. I hope and believe that one day I will be able to visit them again in a free and peaceful Ukraine.

Without the love and support of family this book would not exist. I read portions of it to my mother Dorothy (1927–2019) after her eyes failed her – I know it made her proud. The support of my siblings Chuck, Anne, and Norah is a constant in my life that I treasure.

In 1999 my world and family expanded. My son Duncan has seen me through two books now! My parents-in-law, Mary (1925–2014) and Les, and the entire Carmichael clan, accepted without question my strange obsession with tsarist Mennonites. I thank them all.

This project has stretched over twenty years, and I owe more debts of gratitude than I can ever repay. I particularly thank Harvey Dyck and Anne Konrad Dyck for their friendship and guidance. Thanks also to Leonard Friesen, who read the manuscript and offered good advice at a particularly low point. Ingrid Epp (1938–2016) was as insightful as she was kind – she is deeply missed.

Thank you to my colleagues at the State University of New York at Fredonia. The history department read and discussed portions of the manuscript at brown bag lunches, and their observations have improved the book immeasurably while their friendship has helped make the long slog bearable.

Parts of this book have appeared in various publications, and I thank the editors for their permission to reprint this material. Chapter 2 employs

"Romance, Marriage, Sex, and the Status of Women in Nineteenth-Century Tsarist Russian Mennonite Society," published in Mirjam van Veen, et al., eds., *Sisters: Myth and Reality of Anabaptist, Mennonite, and Doopsgezinde Women, ca. 1525–1900* (Leiden: Brill, 2014). Chapter 5 employs "Johann Cornies, Money-Lending, and Modernization in the Molochna Mennonite Settlement, 1820s–1840s," published in the *Journal of Mennonite Studies* 27 (2009). Chapter 6 employs "'On Civilizing the Nogais': Mennonite–Nogai Economic Relations, 1825–1860," published in *Mennonite Quarterly Review* 74, no. 2 (2000). Chapter 8 employs "Religion, Politics, and the Mennonite Privilegium: Reconsidering the Warkentin Affair," published in the *Journal of Mennonite Studies* 21 (2003). Chapter 9 employs "Iogann Kornis i osnovanie Berdianskogo Lesnichestvo," *Voprosy Germanskoi Istorii* (2017). Several chapters employ "Afforestation as Performance Art: Johann Cornies's Aesthetics of Civilization," published in Leonard L. Friesen, ed., *Minority Report: Mennonite Identities in Imperial Russia and Soviet Ukraine Reconsidered, 1789–1945* (Toronto: University of Toronto Press, 2018).

The COVID pandemic cast a long shadow over the final stages of this project, and my wife Barbara and daughter Emma provided daily light in dark times. I am forever grateful for their encouragement, sharp critiques, and most of all their love.

Abbreviations and Maps

ARAN	Arkhiv Rossiskoi Akademii Nauk
d.	delo
DADO	Derzhavnyi arkhiv Dnipropetrovs'koi oblasti
DAOO	Derzhavnyi arkhiv Odes'koi oblasti
f.	fond
l.	list (page)
op.	opis'
RGIA	Rossiskii Gosudarstvennyi Istoricheskii Arkhiv
ZhMGI	*Zhurnal Ministerstvo Gosudarstvennykh Imushchestv*

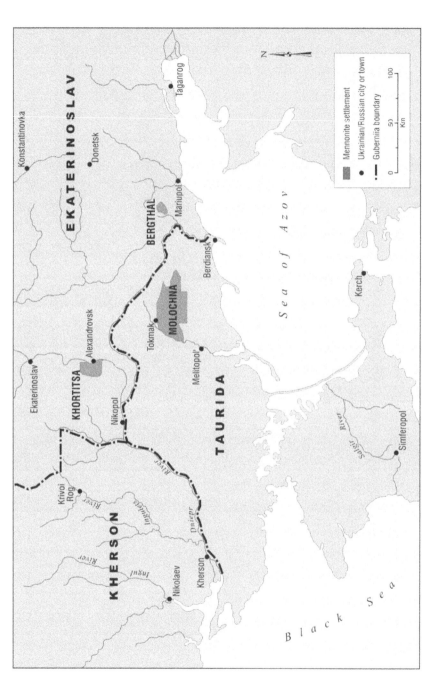

Map 1. Mennonite settlements in New Russia, ca. 1880. Source: Harvey L. Dyck, translator and editor, *A Mennonite in Russia: The Diaries of Jacob D. Epp, 1851–1880* (University of Toronto Press, 1991).

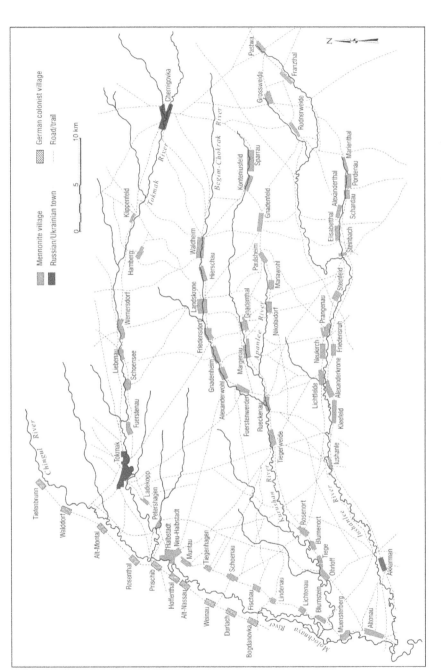

Map 2. The Molochnaia Mennonite settlement. Source: William Schroeder and Helmut Huebert, eds., *Mennonite Historical Atlas*, 2nd ed. (Springfield Publishers, 1996). Used with permission.

JOHANN CORNIES, THE MENNONITES, AND RUSSIAN COLONIALISM IN SOUTHERN UKRAINE

Chapter One

Introduction

In 1804 the Cornies family packed their belongings and travelled by wagon to the Molochnaia River basin in southern Ukraine to help found the frontier village of Ohrloff. Johann Cornies, the family's eldest son, turned fifteen that year. They were Mennonite peasants from the Vistula delta of Polish Prussia, pursuing the land and religious freedoms that Russia promised.

By the time Johann died in 1848, Russia had experienced profound changes, and this German-speaking Mennonite peasant had played a remarkable role in shaping and recording the transformation. Powerful and influential, he was widely known in the empire. He had met Tsar Alexander I, Tsar Nicholas I, and the future Tsar Alexander II, who dined at his home in 1837. Pavel Kiselev, Nicholas's Minister of State Domains, visited Cornies and corresponded with him about regional and empire-wide issues. Nikolai Miliutin, the most important architect of Russia's Great Reforms in the 1860s, visited and consulted Cornies about peasant affairs. August von Haxthausen, author of a hugely influential nineteenth-century account of Russian peasant life, stayed at Cornies's home and described him as "one of the most influential men in Southern Russia."[1]

Cornies's network of friends stretched from the Caucasus and Trans-Volga to Moscow, St. Petersburg, Odesa, and Danzig and enabled him to track the winds of change and influence decisions with far-reaching significance for the tsarist Mennonites. His work for the Guardianship Committee – the bureaucracy that oversaw foreign colonists in New Russia – and for the Ministry of State Domains makes him an invaluable window onto the Russian colonial project in the first half of the nineteenth century.

Russian colonial policy is conventionally portrayed as contingent – as constantly adapting to the remarkable diversity of the empire, cutting deals with local elites, and seeking little more than security, stability, and revenues. On the surface, the empire's Mennonite subjects may seem to be just one more in a long list of examples of such diversity, contingency, and co-option. A deeper look, however, reveals something much more interesting: in their Molochnaia settlement in New Russia the Mennonites became a colonial laboratory of modernity, where the tsarist state sought universal answers for the empire.

One particular value of the Mennonite case is that it *permits* a deeper look at the evolution of colonial policy. Accounts of Russia's interactions with its colonial subjects have been written largely from the perspective of the imperial centre, which is often the only source of documentary evidence.[2] However, Cornies kept voluminous records, both of his correspondence with imperial bureaucrats and of his workaday administrative activities. Through his eyes we gain a unique view, from the periphery, of the core policies that evolved during the reigns of Alexander I and Nicholas I.[3] These policies began as local and contingent, but, beginning in Alexander's last years and increasingly under Nicholas, they gradually coalesced into a national vision.

While this perspective on the Russian colonial enterprise is invaluable, Cornies himself is also important for what he reveals about the challenges of life on the New Russian frontier and the impact of those challenges on Mennonites. In the late nineteenth century, Russia's Mennonites experienced a religious schism that did much to shape the international Mennonite community as it exists today. Cornies was deeply involved in the religious disputes that troubled his community in the first half of the century, and his story reveals important precursors of the later schism, showing how Pietism first took root among Russian Mennonites. Just as Mennonites lived on the periphery of the Russian Empire, they were also a frontier outpost in the Second Great Awakening, and the struggles within their settlement reveal both the power and the limitations of the Pietist movement.

This study offers a unique view of Russian imperial history from the southern frontier, through the eyes of a peasant-born, German-speaking sectarian. It is, first and foremost, a microhistory that employs Cornies's life to shed light on his Mennonite community, the New Russian frontier, Russian colonial policy, and international religious currents. To that end I look closely at Cornies's personal life. Mennonite minister and historian P.M. Friesen wrote in 1911 that Cornies stands alongside Menno Simons as a cornerstone of the "ecclesiastical and cultural character" of tsarist Mennonites.[4] A modern biography of Cornies is long overdue, and while my sights are set on a broader horizon, I hope that those seeking Cornies's life story will find some satisfaction in these pages. Cornies's personal relations with family and friends, his reflections on religion, and his attempts to balance his pursuit of wealth with his sense of responsibility to his community offer a compelling look into one particular life on the New Russian frontier, and this too is valuable to our understanding of the world he inhabited.

Cornies today is known mainly to Mennonites, and even then, most accounts of his life rise little above caricature. Perhaps this study will restore some small part of his earlier fame.

Mennonites on the Move

Cornies's mother Maria was forty-five and his father Johann Sr. was sixty-four in the summer of 1804 when they packed their belongings and left the village of Mühlhausen in the Vistula River delta of West Prussia to make the long overland trek to New Russia.[5] The family had rattled around the Vistula since Johann Sr. and Maria (née Klassen) married in 1786. They first lived in Schönbaum on the Vistula Spit, but by the time their eldest son Johann was born in 1789 they were in Bärwalde, a small agricultural village halfway between Danzig and Elbing.[6] Between 1791 and 1797 they were back in Schönbaum, where Peter (1791) and David (1794) were born. In 1797, apparently fleeing tax collectors, they moved on to Mühlhausen, where the couple's only daughter, Katherina, was born in 1800; she died in Ohrloff in 1808. Their seventh child, Heinrich, was born in Ohrloff in June 1806.[7] In all, Johann Sr. and Maria had four children who lived to adulthood, and three who died in infancy or childhood – a typical family history for their time.

Little is known about Maria, nor about any of the other women who figure in this study. Letters and reports from the period, almost exclusively authored by men, largely ignored women's important contributions to Mennonite life. We know a little more about Johann Sr., which suggests that he was an unconventional risk-taker. David Epp, Johann's first biographer, tells a colourful tale of Johann Sr.'s life in the merchant marine, during which he sailed out of Danzig and around the Horn of Africa to the far-off "paradise" of India, and survived the great Lisbon earthquake of 1755. He was, Epp wrote, "a gnarled old tree ... a man with great strength of will, the kind of man we seldom see in these later, decadent times."[8] Epp assured his readers that "in spite of the rough, sometimes barbaric life he led as a sailor, he was able to also preserve his personal integrity. Upon his return to his home harbour after a long sea voyage he wouldn't waste time in wild celebrations ... but would hasten to his house as behoves a faithful married man."[9] Whether or not Johann Sr. avoided harbour taverns, by the time he left Prussia they provided him with a living as a distiller. This was profitable enough that he was able to raise the 300 guilders (roughly 1,000 rubles) that Russia required Mennonite families immigrating to Russia to produce as evidence that they would be self-supporting.[10]

When the Cornies family departed Prussia they became part of a worldwide phenomenon of human migration. In the eighteenth and nineteenth centuries, the grasslands of the world opened to agricultural settlement. In places as diverse as Argentina, the United States, Canada, South Africa, and Russia, people set out to colonize "promised lands," dreaming of peace, plenty, and escape from their overcrowded homes. They came at the urging of imperialist governments that viewed the grasslands as both a ground-spring of national wealth and a blank slate upon which to create new moral orders and shape new national identities.[11]

Russia's expansion east to Siberia and south onto the steppe was born of this vision, but in southern Ukraine – "New Russia," as Empress Catherine the Great named it – the Russian imperial project intersected with geopolitical realities that gave it unique shape. Beyond New Russia lay the Ottoman Empire, a powerful competitor with its own imperial ambitions. Expansion toward the Black Sea and the Balkans meant certain conflict between the two great powers.[12]

Geopolitics shaped the contours of Russian imperialism. Its southward expansion was a carefully managed affair, constrained by the need to create communities that could support the Russian military. The clearest examples were the "military colonies" of peasant conscripts, whom the state relocated with their families to the New Russian frontier, ordering them to build their own villages and grow their own food, all under harsh military discipline.[13]

The Russian administrative ideal was cameralism, a theory of centralized planning with tight control, administered through an obedient and well-trained bureaucracy. It relied in part on providing models of "proper" behaviour to the Slavic peasants who were moving to the empire's new territories. Russia recruited settlers from the German states as model colonists who could teach their progressive agricultural methods by example. Prussian Mennonites, renowned for their work ethic and agricultural successes, became a central target for such recruitment.

The Mennonites who immigrated to the Russian Empire in the late eighteenth and early nineteenth centuries brought little with them beyond a deep-rooted Christian Anabaptist faith and a tradition of hard work. As they settled in New Russia, they built villages, ploughed the rich prairie, and established model farmsteads. They crafted farm machinery, milled grain, and manufactured cloth, creating a bustling, prosperous community that in the late nineteenth century would lead the way in Russia's nascent industrial revolution.[14]

The tsarist Mennonite story remained alive in the émigré communities that left Russia beginning in the 1870s and continuing into the 1940s. They settled in Canada, the United States, and Paraguay, built new villages, and transplanted their Russian successes – and religious disputes – to their new homelands.[15]

The story these Mennonites preserved was mainly one of faith and suffering. Filtered through their Russian and Soviet experiences, it stressed their religious values and sense of community. It ignored (or did not understand) their role in the larger Russian story of colonization and economic development. This was true even in the work of secular historians, who depended heavily on in-group Mennonite accounts.

This study examines the first period of Mennonite settlement. It explores the foundations of Russian Mennonite prosperity: their hard work, self-discipline, and entrepreneurial spirit, but also the privileges they enjoyed as colonial agents of the state. It likewise reveals the fermentation of religious beliefs in their community. Significantly, it depicts a sometimes contentious, sometimes cooperative, constantly evolving relationship to surrounding peoples and to the state.

Through Johann Cornies's eyes the Russian colonial world comes alive. He was a leading figure in his community, an ambitious, entrepreneurial, and energetic reformer. He accrued great wealth and power, and he devoted himself to transforming New Russia. In Moscow, St. Petersburg, and the West his keen mind and tremendous work ethic brought him acclaim. In the Mennonite community he earned respect, but his imperious manner and his reform agenda also created deep controversies.

Mennonites in Poland and Prussia

The Mennonites are pacifist Christian Anabaptists. Their religion, which originated in Switzerland and the Netherlands in the sixteenth century, owes its name to one of its founders, Menno Simons. The Catholic Church, allied with the Dutch crown, persecuted Mennonites in the sixteenth and seventeenth centuries, causing many to flee to the delta of the Vistula River in Poland. There they prospered in the relatively tolerant Polish state until the region came under Prussian control between 1774 and 1794. Most Mennonites who migrated to the Vistula settled within sight of the walls of Danzig, a Hanse city with a bustling trade and craft economy. These Mennonites were artisans, traders, and farmers and had little trouble adapting to local economic circumstances. Their skills, whether in draining swampy delta land for farming or as artisans and merchants, ensured that they would be welcome additions to their new homeland, although most were denied the right to live within the city walls because of their sectarian religious beliefs.[16]

A key element of the modern Mennonite story in both the Vistula delta and tsarist Russia is the relationship between pacifism and land. It is important to stress that this is the *modern* story, for before Prussia annexed the Vistula other theological issues stood alongside pacifism as important collective concerns of Mennonites. Pacifism is just one element of the complex, multifaceted Mennonite religion, but because it has generated so much controversy it has become symbolically central to Mennonite history. Most people in Europe gained access to land in exchange for services to a state, or at least to the landowning elites of the state. A basic duty of all subjects to their ruler was military service, whether by direct enlistment in the military or by supplying food and lodging to troops. By refusing military service Mennonites placed themselves outside of normal state structures. The issue that most directly engaged them with governments was the right to use land without providing military service in exchange. That right had to be negotiated and defended.[17]

While pacifism was the most obviously controversial element of Mennonite beliefs, adult baptism and the commitment to a self-disciplined Christianity that it symbolized was an equally important source of tension between the Mennonites and the states where they made their homes. Mennonite religious doctrine begins with the personal decision of each adult to join the church through the ritual of baptism. That decision is influenced by myriad family and community pressures that encourage conformity in all aspects of life, but the centrality of the personal commitment to live in accordance with biblically defined Christian practices places self-discipline at the very centre of Mennonite values. Yet at the time, Mennonites lived in autocratic states, and in the eighteenth and nineteenth centuries, many of those states were becoming increasingly absolutist. Both the tsarist state that the Cornies family migrated to and the Prussian state they left behind sought *state* discipline, not *self*-discipline. Where Mennonites' self-discipline did not challenge state interests this was not a problem, but by the end of the eighteenth century the militarized Prussian state found their self-disciplined pacifism unacceptable, and this stimulated the Mennonite migration to Russia. Though nobody yet recognized the danger, Russia was looking admiringly at Prussia's successes, and as Russia tried to emulate Prussian absolutism in the nineteenth century the self-discipline of its Mennonite immigrants loomed as a major problem.

Mennonites had prospered in Poland because of the unique political situation there prior to the Prussian annexation; but at the same time, shifting political, economic, and religious forces in Poland exerted constant pressure on the Mennonite community. Poland was a sharp exception to Europe's absolutist trend; by the sixteenth century it had emerged as a highly decentralized state with a weak monarchy. Poland was positioned at a crossroads in Central Europe, a place where Germanic, Slavic, and Jewish peoples, and Protestant, Catholic, Orthodox, and Jewish religions, all intersected. To unite this diverse group and build a state that could protect them from the surrounding Austrian, Ottoman, Swedish, and Russian states, the Polish crown had to grant unparalleled levels of autonomy to its various constituents. Thus, the crown required the consent of the Polish nobility, granted through the Sejm (the noble assembly), to institute any new law, and any single member of the nobility could veto legislation by employing the notorious *Liberum Veto*. Because of this political arrangement, the nobility enjoyed substantial autonomy on their own lands, and the Catholic Church and several large cities enjoyed equal autonomy on their lands.

Poland had no strong central government capable of dictating policy, and it was constantly having to negotiate among its various constituents. At times these "negotiations" ended in brute force, and some of the great Polish noble magnates retained large private armies to defend and extend their interests. More often, though, the negotiations addressed economic issues and found economic solutions. The Polish economy was largely agricultural, centred on the Baltic grain trade. Grain flowed down the Vistula to Baltic ports like Danzig and Elbing and then was shipped to Western European markets. For Polish landowners to prosper they needed reliable tenants to work their land, and because Poland was less densely populated than Western Europe, good tenants could negotiate favourable leases. In the long term they could even acquire property of their own, and many Mennonites did. But this did not remove Mennonites from the constant process of negotiation, because questions of taxes, tariffs, tithes, and other contributions to local, regional, and national authorities were perpetually in flux in the unstable Polish state.

An account of Danzig Mennonites from the late seventeenth century reveals the interplay of religion, politics, and money that Mennonites negotiated so adeptly along the Vistula. In 1678, Mennonites found their religious privileges under attack when King John III Sobieski ordered the Catholic Church to investigate Mennonite beliefs. Elder Georg Hansen represented the Danzig Flemish Mennonite Congregation and skilfully defended his congregation, insisting on New Testament authority for Mennonite pacifism. However, he acknowledged that the success of his defence was in no small part secured by "a significant financial contribution."[18] As historian Mark Jantzen writes, into the nineteenth century "haggling over the price of principles constituted a crucial element of the relationship of the Mennonites to the larger political and social entity in which they lived."[19]

Such negotiations, conducted by wise leaders and lubricated by community coffers, were a constant factor in the lives of Vistula Mennonites. The sudden arrival of Prussian rule after the first partition of Poland in 1774 disrupted the pattern but did not altogether eliminate it, for local officials often retained their positions despite the change in government. The Mennonites who left the Vistula for the Russian Empire brought with them this experience and all of the political understanding that came with it. They had been neither naive nor puritanical in their attitude toward the Polish state, and they would approach the Russian state with the expectation that the same strategies and tactics that had worked in Poland would work in Russia. However, the personal, business, and political relations that had evolved over centuries in Poland did not yet exist for them in Russia, and the Russian administration was far more hierarchical than the Polish one, so Mennonites would need to find the pressure points that would permit them to negotiate their rights in Russia.

While the Vistula experience gave the Mennonite immigrants to Russia a significant shared past, there were also significant divisions within the community. All Vistula Mennonites shared the same basic religious doctrine, and when circumstances demanded it, they presented a united front to the larger world. Internally, however, Mennonites were divided between the liberal Frisian and the conservative Flemish congregations, and this division would survive to play a central role in the controversies that later shaped Johann Cornies's life in New Russia. Flemish congregations dominated the Vistula delta, including the villages where the Cornies family lived, while Frisian congregations dominated the upper parts of the river valley, where Mennonites were only a small percentage of the population. Overall, the Frisians were a distinct minority.[20]

The most significant point of discord between the two congregations revolved around the application of the ban, that is, the practice of excommunicating members who violated congregational or community rules. In a community that forswore corporal punishment, the ban was the main instrument for enforcing community discipline. Frisians favoured a relatively lenient application, not demanding, for example, that spouses shun their banned mates; the Flemish were far more strict.[21] Frisians were also open to dialogue and even intermarriage with members of other religious confessions, and this openness permitted Pietism to gain powerful influence in the Frisian communities in the late eighteenth century. The Flemish, by contrast, strongly opposed religious dialogue with other confessions, especially the emotionalism and universalism of the Pietist movement.[22]

Pietism, which emphasizes inner spiritual regeneration and evangelical activities, emerged as a significant force in Prussia and the other German states in the eighteenth century. Originating as a reform movement within the Lutheran Church, Pietism promoted the cultivation of personal piety through an individual exploration of faith, and it consequently challenged the authority of the established church. Because Bible-reading was so central to this individual exploration, Pietism also promoted literacy and education. Beginning with the founding of Philipp Jakob Spener's Ritterakademie in Halle in 1694, systematic Pietist education cast its net across Central Europe, harvesting generations of literate, numerate, serious young men to fill the ranks of the Prussian bureaucracy.[23] Under Frederick the Great they became key players in Prussia's highly disciplined state system, as well as an essential element of what has been labelled the world's first modern police state.[24]

The Pietist emphasis on evangelism was especially controversial among conservative Mennonites, whose traditional beliefs promoted separation from the secular world. Their goal was to live ascetic lives in imitation of early Christian communities, in anticipation of securing their future in the next life. Their early history of martyrdom had given emphasis to this belief, in that Mennonites had learned to keep their heads down if they wanted to survive. Pietism, in contrast, demanded engagement with the larger world, leading implicitly toward the creation of the Kingdom of God on earth. By the late eighteenth century Pietism was exerting a significant and contentious influence within Mennonite society.

Russia's "Foreign Colonists"

Whatever their internal differences, Vistula Mennonites faced the 1774 partition of Poland and subjection to Prussian rule as a common threat to their religious rights and economic security. The militarist Prussian state had little tolerance for pacifist Mennonites, and the reign of Friedrich Wilhelm II (1786–97) saw a concerted attack on their rights. Prussia linked permission for Mennonites to purchase land to military service, thus impeding expansion of Mennonite landholdings.[25] The new

Prussian laws were the impetus for the Mennonite migration to Russia that began in 1789. The migrants looked to Russia, with its promise of plentiful land and guarantees of religious freedom, as a refuge.

In the late eighteenth century, Russia seemed as eager to attract Mennonites as Prussia was to push them away. Russia's recruitment drive began during the reign of Catherine the Great (1762–96), when the empire expanded to encompass southern Ukraine. Catherine justified southern expansion with a mixture of security concerns and imperial ambitions.[26] Before 1783 the Khortitsa and Molochnaia regions, where the first Mennonite immigrants settled, were on the frontier with the Crimean Khanate, a hostile vassal state of the Ottoman Empire and Russia's major competitor for power on the southern steppe and in the Balkans and Caucasus. Catherine viewed herself as rightful protector of the Orthodox peoples of the Ottoman Empire. She openly acknowledged her ambition to wrest control of the Balkans from the Turks, and in 1779 she famously hinted at her desire to capture Constantinople itself when she named her grandson Konstantin.[27]

By the time of Catherine's reign, Russia was beginning to gain the upper hand in its long series of wars with the Ottoman Empire. In the Russo-Turkish War of 1768–74, Russia seized the city of Azov and the Black Sea coastline between the Dnieper and Bug Rivers, and gained formal Ottoman recognition of the independence of the Crimean Khanate, including the Molochnaia region. In 1783 Catherine annexed Crimea, provoking the Russo-Turkish War of 1788–91. Catherine's victory in that war secured Russian control of Crimea and helped start the Ottoman Empire down the long road to its demise in the twentieth century. She labelled the newly gained territories "New Russia," a powerful metaphor for her imperial ambitions. Catherine saw the south as a blank slate where Russia might create a modern economy as a model for the transformation of the empire's interior.

For Catherine, military subjugation of the south was simply a first step toward enlightened administration; her goal was to exploit the agricultural and commercial potential of her new territories in the interests of the state. Influenced by the Enlightenment belief that national wealth was a function of population size, Catherine set out to populate her new domains.[28] Russia did not have enough peasants to populate its vast new territories, a problem compounded by its serf and state peasant economy, which sharply restricted peasant mobility and made impossible the type of spontaneous settlement of the prairies that would soon take place in North America.[29] Catherine therefore looked to foreign migrants, in 1763 creating a special Chancellery for the Guardianship of Foreigners and issuing an open invitation for immigrants to populate the southern steppe on attractive terms. She commissioned recruiting agents to lure Western European peasants with promises of money, tax exemptions, and large land grants.

Peasants from the German states were prime targets of this recruitment campaign. Catherine knew that German peasants were skilled agriculturists and experienced craftspeople and tradespeople. They were an ideal population for her grand project, and she hoped they would serve as models for the Russian and Ukrainian peasants she intended to settle alongside them. Mennonites figured prominently in these plans, for Catherine and her most able administrators were well aware of the reputation of the Mennonites as sober, hard-working, prosperous, and progressive. Catherine and her successors founded German peasant settlements across Russia. The most extensive were along the Volga and in New Russia, where, by the early nineteenth century the German language could be heard in cities and villages from Odesa to Ekaterinoslav.

Historian Roger Bartlett has described the Russian model colonies as an example of "didactic" colonization.[30] The assumption had been that the German colonists would by their example teach Slavic peasants and nomadic Tatars the advantages of modern peasant agriculture. Bartlett writes that by the end the eighteenth century the tsarist state saw this approach as a failure: Slavic peasants had not imitated their new, modern neighbours; instead, the foreign colonists had adapted to Slavic peasant ways. Emblematic of this, in 1806 the duc de Richelieu, New Russia's Governor General, described the German colonists (with the exception of the Mennonites) as "intolerable."[31] By the nineteenth century the didactic model survived only in the Mennonite settlements, where the immigration waves of 1818–22 and 1836–9 were exceptions to a broader policy that sharply restricted immigration.[32]

Even among the Mennonites the didactic model had begun to change by the 1820s. Catherine's New Russian project is a prime example of what anthropologist Ann Laura Stoler has labelled a colonial "laboratory of modernity."[33] In that phrase, Stoler captures the essence of a growing anthropological and historical literature which suggests that "transformed by force, the colony could also become a laboratory of experiment for new technology and new ways of thinking."[34] Often, "laboratory of modernity" is used as an interpretive, even metaphorical framework for analysing how colonial experiences have influenced development in metropoles. A weakness of the metaphor is that such laboratories sometimes lack the intentional experimental character of real laboratories. Other times there is a more conscious experimental process, as for example in experiments with unproven vaccines forced upon colonial populations, a process that anthropologist Shiv Visvanathan grimly labels "the vivisectional mandate."[35] The role of force in the colonial laboratory is controversial in the historiography, for it suggests that colonial subjects lack the agency to affect outcomes.[36] The Mennonites' story reveals their agency, but also its limits. After the Napoleonic Wars, and particularly after the ascension of Tsar Nicholas I in 1825, the Mennonite settlements were pushed to become active laboratories where the state closely observed new experiments in agriculture and social organization and, when they were successful, promoted them throughout the empire. Johann Cornies made his name as Russia's chief laboratory technician – a process that brought him fame, fortune, and controversy and that had a profound impact on both his adoptive country and his Mennonite community.

Willard Sunderland, in his influential study of Russian settlement of the steppe, shows that from the perspective of the imperial metropole the occupation of New Russia was at most ambiguously "colonial" and that in practical terms Russian leaders often perceived the region as an extension of the Russian metropole.[37] Kelly O'Neill, writing of Russia's absorption of Crimea, echoes Sunderland, suggesting that the southern part of the empire was not "the product of a binary relationship ... but ... an arrangement of interrelationships – a topology capable of stretching and bending, growing compact or attenuating, defined by connection rather than rupture."[38] John LeDonne labels the process an expansion of the Russian core.[39] The present study, focused tightly on the view from one small corner of the periphery, shows one extreme of this ambiguous situation, for the use of the Mennonite settlement as a laboratory of modernity was emphatically colonial; moreover, by the second quarter of the nineteenth century it reveals a hardening of the lines of demarcation between metropole and periphery.

Adapting to New Russia

The New Russian laboratory gained its first cohort of Vistula Mennonite immigrants in 1789. They established the Khortitsa settlement on the banks of the Dnieper River near present-day Zaporizhzhe. In 1803–6 a second cohort established the first eighteen villages of the Molochnaia settlement along the Molochnaia River, just north of present-day Melitopol. Two more waves of Mennonite settlers came to the Molochnaia in 1818–22 and 1835–9 before intensifying Russian nationalism, coupled with Tsar Nicholas I's fear of liberal Western ideas and concerns about the emerging German state, caused Russia to slow and finally stop immigration in the latter half of the nineteenth century. Springing from these original settlements, by 1914 Mennonite settlements had spread across European Russia, Siberia, the Caucasus, and Central Asia, and the tsarist Mennonites numbered more than 100,000.

Mennonites based the administration of their New Russian settlements on that of their Vistula communities, which were governed internally by church congregations. All members of a congregation were subject to its ethical rules, which were enforced by an elected elder (*Ältester*), assisted by elected preachers (*Lehrer*) and deacons (*Diakonen*). Collectively a congregation's religious leadership was called the Teaching Service (*Lerhdeinst*).[40] These internal structures set Mennonites apart from other German immigrants to Russia. Catholic and Lutheran immigrants were accustomed to accepting church and state as part of a single social and political system. By comparison, Vistula Mennonites had been separated legally and religiously from their neighbours and state, and this separate existence helped build a strong sense of community identity that survived and flourished in Russia.

A key challenge for tsarist Mennonites was to adapt their imported practices to their new circumstances. Russia required Mennonites to adopt the district (*volost*) administrative system created by Paul I in 1797, of elected village mayors (*sels'skii vybornyi*) and ten-men (*desiatskie*). The Mennonite equivalent of a *volost* was the *Gebiet*, and just as Ukrainian and Russian state peasants had an elected *volost* mayor (*volost'noi golova*), the Mennonites had an elected *Gebiet* mayor (*Oberschulz*). The mayor and his deputies were collectively referred to as the district administration (*Gebietsamt*). The congregational system came to coexist with the Russian administrative system, with elders, preachers, and deacons exercising significant influence over the election of local secular officials, and secular officials relying on the support of congregational officials when enforcing regulations.

The state assigned local officials the responsibility for publicizing new laws, encouraging church attendance, taking measures against epidemics and fire, maintaining roads and bridges, and arbitrating minor disputes. It also gave them authority over important aspects of the economy such as agricultural practices and grain reserves. In other words, those officials held secular authority over economic affairs in the Mennonite villages.

The state agency that directly oversaw Mennonites and other foreign colonists was the Guardianship Committee for Foreign Settlers in New Russia, which answered to the Ministry of Internal Affairs until 1838 and to the Ministry of State Domains after its creation in that year.[41] The Guardianship Committee became a gathering place for some of the most reform-minded bureaucrats in the Ministry of State Domains, and Cornies's association with such people strongly affected him. The committee was headquartered in Kishinev until 1834, when it relocated to Odesa. Until 1834 a local Guardianship Committee bureau in Ekaterinoslav oversaw New Russian Mennonite affairs with considerable autonomy from Kishinev; after 1834 the Molochnaia and Khortitsa Mennonites answered directly to the central offices in Odesa. This administrative system survived virtually unchanged until the Great Reforms of the 1860s, at which time attempts were made to more fully integrate Mennonites into the Russian state system.

The Russian state did not intend to isolate Mennonites, and Mennonites were divided in their attitudes toward self-isolation when they arrived in southern Ukraine, but the conditions they encountered upon arrival inevitably shaped their subsequent development. Their new frontier home was strange and foreboding, filled with the babble of unfamiliar languages (Russian, Ukrainian, Tatar) and unfamiliar customs and religious practices. There were no cities like Danzig and Elbing to provide them with markets, and the nearest ports were too distant to support the market-oriented crop agriculture that many had practised in the Vistula. The howling blizzards that sometimes decimated Mennonite livestock, and the summer "black blizzards" – moisture-sapping dust storms – had no precedent in their Vistula lives. The Molochnaia region provided rich agricultural soil, but it was also a semi-arid zone where inconsistent precipitation made crop agriculture a boom-or-bust proposition and where careful land management was essential for future prosperity. The understaffed Russian bureaucracy was a distant influence, quite unlike the intrusive Prussian bureaucracy of their final Vistula years. At first, the Mennonite migrants had little choice but isolation as they struggled to survive in their new homeland.[42]

This moment of relative isolation contributed to the strong community identity that developed among tsarist Mennonites in the nineteenth century, shaping their self-image as a distinct Russian-Mennonite people.[43] But forces of integration were just as central to the tsarist Mennonite story from almost the moment of their arrival. The immigration of Slavic and German peasants to New Russia, the evolution of regional and national markets, the establishment of nearby ports, the influx of new religious currents, and the growth of the tsarist bureaucracy all intruded upon their lives. They soon moved beyond the gates of their tightly knit communities into a larger Russian world, where they encountered and integrated into a complex and changing multi-ethnic and multicultural empire. Their experiences in Poland had provided them with important tools to begin negotiating their relationship with their new neighbours and the state, but they also needed to learn new lessons. It was through this process of negotiation and learning, as much as through the experience of isolation, that their collective identity developed.

The Mennonites' status in Russia was spelled out in a Privilegium, a document Catherine had promised to the first immigrants in 1787 and that Tsar Paul I granted in 1800. Mennonites regarded the Privilegium as a fundamental, God-willed guarantee of their rights and privileges. It granted Mennonites "the liberty to practise their religion according to their tenets and customs," and – crucially important, given their pacifist beliefs – a complete exemption from military service. Economically, besides temporary tax exemptions shared by all settlers in New Russia, the Privilegium granted each Mennonite family "incontestable and perpetually inheritable possession" of a sixty-five *desiatina* (seventy-one hectare) land allotment as well as the right to build factories, enter trade guilds, and engage in commercial activities.[44]

In the Privilegium's concluding clause, Paul ordered "all our military and civil authorities and government offices not only to leave these Mennonites and their descendants in unmolested enjoyment of their houses, lands, and other possessions, not to hinder them in the enjoyment of the privileges granted to them, but also to show them in all cases every assistance and protection."[45] This seemed to guarantee very significant freedoms, but they came at a price, for Russia was pursuing its own modernization agenda and the Mennonites were part of it. The Privilegium made clear in its opening phrases that the Mennonites had received their special status because their "excellent industry and morality may ... be held up as a model to the foreigners settled [in New Russia]."[46]

Russia assumed that Mennonites would promote improvements in agriculture, forestry, and trade and industry. In essence, the state was granting Mennonites religious freedoms in exchange for economic services. It expected Mennonites to serve as a bridge from East to West across which modern economic ideas would flow. The trouble was that some Mennonites retained a religious ideal of withdrawal from secular entanglements. Mennonites possessed a foundation myth of agricultural life as the proper expression of this withdrawal; life in their agricultural villages permitted physical isolation to match the ideal of spiritual seclusion. This religiously inspired tendency toward isolation was reinforced by various other factors. The late eighteenth and early nineteenth centuries were a time of enormous social, economic, and religious upheaval in Europe. The Enlightenment with its secularizing undercurrents, the counter-currents of Pietism and the Counter-Reformation, the aggressive expansion of Prussia, the French Revolution, and the Napoleonic Wars all provided strong stimulus for some Mennonites to seek escape into religiously sanctioned isolation. Clearly the ideal of withdrawal did not sit easily with the modernizing role envisaged in the Privilegium, and from the outset it seemed certain that tensions would arise among the Mennonites regarding their relationship to the state.

Counter to this isolationist tradition, a practical need for economic and political engagement had penetrated deeply into the Mennonite world view by the late eighteenth century. The Mennonites who immigrated to Russia were not unanimous in their attitudes toward the Russian state and society; countervailing forces pushed them to engage with the tsarist government, society, and economy.[47] Most importantly, Vistula Mennonites were by then integrated into a market economy. Their understanding of their own economic existence was founded on the relatively mature market conditions of the Vistula, where their agricultural production and their crafts found ready buyers in the cities of Danzig and Elbing and in export markets in Western Europe. Families like the Cornies lived side by side with Lutherans and Catholics in their Prussian villages, embracing the German language and trading and socializing with their neighbours.[48] Many Mennonite immigrants were coming to Russia not to isolate themselves but to find new and better economic opportunities. The Cornies family fit comfortably into this latter group. Johann Sr. had travelled far beyond the confines of conservative Prussian Mennonitism. Progressive Mennonites like the Cornies were precisely the bridge to the West that Russia sought.

The existence of this outward-looking element among the Mennonite immigrants is apparent from the activities of the advance parties that had been sent to survey potential settlement sites in New Russia. They focused on finding economically viable locations, and the Privilegium they negotiated sought not to isolate the Mennonites but to define the terms of their engagement with Russia.[49] It reflected all of their experiences in the complex Polish state they had left behind. Mennonites undoubtedly favoured exclusively Mennonite settlements, in contrast to being scattered among other religious denominations as they had been in the Vistula, but there was no explicit attempt to cut these settlements off from the surrounding world. In 1806, visitors to the Molochnaia noted that within two years of the settlement's founding, Mennonites were already sending out representatives to explore market opportunities in the nearby cities of their new homeland.[50] They were not so much pursuing isolation as building a community. Mennonites were willing to engage with the tsarist state, economy, and society, but they wanted a say in the terms of engagement.

The Privilegium was a first step in the process of Mennonite engagement, and it would help shape Mennonite existence in Russia for more than a century, but by the time the ink dried on the agreement a problem already loomed. As the old conservative order began to collapse in Europe in the nineteenth century, Russia's attitude toward the West came to parallel Mennonite attitudes toward the secular world. Mennonites were a people torn between their desire to isolate themselves from the corrupting influences of the secular world and their desire to enjoy the economic benefits of modernization. They found themselves subjects of a state torn between its fear of the corrosive influences of new Western political and social ideas and its desire to enjoy the benefits of Western economic modernization. Even as Mennonites attempted to negotiate a relationship with the Russian state that would permit them to enjoy the economic advantages of citizens while preserving the religious and cultural markers of a people apart, the Russian state was seeking ways to enjoy the economic advantages of Western modernization while preserving the political and cultural markers of a state apart. Neither goal was realistic: In order to move out into the economic world of the nineteenth century, Mennonites had to engage with the Russian state in which they lived, and that engagement necessarily shaped and changed their identity. At the same time, the Western economic advantages that the Russian state wanted to imitate were in part a product of the breakdown of old social and political conventions in the West, and Russia could not enjoy the economic benefits without dealing with the social and political consequences. Because Mennonite engagement with the Russian state made Mennonites a conduit for Western ideas into Russia, they helped shape and change Russia.

Russian Colonialism through Mennonite Eyes

The curious position that Mennonites occupied in Russia, as both valued representatives of progressive Western economic ideas and potentially dangerous representatives of progressive Western political ideas, makes their story particularly useful for understanding Russian colonialism. Mennonites came to New Russia as representatives of the Russian colonial state; they were meant to create a model community that would "civilize" Russia's new colonial possessions. In practice, they were Russian colonists. But they were not Russian, and as the state changed its colonial policies, and consequently its demands on Mennonites, the Mennonite community found itself forced to defend its own cultural identity. In this sense, they were not colonists but colonial subjects. Through them the Russian colonial enterprise is portrayed both from an insider's and an outsider's perspective.[51]

These multiple perspectives are refracted through the gaze of Johann Cornies, who wrote a vast collection of documents about New Russia and collected tens of thousands of pages of information about both his own Mennonite community and its neighbours. He also wrote reports and letters that directly influenced state policy toward peasants. His knowledge and expertise won him appointment to the prestigious Learned Committee of the Ministry of State Domains in 1838, and his reports appeared regularly in *Journal of the Ministry of State Domains* and in newspapers in Odesa and St. Petersburg.

The materials authored or collected by Cornies are invaluable. Most of Russia's colonial subjects in the nineteenth century were illiterate, and consequently sources originating from such people are extremely rare. Sources regarding these populations were almost exclusively authored by members of the nobility or members of the state bureaucracy – categories that are often coterminous. Cornies was legally classified as a peasant and he never held an official post in the state bureaucracy. Despite his wealth and power, he lived throughout his life in Russia in the small frontier village of Ohrloff that his family helped establish when they immigrated. He had intimate knowledge of the people and places he described that nobles and bureaucrats never acquired. His records are a unique resource for the history of Imperial Russia.[52]

The problem with Cornies as a historical source is that he was the quintessential outlier, whose accomplishments mean that he was anything but representative of the average New Russian peasant. He was not an Orthodox Christian like most peasants in the region; he spoke only German in a place where Russian was the language of official communications; in a peasant society oppressed by poverty (two rubles was a good daily wage) he accrued a fortune estimated at more than 3 million rubles; in a place where the nobility enjoyed an almost complete monopoly on political power, he had the ear of high officials in the Russian capital of St. Petersburg. How can his life be used to understand the larger milieu in which he lived?

Understanding Cornies's political views is particularly important when assessing his value as a historical source, for he had a political agenda, at times promoting his own economic interests and at times promoting the interests of his Mennonite community. This raises questions about the purpose of his correspondence and the intended audience for his reports. Undoubtedly his political and personal agenda affected his perspective. Anyone wishing to employ the vast trove of documents that Cornies preserved must think hard about his motivations, and this itself is a clear justification for studying his life.

There is a second good reason to focus on Cornies: outliers often do a great deal to shape history. Cornies's Mennonite community, which never made up more than a tiny proportion of the tsarist Russian population, is a good example of what might be called the "outlier thesis."[53] Mennonite economic accomplishments were subjected to intense state scrutiny in the mid-nineteenth century as the state sought ways to imitate their success in other peasant communities. The Ministry of State Domains devoted extraordinary amounts of attention to this tiny, isolated sect. The first article in the fourth edition of the ministry's journal was a long description of Mennonite history, social organization, and agricultural practices, and a description of the Mennonite administrative system – authored by Cornies – was distributed to ministry offices throughout the empire.[54] Such documents tell us important things about the Mennonites, but they equally reveal important things about state aspirations and policy-making. The state used Mennonites as a standard by which to judge others, so its attention to Mennonites inevitably reflected light onto other groups.

The outlier thesis applies as much to Cornies as it does to his Mennonite community. Cornies gained attention because he was an anomaly. Descriptions of his accomplishments, authored by Russian officials, foreign visitors, and other Mennonites, described what was eccentric about him and, in doing so, defined what others perceived as "normal." Microhistory, in the guise of biography, shows that the life of an eccentric individual is like a photographic negative of a society; the sharper the image appears, the sharper the world its subject inhabits.[55]

Cornies became the Mennonites' chief negotiator, promoting and defending Mennonite rights vis-à-vis the state, promoting and defending state demands within the Mennonite community, and promoting and defending his own reform agenda vis-à-vis both state and community. Despite his lack of a formal education, Cornies acquired a remarkable self-education, reading broadly on agriculture, forestry, economics, pedagogy, government, and theology. Limited by his rudimentary formal education, he read only in German, and his understanding of all of these subjects was a Western one. Yet his arena for implementing reforms was the southern frontier of the Russian Empire. Consequently, while he gained his formal expertise in the German language, he gained his practical expertise in a Russian context. More than anyone in the Mennonite community, he understood the Russian administrative world that constrained Mennonites. More than anyone in the Russian administration, he understood the Mennonite cultural world that shaped his community's responses to Russian policies. More than most Mennonites or Russians, he understood the opportunities (and dangers) presented by the West. Cornies's unique experiences, ambitions, and insights made him both insider and outsider to the Mennonite community, the Russian state, and the Western world. If the Russian Mennonites provide a unique perspective on the Russian colonial enterprise, Cornies provides a unique perspective, as insider and outsider, on both the Russian state and Mennonite society.

Chapter Two

Land of Opportunity, 1804–1817

When Johann Cornies arrived in New Russia in 1804 he was fifteen years old and fast approaching adulthood. Although there is no record of the event, his congregation probably symbolically recognized his majority by baptizing him in 1806 or 1807, and his parents would have recognized his adulthood in much more practical terms, relying upon their eldest son to take on important responsibilities as they established their new home on the frontier. The details of Cornies's life from 1804 until he emerged as a public figure in 1817 are hazy, but the main outlines are clear enough. He married, had his first child, moved with his wife and son into his own home in Ohrloff, became fast friends with Wilhelm Martens, got rich, and earned the respect of his community. By the age of twenty-eight he was a person of consequence.

Cornies only returned to the West once, briefly, in 1827. That story is detailed in chapter 4, but a striking observation he made during that trip fits here. For all the new and impressive things he encountered on his travels, he could not wait to return home to the Molochnaia. As he recorded in his travel journal, the German states were overcrowded and overregulated; New Russia, by comparison, was a land of opportunity.[1]

"Land of opportunity" is a cliché, but the land it usually refers to is the American frontier. The tsarist empire, by contrast, is firmly entrenched in historical literature as a land of heavy-handed bureaucracy and peasant servitude. The story of Cornies, and the broader Mennonite story it unveils, demands a reassessment of this assumption about Russia. This is a story about the unique experiences of an unusually successful individual in an unusually successful community. That success, however, could not have occurred without the opportunities the Russian Empire provided.[2]

The Molochnaia Immigration

Cornies's first years in the Molochnaia were a time when both the Mennonites and the tsarist state were feeling their way in the colonial experiment. The Napoleonic Wars had distracted Russia from Catherine's New Russian dreams, and the state mainly offered its new colonists advice, along with just a little material support.[3] For the Mennonites the struggle to establish a frontier community was all-engrossing and left little time to worry about their obligations to the state or whether they were building God's heaven on earth.

Under the circumstances it is remarkable how quickly the Molochnaia Mennonite settlement took root. In this it benefited from two things: the experiences and advice of members of the Khortitsa Mennonite settlement, which was founded in 1789 and was still struggling to survive in 1803; and the relative prosperity of the Molochnaia immigrants. That prosperity was no accident. In 1789 Russia was not picky about whom it permitted to immigrate, and many of the first Mennonite settlers were drawn from families that did not have the financial resources to easily establish a new community.[4] Khortitsa and the other eighteenth-century immigrant communities were an expensive experiment for Russia, which found itself investing scarce resources just to keep the colonists alive. In the early nineteenth century the tsarist administration began placing more stringent conditions on immigration. Molochnaia families had to prove that they could support themselves by providing evidence that they were arriving with at least 300 guilders in assets (roughly 1,000 paper rubles).[5] They brought with them livestock, agricultural equipment, and cash, all of which made their first years in New Russia easier than they had been for the Khortitsa Mennonites.[6]

The Cornies family left Mühlhausen in late June 1804, crossing the border into the Russian Empire at Grodno on 1 July. They left Grodno for Khortitsa on 4 July. In Grodno the Russian government issued them 47 silver rubles to cover food during their journey, which was expected to take forty days. They also received 50 paper rubles to buy food for their livestock.[7] There is no precise record of what the Cornies family brought with them to New Russia, beyond the 1,000 rubles in cash and assets they produced to meet Russian requirements.

The family spent their first year and a half in New Russia in the Khortitsa settlement. The precise dates are not recorded, though barring major delays they probably arrived in Khortitsa in late August 1804. They almost certainly moved on to the Molochnaia as early as the weather allowed in the spring of 1806 to give them time to build and plant before winter. They were definitely in the Molochnaia by 12 June 1806, when Heinrich was born.

There is no indication why the family stayed so long in Khortitsa. Many of the immigrant families spent their first winter there, but the Cornies family lingered for nearly two years. It seems unlikely that they intended to stay permanently – there was little land to be had in the original settlement, and the state had promised them land in the Molochnaia. More likely the shortage of building materials in the Molochnaia prompted the delay. The first twelve families who established the village of Ohrloff (the Cornies family's final destination) in 1805 found that there was not enough lumber available to build homes for everyone, and they spent the winter of 1805–6 with two or three families crowded into each completed home.[8]

Ohrloff was at the southern end of the Mennonite settlement, at the confluence of the Iushanle and Molochnaia Rivers. The Molochnaia flows out of the Azov Uplands – the southern edge of the Ukrainian Crystalline Shield – and into the Azov Lowlands, terminating at the Molochnaia Estuary, a saltwater lake separated from the Sea of Azov by a narrow spit of land. To the west of the Molochnaia River, a low ridge dotted with ancient burial mounds marks the western border of the lowlands. The Mennonite settlement as a whole sat in the transition zone between highlands and lowlands on a rolling, treeless steppe.[9]

The soil of the lowlands is less fertile than the famed chernozem (black soil) that made the Ukrainian Crystalline Shield the "breadbasket of Europe"; however, the floodplain of the Molochnaia River formed a narrow ribbon of chernozem cutting across the lowlands. Provided the rains came, the land would support the type of crop agriculture the Mennonites had known in the Vistula. However, those rains were anything but reliable; the region was semi-arid, and – particularly at the southern edge of the settlement, where Ohrloff was situated – drought was a frequent occurrence.[10]

The Mennonite land grant stretched east from the Molochnaia River, encompassing the smaller Kurushan and Iushanlee Rivers. The Mennonites established their first villages on the prime settlement sites along the east bank of the Molochnaia, but as the settlement grew, they founded new villages up the Kurushan and Iushanle Rivers on more marginal land. East of the settlement, Ukrainian and Russian peasant villages were springing up, particularly along the Tokmak River.[11] To the west, the land between the Iushanle River and the Sea of Azov was assigned to the semi-nomadic Nogai Tatar Horde, who numbered roughly 30,000 people. The Nogai land was suited for little but grazing, and in the summer the Nogais, with their large herds of sheep and horses, migrated through the region in search of good pasturage. In winter they settled in encampments along the Molochnaia River, and before the Mennonites arrived their winter homes were often well to the north of their official land allotment. When the Mennonites arrived, the Nogais lost access to these prime settlement sites, one of which became the village of Ohrloff.[12] West of the Molochnaia River along its lower reaches were nine Doukhobor villages. A persecuted sect, the pacifist Doukhobors, most of them Russian and Ukrainian peasants, believed that their leader was a "personification of Christ."[13] They began arriving in the region in 1802, a year before the Mennonites, after Tsar Alexander suspended their persecution and granted them the right to live in peace on their own land grant. Beginning in 1822 they were joined by a small group of Molokans, another pacifist sect.[14] On the upper reaches of the Molochnaia, across the river from the Mennonite settlement, Catholic and Lutheran settlers from the German states, part of the recruitment drive that brought the Mennonites to the region, began founding their own villages in 1803.[15]

The Cornies family took possession of fullholding number seven in Ohrloff in the spring of 1806.[16] The village was on the southern edge of the Mennonite settlement, its hearth sites facing a single street that ran along the south bank of the Kurushchan just east of its confluence with the Molochnaia. The Cornies hearth site was on the north side of the street, backing onto the Kurushchan. The Iushanle marked the southern edge of the Ohrloff land allotment and formed the border between the Mennonite settlement and the land of the Nogais. While this location received less rain than the northern villages in the settlement, Ohrloff had the advantage of water access on two fronts. It was prime agricultural land.

There were twenty fullholdings in the village, twelve settled in 1805 and eight in 1806. A fullholding was sixty-five *desiatinas*, but this included common pasturage and land reserved for planting trees. Hearth sites consisted of one and a half *desiatinas* of land, where the new settlers built their distinctive housebarns and planted gardens (a housebarn was a combination house, barn, and implement shed).[17] Behind the houses on the south side of the street the village's ploughland and pasture stretched to the Iushanle River. Each fullholding was permanently assigned twenty-five *desiatinas* of crop land, much of which remained untouched for several years. Eventually a *desiatina* of land behind each hearth site would become a tree lot. The rest of the village land was common pasture and, along the Iushanle, hay meadows.

Two Moravian Brethren missionaries from the village of Sarepta on the Volga visited the Molochnaia on 15 September 1806, and they provide the first detailed description of the Mennonite settlement. Reflecting the speed with which the Molochnaia Mennonites had settled into

Land of Opportunity, 1804–1817   27

Photograph 1. The gravestone of David Cornies (1794–1873), looking east from the Ohrloff village cemetery. The line of trees in the background was the location of the village of Ohrloff. Source: Maryna Belikova, "David Cornies's Gravestone," 2016, photograph, provided by photographer.

their new homes, the description hardly seems to portray a frontier outpost at all:

> The order and cleanliness of the interior and exterior of their houses, and of their stables, barns, gardens, and fields, proves that this must be an extremely self-disciplined folk … [The Mennonites] have accomplished so much in two years, and so little remains to be finished, … that one realises how very much work they have done … All of their buildings and everything in them is very orderly, and they also have several beautiful windmills equipped with storage hoppers that produce wonderfully fine flour, although it is still not sold outside of the settlement. They have wisely sent a man to Taganrog with butter to sell, and soon they will export other products. The Mennonites understand unusually well that they must take notice of their opportunities.[18]

The Molochnaia region presented both challenges and opportunities to its new colonists. The soil and climate were altogether different from what the Mennonites had known in Prussia. The soil along the river was rich, but the thick sod was a serious physical obstacle for the first settlers, and as late as 1813 the Mennonites had still barely ploughed enough land to grow food for themselves and their livestock.[19] Inconsistent precipitation meant that in bad years the region sometimes failed to produce even seed grain for the following year. This was the most critical first hurdle for the Mennonites: until they could build up enough grain reserves to survive bad years there would be little opportunity to really prosper. The long-term challenge was to learn what agricultural practices would work best in their new circumstances, but first they had to figure out how to manage community resources to ensure that there was always enough grain set by to allow them to survive droughts. The back-breaking work of breaking the sod and sowing and harvesting crops dominated their first Molochnaia years, leaving little room for other pursuits.

Mennonites survived these years in part through state subsidies and tax exemptions. Each family received 444 rubles in subsidies to cover travel costs, build and furnish homes, and buy agricultural implements. The money the Cornies family received in Grodno came from this fund. They also received eight kopeks per person per day for food until the first harvest came in. This money was an interest-free loan to be repaid over the following ten years, although the state eventually extended the repayment period to fifteen years.[20] In the late nineteenth century, as Germany came to dominate European diplomatic affairs, Russian nationalists would claim that these subsidies were the sole basis of the exceptional wealth of the "German" Mennonites, and this explanation survives and flourishes in some modern Mennonite historiography. In fact, colonial subsidies were shared by all manner of New Russian settlers, including Ukrainian peasants resettled to the frontier from Smolensk.[21] It is true that subsidies differed by group, with immigrants from the German states receiving more generous support than Slavic immigrants, and it is equally true that without the subsidies the Mennonite settlement might not have survived, but subsidies by themselves do not account for the Mennonites' later exceptional prosperity.[22]

Apart from contributing to their survival, the subsidies had one important additional effect: they tied Mennonites into the state administrative system and thus helped establish the basic framework of the colonists' relationship to the tsarist government. That framework had little to do with the ideal relationship imagined in the Mennonite Privilegium, for local circumstances and international conditions imposed their own order on things.

The Guardianship Committee that oversaw the Mennonites was briefly described in chapter 1. Its name indicates its intended function:

it was supposed to be a paternal institution, protecting colonists and in return enjoying their unquestioning obedience. In practice, the committee was understaffed and underfunded, and it depended on the cooperation of colonists as much as on that obedience. The first years of Mennonite settlement coincided with the Napoleonic Wars, and the state lacked the resources or energy to closely oversee its colonial projects. So instead, it offered the Mennonites a small amount of money and other resources, and a lot of advice. It provided opportunities for Mennonites but could hardly insist that they seize upon them.

The Cornies Family in Ohrloff

Johann Cornies is a striking example of a Mennonite who did seize upon new opportunities. Other Mennonites also grew wealthy quickly – Cornies's close friend Wilhelm Martens was one of them – and most Mennonites prospered, so that by 1817 the Molochnaia Mennonites were already a notable success story. Cornies's experiences help reveal why this was possible.

Johann Cornies Sr., at sixty-five, was one of the sixteen oldest people in the entire Molochnaia settlement when the family arrived, but he had a much younger wife (Maria was forty-six) and three sons to share in the exhausting agricultural work.[23] Women took on a full load of the work, which meant that Maria, who was pregnant with Heinrich when the family arrived in Ohrloff, and who also had six-year-old Katharina to care for until her death in 1808, had a double burden.

According to David Epp, the Cornies family was very poor in those first years. The money they brought with them was soon exhausted. Johann Sr. during his travels had learned naturopathic medicine, and he had brought basic medical books with him from Prussia. He now supplemented the family's income by serving as a community doctor. Nogais from south of the Iushanle, settlers in the Catholic and Lutheran German settlements west of the Molochnaia, and Russian and Ukrainian peasants also found their way to his door for treatment.[24]

Johann went to work making money for the family in various ways, and it is likely that his first ventures were at his father's bidding. David Epp, writing one hundred years later, provides the only details from these early years, and he does not identify his sources.[25] Epp strikes a romantic tone, writing that already during the family's time in Khortitsa, Cornies, supervised by his father, "took over the brandy distillery."[26] Johann Sr. had been a distiller in Mühlhausen, and he and his son may well have turned to that skill while in Khortitsa, but the notion that his teenaged son ran the entire operation is far-fetched. Epp seems on firmer ground about the period after the family arrived in Ohrloff; he writes that Cornies went to work as an apprentice at an Ohrloff flour mill. According to Epp, at the age of nineteen (so probably in 1808), Cornies left the mill to become a trader, carting butter, ham, and cheese to markets in Crimea.[27]

In one of his most vivid passages, Epp describes Cornies's encounters with the Nogais in this period, claiming that Cornies "was often forced to ride for his life [from] those barbaric tribesmen."[28] Epp was almost certainly indulging his imagination; although the state disarmed the Nogais after a violent incident in 1811, there is no record of bandits roving the steppe. If they existed, it is difficult to believe that Cornies, driving a cart loaded with butter, could have outrun them!

While Epp may have embellished, it seems certain that soon after the Cornies family arrived in the Molochnaia, Johann began the entrepreneurial activities that would eventually make him one of the richest people in New Russia. Epp's account of Cornies carting butter to market in Crimea fits with Johann Eck's 1806 account of anonymous Mennonite traders. A second, slightly different account confirms Cornies's merchant ventures. It comes from Auguste de Marmont, a French nobleman who visited the Molochnaia in 1834 and lodged with Cornies during his brief stay. Marmont claimed that Cornies became a merchant only after his father's death in 1814. In this version, Cornies used a 4,000-ruble inheritance to finance his merchant activities, which "lasted three years, and after that time, its capital amounted to seven thousand rubles."[29] Marmont's version seems less likely than Epp's, for Cornies purchased a fullholding immediately after his father's death, and it is difficult to imagine how he found the money to do so if he used his inheritance to fund his merchant activities. Moreover, once he leased his land on the Iushanle in 1812 he would have had less time to travel. When Cornies received a copy of Marmont's account he wrote that it was "not quite accurate," perhaps referring to this apparent error.[30]

Mennonite accounts of Cornies usually credit his early economic successes to a unique character that destined him for greatness. Epp writes of his "almost impudent boldness, paradoxically coupled with a genuine trust in God ... Honesty, diligence, frugality, and, above all, reliability enabled Cornies to amass, in a relatively short period of time, a tidy sum of money ... He was a born pioneer in almost every sense of the word. He was one of those who see opportunities everywhere, and prosper in almost everything."[31] It is true that Cornies's many achievements distinguished him, but family circumstances helped make his accomplishments possible. Johann Sr., who lived on into his seventies, was still healthy and robust.[32] With his father at home to manage the household, Cornies was freer than many Mennonites of his age to pursue other activities. It helped that his brothers Peter and David were already old enough in 1806 (fifteen and twelve respectively) to do a significant share of the farmwork. His mother Maria undoubtedly also did more than her share. As noted earlier, Johann's early entrepreneurship was probably a matter of family duty.

We know almost nothing about the relationship between Cornies and his parents. He referred lovingly to his mother in letters from the late 1820s and early 1830s (she died on 4 July 1833), but Johann Sr. died on 24 June 1814, before his son became an active letter writer, and Cornies only mentions his father once in his surviving correspondence: in the last year of his own life, he fondly reflected that his beloved grandson, another Johann, resembled his great-grandfather "entirely in regard to his features, characteristics and behaviour."[33]

As for Johann's relationships with his brothers, he was seventeen when Heinrich was born and their relationship appears to have been more paternal than fraternal, hinting that Cornies inherited the role of father figure when Johann Sr. died. Even in his relationship to David, just five years his junior, Johann frequently adopted a paternal tone. In almost all of his surviving letters to David and Heinrich and eventually to his own son Johann, Cornies strikes a cold, stern, critical note. Perhaps this echoed his relationship to his own father.[34]

Cornies's relationship to his brother Peter is harder to discern. Both lived their lives in Ohrloff, and while Johann clearly overshadowed his brother in every way, Peter was a reputable fullholder and held office as Ohrloff village mayor in the late 1830s and early 1840s. Almost no correspondence between the brothers survives; even when Johann travelled and wrote letters home to the rest of the family, he did not write to Peter. In his later years, as Johann became preoccupied with public affairs, David, Heinrich, Johann Jr., and Johann's daughter Agnes all played a part in managing Cornies's extensive landholdings, but not Peter. When Peter died in 1847, Johann mentioned his brother's death only in passing, deep in the last page of a letter to a friend in Prussia.[35] Did those early years, when Johann travelled and made his fortune while Peter was stuck at home to do the farmwork, set the tone for their later relationship? The answer must be left to conjecture.

In 1811 Cornies married Aganetha Klassen (1792–1847), the daughter of Cornelius Klassen from the Molochnaia village of Rückenau. There is no record of how they met or courted, or even the exact date of their marriage, but general Mennonite practices in the period offer some expectations. Opportunities for young men and women to meet and become acquainted were limited. Men typically identified a prospective bride from their own village, though sometimes from other villages within the settlement. The father of the prospective groom carried the marriage proposal to the parents of the prospective bride, and if the woman accepted, the marriage followed at the home of the bride's parents, usually within two weeks of the engagement.[36]

Johann's mother Maria was also a Klassen, so there may have been a family connection that led to the acquaintance; it is unlikely that the two were first cousins, but second cousins would not have raised any eyebrows. Johann's three brothers also married Klassen women, and Peter's wife Agatha and Heinrich's wife Margaretha were Aganetha's sisters. The temptation to imagine some matchmaking at work is irresistible, though unsupported by any direct evidence.

Aganetha required her parents' consent to accept a proposal, but she had the right to reject a proposal on her own, and there are enough documented cases to show that this right was sometimes invoked by women in the tsarist Mennonite community. Many factors would have influenced such a decision, including the opinion of the prospective bride's parents and the economic prospects of the prospective groom. There were neither bride prices nor dowries, but in small communities like Ohrloff, where every family knew the details of their neighbours' lives, the prospects of a potential husband must have been a consideration.[37] Apparently Aganetha and her parents found Johann acceptable on this front – by 1811 his merchant adventures were probably already turning a tidy profit.

The newlyweds moved into a cottage on Johann Sr.'s fullholding, and on 10 December 1812 they had a son. Following Mennonite customs, he too was named Johann (1812–1882). Over the following seven years, they would see three children die in childbirth before their last child, Agnes (1819–1858), was born on 11 December 1819.[38] As with so much from this period, we have no idea what toll these three infant deaths took on Johann and Aganetha, but they must have caused deep sorrow.[39]

Romantic love seldom played a significant role in marriage decisions. It was a relatively new concept in early nineteenth-century society except among the elite.[40] A woman's right to make decisions about marriage based on love was virtually unknown in pre-modern agrarian societies. The survival of the entire community hinged on the creation of economically viable families, which formed the basic economic units of the community. Under such conditions, romantic love could not be permitted to play a central role in matchmaking.[41]

This seems a grimly utilitarian perspective on marriage, and there is evidence that Cornies did not share it. His correspondence from later years shows that he loved Aganetha deeply. In the last decade of her life he agonized over her declining health, and when she died in 1846 he wrote that it left him "shattered."[42] Cornies also – in a manner perhaps unique for his community at the time – left a number of reflections on the importance of romantic love. Writing about the Nogai Tatars in 1825 he described their customs of matchmaking and bride price with deep disapproval, saying that "the girl's wishes do not count, though there are sensible parents who love their child more than money and consider what she desires. However, a girl is rarely asked, and objects just as rarely. Completely submissive to the customs of her people, she moves toward every fate, unacquainted with the wishes and requirements with which we conduct such steps."[43] The practice of matchmaking without reference to the wishes of women, he went on, was a consequence of a Nogai society in which "men are not aware that they can touch the tender cords which open to love the eye and heart of the wife or young woman."[44] Here, clearly and very unusually for Mennonite sources from the period, is an explicit endorsement of romantic love and of the right of women to choose their marriage partners based on love.

These were principles that Cornies eventually applied to his own children, both of whom married at a relatively late age, Agnes at twenty-six and Johann Jr. at thirty. This was sufficiently unusual to attract the attention of Cornies's friend Andrei Fadeev, who in 1840 asked him when he planned to "marry off" his children. Cornies replied that according to the practices of the Mennonites, "parents are not allowed to marry off their children. It is one of their principles that they do not try to arouse a desire to marry in their children."[45] In 1847, when the recently widowed Johann Jr. travelled to Prussia and found, courted, and married his second wife, Cornies expressed deep concern about the nature of the relationship between his son and his future daughter-in-law. When he learned from a Prussian friend that "mutual attraction is supposed to have caused this connection," he replied that "such a union, where true love and delicate inclinations are paired with honest mutual love, is a genuinely blessed marriage. What can the person fear who loves and is loved?"[46]

Entrepreneurship and Wealth

Soon after his marriage, on 1 January 1812, Cornies leased 3,500 *desiatinas* of unoccupied Mennonite reserve land from the Guardianship Committee for 300 rubles per year.[47] That he signed this lease at a time when most Molochnaia Mennonites were still struggling to break sod reveals that he had managed to accrue a little bit of money quickly and that he had already recognized that raising sheep (his lease lands were suited to little else) made more economic sense than growing grain. The land, along the Iushanle twelve *versts* (12.8 kilometres) east of Ohrloff, became Cornies's Iushanle estate and eventually the headquarters for his administrative empire.

Before 1812 Cornies had focused his attention on the frontier market cities to the south, on the Sea of Azov and the Black Sea. He enjoyed some success, but he also learned that the Molochnaia was a long way from those markets and that carting perishable goods over bad roads through sometimes hostile territory was no way to make a living. Also, while Mennonites needed to grow enough grain to feed themselves, unreliable weather and the lack of good roads and local ports meant there was little point investing the time and energy it would require to produce large surpluses. So Cornies turned his attention away from the relatively free but limited southern trading economy and looked north instead, toward the Russian state. That decision had real symbolic and practical significance for him: the Iushanle lease came from the Guardianship Committee, the principal New Russian agent of the Russian state, and Cornies's control of this land was conditional, in that it depended upon his good relationship to that committee. Thus, he had tied the centrepiece of his economic empire to his relationship to the state.

In choosing to raise sheep Cornies was buying into the state's economic policy. Since 1804 the Guardianship Committee had been promoting sheep in colonist communities in New Russia with all of its energy. The state offered cheap leases as well as a small breeding stock of valuable merino sheep. An 1809 pamphlet commissioned by Minister of Internal Affairs Aleksei Kurakin promised that eventually colonists who took up sheep rearing would be rewarded with permanent land grants.[48]

The sheep improvement program was one of the first manifestations of the state's changing attitude toward New Russia. Rather than the passive didactic role as model colonists that Catherine the Great had envisioned, this was a plan to employ the colonies as a laboratory for new agricultural experiments. It did not yet insist that the colonists participate, instead offering rewards for volunteers. That merino sheep were introduced to the region testifies to the experimental nature of the project. Most sheep in New Russia were of the kurdiuch breed, hardy and inured to the regional climate, but with a coarse wool that had little market value. People raised them for their hides and for rendering tallow. Purebred merinos were badly suited to the steppe climate and required more care and attention than most settlers could offer. The new program intended to interbreed the merinos with kurdiuch in order to produce sheep that could survive on the steppe but produce fine wool that could be sold on international markets. This was a specialized, painstaking process that required carefully segregating the purebred merinos and each subsequent generation of interbred sheep through five generations. Sheep of the fifth generation produced wool of a quality approaching that of the original merinos, but they had to be permanently segregated from unrefined kurdiuch sheep to prevent a reversion.[49]

The state provided Cornies with an attractive lease on a huge swathe of land; Cornies provided the venture with local knowledge. His travels had allowed him to assess regional conditions and to learn the practices of the neighbouring Nogai Tatars, who kept large flocks of sheep and herds of horses. He also knew the regional markets for wool and the local labour markets for the shepherds he would need to hire. Already in 1812 he brought something important to the bargaining table, and when the Guardianship Committee approved the lease, a partnership began that would pay off for all concerned.

Secular Authority and Religious Tensions

Cornies's entanglements with the Guardianship Committee involved him in the most significant source of tensions between Mennonites and the tsarist state. The state wanted two things from the Mennonites. The first was that they be orderly and prosperous so that they did not draw upon state resources, either by demanding excessive economic support or by fomenting internal disputes that might force the state to waste scarce administrative resources intervening in their affairs. The Mennonites established this type of internal order by applying their traditional congregational administrative structures. The state's second requirement was that the Mennonites be responsive to its reform policies and indeed serve as technicians in the state's New Russian laboratory of modernization. That meant it needed a secular Mennonite administrative system through which to pass orders and assess results. Mennonites had such a secular administration, but the boundaries between it and the congregational system were amorphous; even the authority of congregational leaders over individual Mennonites was far from clear.

The secular administrative system described in chapter 1, of *volosts* with their elected mayors, and villages with their elected mayors and ten-men, represented the state's attempt to bolster its inadequate administrative structures by co-opting local people into the system. The state did not intend the system to be in any sense representative: the role of local officials was to communicate and enforce official state policies, not to represent local concerns to the state.

Secular administrative agencies were not new to the Mennonites, for while their religion forbade them to swear oaths or hold public office, in Prussia they had participated in local organizations such as dike societies. One of the peculiarities of the first fifteen years of the Russian colonial period is that the secular Mennonite administration took on a practical representative role that was quite unintended by the state. Most Mennonite contact with the state revolved around requesting and distributing aid, rather than following government orders. This must have sent false signals to the Mennonites about their position. Certainly they showed few signs of understanding their elected secular representatives as authoritative voices of state policy in their communities, at least before the 1820s. Indeed, when the first Molochnaia congregational elder, Jakob Enns, quarrelled with the first *Gebietsamt* mayor, Klaas Wiens, the mayor came out the clear loser, finding himself under the ban until he relented.[50] It would later come as a surprise to many Mennonites when the state began to assert that the secular leadership was the state's authoritative voice in the settlement. It was equally a surprise to the state when it encountered resistance to its assertions of secular power.

The settlement's elected administration, the *Gebietsamt*, was more important in the Mennonite settlement than in other colonial settlements, for the Mennonites had a Privilegium that formally granted them rights as well as obligations. While this arrangement was not unique to the Mennonites – the Crimean Armenian communities had a comparable charter – most foreign colonists were subject only to Catherine the Great's 1763 decree defining the terms of immigration. Charters were rare, and the Mennonites' strong sense of corporate identity helped them use their Privilegium as both a precedent and a framework for negotiations with the state.[51] Their most important right was their exemption from military service, and the Mennonites' historical willingness to assert that right even in the face of harsh punishment meant that the state's power over the Mennonites, while enormous, was not unlimited. Because members of the *Gebietsamt* had the power to represent Mennonite interests to the state, elections in the settlement were sometimes hotly contested. The most significant elections in the late 1830s and early 1840s – described in chapters 7 and 8 – gave rise to major crises with far-reaching effects.

Ohrloff, the Cornies family's new home, was particularly important in the early settlement's religious life and provided the stage for the first major conflict between religious and secular authority. Jakob Enns, the elder of the first Molochnaia Mennonite congregation, made his home there, and in 1809 the village built the settlement's first church (a second was built in Petershagen in 1810). In 1806 the Cornies family arrived at a village that was at the centre of religious controversy. That spring, when Enns assembled his preachers and deacons in Ohrloff to discuss church business, one of the deacons, Johann Huebert, reported on disputes in the village of Muntau that had led to open fighting among the settlers. This fighting was a serious violation of Mennonite pacifist beliefs. When Enns responded by saying that he had already referred the matter to the *Gebietsamt*, another deacon, Klaas Reimer, was outraged, protesting that "according to the holy scriptures it was incumbent on us to rectify the situation and not the *Gebietsamt*."[52]

Klaas Reimer's accounts of religious disputes in the Molochnaia reflect a particular, strongly conservative religious perspective, and it is difficult to know how deeply such divisions ran. Indeed, little is known about everyday religious life because most of what we know comes from reactions to crises, and the sources inevitably highlight the extremes and ignore the mundane. We are left with a handful of reasonable assumptions, of church on Sunday mornings with silent prayer, the singing of Psalms, seated elders reading sermons from published collections brought with them from Prussia, and daily prayers and Bible readings at home. Theirs was a life of conscious, disciplined Christian devotion.

The Polish Mennonite communities from which the Molochnaia Mennonites came provide more evidence about religious life, but these sources too have their weaknesses. At the time the first Molochnaia settlers emigrated, the Polish Mennonite community was in the midst of major changes. By the 1790s the Frisian and Flemish congregations were beginning to merge, signalling a liberalization of Flemish beliefs and practices. The first wave of Molochnaia Mennonite immigrants were members of the Flemish congregation, which raises (but does not answer) the question of whether their immigration was partly motivated by a rejection of this merger.

A second problem with assumptions based on the Polish Mennonite religious milieu is that Mennonite congregations were notoriously idiosyncratic. Before the late nineteenth century their elected elders were distinguished by their reputations for faith and wisdom but seldom by their formal education. Consequently, while all congregations shared a basic set of values, they could differ markedly in everyday practices. One source of tension in the early Molochnaia years was that the settlement threw together Mennonites drawn from across the Prussian Flemish congregations, whose different religious expectations made it difficult for them to agree on elders and practices.[53] When the Molochnaia settlement was established, the eighteen villages formed a single congregation with Jakob Enns as its elder. He was a controversial figure, described by Heinrich Goerz as "prone to anger" and with a "lust for power."[54]

The reputation of the Flemish congregation was one of religious conservatism, quietism, and formalism. A typical account, this one from Mennonite historian Cornelius Krahn, says of the first Molochnaia settlers that "in educational and religious practices the pioneers in Russia were extremely conservative, preserving the practices of the old homeland. Ministers read their sermons monotonously. Very little progress was made in challenging the congregations and individuals in their ethical and religious practices and in awakening their social, missionary, and evangelistic responsibilities."[55] Daniel Schlatter, who passed through the Prussian Mennonite communities on his way to the Molochnaia in 1822, was far from impressed, writing that their faith was "superficial," formalistic, and showed little evidence of "true belief."[56] He reported much the same of the Mennonites he encountered in the Molochnaia. The problem with such accounts is that they were written from a Pietist religious perspective that saw "proper" religious life as rooted in an aggressively evangelical world view. From such a perspective, the first Molochnaia Mennonites were the antithesis of a true, living faith.

A second, equally reproachful group of accounts decries the first settlers for being too religiously liberal. In 1812 a small group of Mennonites broke away from the Molochnaia Flemish congregation and founded the unsanctioned Small Congregation (*Kleine Gemeinde*). Their leader, Klaas Reimer, criticized the Molochnaia Mennonites for their contributions to the Russian government during the Napoleonic Wars and for their use of secular punishments for Mennonites who violated laws. If Pietists condemned the Molochnaia Mennonites for their quietism, the Kleine Gemeinde condemned them for being too worldly.[57]

Johann Cornies tells us nothing directly about religious life during the first fifteen years of the Molochnaia Mennonites, but his and his father's interactions with the Nogais, Slavic peasants, and Catholic and Lutheran German peasants raise questions about how insular the community really was. Certainly there is not even a hint that their activities attracted scrutiny or condemnation from the religious hierarchy, and Cornies's growing status within his community, leading to his appointment as land surveyor in 1817, indicates at least a passive endorsement of his engagement with "the world." The same can be said of other entrepreneurial Molochnaia Mennonites. Johann Klassen, who built a cloth mill in the village of Halbstadt in 1817, is absent from the records of religious disputes in the period. Whatever the nature of their religious conservatism, Molochnaia Mennonites apparently had room for broad engagement with their local New Russian world. They countenanced travel, entrepreneurship, and negotiations with the state. While their formal religious practices were insular, in their day-to-day lives their religious beliefs did not erect barriers to a larger engagement with the communities that surrounded them.

The Prussian Mennonite immigrants brought with them to the Molochnaia a congregational administrative system. In Prussia most had been members of the Flemish congregation, and they consequently arrived in New Russia with a substantial bond of agreement as to their basic community structures. These were described in chapter 1: Mennonites elected congregational elders, preachers, and deacons. These figures were respected members of the community who served without pay and supported themselves by working their own fullholdings. Apart from their religious functions, congregational authorities enforced the moral code of their society, but they had a limited repertoire of mechanisms to assert their authority, and they operated largely through moral suasion. When improprieties came to their attention they counselled, advised, and reprimanded community members, and when these actions failed to resolve problems, they referred the transgression to the *Bruderschaft* (Brotherhood), an assembly of all male members of the congregation, which could resort to the community's strongest disciplinary mechanism: banning the transgressor from community fellowship. The ban excluded the transgressor from the Holy Sacraments and from all interaction with the rest of the community. In the Flemish congregation even spouses were forbidden to speak to their banned mates. The ban usually only lasted for a few days, or at most a week or two. Then, so long as the transgressors publicly repented, the *Bruderschaft* accepted them back into its fold.[58]

The ban was an effective means of asserting social control, and it was probably even more effective in New Russia than it had been in Prussia, where Mennonites at least had the option of leaving their church and community. In New Russia, Mennonites could not live outside of the Mennonite settlement without the explicit permission of the state, so the ban utterly isolated them. However, the ban also had significant limitations. Because Mennonites were pacifists who rejected all forms of corporal punishment, if a member of the community was willing to accept the isolation brought on by the ban, there was little else the community could do. Moreover, when Mennonites committed serious crimes against one another, the ban might amount to an inconsequential punishment in no way proportionate to the crime. One vivid example of this is the case of Cornelius Janzen, a preacher who raped an unidentified woman sometime between 1816 and 1819. Klaas Reimer recounted the incident in his autobiography:

> God made manifest [Janzen's] disgrace ... Janzen had forcibly committed his shame on the open steppes giving [his victim] no peace of conscience.

Instead she came to him during the night from a distance to discuss the matter with him ... Janzen was very casual regarding the entire affair and simply advised her that he had committed the matter to God and that she should do likewise ... [The congregation] then removed [Janzen] from his office as preacher as they did not know what else they could do. Later they also placed him under the ban for three or four days.[59]

Clearly, removal from his ministerial position and "three or four days" under the ban was a punishment in no way proportionate to Janzen's serious crime.

Also, the congregational officials were extremely limited in their ability to interfere in internal family matters. The Mennonite family was strongly patriarchal. Only rarely did wives or adult children turn to congregational officials to ask for intervention in family disputes, and the congregation usually limited its intervention to stern admonishments. It required family members to admit their infractions before it would employ public censure, and because families seldom were willing to air their dirty laundry in public, community authority over the family was sharply constrained, even where the infractions were serious.[60]

The inability of the congregational authorities to discipline their members effectively meant that Mennonites were faced at times with the difficult question of whether and to what degree they should permit the Russian state to intervene in their internal affairs. A second example highlights the challenges. Sometime around 1820, Franz Thiessen raped his daughter Anna, and both were accused of incest. When Franz Thiessen would not bend to congregational discipline, the *Gebietsamt*, with the approval of congregational authorities, turned both Franz and Anna over to Russian civil authorities. They were imprisoned in the regional administrative centre of Orekhov. A Kleine Gemeinde leader, Abraham Friesen, protested this use of Russian secular authority in the settlement and appealed to Elder Bernard Fast to intervene. Fast refused, and Franz Thiessen died soon after in the Orekhov prison. The plight of poor Anna is described in a second Friesen letter: "She languishes away because of starvation and lack of clothing. In addition she has been terribly savaged by lice. Yes, so that she is weeping night and day and has no hope."[61] Anna was ultimately exiled to Siberia, never to return.

The cases of Janzen and the Thiessens reveal an underlying problem in the Molochnaia settlement. The community wanted to be independent and self-regulating, but its self-regulating system was not always up to the job. The enormous emphasis that Mennonites placed on individual conscience was at the core of the problem. Congregational discipline was based on transgressors confessing their sins, repenting, and being readmitted to the fellowship. If transgressors would not confess, congregational authorities could not punish them. When transgressors did confess, the punishment – exclusion from the community – obviously emphasized community over individual, but still, the prerequisite of confession emphasized the primacy of the individual's relationship with God. This was consistent with that basic tenet of Anabaptist faith, that adults make the personal choice to be baptized into the congregation.

In the autocratic Russian state, this streak of individualism had the potential to become extremely controversial. The Privilegium was an agreement between the state and the Mennonite community, and it assumed that the community would act as a single, cohesive unit in its relationship to the state. If Mennonites had such limited means to assert community authority over individuals even as it related to internal matters of morality, it would be very difficult to assert authority in response to external orders.

The Thiessen case also reveals that the Molochnaia congregation was far from united. While the settlement officially had just one congregation until 1819 (see chapter 3), a second, unofficial congregation, the Kleine Gemeinde, had emerged in 1812. Its leader, Klaas Reimer, had immigrated to New Russia to escape what he viewed as the worldly attitudes of Mennonites in Prussia. He soon concluded that the Molochnaia was little different from Prussia, and he criticized both the laxity of church discipline in the new settlement and the authority of the *Gebietsamt*. From 1812 Reimer led a small but clearly defined unofficial congregation. The Kleine Gemeinde demonstrates that the community unity that the Russian state took for granted was not a reality.[62]

The preceding examples reveal the tensions the Molochnaia Mennonites experienced in their starkest, most serious terms, and they are indicative of a broader problem. As long as the state was preoccupied with international affairs and the Mennonites were preoccupied with basic frontier survival, Mennonites enjoyed substantial autonomy. Once the community was firmly established and the Napoleonic Wars were over, the state would try to reassert itself. By 1817 it was ready to demand that Mennonites live up to their bargain and play the role of model colonists that their Privilegium defined for them. Because the community was not united in its attitude toward the state, this led to conflict.

Growing Wealthy

In the midst of these community disputes, Cornies established himself as a prosperous merchant, landowner, and entrepreneur. In 1813 he erected a Mennonite housebarn on his Iushanle estate, and by 1820 he had added a small cottage, a sheep barn to protect his merino stock in winter, and a corral. The Iushanle sheep ranch became the springboard to Cornies's future wealth. The details of his Iushanle business affairs in these early years are unclear, but the general outline is unmistakable. In 1811 the Cornies family – Johann Sr., Maria, Johann, Peter, David, and Heinrich – was slightly better off than average: it owned eight horses (the average Molochnaia Mennonite family had six), twelve head of cattle (the average was nine), and seven sheep (the average was also seven). By 1813 the Cornies household – now including Aganetha and Johann – owned twice as much livestock as the village average, and by 1820 Cornies kept a herd of 1,425 sheep, 100 cattle, and 180 horses at Iushanle.[63]

Johann Sr. died on 28 June 1814, leaving each of his sons an inheritance of 4,000 rubles. That was enough to permit Johann and Peter to purchase their own fullholdings in Ohrloff. Maria retained the original family fullholding. David, who was still single (he married Helena Klassen in January 1821), stayed home and worked the original fullholding, and Heinrich, just eight, also remained home with his mother. As fullholders, Johann and Peter gained the important right to vote in village and settlement elections.

After 1813, fragments of Cornies's rudimentary bookkeeping records offer a hazy picture of his business activities. These early records, quite different from his detailed accounts in the 1830s and 1840s, are a chaotic collection of chits, scratched in his almost illegible hand on small sheets of paper, with hurried calculations and crossed-through notations scrawled at odd angles.[64] They are a reminder that Cornies's formal education probably extended no further than what was needed to permit him to read the Bible and keep his household accounts. David Epp describes the teenage Cornies reading insatiably during long wagon rides to market, and this may be true, but what books his community possessed were largely religious; he certainly was not reading *Business for Dummies*.[65] After 1812, as his affairs grew more complicated, Cornies taught himself to run a business even as he created it.

The records may not reveal details, but they do reveal the way that Cornies did business. Most of his Iushanle land was on the high steppe, suitable for grazing sheep and not much else. At first Cornies did not closely oversee the land, instead contracting shepherds to take care of the sheep in small lots of fifty or a hundred, grazing them at Iushanle. The herders who contracted to Cornies reflect the ethnic diversity of New Russia. They were Tatars, Armenians, German colonists, Ukrainian peasants, and an occasional Mennonite.[66] In these early years, Cornies was not only getting the lay of the physical environment, he was also parsing the cultural contours of New Russia.

By 1816 Cornies had accrued enough money to add a second important venture to his business pursuits. In partnership with Wilhelm Martens he purchased the rights to the state monopoly on the sale of spirits in the Molochnaia.[67] The Russian state maintained a monopoly on the sale of all spirits, selling the distribution rights to the highest bidders, and Cornies and Martens acquired the right to buy and resell all spirits produced in the Mennonite settlement. Cornies did no better in his bookkeeping for the "brandy monopoly" (as it was called) than for his sheep ranch; the most that we can say is that it was highly profitable. Eventually they would build their own distillery in Halbstadt. This business provided a steady income to Cornies for the next three decades. By the late 1820s it was turning a profit of more than 10,000 rubles per year.[68]

Cornies's friendship with Wilhelm Martens was particularly important. As with many of Cornies's personal relationships there is little evidence to go on, and most of their interactions were undoubtedly verbal. There is enough extant correspondence from their later years to show that they were good friends, but before the late 1830s the main evidence of their relationship is their joint business ventures. These were substantial and successful – by 1841 Martens was reputedly the wealthiest Molochnaia Mennonite, and Cornies was not far behind.[69] Besides their brandy business, the two worked together to market wool, and they jointly contributed large "gifts" to government officials when community interests dictated.

By the age of twenty-eight Cornies was well on his way to being a wealthy man. He already owned his own fullholding in Ohrloff. His Iushanle land, though leased rather than owned, gave him control of one of the largest single landholdings in the region – only a handful of Russian noble estate owners had more land – and his sheep-raising venture was turning a tidy profit. His brandy lease provided him with a share of one of the biggest money-making government contracts the region had to offer.

The Mennonite Oasis

To keep Cornies's success in context, it is worth remembering that his Mennonite community was already something special too. In the broad desert of struggling colonial communities, by 1817 the Molochnaia Mennonite settlement was a thriving oasis. This "desert and oasis" metaphor was a favourite of travellers to the Molochnaia throughout the nineteenth century, and the account of one visitor in 1819 confirms the prosperity the Mennonites had achieved just fifteen years after their arrival. The Quakers Stephen Grellet and William Allen visited the Molochnaia in May 1819, accompanied by Samuel Contenius, who acted as their guide and interpreter. The southern steppe appeared to Grellet to be a barren place – he called the region southwest of the Molochnaia a "desert" – and that made his impression of the Molochnaia Mennonites all the more vivid. "Their land," he wrote, "is in high cultivation; formerly, not a tree or shrub was to be seen on their vast steppes; now they have fine orchards of various kinds of good fruit. Travelling over these steppes, we saw, as we thought, at a distance, large groves of beautiful trees, and to our astonishment, the scenery continuously changed; at first it appeared as if the groves were in motion; on coming nearer, we found that they were flocks of cattle feeding."[70]

Grellet's description is reminiscent of Johann Eck's 1806 account: both travellers perceived the Mennonite settlement as a remarkably orderly, developed community. There is, however, an important difference between the two descriptions. Eck describes well-built houses and neatly laid-out yards, while Grellet describes orchards and pastures. The Mennonites had moved beyond the village streets and onto the steppe in the thirteen years that separated these accounts, building an orderly agricultural economy upon their orderly village foundations.

Grellet also describes the Mennonite settlement's administration: "The Emperor grants them every privilege, and liberty of a civil and religious nature. They choose their own magistrates, and are not under the authority of the police of the empire. This is exercised by themselves. They are exempt from military requisitions, and have no taxes, except those requisite among themselves, for their own government, and they are placed under the superintendence of those persons who preside over the colonies in the Crimea generally. Contenius is the chief person on whom that care now devolves."[71]

Grellet was suggesting that Mennonites enjoyed a degree of independence far beyond anything promised in their Privilegium. It seemed to him that the Mennonite oasis was not just a physical anomaly – it was also politically apart, an autonomous district, and perhaps even the "refuge from the world" that conservative Mennonites had dreamed of as they departed from Prussia at the turn of the century.

In this, Grellet was half right. The Mennonites, like all other New Russian colonists, experienced a remarkable degree of freedom in the early years of the nineteenth century. Most of Russia's energy and resources were focused on the West, on Napoleon. To the extent that Mennonites had engaged with the state, it was the Mennonites and not the state who were the initiators, pursuing subsidies and extensions on the repayment periods for their loans. The state did have an Inspector of Colonies who was responsible for the Mennonites, but that person covered a huge region and oversaw a large number of other colonists as well.[72] Colonists who did not ask for state interference or cause trouble were likely to draw little attention. So in these early years it was possible for Mennonites to delude themselves into thinking they were to receive their privileges without offering any services in return. It was this perception of autonomy that Grellet recorded.

What Grellet did not see was that after the Napoleonic Wars ended in 1815, the tsarist regime was poised to re-engage on the home front. Tsar Alexander I's transformation from liberal reformer to mystic reactionary after the Napoleonic Wars is well documented. Even as he promoted constitutional reforms in the West he turned away from the same ideals in Russia, leaving his elites disappointed and bitter. While Grellet was visiting the Molochnaia, in St. Petersburg and Kyiv disillusioned young military officers and intellectuals were already forming Russia's first secret revolutionary societies.[73] Although Alexander continued to promote religious toleration in the last years of his reign – it was he who sponsored Grellet's expedition, motivated by his interest in Quaker beliefs – the tsar and his administrators were readying themselves to take firmer control of colonial communities.

The consequences of this renewed state attention were felt by everyone in New Russia, and perhaps the group that best demonstrates it is the Doukhobors. A pacifist Christian sect, the Doukhobors had formed in the mid-eighteenth century. Archbishop Amvrosii Serebrennikov of Ekaterinoslav labelled them "Doukhobors" – Spirit Wrestlers – in 1785 as a derogatory epithet, implying that they wrestled against the Holy Ghost, but the Doukhobors embraced the name.[74] According to historians George Woodcock and Ivan Avakumovic, their core belief was in

> the immanence of God, in the presence within each man of the Christ spirit, which not only renders priesthood unnecessary, since each man is his own priest in direct contact with the divine, but also makes the Bible obsolete, since every man can be guided … by the voice within … Since the direction of their behaviour must come from within, they naturally deny the right of the state or other external authority to dictate their own actions. And, since all men are vessels for the divine essence, they regard it as sinful to kill other men, even in war.[75]

The Doukhobors experienced harsh state persecution in the eighteenth century, before Alexander relented and allowed them to settle as colonists on land southwest of the Molochnaia Mennonite settlement, along the lower reaches of the river. From 1803 to 1815 the Doukhobors, like the Mennonites, were largely left to their own devices, and they prospered. When the war ended they suddenly found the baleful eye of the Orthodox Church turned their way, and at the church's behest the state conducted the first of a series of investigations that ultimately led to their exile to the Caucasus in the 1840s.[76] The 1815–17 investigation resulted in the arrest of Doukhobor leader Savelii Kapustin and sixteen of his followers.[77] The accusations were groundless, and Alexander I intervened and ordered their release. Even so, the renewal of state attention signified by the Doukhobor investigation was an important sign of the changing times for all colonial communities.[78]

The Mennonites did not experience any of the hostile attention directed at the Doukhobors. Even so, the Doukhobor story clearly indicates that the Russian administration, freed from the distractions of the Napoleonic Wars, was ready to pay close attention to New Russian colonists once again. Grellet had no sense of this shifting situation. He described Samuel Contenius, head of the Guardianship Committee, as though he were a missionary who "from religious motives ... has devoted the last thirty years of his life to endeavours to promote the well-being of the several colonies."[79] There might be some truth to this characterization: Contenius was the son of a Westphalian Separatist minister, and he seemed fully at home with the Pietist sensibilities of his Quaker guests. He even acted as their interpreter at church meetings in the Molochnaia, where he was "so feeling in his manner of interpreting" that Grellet characterized him as "a faithful helper."[80] But Contenius was also the most important government official in the New Russian colonial settlements, one of the most effective tsarist administrators on the frontier, and a demanding taskmaster who in the coming years would drive the Mennonites to conform to state demands. If he came to the Molochnaia to guide and interpret for Grellet, he was also there with his eyes wide open, assessing the potential of his Mennonite charges to take up the active role envisaged for them in their Privilegium.

Conclusion: New Pathways

The ambiguities between individual autonomy, family authority, congregational authority, secular Mennonite authority, and secular state authority described in this chapter had one further implication that is important to the Russian Mennonite story. In the fissures between the responsibilities of each of these authorities there was space for real freedom.[81] There is an important distinction to be made between the individual autonomy that Mennonites asserted as a matter of private conscience and the freedom to publicly act upon that autonomy that grew out of ambiguity. In New Russia, Mennonites had found freedom to act and grow without punishment, as long as that growth was channelled along the fissures within defined authority. The prosperity that Mennonites achieved in Russia is often portrayed as developing in spite of the Russian state's interference and as a consequence of the community's unity. Mennonites are supposed by their historians to have created, by the late nineteenth century, a "Mennonite Commonwealth," a "state-within-a-state" that sheltered them from the dictates of the tsarist regime and accounted for their conspicuous prosperity.[82] While this is a convenient way to look at the community from the outside, looking from within reveals endless fissures in the unified facade.

Already in the first years of the Molochnaia Mennonite settlement, Johann Cornies was finding these fissures and exploiting them. When Cornies suggested in 1827 that New Russia was a land of opportunity, he showed how clearly he recognized these liberating opportunities. It was freedom, rather than community unity or state systems, that led him southward to coastal communities, where he traded butter and made a little money. It was freedom, too, that turned him to the north, where he seized the opportunities offered by the state in the form of leased land and the brandy monopoly, to make quite a lot of money.

Cornies spent the first decade of his adult life exploring his new homeland and learning to bring physical and economic order to his own small piece of the New Russian frontier. This readied him to move on to the personal, intellectual, and cultural frontiers of encounter with the Russian state, his own community, and the West. The orderly personal, business, and administrative practices he developed in his early years would synchronize easily with the orderly ideals of the Russian state. They would be tougher to synchronize with the religious and cultural diversities of his community.

Chapter Three

A Public Life, 1818–1824

The end of spring planting is always a time for celebration in agricultural communities, but Molochnaia Mennonites had more than the usual cause for excitement in 1818: in May the tsar himself visited the settlement. Alexander I was on his way to the Crimea, but his curiosity about the Molochnaia colonists led him to detour and see the Mennonite oasis with his own eyes. Mennonites prepared for his visit for weeks, and on the great day they lined the streets to see their sovereign. He did not disappoint, warmly greeting the crowds and stopping for breakfast at the home of David and Agatha Hiebert in the village of Lindenau. Hiebert later recounted Alexander's visit with obvious awe:

> The tsar did not take the place of honour at the head of the table. Instead he took an ordinary chair and sat at the side ... I asked him to sit on a better chair, but he responded, "No, my hosts shall have the place of honour." These words confused us and my wife said, "I am far too humble a servant to sit next to the Lord's anointed!"
>
> "No, dear child," replied the Emperor and took her hand and led her to the place of honour. "Sit down next to me for we are all only humans, created equal by God." I had to sit across the table from the Emperor. Then the general Gorchakov and the old Contenius were invited to come to the table.
>
> His Majesty ate with apparent appetite, drank beer and coffee during the meal and cordially inquired about our circumstances: how long had we been in his empire, how we liked it and whether we had any complaints about anyone. We thanked him for everything. Furthermore we implored his continued protection and the reception of our co-religionists who still remained in Prussia and apparently were in serious difficulty because of the war. Then the tsar said to my wife, "Yes, dear child, it shall be done."[1]

The tsar's visit was pregnant with implications for the Molochnaia Mennonites. Alexander was deeply impressed with what he saw: here was an orderly, prosperous Russian colonial community that could be held up alongside the best that the West had to offer. Indeed, after the devastation of the Napoleonic Wars, the Molochnaia settlement must have looked progressive even by Western European standards.

What Hiebert could hardly have known was that Alexander had a larger vision. As impressive as the Mennonite oasis was, the desert that surrounded it was of far greater concern to the tsar and his administration. Alexander had already launched a grand scheme to create military colonies in New Russia, and if the Mennonites had possessed a clearer sense of it, this might have given them pause.[2] The tsar was preparing to tighten his control of the empire's frontiers, and while the Mennonites were not about to be militarized, they would soon be called upon to expand the role that their Privilegium had originally defined for them as model colonists.

Samuel Contenius travelled with Tsar Alexander in 1818, but Hiebert barely mentions him. Of course, with the tsar at the breakfast table, "old Contenius" did not take the spotlight, but he should not be forgotten. Alexander's attention soon shifted elsewhere, but Contenius remained closely focused on the Mennonites. It was his job to make sure that Alexander's new colonial vision was realized, and in 1818 he was getting ready to put the Mennonites in harness.

Johann Cornies is not mentioned in any account of Alexander's 1818 trip to the Molochnaia, but in retrospect Hiebert's description places Cornies squarely in the frame. The tsar was sincere when he promised his hosts that he would not forget their fellow Mennonites in Prussia. In 1818 Russia was preparing to let a large new group of Mennonites immigrate to the Molochnaia, and Cornies would play a key role in the Mennonite Settlement Commission. This new role would transform Cornies's life, moving him into the heart of Mennonite public affairs and placing enormous demands on him. Cornies had experienced freedom and opportunity from 1806 to 1817; from 1818 to 1824, as the demands of the state placed greater and greater constraints on the Mennonite settlement, the demands of the settlement would close in upon him.

During those years, Cornies would become the most publicly and broadly engaged person in his community. In 1818 he was twenty-nine and still had much to learn. The experiences now thrust upon him were transformative, and the friends and acquaintances he met became his teachers and allies. The simplest lesson was about administrative practices. He saw and accepted the precepts of cameralism, based on Prussian practice tempered by Russian circumstances. He also encountered a more difficult human lesson, tied up with personalities, religion, belief systems, culture, and society. His efforts to act as an effective administrator embroiled him in controversy and at times left him frustrated, disillusioned, and undoubtedly a bit befuddled. He began with a set of clear and easy answers – cameralist administration in service to state objectives – but discovered that the underlying questions were very complicated.

The 1818–22 Immigration

When Agatha Hiebert begged the tsar to look out for the interests of Mennonites in Prussia she identified an important issue for the Molochnaia settlement. Napoleon's armies had swept through Prussia in 1812, and Alexander's armies had chased them back out in 1813. Mennonites knew, through letters and personal visits with family and friends, that their co-religionists in Prussia were in dire straits.[3]

Russia had always planned to attract more Mennonites from Prussia to the Molochnaia and had set aside a large land grant for future immigrants. The original Molochnaia settlement comprised eighteen villages, which were allotted 26,619 *desiatinas* of land. This amounted to sixty-five *desiatinas* per fullholding and an additional 3,803 *desiatinas* of what was called surplus land, distributed among the villages to provide for future population growth. Beyond this, the state set aside 96,621 *desiatinas* of reserve land for future immigrants.[4]

By 1818 the Russian state was less eager to attract foreign immigrants than it had been in the eighteenth century, but Mennonites were an exception. While many other foreign colonist communities were struggling to survive and placing unwelcome demands on the strained tsarist treasury, the Molochnaia settlement was a shining success story, fulfilling the role of model colony that had been envisaged for it in the Privilegium. When Tsar Alexander promised Agatha Hiebert not to forget the Prussian Mennonites, he meant it: plans were already afoot to double the population of the Molochnaia settlement with immigrants from Prussia.

Bringing new settlers to the Molochnaia was a major undertaking, and it provided a practical justification for the state to take a more direct interest in the settlement at precisely the time when Alexander was determined on principle to become more engaged in colonial policy. The Mennonites understood that the immigration process posed a danger to their position in Russia by entangling them with the administration's plans, and in advance of it they took two actions to protect their status. First, they asked Alexander to reconfirm the Privilegium, securing their status and ensuring that the new immigrants would share in it.[5] This Alexander did willingly – after all, from his perspective the Privilegium bound the Mennonites to state service. Second, the Mennonites designated a special Settlement Commission to represent their interests to the Guardianship Committee and act as their agents in settling the newcomers. Eventually Cornies would emerge as the central figure on that commission.

Cornies's new status in the settlement is difficult to define. In 1817 he had accepted the responsibility of representing Mennonite interests to the Guardianship Committee's general surveyor in a long-running border dispute with the neighbouring Doukhobors. The trust that Cornies had gained from his community by 1817 is evident in the terms of his appointment, which granted him complete discretion in representing the settlement.[6] Cornies had earned the respect of his fellow Mennonites through his business successes beyond the settlement, suggesting there was no strong opposition to his engagement with the outside world; indeed this appointment can be seen as the settlement's stamp of approval on his activities.

In 1818, when the Guardianship Committee called for the creation of a Mennonite Settlement Commission to oversee the new immigration, the *Gebietsamt* designated Cornies as the commission's land surveyor, a menial-sounding position on a commission that included a senior representative from the original colonists as well as a senior member of the immigrant group, Heinrich Balzer.[7] Cornies eventually emerged as the leading Mennonite figure in the immigration process; indeed, most accounts of the immigration make no mention of the commission, instead identifying Cornies as the Mennonites' "plenipotentiary" to the Guardianship Committee. This exaggerates Cornies's role, at least in the initial stages of the immigration process. The Guardianship Committee itself contributed to this exaggeration in the 1820s by sometimes referring to Cornies as *Oberschulz*, a title he never held.[8] The confusion perhaps stems from the fact that land surveyor was an official title and could only be held by a state employee, which Cornies was not. The Mennonites' secular administration was delineated by the 1797 laws governing state peasants, and the state had never imagined peasants having the authority or expertise to survey their own land, nor had it defined any such position as land surveyor. That title, then, described Cornies's role on the commission, but it never existed as a formal title. Notwithstanding, over time, Cornies came to dominate the commission.

Land surveying, both in practical terms and as a metaphor, became central to Cornies's life. Its purpose was to bring order by taking undivided land and imposing formal borders upon it. The results were transposed onto maps, decrees, deeds, and other formal representations. It defined who lived where and who paid what taxes. It was one of the means by which the state exerted control over people; moreover, as Steven Seegel observes, in mapping the Ukrainian frontier, Russia "imagined new colonial regions."[9] As land surveyor, Cornies served as a colonial agent entangled in the state's legal processes, and he was formally identified in the paperwork that defined who belonged where. He was the Mennonites' agent and not an employee of the state, but his work situated him at the border between the two.

As land surveyor, Cornies found the opportunity to bring order to a frontier world that he viewed as fundamentally disordered. This helped give purpose to his life, and he eventually broadened his horizons beyond the Mennonite community, aiming to "civilize" what he saw as the uncivilized world of New Russia. At the same time, the ambiguity that characterized his position on the Settlement Commission would dog him for the rest of his life. The state always regarded him as its agent in the Mennonite community, while the Mennonites always regarded him as their agent in dealing with the state. When he chose to press community interests in opposition to state policies, the state exerted enormous pressure on him, and when he chose the state, his community was no less insistent. At times the pressures threatened to overwhelm him, yet that very ambiguity also potentially opened to freedom for Cornies: both sides needed him, and as he matured in his appreciation of the challenges that faced community and state, he would take advantage of that ambiguity to exercise substantial autonomous power in finding solutions. First, though, he needed to learn his way through the new challenges he faced.

The most basic of those challenges was where to put the new villages. The Mennonites had almost 100,000 *desiatinas* of land to choose from. The problem was that much of it was arid steppe, unsuited to crop agriculture and often without sufficient water for livestock. The original colonists had already occupied all of the viable land along the Molochnaia River, so the new villages would have to be located along the smaller rivers and streams that flowed into the Molochnaia from the east. It was essential that the villages be located where the streams did not dry up in summer and the surrounding steppe was not rocky or alkaline. For the immigrants – and for the settlement as a whole – Cornies's decisions about village placement were enormously important. If he made mistakes, the villagers who settled on bad land would suffer, and the community, which would have to support them, would suffer as well.

What made Cornies the Mennonites' best candidate to act as land surveyor was his understanding of the environmental characteristics that shaped settlement options in the region. He had no formal training as a surveyor or an agronomist, but he had travelled locally much more than most Mennonites. His Iushanle lease had forced him to pay close attention to conditions beyond the original village allotments, in the upstream locations where most of the new villages would be located. The long-term prosperity of the new villages is a testament to his success in selecting sites. Except for the village of Alexanderwohl, which had to be relocated in 1825, Cornies carried out his main task admirably, and the decisions he made left an imprint on the human geography of the Molochnaia that is evident to this day.[10]

This surveying work played a vital role in Cornies's ongoing self-education. He did not do the formal surveying – the state provided a professional surveyor to do the technical work – but he was forced to think seriously about the capacity of his New Russian environment to support new settlers as he made the key decisions about village placement. Russia's central provinces were overcrowded, and the state viewed its southern frontier as a potential outlet for its excess population. Cornies was not aware of the state's broader goals, but his work as surveyor taught him that all land was not created equal – there were significant environmental constraints on his region's ability to absorb more settlers. This knowledge would shape his activities in the 1830s and 1840s when he pressed his community to use its land more efficiently and offered advice to the state about reforming the administration of state peasants throughout the empire.

Cornies was the main architect of the Molochnaia settlement's physical landscape as it expanded from nineteen villages to thirty-nine between 1819 and 1824, but while he could control the location of the villages, the immigration brought with it a new cultural landscape over which Cornies initially had little influence and which he did not even particularly understand. The physical challenge absorbed Cornies's energy in the moment; the cultural challenge would sweep him and his community into controversies that were far more significant in the long run.

A City upon a Hill?

The new migrants had lived through the defeat of Napoleon and the rapid growth of Prussian German nationalism with its accompanying economic and political modernization. Their experiences under Prussian rule had made them better educated and more open to progressive economic reforms than the first settlers. Most of them belonged to a Pietist Frisian congregation that had its own elder, Franz Goerz, but some were members of a relatively liberal Flemish congregation led by Elder Peter Wedel. Thus their arrival meant that the Molochnaia suddenly had three separate official congregations, plus the unofficial Kleine Gemeinde. The newcomers were even linguistically distinct, for some among them had begun to prefer High German to their traditional Mennonite Low German. They brought to the Molochnaia an impetus for economic, religious, and cultural change. They also brought deep controversy, for the original Molochnaia settlers were members of the religiously conservative Flemish congregation, for many of whom Pietism was anathema.

These Pietist immigrants came at a time when Russia was uniquely open to their religious beliefs. Andrei Fadeev, who became chair of the Ekaterinoslav bureau of the Guardianship Committee just as the first Frisian immigrants arrived in 1819, later wrote that this immigration was part of an insidious Pietist plot.[11] Tsar Alexander had emerged out of the Napoleonic Wars with a messianic sense of mission and a fascination with mysticism, and he surrounded himself with advisers who shared and promoted his views. Most important among them was Prince Aleksandr Golitsyn, a close personal friend who had served as Russia's Procurator of the Holy Synod – the secular head of the Orthodox Church – since 1803. In 1810 he also became the director of the Central Directorate for the Spiritual Affairs of Foreign Confessions, which brought all religious matters in the empire under his authority. In 1817 the tsar further expanded Golitsyn's authority by placing him in charge of a new Ministry of Religious Affairs and Public Instruction – usually called the Dual Ministry – a position from which Golitsyn could promote his Pietist vision of spirituality for Russia.[12]

Golitsyn helped found, and served as president of, the Russian Bible Society – a Russian branch of the British and Foreign Bible Society (BFBS) – which in 1814 was formally incorporated into his directorate. He lent his full authority to the expansion of the society's work.[13] The BFBS holds an important place in the history of the tsarist Mennonites.[14] Founded in 1804, it was one of the most influential products of the evangelical Second Great Awakening that swept through Britain, Europe, and North America in the early nineteenth century. It was an ecumenical organization supported by Catholics, Anglicans, Lutherans, and other denominations and sects. The secret to its success was that it avoided doctrinal controversies and focused on translating and distributing cheap Bibles "without note or comment."[15]

The BFBS came to Russia in 1812 when John Paterson, a Scottish Congregationalist and agent of the society, travelled to St. Petersburg and Moscow to explore its prospects in the Russian Empire. He arrived just weeks before the Napoleonic invasion, and his timing could not have been better, for it was in the heat of this invasion that Alexander experienced his famous conversion to mysticism. In 1818 the tsar described the experience to a Prussian bishop: "The fire of Moscow enlightened my soul, God's judgement on the frozen fields of Russia filled my heart with a warm faith. Then I came to know God as he reveals himself to us in His Holy Scripture. From then on I accepted His will and law, and there arose in me the firm determination – to dedicate myself and my entire kingdom to Him and His glory."[16]

In St. Petersburg, Paterson pitched his proposal for a Russian branch of the BFBS to Golitsyn and Count V.P. Kochubei, one of the tsar's closest friends. Kochubei had been a member of the Secret or Unofficial Committee that dominated Russian politics during the first few years of Alexander's reign, and from 1819 to 1825 he served as Alexander's Minister of Internal Affairs.

Golitsyn and Kochubei enthusiastically supported Paterson's proposal for the Russian Bible Society, which was created in December 1812 with Golitsyn as its president and Kochubei as its vice-president. In February 1813 the tsar enrolled in the society, donating 25,000 rubles and promising annual contributions of 10,000 rubles. His brothers Nicholas and Konstantin also joined. The society's directors were drawn from the Russian elite and included luminaries like Sergei Uvarov, the principal architect of Nicholas's Official Nationality doctrine in the 1830s, and Count A.K. Razumovskii, the Minister of Public Instruction. It also included a number of prominent leaders of the Orthodox Church, including Archbishop (later Metropolitan) Filaret, who personally oversaw the translation of the Bible into modern Russian. According to Elena Vishlenkova, a historian of religion and politics under Alexander, Christian ecumenism became Russia's "official ideology" during his reign. The Russian Bible Society was the main agency for promoting this ideology and thus influenced the empire's economic, political, and international policy.[17] The tsar believed that the Russian Bible Society would help create a cadre of educated people to serve in his bureaucracy; he also expected it to help secure "internal peace for the polyethnic Russian Empire."[18]

Across the empire in regional administrative centres more than 250 Russian Bible Society branches sprang up. In Siberia its director was Mikhail Speranskii, the great advocate of constitutionalism. In Odesa, Civil Governor Count Langeron was vice-president and I.M. Inzov, director of the Guardianship Committee, was among its most "zealous activists."[19] In Ekaterinoslav, Archbishop Iov, a vice-president of the society, oversaw the most successful regional branch in the empire, selling more than 25,000 rubles worth of Bibles in 1816 alone.[20] With the aid of these regional branches, between 1813 and 1826 the Russian Bible Society distributed more than 700,000 Bibles in forty-one languages.[21]

There is an important distinction to be made between the size of the Russian Bible Society's membership and the extent of its long-term impact on Russia. Historians of the society have always struggled to ascribe to it any lasting influence after Golitsyn's sudden fall from grace in 1824 and its closure in 1826.[22] By the 1830s, conservatives within the Orthodox Church had regained their stranglehold on religious attitudes in the empire and it was hard to find anywhere a leading Russian administrator who would admit to having been a member.[23] Undoubtedly many of the society's adherents only joined in the first place because it provided access to the tsar and his most trusted advisers. Membership was a way of currying favour.

There is a case to be made that the Russian Bible Society's influence on frontier administration was more lasting. Colonists had always been at the bottom end of a very long chain of command, and in the hierarchical, socially stratified Russian system there was little chance for them to have a say in administrative affairs. The lack of a strong administrative presence on the frontier allowed colonists a degree of freedom in their own affairs, but it also left them with few means to influence government policy or even voice their concerns. The Russian Bible Society, with its ecumenical message, opened important doors for interaction between colonists and administrators.[24]

For regional administrators like Contenius and Fadeev, the Russian Bible Society provided vital contacts within colonial communities. They were almost certainly members of the society (despite Fadeev's later denunciation of it), and it provided the opportunity for them to work and form friendships with Mennonites outside of the normal hierarchical administrative setting.[25] For Mennonites the society provided a venue for interaction with administrators that did not demand direct involvement in the bureaucratic system. Although the Russian Bible Society closed in 1826 (a much smaller Protestant Bible Society formed in 1831), the network of friends, acquaintances, patrons, and clients that it created survived.

The ecumenism promoted by the Russian Bible Society, together with the evangelical phenomenon it represented, posed a particular challenge to religiously conservative Molochnaia Mennonites, for whom living apart from the world had significant theological implications. Their religion demanded that they live their lives among fellow believers in open and conscious obedience to biblical precepts. Their communities were intended to be, in historian Robert Friedmann's words, "a nucleus of the Kingdom [of God] to which men were to be invited and which was open to everybody. By this, it was hoped, the brotherhood of the regenerated would grow until the last days and thus gradually overcome the Prince of the World."[26] However, while they were "open to everybody," Mennonites insisted that joining their congregations be the voluntary act of adults, which meant they would not proselytize.

Nothing in this prohibited Mennonites from distributing Bibles, and because they believed Bibles to be the manifest word of God, they viewed distribution of them *among Mennonites* as clearly desirable. The BFBS insisted that the Bibles come "without note or comment" as this would "cut off the occasion of theological hostilities, and invite Christians in general to associate for the more extensive propagation of their common faith."[27] This was problematic for religiously conservative Mennonites, for they had utterly no desire to associate "in general" with other Christians, and they were particularly opposed to the "propagation" of their faith among non-Mennonites, whom they hardly accepted as holding a "common faith."

While the Russian Bible Society's Bibles were printed "without note or comment," the agents who distributed them were evangelical Christians, chock-full of missionary zeal. Emissaries of the racial and religious chauvinism that flourished in the early nineteenth century, those agents saw the Molochnaia Mennonite settlement, perched on the frontier of Nogai country, as an ideal beachhead for missionary work among the "heathen" Islamic Tatars, who were one of the main targets of British and European evangelical missionaries. As BFBS representative Ebenezer Henderson wrote, "placed in the centre of an extensive territory, where they are surrounded by Russians of various sects, Germans, Greeks, Bulgarians, Tatars, and Jews, we could not but regard them as destined by Divine Providence to shine as lights in a dark place."[28] This language is a vivid evocation of the civilizing role claimed by Pietism, in that it echoed the modernizing agenda of the Enlightenment even as it tried to reject the secularizing implications of that agenda.[29] The missionary discourse characterized Indigenous peoples as part of a "vast moral waste" and viewed the incorporation of such people into the peasantry as the Christian antidote.[30]

The state-prescribed role of the Mennonites as model colonists echoed the Christian idea of a "city upon a hill." In the Sermon on the Mount, Jesus told his audience that "You are the light of the world. A city that is set on a hill cannot be hidden."[31] The city upon a hill, as a depiction of a model Christian community, similarly echoed the Russian state's ambiguous injunction to the Mennonites to be model colonists. It was most famously invoked by John Winthrop's sermon "A Model of Christian Charity," given to Puritans fleeing the religious constraints of England. In that context it clearly envisioned a static model, for the early Puritan colonization of America was not a missionary enterprise. The relevance of this example for religiously conservative Mennonites fleeing Prussia for the Russian frontier is obvious. However, in the hands of Pietist leader August Hermann Francke the city upon a hill took on new, evangelical significance. Francke envisioned Halle as the city upon a hill from which a second Reformation would emanate. His plan was to educate and send forth an army of clergy to win over the world to a renewed faith. This explicitly missionary vision saw the city upon a hill not as a static model but as a beachhead for transformative Christian missionary work.[32]

The Mennonites' signal success in establishing an orderly, prosperous frontier community made them an irresistible recruitment target for both secular and religious civilizational projects. Mennonite religious conservatives probably did not see much difference between the two: whether Russian officials or Russian Bible Society agents, they were unwelcome worldly intruders. And of course, in 1818 the society came with the clear support of the state, which itself did not seem to differentiate between its own goals and those of the Russian Bible Society.

The Russian Bible Society and its evangelical agents realized that before they could use the Mennonites to evangelize the Nogais, they would first need to recruit Mennonites to their cause. Happily for the society, they could hardly have picked a more propitious time to launch their Molochnaia efforts, for on the one hand, the tsar himself was promoting their cause, and on the other, the 1818–24 Mennonite immigrants provided a constituency in the Molochnaia that was open to their message.

The Quakers Grellet and Allen visited the Molochnaia in 1819 specifically because of the Russian Bible Society's interest in the settlement. Allen was a founding member of the BFBS, and while he and Grellet were officially in Russia to promote Quaker school and prison reform projects they were also unofficial agents of the society. The two had enjoyed a personal audience with the tsar when he was in London the previous year, during which they had promoted the Quaker agenda of hospital, school, and prison reform as natural extensions of the society's mission. Alexander invited the Quakers to come to Russia to survey conditions there, and when they arrived in November 1818, between religious meetings and inspection trips they circulated in the highest society, frequenting the home of Golitsyn, visiting Alexander's mother, and, after his return to St. Petersburg in February 1819, again meeting with the tsar. They also dined regularly with John Paterson, and at his home they encountered a wide variety of local and foreign Pietists.[33]

In Russia, Grellet and Allen found genuine support for their ideas about prisons and hospitals, but when it came to schools the story was more complicated. Allen wrote in frustration about the perspective among the Russia elite "that learning, being an instrument of power, should be kept from the poor, lest they make a bad use of it."[34] As he protested to an apparently sympathetic tsar, the distribution of Russian-language Bibles to Russian peasants was a meaningless gesture if the peasants could not read them.[35]

According to Grellet and Allen, when they arrived in the Molochnaia they met with a universally friendly reception from the Mennonites. If this is true – and there are no Mennonite accounts to suggest otherwise – then opposition to the Russian Bible Society had not yet emerged in the Molochnaia. This complacency would not last. The school reforms that were so dear to Grellet and Allen were as controversial to Mennonite religious conservatives as they were to some conservative Russian noblemen. Mennonite villages already provided their children, both male and female, with primary education, but its purpose was limited to ensuring rudimentary literacy and numeracy. While all Mennonites needed to be able to read the Bible, religious conservatives, just like conservative Russians, feared that any further education would encourage children to question traditional beliefs. Moreover, religious education was the prerogative of elders, and the creation of independent secondary schools challenged this prerogative. Also, conservatives associated the expansion of formal education with Pietism, and as they well knew, Pietism had secured its influence in Prussia by providing the state bureaucracy with foot soldiers, who would fill the administrative ranks and permit cameralism to function efficiently. In other words, conservative Mennonites correctly recognized that Pietism, education, and the state's intrusion into their affairs went hand in hand.

In 1821, Ebenezer Henderson, a leading agent for the BFBS in Russia, followed up on Grellet and Allen's visit to the Molochnaia, where he promoted the creation of a local branch of the society. Like other visitors, Henderson admired the Mennonites' "industry and prosperity," but more than that he saw in them a golden opportunity to further the Russian Bible Society's evangelical mission. He convinced a group of prominent Mennonite leaders to create a Molochnaia chapter of the society, with Cornies as its secretary and treasurer.[36] The Mennonites also consulted Henderson on their planned secondary school, and he promised to help them attract a qualified teacher. He had in mind Daniel Schlatter, a Swiss Separatist and nephew of the famous Pietist Anna

Bernet-Schlatter. Schlatter's cousin, Kasper Schlatter, taught at the Basle Mission Society School, and it may have been he who recommended Daniel to Henderson.[37]

The Christian School Association was founded in 1820 and opened its secondary school in 1822.[38] Its first teacher was not Schlatter, but Tobias Voth, a zealous Pietist whom the association recruited from Prussia. Schlatter also arrived in the Molochnaia in 1822; finding that the teaching position was already filled, he stuck around to study and evangelize the Nogai Tatars. Eventually he would exert a strong influence on Cornies, but for the time being Cornies was too entangled with his duties as land surveyor to pay close attention to Schlatter.

Cornies, already a leading figure in the Molochnaia branch of the Bible Society, was the driving force in the creation of the Christian School Association. He not only served as its chair but also generously funded the school with what he characterized as loans (they were never repaid) that totalled 2,888 rubles – 56 per cent of the school's total budget – between 1822 and 1827.[39]

The Ohrloff school was the start of Cornies's lifelong commitment to education, which would be one of his most important legacies. The school was built in his own village of Ohrloff, and his children were among its first beneficiaries. Cornies had the same rudimentary education as most of his contemporaries, but he had a better appreciation than most for the value of education. His business pursuits had impressed upon him the inadequacies of his own education, and his survey work had shown him there was technical expertise that could only come from formal education. The creation of the Ohrloff school ensured that his children would have access to the formal education he had never received.

The Frisian immigrants provided an important constituency to support the creation of the new school, and without their arrival it might never have happened. Cornies provided leadership and influence in the established community to see the plan through. His appointment to the Settlement Commission indicates the status he had already earned in his community before the new immigration, and his successful oversight of the immigration increased that status. Because he oversaw the allocation of land – that most vital Molochnaia resource – the new arrivals looked to him as their representative in the community. As his reform agenda grew, the Frisians continued to support Cornies, and this constituency would be essential to his future success.

The Frisians were more than just a political constituency; the newcomers, along with his new Bible Society colleagues, also provided Cornies with access to the world view that engagement with the secular world was acceptable. Through them he opened a correspondence with David Epp, one of the most prominent Pietist Mennonite elders in Prussia and a member of the BFBS. Epp's letters in the 1820s and early 1830s kept Cornies informed about developments in the Prussian Mennonite Church, and Epp, along with the BFBS, provided Cornies with an entrée to other leaders in the western Pietist community.[40] In the 1830s Epp also served as intermediary for the immigration of the Pietist Gnadenfeld community to the Molochnaia settlement.

For Cornies, Pietism must have been a welcome relief from the constraints under which he lived and laboured. He was an innovator, but he lived in a conservative community explicitly dedicated to quiet withdrawal from the bustling world. This is of course a caricature of the first Molochnaia Mennonites; when they chose to immigrate to Russia they showed themselves to be risk-takers, and, as argued in chapter 1, the community had never intended to close itself off from the world entirely. Still, religiously the community was conservative, and its quietism made it a difficult place to promote change. Not only that, but traditional Mennonite religious beliefs were explicitly inward-looking. Most importantly, the emphasis on adult baptism, which demanded that individuals consciously choose membership in the community, forbade proselytization and discouraged religious engagement with outsiders. For Cornies, who at an early age had moved beyond his community into marketplaces and administrative offices, the conservative mindset was a terrible constraint. Pietism, which looked outward and encouraged engagement, opened new vistas for him.[41]

Congregational Schism

The initial response of the mainstream Flemish congregants to the arrival of Pietists was restrained but friendly. In 1819, Grellet and Allen, introduced by leading members of the Flemish congregation, addressed church meetings attended by hundreds of Mennonites. Elder Jacob Fast, leader of the Flemish congregation, worked hard to establish good relations with the Frisian newcomers, even supporting the creation of the Christian School Association. Soon, however, the more conservative members of the Flemish congregation began to see the Pietists as a threat to their values. The Russian Bible Society, the Christian School Association, the visits by Henderson and then Grellet and Allen, and the arrival of Frisians came in rapid succession, contributing to a sense that the values of the original community were under assault.

Two events pushed the tension to the breaking point. First, Bernhard Fast, who succeeded Jakob Fast as Flemish elder in 1820, broke with tradition – and angered many members of his congregation – when he allowed himself to be ordained by Frisian elder Franz Goerz. Custom dictated that the new elder be ordained by an elder in his own congregation, the closest available being the senior Flemish clergyman from Khortitsa.[42] In breaking with this custom, Fast seemed to have ceded a significant measure of authority to the Frisian congregation. The second controversial event came in 1822, when Fast, supported by the elders of the new immigrants, permitted a visiting non-Mennonite missionary, Johann Moritz, to address a prayer meeting and take communion in Ohrloff. Moritz, a convert from Judaism, was officially employed as the "Spiritual Superintendent of the Emperor of Russia's Colony of Christian Israelites," but he was also hard at work promoting missionary prayer meetings in the Molochnaia.[43] The anger his 1822 visit provoked indicates how much the relations between the Flemish and Frisians had eroded in just three years. Sermons by Allen and Grellet had excited no protests in 1819, but in 1822 the Flemish congregation regarded Moritz's sermon as a major provocation. Fast apologized, but conservative leaders would not be placated. In 1824 they formed a new congregation, the Large Flemish Congregation, which roughly three quarters of the members of the original Flemish congregation joined.[44]

The leader of the religious conservatives was Altona preacher Jacob Warkentin. Warkentin left few written records to reveal his beliefs and motivations, so he is mainly known to posterity by the controversies he helped create and by denunciations from his opponents. These paint him as a harsh and unreasonable opponent of innovation of any kind who unrealistically demanded that Mennonites reject state interference in their community and who sometimes stooped to false accusations and dirty tricks to undermine his opponents. Some of these accusations will be explored in later chapters, but in fairness to Warkentin his success and popularity must also be acknowledged. For two decades he was the leader of the largest congregation in the Molochnaia, representing the views of a clear majority and providing a spirited defence against changes that represented a real danger to traditional Mennonite beliefs. He was an important foil to Cornies, and to some degree the dimensions of Cornies's reform vision were defined by the dimensions of Warkentin's opposition.

Warkentin represented a conservative Mennonite world view closely linked to the eighteenth-century rural Prussian communities from which most of the first Molochnaia settlers had come. He promoted a quietist theology of strict withdrawal from the secular world, and by the 1830s he would encourage his followers to extend the religious autonomy they already enjoyed to include administrative and economic autonomy. At first, however, his movement was primarily a reaction against the Pietist religious innovations that had arrived since 1818.[45] His anger focused on the Frisian elder Franz Goerz, who he claimed had introduced religious innovations that were "wholly contrary" to Mennonite religious beliefs.[46]

In the early 1820s Warkentin did not explicitly identify Johann Cornies as an opponent, but he must have been aware of Cornies's activities. Warkentin particularly singled out for criticism the Christian School Association that Cornies led, and he knew that Cornies was the treasurer of the Molochnaia branch of the Russian Bible Society as well as a member of the Settlement Commission for the Pietist newcomers. Cornies, who encouraged the new Pietist schoolteacher Tobias Voth to hold mission prayer meetings at the school and prayed aloud at one of the meetings, was emerging as a central figure in what might fairly be termed the Molochnaia Pietist movement.[47]

The deep community rift that developed in the wake of the 1818 immigration would define the Molochnaia Mennonite community for decades to come, drawing the main party lines of Molochnaia politics for at least the next twenty-five years. The Large Flemish Congregation, led by Warkentin, representing the original settlers, opposed Pietism and Russian state interference. Its members were the majority in the community, but because of its quietist position it had few links to outside sources of influence apart from leaders of the Flemish congregation in the Khortitsa settlement. The Frisian congregation represented the newcomers and promoted Pietism and Western innovation. At first the Frisian congregation lacked strong influence within the Molochnaia community, but it retained close ties to the Prussian Mennonites, which lent it some influence, and in Cornies it found a champion in the old community. There was also a constituency of moderates who remained loyal to the original Molochnaia Flemish Congregation, now known as the Old Flemish Congregation. They were willing to accept economic changes, and eager to get along with the newcomers, but unwilling to buy into Pietism. Cornies was not wholly aligned with either the Frisians or the Old Flemish. He remained a member of the Old Flemish Congregation throughout his life, but he frequently used his influence, both locally and with the Guardianship Committee, to promote Frisian interests. He equally used his influence in the 1830s to defend the rights of the Kleine Gemeinde, the small, unofficial, and extremely conservative congregation in the Molochnaia.

Activating the Mennonite Model

At its core the political issues in the settlement were religious, but they had significant implications for the Russian state and its secular colonial policies. The Mennonites' internal debate arose as the state re-engaged with the colonial process after the Napoleonic Wars. Warkentin's conservative position directly challenged the state, for by committing themselves to isolationism, the Mennonites – Russia's star colonists – would be placing themselves in direct opposition to official policy. The state had a keen interest in the outcome of the dispute, and as the battle lines formed the Guardianship Committee identified Cornies as an important ally. Cornies's engagement with the state that flowed from his position as land surveyor was every bit as important as his engagement with Pietism: if Pietism provided a belief system, the state provided a means to influence settlement politics.

The Russian policy the Guardianship Committee promoted was cameralism, which is both an administrative theory and a political ideology. Ideologically, it is a belief in the ability of humans to organize their world to ensure progress and in the role of the sovereign as the leader toward progress. Administratively, it is a hierarchical bureaucratic system that calls on the government and educated elites to organize society in order to achieve progress. The objective of cameralism, as historian Marc Raeff asserts, is to create a "well-ordered police state" in which sovereigns, through their agents, control every element of public and private life as the "active proponent of a deliberate, methodical policy, the purpose of which is to maximise [their] country's productive potential, increase its wealth and power, and promote its material well-being."[48]

Cameralism came late to Russia. Peter the Great had tried to impose it, and Catherine the Great had made great strides toward creating a new administrative infrastructure, but the country lacked the educated human resources to implement it before the nineteenth century. Catherine saw New Russia as part of a grand cameralist vision, as a place where progressive policies could be imposed on a blank canvas, thus offering a model that would propel the rest of the country forward. Mennonites, as "model colonists," were part of this vision, the bottom rung of the intended bureaucratic structure.

With the Napoleonic Wars over, Alexander and his administration could begin their efforts to put the cameralist plan in force on the frontier. The state's expectations of the Mennonites were spelled out in the Privilegium: they were to be a model community, who by their example would show other colonists how to conduct their lives. There was a critical ambiguity in this plan: many Mennonites quite reasonably understood themselves to be required only to live as they always had, in a self-disciplined, orderly fashion. What they had achieved by 1818 was already exemplary, and from that point it was up to other colonial communities to emulate them. That is how Jacob Warkentin and his followers viewed themselves.

The main obstacle the state faced in extending cameralism to the frontier was that it lacked bureaucrats. Andrei Fadeev provides a vivid description of the inadequacies of the frontier administration as he encountered it when he took up his post as Deputy Chair of the Guardianship Committee bureau in Ekaterinoslav in 1815: "What can be said about the other [bureau employees]? With few exceptions these were people of whom only the best had even a modicum of education, and even those had no real merit; almost all of them were feckless people, and most were antagonistic toward Contenius, hating him and putting all possible obstacles in the way of his efforts to serve society."[49] In such circumstances it was almost impossible to introduce reforms without local cooperation. The Guardianship Committee expected Mennonites to be its main agents in the Molochnaia, but as it would learn, it first needed an agent among the Mennonites to ensure that the divided community would unite in service to the state.

The precise point in time when the Guardianship Committee identified Cornies as its prospective agent is impossible to pinpoint; probably it happened gradually as he proved himself through his work on the Settlement Commission. He received no special mention in accounts of Tsar Alexander's 1818 visit or Grellet and Allen's 1819 visit, but as the new immigrants began arriving, his contact with the Guardianship Committee grew. In 1821 his name began to appear regularly in committee correspondence as the *Oberschulz* responsible for looking after the new settlers, but still he only appeared as a local functionary and not as the committee's principal Mennonite agent.[50] Only in 1823, as the Warkentin-led opposition to reforms swelled in the settlement, did Cornies's status with the committee also grow.

Cornies's most direct contact with the Guardianship Committee should have been through the regional inspector of colonies. The inspector, who lived in Halbstadt in the heart of the settlement, was the official with whom Cornies had the most interaction in his earliest years as an administrator. By 1823, however, as Cornies's status rose, he increasingly dealt directly with the Ekaterinoslav bureau.

Cornies's relations with the chief figures in the Ekaterinoslav bureau, Samuel Contenius and Andrei Fadeev, had a profound impact on his life and that of his community, and the Mennonite successes he engineered equally served the career ambitions of his benefactors. The elderly Contenius was the chair of the Ekaterinoslav bureau from 1800 to 1818, and thus he was the most important state administrator for early Molochnaia Mennonite affairs.[51] Born and educated in Westphalia, Contenius was an energetic proponent of agricultural modernization, and his wide contacts with the central Guardianship Committee administration in Kishinev and with senior government authorities in St. Petersburg allowed him to bypass administrative red tape and push through reforms among the foreign colonists under his supervision.[52] Contenius was a domineering cameralist bureaucrat. He placed enormous demands on everyone he commanded, and Cornies both feared and admired him. Contenius officially retired in 1818, but he retained an office and staff in Ekaterinoslav until his death in 1830 and would be a driving force in colonists' affairs until almost his last days. Cornies modelled strategic aspects of his own economic agenda and administrative practices on Contenius's example.

Fadeev, deputy chair of the Guardianship Committee from 1815 to 1818 and chair from 1818 to 1834, was equally important for Cornies.[53] Born, like Cornies, in 1789, he married Princess Elena Pavlovna Dolgorukaia, a member of one of Russia's most powerful aristocratic families. This gave Fadeev important contacts in St. Petersburg, not least with Golitsyn, a close family friend of the Dolgorukiis. First as Contenius's deputy, and then as his replacement, Fadeev became Cornies's friend and mentor, helping him to enlarge his economic vision and to navigate the channels of officialdom even after being transferred to a new position in the Caucasus in 1836. Fadeev's willingness to use his influence to promote Cornies and his various projects helped open the way for Cornies's success. Fadeev and Contenius both recognized Cornies's potential, recruited him, employed him for their own interests, and became powerful patrons for him in Mennonite community disputes as well as in negotiations with the state. They imposed upon Cornies but also offered him leverage with which to pursue personal and community goals.

Between 1819 and 1830, Contenius's most important project was the creation of wool improvement societies in colonist settlements. In this he had the full support of Fadeev and the Guardianship Committee. In 1823, with all but three of the planned twenty new Mennonite villages established, Contenius took the first step in expanding Cornies's role in the colonial program when he ordered the Mennonites to create a Molochnaia Mennonite Wool Improvement Society (often called the Sheep Society), with Cornies as its chair.

The Wool Improvement Society amounted to a Guardianship Committee outpost in the Molochnaia Mennonite settlement, with a handpicked chair to do the work and one or two other respected Mennonites as members to lend it legitimacy. Contenius had been trying to promote sheep breeding in the settlement since the arrival of the Mennonites, but with limited success. Although Cornies and a handful of other Mennonites established large sheep flocks, in 1823 the average fullholder still owned just seventeen sheep.[54] Contenius believed that the best bet for creating a commercial agricultural economy in New Russia lay in promoting the production of high-quality wool, and to that end he needed to convince Mennonites to raise sheep, which in turn meant investing in expensive breeding stock so that they could improve the quality of the wool they produced.

Contenius wanted to introduce fine-wooled Spanish merino sheep into the Molochnaia herds as breeding stock. Merino wool was in great demand in the West and was one of the few agricultural products that could be sold for high enough prices to pay for the costs of transporting it from the Molochnaia to distant markets. The problem was that merinos had difficulty surviving the harsh climate of New Russia and had to be kept close to home, where they could be sheltered and fed in barns when the weather turned bad. Contenius understood this difficulty, and his goal was to interbreed kurdiuch sheep with merinos, thus creating a breed that was adapted to local conditions and that produced a finer wool to satisfy commercial demand.

As described in chapter 2, this inter-breeding process required years of careful management. Given the costs and complexities, few Mennonites were eager to invest their time and money in it. In the early 1820s most fullholders practised a mixture of grain growing, sheep and cattle raising, and gardening. This balance provided a measure of security against drought years and offered a slow but sure path to prosperity. Sheep raising on the scale that Contenius proposed was a risky departure that only the rich or the foolhardy might attempt.

Contenius's plan relied on the cooperation of Mennonites. By itself this did not amount to a major shift in Mennonite relations to the state, but it did have important implications. Since the Mennonites' arrival, the Molochnaia settlement had been allowed to develop with relatively little interference from the state. That reflected the state's ambiguous colonial policies. The result was a model settlement that seemed to fulfil the terms of the Privilegium, but it was a model largely of Mennonite design. When Contenius asked the Mennonites to model sheep raising, his request reflected the empire's emerging search for a more standardized imperial model. He was asking them to become active agents in the state's vision of a modern New Russian economy. This presaged the shift from a static model to an active laboratory. As long as Contenius was asking and not ordering, this shift did not need to be controversial, but in later years, as the state became more insistent about its reform agenda, it would have serious implications.

The Wool Improvement Society, in both its aims and its methods, was very much Contenius's personal project. This reveals the weakness of the cameralist system on the Russian frontier. The understaffed, underfunded, and overburdened Guardianship Committee could barely keep up with its basic administrative tasks, and it had no hope of extending itself to the kinds of ambitious projects that Contenius promoted. Consequently, although the state's ideal was top-down cameralist bureaucratic control, the reality was that Contenius, a particularly gifted and progressive administrator, was promoting his own vision of progress through a special office working outside of normal bureaucratic channels, though backed by the Guardianship Committee. While this led to some notable successes, it did not provide the kind of replicable administrative model for the entire empire on which cameralism depended. Instead, it was dependent on the ability and energy of one individual in one region.

Contenius's position on the Guardianship Committee of the 1820s was extraordinary, and so was Cornies's role as chair of the Wool Improvement Society. As with the position of land surveyor (which he continued to hold), the new position of Wool Improvement Society chair was not defined by law. Cornies was an unpaid volunteer, and the society had no formal authority in the settlement. Its success depended on the personal status of Contenius and likewise on the status of his chosen representative Cornies.

The relationship that was forming between Cornies and Contenius by 1823 had less to do with cameralism than with the older administrative expediency of patronage.[55] Cornies operated as a client to his patron Contenius, and his authority within the settlement was reinforced by his personal relationship with Contenius, who was highly respected by the Mennonites. Contenius, meanwhile, relied on Cornies's authority in the settlement, and because Cornies did not have a formal administrative position, he needed to develop his own system of patronage. That patronage network operated in parallel with the formal cameralist system. The tsarist administration defined goals and ordered its colonial administrators to achieve those goals; then those administrators, lacking the efficient ground-level bureaucracy to achieve those goals, resorted to patronage.

The patronage system must have seemed familiar to the Mennonites, for it looked precisely like the type of administrative system they had known in Poland and Prussia. This familiarity concealed a dangerous trap, for in the Vistula local authorities had possessed a degree of regional autonomy that Russian officials did not. Officials like Contenius and Fadeev were not members of a local landed gentry with independent authority and connections to protect and promote Mennonite interests. No matter how real their personal support for the Mennonites was, they worked in a Russian administrative system that, at its higher levels, was increasingly functioning as a cameralist bureaucracy.

Russia had always relied upon its landed nobility to administer much of the country. Serfdom placed 40 per cent of the country's population under the direct control of the nobility, who consequently took on administrative functions for this population that would otherwise have fallen to the state. Another 40 per cent of the population were state peasants, officially wards of the state. Most state peasants lived in the peripheral provinces of the empire, and because Russia had never possessed an adequate professional bureaucracy to administer them directly, it relied upon the regional nobility to perform administrative functions for these peasants as well. The system was riven with inefficiency, corruption, and tyranny and was every bit the paradise for patronage that Mennonites had known in Poland.

Peter the Great had begun to modernize Russia's administration, attacking traditional noble prerogatives and trying to implement central control, and Catherine the Great had gone further with her large-scale reforms of Russia's central and provincial administration. However, lacking the large numbers of educated people necessary for true cameralist control of their massive empire, neither Peter nor Catherine could go far beyond sketching the outlines of a new system. As the Russian Empire entered the nineteenth century, outside of its central provinces much of it was still administered by the local landed nobility.

The rapid expansion of Russia in the eighteenth century posed major challenges to the traditional Russian system. The tsars relied upon the nobility's loyalty to them, and in newly acquired territories this loyalty was not guaranteed. Wherever a local landed gentry already existed, Russia tried to co-opt them by confirming their positions and privileges. However, where that nobility's customs and practices were too different from Russia's to make them easily co-optable – as was the case in much of Central Asia – or where there was no landed nobility at all – as was the case in much of New Russia – the problem was more difficult.[56]

One attempt to solve to this problem involved granting large swathes of the new territories to members of the extant Russian nobility. Catherine had done this, so even in the remote Molochnaia region there was a large noble estate owned by a nobleman named Granobarskii. The problem was that giving the land to the nobility did not necessarily create a local pool of noblemen to serve as administrators, because most recipients of Catherine's largesse never personally occupied it, choosing instead to live in distant cities (St. Petersburg if they could afford it) as absentee landlords.

Beginning with Peter the Great, Russia shored up its administrative system by recruiting from Western Europe. Most infamously, Tsarina Anna filled her court with Baltic Germans and allowed her closest adviser, Count Ernst Johann von Biron, to oversee a reign of terror for ten years. These foreign helpers played key roles in the Russian court throughout the eighteenth century, but they seldom filled the less attractive provincial administrative positions that would become so crucial to Russia as it expanded under Catherine.

Catherine and her successors benefited from the turmoil brought on by the French Revolution, as suddenly there was a flood of well-educated Western European noblemen looking for places to flee, and they could not afford to be picky about where. One French expatriate, the duc de Richelieu, provided brilliant leadership to New Russia as its governor general from 1805 to 1815; his successor from 1815 to 1823 was another French nobleman, Count Langeron, who also served as vice-president of the Odesa branch of the Russian Bible Society. French noble refugees could even be found in remote places like the Molochnaia, where the comte de Maison served from 1809 to 1821 as the guardian of the Nogai Tatar Horde.[57]

Samuel Contenius had found his way to Russia before this flight from revolutionary Europe, but his role as a foreign expert was similar. His life before he came to Russia in 1785 is mysteriously vague. He claimed to be the son of a Separatist minister in Westphalia, and according to Grellet it was religious zeal that led him to immigrate. Fadeev, who worked with Contenius for fifteen years and revered the older man as both mentor and friend, hinted that something else may have caused Contenius, at the age of thirty-eight, to suddenly leave Westphalia. Fadeev was in St. Petersburg in 1830 when Contenius died, and in his autobiography he provides a dramatic description of how the dying man summoned Fadeev's wife Elena to his side. The old man, failing rapidly, clasped Elena's hand and gasped that he needed to confess ... and then died before revealing the dark secret of his past.[58]

This dramatic story of Contenius's death may be nothing more than Fadeev's attempt to spice up his own autobiography. Whatever the case, like Richelieu, Langeron, and de Maison, the expatriate Contenius owed his position in New Russia to his loyalty to the tsar and not to a local power base. Other senior Russian administrators in New Russia were in the same position. Fadeev was born in a regional administrative town near St. Petersburg, the son of a mid-level bureaucrat in the Department of Water Transport. His mother, a Baltic German, taught him German, and his father found him a junior post in the department. In 1812 he was stationed on a canal connecting the Dnieper River to the Western Dvina, squarely in the path of Napoleon's invasion. Unable to find lodging in refugee-packed Kyiv, he had the good fortune to stumble upon the country estate of Countess Dzialynskaia some 70 kilometres south of the city. There he met and fell in love with Princess Elena, granddaughter of the countess. Fadeev was a penniless member of the petty nobility, by no means a good match for Elena, and it took him two years to win her grandmother's approval, but they finally married in 1814. The couple did not have the money to live the life of the idle rich, so Fadeev had to find work. Family connections, combined with Elena's insistence on living close to her grandmother, were the key factors in his decision to accept a post in Ekaterinoslav. Fadeev thus also came to New Russia as a product of the dislocations caused by the French Revolution and Napoleonic Wars.

Because they lacked any local ties of the kind that make patronage work, Fadeev and Contenius were not the type of local authorities that Mennonites had learned to deal with in Poland. Both men were undoubtedly familiar with how patronage functioned – Fadeev, after all, owed his appointment to the influence of his Dolgorukii in-laws – but neither held land or independent wealth, so the only advantage they could offer as patrons was their influence with a central government that was beginning to professionalize. Officials like Fadeev and Contenius were liable to be transferred to more important positions if they were successful or removed from their positions if they did not achieve state goals, so their patronage had significant constraints. Not only that, but while their relationship to Cornies was often as patrons to a client, their relationship to higher authorities was evolving into one of employees to their bosses. Cornies and the Mennonites would need to figure out this new administrative reality.

St. Petersburg: Walking the Halls of Power

The Wool Improvement Society provided Cornies with the opportunity to learn first-hand how the Russian administrative system was evolving. His first major task as society chair was to travel to St. Petersburg to select sheep from the state's special breeding herd and bring them back to the Molochnaia, where they would become the core of a community sheep flock and provide breeding stock to the settlement. The trip gave him the opportunity to experience the Russian capital and walk the corridors of imperial power.

The trip could not have come at a better time for Cornies. By the time he left in 1824 the religious disputes in the Molochnaia settlement had peaked with the formation of the Large Flemish Congregation. The main issue was religious; but at a time when the state, with its renewed economic agenda, was intruding ever more deeply into community affairs, the political implications of Warkentin's position were also already evident. The worldliness that Warkentin and his followers objected to when they opposed the Christian School Association and the Russian Bible Society had secular dimensions, and the Wool Improvement Society, led by Cornies and devoted to convincing Mennonites to adopt state agricultural goals, was yet another extension of that worldliness. The trip allowed Cornies to temporarily distance himself from the controversy and to regroup and marshal new allies before he returned to the fray.

Cornies travelled as an official representative of the Molochnaia and Khortitsa Mennonite settlements, which paid his travel expenses, but the significant cost of buying the sheep was covered by the state. Cornies had been ordered by the Guardianship Committee to travel to Tsarskoe Selo, the tsar's personal agricultural establishment just south of St. Petersburg, to select sheep from the tsar's flock. He would receive the money to pay for them from the Department of the Imperial Economy in St. Petersburg.[59]

This assignment evidenced the high regard that the Guardianship Committee had for Cornies by 1824. The sheep were expected to cost 17,000 rubles, a substantial sum that could not lightly be entrusted to just anyone. Beyond that, the trip shows how Cornies's relations with the various people and agencies in New Russia were evolving. For the first time, he was representing not just the Molochnaia settlement but Khortitsa as well. This made good business sense, but it also showed that the Guardianship Committee was beginning to identify Cornies as a representative of Mennonites broadly, not just his own settlement. This foreshadowed the much larger role Cornies would take on in the 1840s.

Cornies took two other commissions with him to St. Petersburg in 1824. The first, also from the Guardianship Committee, was to buy a year's supply of stationery for the bureau in Ekaterinoslav.[60] The committee provided Cornies with a shopping list and 1,000 rubles, but it acknowledged that this might not be enough money and urged him to use his own discretion – and his own funds – and pay more if necessary. They promised that the difference would be made up on his return. The request is a striking indication of the day-to-day difficulties of colonial administration. Ekaterinoslav might have been the big city for Molochnaia Mennonites, but as Fadeev wrote with dismay of his first impressions in 1815, to him it was little more than a "big peasant village ... with livestock grazing in the streets."[61] The inability to find paper, that most basic instrument in the bureaucratic toolbox, hamstrung the state's cameralist goals, and the shortage of ready money – the bureaucrat's other basic tool – was equally crippling. Cornies's other commission was a personal one: appended to the committee's official orders came a personal note from Fadeev, asking Cornies to buy him sugar, tea, and other hard-to-find luxuries.[62]

Collectively these commissions illuminate the ambiguous position Cornies occupied by 1824. In buying sheep he represented the Mennonite settlements, which paid his travel expenses, but he also represented the Guardianship Committee, which had initiated the plan and was paying for the sheep. In buying stationery he acted almost as an employee of the committee, but when the committee asked him to front his own money if necessary, it revealed how Cornies's personal wealth gave him status and potential influence with the committee. Finally, when Fadeev asked Cornies to buy him sugar and tea, he revealed an emerging friendship between the two, but – given Fadeev's position of power as chair of the committee – this also must be seen as an assertion of Cornies's obligations rooted in patronage.

Cornies and his companions set out from Ohrloff in mid-April, travelling via Moscow to St. Petersburg.[63] They left no personal recollections of the trip, but Red Square and the multicoloured domes of St. Basil's Cathedral must have been a dazzling sight for the New Russian travellers. And what did they think when they walked along Nevsky Prospekt in St. Petersburg and through the triumphal arch onto Troitskaia Square (today Palace Square), where the massive new General Staff building celebrated Tsar Alexander's victory over Napoleon and provided dramatic balance to the Winter Palace across the way? Did Cornies, a wealthy man in his own right, walk through the park in front of the Admiralty, rubbing shoulders with the aristocracy and stopping to admire the famous statue of Peter the Great?

We will likely never know the answers to these questions, although Cornies, famously dour and deeply pious, was an unlikely candidate to let his hair down on a business trip. Many years later, Fadeev wrote to a St. Petersburg acquaintance that what Cornies feared most in life was to be summoned back to St. Petersburg.[64] Whatever Cornies's reaction to the big-city glitter, he could not have helped but be impressed by the imperial power it symbolized. When he returned home, this would be a weighty consideration in his future decision-making.

The most definitive expression of imperial power for Cornies came when he visited the Department of the Imperial Economy in St. Petersburg to pick up a letter of introduction to the administrators of Tsarskoe Selo. He later related in a letter to a Prussian friend, "In St. Petersburg I was told in the Ministry, 'If you will not be industrious in that for which you have made yourself responsible to the state, on which basis you have received the Privilegium, you will be in danger of losing your special privileges. The law changes in the short term and in the long term and what have you accomplished?'"[65] Cornies was being told in no uncertain terms that Mennonites would not be allowed to sit quietly by as passive models; it was time for them to take up the state's modernizing agenda.

Cornies's personal, business, and administrative affairs were never clearly delineated, and this was certainly true of the St. Petersburg trip, which brought him into contact with people who would become important allies and lasting friends. Most significantly, in Moscow he met Traugott Blüher, the head of the Moscow trading house of the Moravian Brethren. The Brethren, a Pietist Christian confession founded in the eighteenth century and headquartered in Herrnhut, Saxony, had a missionary network that extended around the world. Like the Mennonites they had taken advantage of Catherine's recruitment drive, establishing their Russian colony of Sarepta on the Volga River in 1765. The Brethren's religious vision was almost the exact opposite of the beliefs of Mennonite conservatives. They were aggressively evangelical, concentrating particularly on missionary work among non-Christians, and they saw Sarepta as a beachhead for their missionary activities among the Muslim and Buddhist peoples of Central Asia. This Brethren outpost was expected to be economically self-sufficient and to use its economic contacts as an extension of its missionary activities.

There is no record of how Cornies found his way to Blüher's door, but probably his new circle of Pietist contacts provided the link. A likely intermediary was William Allen. During his journey to New Russia, Allen had promised Contenius that he would do what he could to help advance the Guardianship Committee's agricultural plans, and after he returned to England he kept up a regular correspondence with Contenius and Fadeev, sending them seeds for various vegetables and grains and offering advice on wool marketing. Allen was acquainted with the Moravian Brethren's activities in Russia, having met frequently with Brethren during his stay in St. Petersburg in 1818–19.

Cornies's visit with Blüher blossomed into a strong friendship. The two corresponded regularly for twenty-four years, and their letters provide some of the clearest glimpses into Cornies's personal life. Cornies demonstrated the depth of their friendship when he entrusted his son's care to Blüher while Johann Jr. studied cartography in Moscow in 1834.[66] Blüher returned the compliment in 1844 when his son Joseph's "excessive inclination toward youthful society" was leading to trouble and he sent the youth to Cornies in order to "distance him from" Moscow social life.[67] As well as a close friend, Blüher became Cornies's business agent in Moscow, selling wool and silk for Cornies and the entire Mennonite community and providing vital information about markets for all manner of agricultural goods. Blüher also bought books, medicine, and even hair tonic for the balding Cornies.

Among the most important things Blüher provided to Cornies was personal insight into a religious world view that was foreign to conservative Mennonites. Although Cornies would never adopt the Moravian Brethren's missionary goals, their message of interaction with the secular world – in particular, economic interaction – came to him as a revelation. The Brethren, he concluded, had succeeded in engaging the modernizing world around them while preserving their Christian faith.[68] When he returned to the Molochnaia in 1824, it was this religious insight, as much as the political realities of St. Petersburg, that gripped him.

Conclusion: Mapping the Imperial Landscape

In St. Petersburg, Johann Cornies saw the power of Russia on full display, and he heard in emphatic terms that, from the empire's perspective, the Mennonites were bound in service to the tsar. This cast the Molochnaia settlement's political debate in sharp relief. Warkentin's determination to preserve Mennonite independence and play only a passive role in the state's colonial plans was at best naive and at worst seemed certain to lead to the revocation of Mennonite privileges. By 1824 Cornies knew that Mennonites could not simply disengage from the state; the only alternative was creative engagement in a way that might preserve the most important Mennonite rights while satisfying the state's main goals.

Cornies also returned home with a religious world view that cast engagement in the most positive terms, as a natural outgrowth of evangelical Christian belief. In Moscow, the heart of old Russia, he found Blüher living the life of a prosperous, respected merchant in the very name of Christian piety. Pietism was not new to Cornies – Bible Society emissaries and Frisian Mennonite immigrants had already won his support and leadership for important Pietist initiatives in the Molochnaia. Still, Blüher's Moravian Brethren version of Pietism promoted a much broader engagement that fully endorsed economic ties beyond the settlement. More importantly, it clearly endorsed engagement with the state, for while the Brethren carried on their missionary fieldwork from their Volga River colony, symbolically Blüher lived and worked in Moscow.

Cornies did not return to the Molochnaia as a Moravian Brethren convert, much less as a Russian cameralist bureaucrat. But his journey into the Russian heartland did force him to see clearly the ambiguous position Mennonites held in the tsar's empire. Their privileges, which they themselves had constructed in order to preserve their independence and distinctive beliefs, had been designed by the state to harness them to its colonial mission, which in the 1820s was becoming more sharply articulated. Pietism seemed to offer a way to balance religious belief and imperial ambition, but Pietism itself came in a bewildering variety of flavours, all of them unpalatable to many Molochnaia Mennonites.

Cornies's experiences between 1818 and 1824 gave him an understanding of the challenges facing the Russian Mennonites that no other Mennonite could have acquired. Through the Frisian immigrants and the contacts they brought with Prussia Mennonite leaders, he now had a grasp of the religious currents that threatened them. He also knew through his own administrative experiences and from his contacts with Contenius and Fadeev the practical regional demands they faced. And he knew, directly from the halls of power in St. Petersburg, the imperial plans that they could not avoid. What he did not yet know was how to resolve all of these conflicting forces. Back home in the Molochnaia, in the midst of turmoil and crisis, he would struggle to find his answer.

Chapter Four

Awakening, 1824–1828

On 22 October 1825, Tsar Alexander I visited the Molochnaia for the second and final time. He was no longer the triumphant leader who had come to the Mennonite settlement seven years earlier. His grand vision of a Holy Alliance to preserve European order had foundered on his allies' irreconcilable ambitions after the one thing they had all agreed upon – the threat of Napoleon – no longer united them. The giddy euphoria that had united the Russian nobility in support of the man they had once looked to as the champion of liberal reforms was gone too, haveing faded away as a result of Alexander's failure to deliver on his promises. Even his religious vision had faded: while he still avowed a mystical spiritualism in his personal life, by 1825 the Orthodox Church had reclaimed its dominance over Russia's religious life, pushing Aleksandr Golitsyn and other Pietist supporters of the tsar out of high office.

Most descriptions of the tsar in autumn 1825 portray him as physically and emotionally exhausted, but for the Molochnaia Mennonites his aura of majesty was undiminished. Out on the frontier, among people for whom he had provided a secure new homeland and a religious refuge, his former glory was still whole cloth. The Mennonites greeted Alexander with all the reverence and love they had shown in 1818, and for a few days their enthusiasm seemed to restore the tsar's old passion. He told his hosts: "I am so contented with you for your peaceful way of life and your diligence."[1]

Six weeks later, Alexander I was dead, probably from typhus. By Christmas, Russia's first revolutionaries, the Decembrists, had launched their feckless attempt to achieve by force the reforms the tsar had failed to deliver voluntarily. In January 1826, with the St. Petersburg wing of the Decembrist movement crushed and the Ukrainian wing in hopeless disarray, Tsar Nicholas I took the throne. Frightened by the Decembrists, he set out to impose tight-fisted control over his empire, and his rule placed intrusive new demands on Mennonites. For Johann Cornies, who had already emerged as the most influential Mennonite liaison with the state, the new situation demanded new strategies.

This need for change came in the midst of hard times in the Molochnaia, which had been battered by a hurricane in August 1824 and by a severe blizzard in February 1825. Tsar Alexander observed the lingering effects of these storms in October 1825, and asked whether it was true that the Mennonites had been forced to use their thatch roofs as fodder for their livestock (it was).[2] Whatever new plans Cornies had when he returned home from St. Petersburg in August 1824 were pushed aside by the need to help his community survive and recover. In 1825 and 1826 he focused his energy on immediate community needs. As he did so, his community's internal disputes grew more and more contentious, and Cornies found himself the target of deeply wounding attacks on his personal integrity.

The Molochnaia Mennonite community crisis of the mid-1820s led to a profound personal crisis for Cornies. His life was at a crossroads, and he had no shortage of options for his future path. His closest friend, Wilhelm Martens, pursued personal wealth, amassing one of the largest private fortunes in New Russia, and Cornies could surely have followed his example. Meanwhile, Samuel Contenius and Andrei Fadeev urged Cornies to take a leading role in the state's colonial mission in New Russia. This had its own appeal, especially after Cornies's encounter with the splendours of St. Petersburg. Perhaps most troubling of all were the religious ideas that now swirled through his life. The Moravian Brethren, Swiss Pietists, Prussian Mennonites, and Frisian Mennonite immigrants – an ever-expanding, all but overwhelming world of Russian and foreign contacts – bombarded him with alternative ways to deal with his increasingly complex world. His conclusions, reached during his extended convalescence following a trip to Saxony and Prussia in 1827, would shape the remainder of Cornies's life.

The Crisis of 1824–5

Cornies returned home to the Molochnaia on 19 August 1824. He had left his business affairs in the hands of his brother Peter during his absence, and he was not pleased with the results, for he found himself "catching up on what was neglected, restoring the damage as best possible."[3] Cornies's criticism of his brother was less than fair, for New Russia was experiencing one of its worst summers on record, of drought, harvest failure, and swarms of grasshoppers, capped off by a massive

August storm. Daniel Schlatter vividly described the storm's destruction: "Many houses, even whole villages were blown down in the old settlement. The misery this has occasioned is very great; many families are without a shelter. The hurricane extended to the Dnieper, into which whole herds of cattle were swept by the violence of the tempest, and even the shepherds were drowned."[4]

On 14–15 February 1825 the already difficult conditions worsened when a powerful blizzard swept through the region. Cornies described the devastation in a letter to Fadeev: "The day grew so dark one could not see twenty *fadens* [38 metres] ... Every communication between houses was almost totally cut off ... My sheep were driven over the fences by the wind and snow. In this way, I lost more than seven hundred head of sheep."[5] A second blizzard followed on 8 March, multiplying the damage.

By 1824, Cornies was wealthy enough that the severe weather posed no threat to his personal welfare. Apart from his 3,800 *desiatinas* of land at Iushanle he now leased another 12,000 *desiatinas* in the local area and 39,000 *desiatinas* to the east of the drought zone in Mariupol district. In 1824–5 he wintered much of his livestock in Mariupol.[6] However, his responsibility to his fellow Mennonites consumed him in the winter of 1824–5; as he wrote, "members of the community come to me daily, and, thanks be to God, I am able to assist them with advice and deed."[7]

Cornies's activities during this desperate winter reveal his ambiguous position in his community. His official positions were limited to the Wool Improvement Society and the Settlement Commission, neither of which had anything to do with overseeing community aid. He gave assistance to neighbours as a private member of the community, employing his personal wealth. He estimated his financial losses at more than 30,000 rubles, and as he told Fadeev, community concerns left him with "almost no time to cast my eye over my own affairs."[8]

Cornies's efforts on behalf of his community grew out of a strong sense of personal obligation rooted in religious belief. His letters during the crisis reveal the strain he was under as he struggled with the ambiguities of a Mennonite belief system that did not take lightly the biblical injunction that "it is easier for a camel to go through the eye of a needle than for a rich man to enter the kingdom of God."[9] Cornies was faced with one of the quintessential questions of modern Mennonite identity: the relationship between personal wealth, community responsibility, and Christian faith.[10]

He recorded his conclusions in a letter to Fadeev: "Because, as a member of the community, I possess its confidence, I consider it to be my inescapable duty to employ it according to my best insights for the well-being of every single individual and for the whole community. This is even more so because the Lord, through His gentle hand, has blessed me with temporal riches to the extent that I have been freed of burdensome worries about survival and ... I am obliged to carry out all responsibilities than can serve the purpose of the general well-being."[11]

Under the pressure of the crisis, significant elements of a personal philosophy that would guide Cornies for the rest of his life began to crystallize. He described the 1824 drought to Blüher as "God's judgment," but this did not mean that its consequences should be accepted passively. Rather, it was a test, intended to benefit people by teaching them to seek solutions in "the Word of God, which is written down for us in the Bible."[12] As Cornies understood it, God had blessed him with wealth and ability, and with these blessings came obligations to his community. Traditional Mennonite beliefs stressed that the individual's relationship to God was mediated through the Bible, and for Cornies the element of individual responsibility in this formula was important. While he accepted his obligations to the community, he did not look to the community to decide for him how he would fulfil them.

Implied by this philosophy – though he did not articulate it as such – was that Cornies was beginning to regard his wealth and his appointments to important administrative roles as signs of God's favour that not only obliged him to help his community but also entitled him to decide how to act without consulting with the settlement's religious or secular leaders. This was not a sign of incipient megalomania: Cornies was demonstrably successful in business and administration, and both his community and the state had recognized his unique talents by giving him ever-increasing responsibilities. As his confidence in his own abilities grew, as his understanding of the challenges that faced Mennonites in their New Russian and Imperial Russian context grew, as his wealth and his contacts in the administrative world grew, and as his knowledge of the varieties of Christian belief grew, he was moulding his faith, understanding, ambition, and sense of responsibility to fit together.

There is one additional insight to be gained from Cornies's reflections on faith, community, and responsibility in 1824–5. They reveal an emotional and compassionate side of his personality that is seldom reflected in records of his public activities. This is not quite accurate – in his later life he was sometimes angry and even violent in his relations with Mennonites who did not follow orders, and this has been used as evidence that Cornies had adopted an arbitrary, autocratic style of administration that betrayed the values of his Mennonite community. The existence, not far beneath the surface, of a positive emotional counterpart to Cornies's outbursts of anger provides a response to these criticisms and helps explain how he attracted the support, loyalty, and friendship of people within his own community, in broader Pietist circles, and in the tsarist administration.

As the crisis of 1824–5 deepened, personal and community efforts proved insufficient to address the needs of the hardest-hit Mennonites, and Cornies's semi-official role as the settlement's representative on the Guardianship Committee merged with his unofficial role as a personal representative to Fadeev. On 5 February he wrote to Fadeev that "even with the best intentions, it is impossible for me to help all those suffering need."[13] He begged the Guardianship Committee to release funds from the community treasury to pay for relief efforts and to create a special Mennonite committee to support the most severely affected.

This appeal opened with a salutation from the "authorised representative of the Mennonite Community, Johann Cornies" to "the Honourable Senior Member of the Ekaterinoslav Bureau for Foreign Settlers, Mr. von Fadeev." It was, therefore, an official request from the settlement to the committee. Beyond the formal opening, however, it was entirely a personal appeal from Cornies to his patron Fadeev. The final lines strikingly reflect this, for Cornies no longer spoke in the guise of a community representative appealing to a government agency, but rather as a personal supplicant: "Most obediently, in the name of those in extreme need, I request that your Honour make arrangements for them very expeditiously … because hunger does not permit any delay. At the same time I also obediently request, that you not receive ungraciously the step I have taken with well-meaning intentions. Your Honour's most obedient servant, J. C."[14]

The *Gebietsamt*'s decision to ask Cornies to write this letter is significant. The formal lines of authority ran from the *Gebietsamt* to the local inspector of colonies and from there to the Guardianship Committee in Ekaterinoslav. This bureaucratic chain of command was never very efficient, and during a broad regional crisis, when all of the committee's other charges were desperately seeking aid, the Mennonites had little hope of gaining quick attention. However, by 1825 the Mennonites knew they could bypass official channels by turning to Cornies, who had personal influence with the Guardianship Committee. This not only acknowledged Cornies's special position in the settlement – it legitimized and strengthened that position.

At this point the surviving records fail us. It is impossible to say whether the *Gebietsamt* received permission to strike a relief committee or divert community funds before the fine weather of summer 1825 ended the crisis. In June 1825 Cornies wrote that the settlement had lost

10,000 sheep, 1,800 head of cattle, and 1,200 horses. The Slavic villages in his region had lost 125,000 head of livestock, and among the human population starvation, disease, and many deaths followed.[15] The toll among the Nogai Tatars and German colonists, though undocumented, was certainly also heavy.

The crisis had a significant impact on Cornies's relationship to both his community and the state: it forced him to take on a new and larger public role, and this ultimately drew him deep into community controversies. At the height of the crisis an utterly unrelated request arrived directly from the Russian Minister of Internal Affairs, Viktor Kochubei, bringing unwelcome additional complications.

Kochubei owned a large estate near Odesa, and in late 1824 he decided to send a representative to Saxony to buy merino sheep on his behalf. The minister had heard of Cornies's trip to St. Petersburg and may also have known him through Bible Society channels (Kochubei was vice-president of the society). Through Fadeev he asked whether Cornies would be willing to oversee the selection of sheep and their transportation from Saxony. Fadeev urged Cornies to take the job, pointing out that he would have an opportunity to buy breeding stock for himself and that by doing a favour for Kochubei, he might gain the minister's support "in obtaining several thousand *desiatinas* of land."[16] A follow-up letter from Contenius pressed Cornies to accept Kochubei's commission, adding that the assignment would be valuable to the entire Mennonite settlement.[17] This correspondence bluntly articulated the mechanisms of patronage that were deeply embedded in regional affairs.

The land with which Fadeev tempted Cornies was the 3,800 *desiatinas* that Cornies had already leased at Iushanle. The pursuit of full ownership of this land would occupy Cornies for more than a decade, from his first formal petition in November 1825 until he finally received a smaller grant of 500 *desiatinas* in 1836 (he retained lease rights to the remaining 3,300 *desiatinas*).[18] By then Cornies had purchased thousands of acres of land, but Iushanle was where he had begun his rise to prominence in 1812. It eventually became the headquarters for all of his activities.

The request from Kochubei could not have come at a worse time, and Cornies apologetically replied to his patrons that he could not leave the Molochnaia: "Many existing arrangements require further and very alert supervision and many other forceful, thorough measures and diligent considerations to prevent them from falling into constantly greater deterioration."[19] To this he added that his own business affairs, much neglected during his years of community service, now demanded his attention. Cornies was not exaggerating the problems the Molochnaia faced, and for the time being the idea of the Saxony expedition was shelved. However, once the crisis ended and his duties as chair of the Wool Improvement Society resumed, Fadeev and Contenius would reintroduce it, pressuring Cornies to reconsider.

In the summer of 1825 Cornies returned to his neglected business affairs, finally pursuing the opportunities he had unearthed a year earlier in Moscow. Now began a long and prosperous business relationship with Blüher, who became both Cornies's and the Molochnaia settlement's main business agent in Moscow. In 1825 this was still an experiment – Cornies agreed to ship his own and the community's wool to Blüher, who would store it in Moscow and sell it when market conditions were most propitious. This did not mean the Mennonites could completely bypass the unpredictable regional markets – the wool buyers who travelled through the region provided ready cash when it was most needed – but it did mean that the best of Mennonite wool could be sold for much higher prices than were offered in New Russia.[20] Blüher profited by his sales commissions and at times sent his own money to Cornies, who acted as his wool buyer in the Molochnaia.

This arrangement liberated the Mennonites from the cash-on-the-barrel-head regional markets. In 1825 the dangers those markets posed were brought home to the Mennonite settlement in a tragic way. In August, four men and a twelve-year-old boy from the Molochnaia travelled to the great annual market in Romny to sell wool and buy supplies for the community. They headed home loaded with supplies and more than 80,000 rubles in cash. Their route led them through the forests near Poltava, where a gang of thieves robbed and murdered them.[21] In November the *Gebietsamt* asked Cornies to travel to Romny to investigate the murders, but the Guardianship Committee refused to authorize the trip, telling him that police work was the state's job. Soon after, the community received official word that a police informant had implicated "two Jewish robber bands" that had staked out the Romny market looking for victims.[22] Months later, the Kremenchug police arrested three Jewish carters, Gigal Gomol'skii, Gershka Bukhbinder, and Iankel Brallovskii, for the murders, and Cornies wrote to Blüher praising the state's "good police methods."[23] However, the community never recovered the supplies and money.

This story of the bandits is a vivid reminder of the challenges of life on the New Russian frontier in the early nineteenth century. People like Cornies were highly prized by the Russian state because it lacked the personnel to adequately administer the frontier. To assert regional control, Russia needed to co-opt the most able colonists. At the same time, frontier settlements needed to cooperate with the state because there had to be someone to assert authority and police the region.

Mennonites, being pacifists, could hardly be expected to deal effectively with armed bandits, and the great annual market at Romny must have provided other easy pickings for thieves. The identification of the thieves as Jewish is also striking, though it mainly raises questions for which there are no ready answers. The evidence against the three was scant – they were found in possession of pants taken from the murder victims, but they claimed to have bought them in a market.[24] Were Jewish robber bands commonplace in New Russia? Was the identification of the thieves as Jewish accurate at all, or did it reflect the well-documented anti-Semitism of the Russian administration? What attitudes did it reflect among Mennonites, and what attitudes did the robbery itself engender among Mennonites toward Jews? This latter question would eventually become an important one for Cornies and will be discussed in more detail in chapter 9. Meanwhile, other minorities were coming to his attention by the mid-1820s.

Imagining Civilization: The Nogai Project

The relationship of all minorities to the Russian state was a growing concern for the Guardianship Committee by 1825, and at the committee's request, Cornies became a source of information on the Nogais, Doukhobors, and Molokans who were the Mennonites' close neighbours. This was a significant step for Cornies, who was asked to expand his horizons beyond the Mennonite settlement to serve state interests in other communities. The committee did not ask Cornies to play a direct administrative role outside the settlement, nor did it ask him to give advice on state policy; rather, he was simply to observe and report. But whatever the state might have wished from him, it was not in Cornies's nature to be a passive observer.

The most important result of the Guardianship Committee's request came in 1826, when Cornies wrote a long, detailed study of the Nogais. This report marks a significant new stage in Cornies's development as an analyst and administrator, showing that he was thinking deeply about the nature of "civilized" society and the role of the state in achieving it. The state's request for the report also reflects an important development: imperial Russia was becoming less willing to accept the diversity that had long been a hallmark of its imperial policy; it was preparing to impose its own vision of "civility" on its subjects.

Cornies's account of the Nogais reflects the deep racial and religious prejudices that shaped European encounters with the "other," in that it imposed typical nineteenth-century European constructs of racial and religious hierarchies. He regarded Europeans – white Christians practising arable farming – as civilized, and all others as occupying lower rungs on the path toward civilization. The Russian version of this debate extended to the very nature of national identity and to the question of whether Russia's identity was "European" or "Asiatic." The relationship between the predominantly Slavic Christian farming population of "European Russia" and the predominantly Islamic Tatar and Mongol pastoralist populations of "Asian Russia" was a core element of the debate.[25] The issue extended to the very question of where Europe ended and Asia began, for an eighteenth-century convention identified the border as the Ural Mountains, and the place of the southeastern steppes in this divide was ambiguous.[26]

Within this "ideological construction of geographical space," to use geographer Mark Bassin's phrase, the Molochnaia Mennonites were perched right on the notional border between Asia and Europe.[27] They were clearly "civilized" white Christian farmers, whereas the Nogais were just as clearly "uncivilized" Tataric Islamic pastoralists. Mennonites both defined the border and seemed to offer the potential to breach it by modelling civility to the Nogais. Because of this, Cornies's detailed description of Nogai society and his projects for "civilizing" the Nogais were critically important in establishing the Mennonites in the eyes of the state as front-line agents for advancing a civilizational agenda. Emblematic of this, Cornies's description of the Nogais was eventually published in the same 1836 issue of the Moscow journal *Teleskop* that contained Petr Chaadaev's notorious first "Philosophical Letter," a landmark in the debate over Russian identity that denied the very existence of a Russian civilization.[28]

Cornies's written description of the Nogais is a valuable source of information about their history, but it is even more important for what it reveals about Cornies's attitudes and understanding in 1826. In structure and argument it is a product of Enlightenment thought and tsarist imperial policy, positing an inevitable human progression from primitive to modern. It thus incorporates the Eurocentric racial and religious prejudices typical of the age.[29] Primitive, in Cornies's terms, meant nomadic and therefore economically unproductive. He described the Nogais in their early, nomadic period as having had a "thieving disposition and ... irregular and unproductive way of life."[30] Modern meant sedentary, and in economic terms it meant people who practised arable agriculture.[31]

Cornies described the Nogais as a people in the process of being "civilized." This implies two important assumptions: first, that the Russian state was the agent of civilization; and second, that the Nogais – and presumably all people – were capable of becoming civilized. According to Cornies the paternalistic state's role in this process was to exhibit "patience and love," but if that failed it should use "severity."[32] In Cornies's view, the key measures for the state to take were to provide wise policies – in particular, to compel the Nogais to become sedentary agriculturists – and to provide a good administrator who would find ways to achieve the state's goals.

Cornies placed heavy emphasis on education as a tool to help "civilize" the Nogais. Education could attack what Cornies identified as the root of the Nogai problem, the Islamic religion, which he saw as "probably the greatest obstacle to [their] moral improvement and increased civilization."[33] Cornies saw Islam as fatalistic and thus leading to "indolence and indifference."[34] In particular, he saw the doctrine of predestination as harmful, for it acted "as a deterrent to those improvements usually developed by normal human nature and intelligence."[35] He wrote that the Qu'ran did not consider "human intelligence and strength ... as a gift from God to be used and applied." The solution began with schooling, for "through institutions of education, the fanaticism, fatalism, superstition and the overwhelming influence of priests and all evils of Islam can be mitigated." This would be a slow process, laying a "better foundation for the future generation ... and [promoting] a better sense of culture and morality."[36]

Cornies suggested that the state begin its civilizing mission by establishing a model school to train a new generation of Nogai teachers.[37] Such a school would not directly question Islam; indeed, "religion should be respected." Positive aspects of the Qu'ran should be stressed and given consideration in political arrangements and in schools, while detrimental aspects should be countered "indirectly."[38] Still, Cornies was suggesting taking schooling out of the hands of the Islamic clergy. This would provide the state with an opportunity to control the content of Nogai education and "counter one of the greatest obstacles to their improvement, namely the stupid, detrimental posture of their inherited pride in nation and ancestors, kept alive by ignorance, and always an obstacle to accepting improvement."[39]

Cornies's emphasis on the role of leadership is especially notable. From 1809 to 1821 the Guardian of the Nogai Tatar Horde – the official responsible for direct administration of Nogai affairs – was the comte de Maison. Cornies was an enthusiastic supporter of the *comte*, whose leadership he characterized as "wise, selfless, mild-yet-stern."[40] He bemoaned de Maison's 1821 retirement, after which "indolence, quarrelling and thievery have increased considerably. There is no support or encouragement for individuals seeking anything useful. The wicked find means to insist on their freedom and escape punishment. Very little, actually nothing, is done toward moral improvement and general civilization, even though the state is very concerned about this."[41]

This praise for de Maison shows that Cornies placed great emphasis on the role of the individual in effective administration. After all, while the state's policies toward the Nogais did not change when de Maison retired, according to Cornies progress ground to a halt. Cornies was not dismissing the role of the state; rather, he was promoting a combination of active, creative local leadership guided by wise state policies. He saw the success of this approach both in de Maison's administration of the Nogais and in Contenius's and Fadeev's administration of foreign colonists, including the Mennonites. By comparison, Cornies saw individual freedom, unconstrained by the state, as a formula for chaos. The Nogais, before they became subjects of the Russian state, had been the obvious example of this: "With no comprehension of the world and the state, of countries and peoples beyond his own circle, every ignorant and proud nomadic Nogai saw himself as lord of the whole world ... Only a few individuals were rich or prosperous under nomadic conditions, and it was very difficult to advance beyond [those individuals]. They absorbed everything for themselves; the majority remained in poverty, more or less dependent."[42]

Cornies's developing conception of the relationship between individuals and the state shaped the ways he approached the Russian administrative world in future years. He would come to see himself as the active, creative local leader, guided by state policy but acting independently to develop strategies to achieve state goals. This again reflects an important reality of frontier administration in early nineteenth-century Russia. The shortage of competent regional administrators meant that where they were found, they would be provided significant scope to develop local strategies to achieve state goals.[43] De Maison, Contenius, Fadeev, and Cornies all benefited from this freedom. Historians have often concentrated on the abuses to which such freedom sometimes led, and this is understandable. De Maison left office in 1821 under a gathering cloud of scandal to avoid further investigation of accusations that he had illegally sold the state's salt monopoly for the Nogai district to a Russian merchant.[44] Still, if the system left local administrators free to abuse their power it also left them free to creatively resolve local problems. Co-opted local elites played a vital role in imperial administration, and the Russian state often folded regional particularities into the imperial administrative system.[45] But Cornies also reflects a state in the process of reconsidering this policy, for his report stresses the need for state intervention to erase Nogai particularities.[46] It reflected the message Cornies had heard in St. Petersburg in 1824 – freedoms were to be tightly constrained by state interests.

Cornies's account of the Nogais provides other evidence of how his world view was developing in 1826. Cornies believed strongly that the Nogais could be "civilized," and implicitly this meant that all people were capable of achieving full membership in the civilized world. In a clear reflection of official imperial attitudes, Cornies saw Nogai incivility as both caused by and reflected in economic "backwardness," revealed most clearly in nomadism.[47] Ending nomadism would destroy "the inclination to a lazy, changeable, unrestrained life still clinging to them. Prejudice, superstition and fanaticism would have been reduced, making the Nogais more receptive to moral improvement, culture of the spirit, and all institutions that contribute to the happiness of human society and therefore also to the state."[48]

Cornies emphasized what he saw as the negative effects of Islam, but he did not think that Islam was an impenetrable barrier to the civilization of the Nogais. He believed that "the more a supervisor penetrates into the spirit of Islam, into the character of the people and into their individuality and is able to utilise this knowledge, the more he will be respected, find entrance into hearts and souls, and accomplish the purpose and effect of established institutions and arrangements."[49] Cornies acquired a German translation of the Qur'an, and he came to the conclusion that if it were properly interpreted it would not be an insurmountable obstacle to progress. At heart, Cornies thought that the Nogais were malleable: the paternalistic state, through good administration, and particularly through good schooling, could erase the cultural and religious characteristics that defined their identity and remould them into "civilized," productive subjects.

Cornies did not connect all the dots in his Nogai essay, but he surely understood the underlying implication: if all humans were malleable, and if good governments and able administrators could mould them, then Mennonites were subject to the same rules as Nogais. It is particularly notable that Cornies saw secular schools as the main instrument in this moulding process. One of his first and most enduring causes in the Mennonite settlement was the Christian School Society. The Ohrloff school's curriculum was hardly secular; what made it controversial among Mennonites was that it was not controlled by the congregational elders, and its curriculum extended beyond religion to mathematics, geography, and the Russian language. If the Ohrloff school was Cornies's first tentative step toward applying his new philosophy of change to his own Mennonite community, in 1826 he did not yet have the power and influence to press through widespread change. Still, his detailed, lengthy reflection on the condition of Nogai society and the solution to its problems undoubtedly led to similar reflections about his own troubled community. By 1826 Cornies was laying the intellectual groundwork to "civilize" the Molochnaia Mennonites.

New Intellectual and Religious Horizons

The Nogai essay shows Cornies's intellectual evolution. He had little formal education, and his work as land surveyor had only required him to prepare limited reports. Suddenly in 1826 he authored a fifty-two-page descriptive and analytical essay filled with complex reflections on moral, cultural, and religious matters. This transformation was undoubtedly heavily influenced by the 1822 arrival in the Molochnaia of Daniel Schlatter, whose lasting contributions to Cornies's intellectual development were vitally important.

As noted in chapter 3, Schlatter was raised in St. Gallen, Switzerland, where he acquired a sophisticated education and underwent a deep immersion in the pan-European Pietist community of the early nineteenth century. His aunt, Anna Bernet-Schlatter, was the most prominent woman in European Pietism. Among her friends and correspondents were luminaries such as Johann Heinrich Jung-Stilling, Christian Friedrich Spittler, Friedrich Schleiermacher, Georg Gessner, and Martin Boos. Her home was a gathering place for a diverse and impressive group that included the Duchess Henriette of Württemberg and the Bishop of Regensburg, Johann Michael Sailer. The main Pietist congregation in St. Gallen was Swiss Separatist, but the Schlatters could not be pinned down to Separatist beliefs, and Bernet-Schlatter's most important contribution to European Pietism was as a champion of ecumenicism.[50]

Daniel Schlatter was strongly influenced by his famous aunt, and he listed as his principal intellectual influences her friends Jung-Stilling and Sailer, along with the Quaker Stephen Grellet, and most importantly Johann Kaspar Lavater. The latter was a prominent Pietist preacher and religious writer, but he owed his greatest fame to his *Essays on Physiognomy*.[51] This influential volume argued that it was possible to understand people's moral character from the scientific analysis of their physical appearance.[52] While this seems to situate *Essays on Physiognomy* in the secular scientific milieu of the Enlightenment, in fact Lavater's work is more often "a sermon on the goodness of God and that goodness as reflected in the constitution and action of created things."[53] Lavater, whose work was foundational to scientific racism, wrote that "God has ever branded vice with deformity, and adorned virtue with inimitable beauty," and he went on to argue that physical appearance could be reshaped by moral improvement through education.[54] His definition of what constituted human beauty versus deformity bridged Enlightenment and religious constructions of race, and as historian Richard Gray details, it was a major contributor to the false science of eugenics and the development of Nazi racial policies in the twentieth century.[55]

Lavater's work was never fully accepted by contemporaries in the scientific community, who noted his lack of scientific rigour. Nevertheless he gained broad popularity in Europe, including Russia, in part because he melded Pietist sensibilities with the rationalist values of the Enlightenment.[56] In Schlatter's hands, Lavater's ideas penetrated to the Molochnaia, where they profoundly influenced Cornies, encouraging him to think that people could be changed at the most fundamental level.

Lavater's ideas are clearly reflected in Cornies's Nogai essay, in which he wrote that the consequences of the Nogais' nomadic economy were revealed, "not only in their behaviour but also very clearly in their stature and physiognomy."[57] Implicitly, a change in lifestyle would lead even to a change in physiognomy. Similar reflections appeared in his later reports on other ethnocultural and religious minorities. In particular, Lavater's belief that education was the key agency through which people could be physically and morally transformed expanded and legitimized Cornies's commitment to educational reform. Cornies explicitly applied Lavater's ideas to the Nogais, but those same ideas must be seen as equally influential on Cornies's reform plans for the Mennonites. Those plans marked an important step away from traditional Mennonite religious attitudes, which emphasized modelling life on biblical precepts. While Mennonites had never been opposed to innovation – indeed, it was their progressive agricultural practices that led Catherine the Great to recruit them – their model of social life was explicitly opposed to transformation through interaction with the state and with members of other religious denominations, the direction where Cornies's vision was leading. Cornies was conscious of this departure, explaining in a letter to David Epp that new conditions demanded new attitudes: "Our relationship to the state takes a totally different form than what you have in Prussia. The constitution of our communities is also totally different ... Here, one can really apply the expression: What is a community without the state and without the general life of the society?"[58] This was a good thing, Cornies stressed, because the Russian "state's blessings consist not simply in a large population but it must also use its fatherly guardianship to keep its people from suffering dearth and want."[59]

This letter reflected Cornies's personal views, but it also offers insights into the evolution of the state's view of its colonial subjects in the 1820s. Cornies was arguing that colonial peoples needed to become more fully integrated into the state; in this, he was moving away from the acceptance of diversity that had always characterized imperial policies. Cornies's Nogai essay would play an important role in establishing his reputation with the state, precisely because it reflected this new direction in imperial policy.

Cornies was moving away from Mennonite tradition in social terms; meanwhile, Schlatter encouraged him to continue his reconsideration of Mennonite religious values. Schlatter exposed Cornies to the false ideas of Lavaterian physiognomy, but equally important to Cornies's evolving world view were ecumenical religious beliefs and a strong avowal of a personal religious calling. Schlatter is usually identified as a missionary, but he had no formal affiliation with any missionary organization or religious denomination. Indeed, both the Basel Institute for the Education of Young People in Missionary Work and the British Baptist Missionary Society rejected him because his beliefs were not doctrinaire.[60] W.H. Angas, the prominent British Baptist missionary organizer, encouraged the British Baptists to recruit Schlatter as a missionary after he investigated the Swiss Pietist's background during an 1823 trip to St. Gallen. According to Angas, it was Schlatter's belief in adult baptism that had caused the Basel Institute to reject him.[61]

Angas's letter sheds light on another important aspect of Schlatter's character that undoubtedly contributed to his influence on Cornies. Schlatter was extraordinarily charismatic, gaining friends and supporters wherever he travelled. Angas painted a romantic picture of Schlatter, who he said "has by nature a constitution of body, for hardihood, and robustness, seldom perhaps or never equalled ... For some years he has never slept in a bed, nor drank anything stronger than water ... His affection for his mother ... is almost proverbial in St. Gallen. She was visited with an indisposition which threatened her life, and ... he set off therefore the same day, a journey of nearly one thousand English miles, without any other means than faith in God ... Thus he walked by faith, literally, nearly all the way home."[62]

While faith may have sustained Schlatter in his travels, it was helped along by generous financial donations. The Basel Institute refused him but still paid his travel expenses to the Molochnaia, and on his way there he visited Königsberg, where the local branch of the Berlin Missionary Institution gave him an additional £9 sterling "by way of rendering his situation more tolerable."[63] In 1824 Angas sent him another £50 in order to sustain him in the Molochnaia. By the time he returned home to St. Gallen permanently in 1828 he had accrued hundreds of rubles in debts to Cornies and other Mennonites that long went unpaid.[64] None of this seemed to undermine the devotion of his many supporters.

Bible Society member Ebenezer Henderson recommended Schlatter to the Molochnaia Mennonites as a teacher, and he probably set out for Russia with the intention of taking up that post, but this was never more than a pretext: from the first, Schlatter's real goal was to evangelize the Nogais. The activities of evangelical missionaries in Russia focused on the conversion of Tatars and other non-Christian groups, and such work had captured Schlatter's imagination. As he wrote, from his earliest years he had been gripped by a "desire to influence and benefit in a moral-religious and economic way such people."[65] By the time he arrived in the Molochnaia in late 1822, Tobias Voth had already filled the Christian School Society teaching position. Schlatter immediately took up his real purpose. He found for himself a position as a servant in a Nogai home, shed his European clothing in favour of Nogai robes, and pursued the religious "enlightenment" of his hosts.

In his own account of his time among the Nogais, Schlatter emphatically denied any missionary affiliation, making no mention of his rejection by the Baptists and the Basel Institute. Before his departure to Russia, Schlatter had spent several weeks in London, where he reported with awe – and apparent disapproval – on the conspicuous wealth of the British. His disapproval extended to the Bible Society itself, and his final word on London was an ironic description of the "toilet-room beneath the huge, magnificent assembly hall of the Bible Society ... It contained everything necessary for washing, brushing, shaving and perfuming, powdering and pomading before entering into the sumptuous assembly hall. Thus are the customs of Londoners!"[66] While Schlatter respected missionaries, writing in 1830 he claimed that he rejected association with any missionary organization because he did not wish to be bound by the congregational constraints under which missionaries worked. He carefully defined his journey to the Molochnaia as a "pilgrimage" rather than a mission, calling himself a layman who, through his individual actions, worked as a "tool in the hand of God."[67] He elsewhere explained that as a "lay-minister" he was not constrained by any organization and had only to answer to his own beliefs.[68]

Schlatter briefly visited the Molochnaia in autumn 1822 before returning home to visit his sick mother. He came back in May 1823 and remained until January 1827, when he travelled to London to interview with the Baptist Missionary Society. He returned in the spring of 1827 before making his final departure in June 1828. During his time in the Molochnaia he and Cornies became close friends, and Schlatter was a frequent visitor at the Cornies home in Ohrloff, particularly on Sundays, when, dressed in flowing Tatar robes, he accompanied the Cornies family to church.[69] Their correspondence in the late 1820s and early

1830s reads as a continuation of a long dialogue about Christianity and the role of the Christian individual in society.

Schlatter's ecumenicism and evangelism made him sharply critical of mainstream Mennonite society. On his way to the Molochnaia in 1822 he had passed through the Prussian Mennonite communities, where he met relatives of the Mennonites in New Russia. He was far from impressed, writing that their faith was "superficial," formalistic, and showed little evidence of "true belief."[70] He reported much the same impression of the Mennonites he encountered in the Molochnaia.[71] That such a harsh critic of Mennonites was so warmly received in Cornies's home, and that Schlatter himself felt so comfortable there, suggests that Cornies was receptive to Schlatter's brand of religion. In the same 1824 letter in which he criticized the Molochnaia Mennonites, Schlatter described Cornies as a friend "to humanity" and commended him to the Baptist Missionary Society.[72] This is not surprising – by the time Schlatter arrived, Cornies was already strongly sympathetic to Pietism. Not only that, but much of what Schlatter had to say about individual agency and "warm" Christian belief reinforced in religious terms the secular philosophy of public service that Fadeev and Contenius were promoting.

None of this should be construed as meaning that Cornies simply adopted Schlatter's religious views. By the late 1820s, Cornies had rejected the extreme individualism of Schlatter's philosophy, for he understood that reform plans could only be realized by working within both the Mennonite community and the secular administrative system. Cornies's personal religious beliefs reflected the strong influence of Pietism, but in public life he worked to maintain friendly relations with moderates in his community, and he remained a member of the original Flemish congregation throughout his life. Schlatter exposed Cornies to a sophisticated understanding of the Western European religious and intellectual world. However replete that world was with paternalism and implicit racism, it expanded Cornies's horizons and honed his analytical skills. That newly acquired sophistication was recognized by Russian officialdom, and in the future it would lend legitimacy to Cornies's views and make his opinions sought after at the highest levels of the Russian administration. Ultimately, however, the vision Cornies promoted was uniquely his own.

Scandal and Alienation

For a time in 1826–7, Schlatter's individualism intersected with Mennonite community disputes and threatened to sway Cornies's attitude toward public service. In those years Cornies found himself under attack within his own community, where the rising power of Warkentin and his Large Flemish Congregation threatened Cornies's influence. Angered by false accusations that he was a horse thief, and equally angered by the failure of the *Gebietsamt* to squelch the accusations, he briefly withdrew from all community duties.

Cornies's troubles in 1826 came as a result of his increasing prominence and personal influence, as well as his ill-defined relationship to the settlement administration. He had no official position in the *Gebietsamt* apart from his role as land surveyor, but by virtue of that work, as well as his role as the community's sheep-buyer in St. Petersburg in 1824 and his relief activities during the crisis of 1824–5, he was a prominent community figure. Cornies's personal connections to the Guardianship Committee, which the *Gebietsamt* had happily exploited during the 1824–5 crisis, further increased his importance. The problem was that his power and status were not clearly defined by any official rank or job description, either within his community or on the Guardianship Committee, and he was being called upon to serve in all manner of capacities that easily brought him into conflict with religiously conservative Mennonites led by Warkentin. Cornies recognized this problem and voiced his concerns in July 1825 when he asked the *Gebietsamt* to clarify his obligations as land surveyor. The *Gebietsamt* replied that his obligations were restricted to surveying and related duties, though in truth, it relied upon Cornies for much more.[73]

In the summer of 1825 the *Gebietsamt* asked Cornies to travel through the Nogai district to try to locate stolen Mennonite horses.[74] In its dealings with non-Mennonites the *Gebietsamt* was supposed to work through the unwieldy New Russian bureaucratic system, which was unlikely to produce justice of any kind, and certainly not quick justice. Cornies had personal and business contacts among the Nogais that might allow him to cut through the red tape and quickly recover the horses. If that failed he could drop the names of his personal friends in the world of Russian officialdom and hopefully intimidate the petty officials in the Nogai district into cooperating.

This worked. In September, Cornies recovered two stolen horses and turned the thieves over to Nogai authorities. The authorities entrusted the horses to Cornies in exchange for his promise that the *Gebietsamt* would follow up with a formal statement to the Nogai district administration describing the theft and identifying the owners of the horses. In the meantime Cornies held on to the horses, pasturing them on his own land.

This minor matter embroiled Cornies in a major controversy. In April 1826, Cornies's enemies spread rumours throughout the Mennonite settlement and the neighbouring German colonist and Slavic peasant communities that he was buying stolen horses from the Nogais. The story had been planted by a Nogai, but Cornies identified four Mennonites from the village of Blumenort as the people responsible for spreading it in the Mennonite settlement.[75] He demanded that the *Gebietsamt* investigate and punish the men for what he characterized as "criminal" behaviour. At the same time, he resigned from his position as land surveyor and renounced all further work for the *Gebietsamt*.

This seems like a dramatic overreaction to a minor provocation, and it can only be understood in the context of the religious controversies of the time. The split in the Mennonite church that had begun to develop in 1820 was reaching its apogee by 1826, with Warkentin's Large Flemish Congregation, unofficially formed in 1824, now petitioning the state for official status. The religious split had important political implications, for in the 1826 elections Warkentin gained control of the *Gebietsamt* when his brother-in-law Johann Klassen was elected mayor. Warkentin was already exerting significant influence over the *Gebiesamt*, and with the election of Klassen, he was now the most powerful person in the settlement. Cornies's reaction shows his understanding of the political implications: "Ice cold shivers travel down my back when I think about our general situation and weigh this against [Klassen's] character."[76]

In the eyes of the state, Mennonites had a single corporate identity defined by their Privilegium, and they were collectively responsible to the state. Mennonite privileges were justified by Mennonite obligations as model colonists, and this formula made no allowance for several separate versions of "the Mennonites." In practical terms, the state simply did not have the human resources to allow its administrative charges to fracture and multiply. The state wanted to deal with a single group that filled a single state-defined role in the imperial system and that was responsive to a single administrative chain of command.[77] The danger for the Mennonites of appearing divided was that their privileges were unequivocally linked to their united role as a model colony. Cornies had heard this for himself in St. Petersburg in 1824, and other leaders of the Molochnaia community understood that the appearance of disunity caused by the religious dispute might constitute a threat to their rights in Russia.[78]

The Mennonites' 1827 request for confirmation of their Privilegium was motivated mainly by their desire to have the new tsar affirm his predecessors' promises, but an additional factor was the Ministry of Internal Affairs' official recognition of the Large Flemish Congregation. The Mennonites thought it important to confirm that their privileges had not been abrogated by the congregational division. There was no way to prevent the Russian administration from learning about the community dispute because the creation of a new congregation required formal permission from the state. Jacob Warkentin, as leader of the new congregation, had to petition the ministry through its provincial offices in Odesa for an official authorization. This was not just a religious matter; in the Molochnaia settlement the political implications of the split magnified the underlying religious dispute.

As an important public figure closely aligned to the Frisian Pietist constituency, Cornies was deeply embroiled in the political and religious controversy. In a March 1826 letter to David Epp in Heubuden, Prussia, Cornies vented his frustrations: "Our community is trying to retain old practices and we are sinking ... Self-will and fanaticism will cause us to limit our rights here in Russia ... How can one remain indifferent when more than four thousand souls will suffer temporal and worldly disadvantage, because they are led by a few obstinate heads belonging to our spiritual and worldly leaders."[79]

The heated community dispute lends context to the intensity with which Cornies reacted to the false accusations of horse theft. Bad enough that his personal integrity was impugned, but because the accusations were of criminal conduct between Mennonites and non-Mennonites – groups that belonged to two distinct jurisdictions – the Mennonites could not address them as an internal community matter. Russian authorities would *have* to be involved, and this had larger implications for the position of Mennonites within the state.

Cornies responded with all of the political tools available to him. The most significant was his role as unofficial liaison between his settlement and the Guardianship Committee. As the crisis of 1824–5 had made clear, the community needed Cornies as its most direct and influential means of communicating with the committee. If Cornies resigned, this avenue would be closed. At the same time, the Mennonite *Gebietsamt* knew that if it permitted Cornies to resign, his Guardianship Committee patrons would not be pleased.

If anyone doubted where the Guardianship Committee's allegiances lay, Contenius clarified the issue by making two fourteen-day visits to the Molochnaia in the spring of 1826. While there, he stayed with Cornies in Ohrloff. Contenius's presence in Cornies's home, at precisely the time when Cornies had publicly and emphatically resigned from community duties, brought tremendous pressure to bear on the *Gebietsamt*, and it reacted decisively in clearing Cornies's name. It circulated a directive to all Molochnaia Mennonite villages that declared Cornies innocent and warned that "in future no one, under any pretext, shall be so bold as to utter this fabricated insult."[80] The *Gebietsamt* ordered the guilty parties to publicly recant, and this prevented the matter from proceeding to the secular courts and hopefully ended the public airing of Mennonite dirty laundry. The same directive emphasized that the leaders of all Molochnaia Mennonite congregations – including Jacob Warkentin – fully supported the *Gebietsamt*'s findings. Church elders were left to punish the guilty parties, presumably by imposing a congregational ban. In a letter to Cornies the *Gebietsamt* informed him of its actions and begged him to return to his community work.[81] So the *Gebietsamt* had vindicated Cornies; even so, the accusation of horse theft and Cornies's resignation from community duties left bitter feelings between him and community leaders – most prominently Warkentin – that did not quickly fade.

Journey to Saxony

The dispute between Cornies and the *Gebietsamt* was exacerbated when Contenius proposed that Cornies travel to Saxony on behalf of the settlement to buy merino sheep as breeding stock for Mennonite herds. As noted earlier, Cornies had refused to make such a trip for the Minister of Internal Affairs in January 1825 because of the agricultural crisis. Contenius had been promoting the introduction of high-quality merino sheep to New Russian colonists' herds since he first came to the Guardianship Committee in 1800, and since his retirement as chair of the Ekaterinoslav bureau of the committee in 1818 he had made improvements in sheep breeding the main focus of his Office of Special Projects. He saw Cornies as the best candidate to advance his projects, and in January 1826 he wrote to Cornies to reintroduce the idea of the Saxony trip.[82] Cornies again refused to take up the project, arguing that in the current Russian political climate it was important that the proposal be made by the *Gebietsamt*: "I consider it not to be good for our future if everything advantageous for us is urged forward only by the administration."[83]

Cornies was keenly aware of the relationship between Mennonite obligations and privileges, and he saw the Saxony expedition as an opportunity to demonstrate to the state that the Mennonites were fulfilling their role as model colonists. By 1826 he understood the machinery of colonial politics, and there was a degree of pragmatic cynicism in his manipulation of this matter. The expedition was Contenius's idea, but Cornies knew that Contenius would be willing to let the Mennonites take credit in the eyes of higher authorities. For all that Cornies was Contenius's protégé, he now felt confident enough in his own political judgment to refuse Contenius's advice and try to force the *Gebietsamt* to propose the expedition as its own initiative. Cornies was moving beyond his earlier role as an agent of his community and of the administration toward a more explicitly political position in which he actively manipulated competing forces to his own ends. It would soon become apparent, however, that no matter how well Cornies understood colonial politics, he still had considerable distance to cover in his understanding of Mennonite politics.

At a spring *Gebietsamt* meeting attended by Contenius, Cornies and Wilhelm Martens offered to lend the *Gebietsamt* 30,000 rubles to buy sheep in Saxony. Still stinging from the accusation of horse theft, Cornies refused to lead the expedition himself. In a letter to his Prussian brother-in-law Klaas Dyck he described the meeting, and complained: "Is it justice that one gives money and then is required to undertake the difficulties involved along with it?"[84] Cornies thought that the *Gebietsamt* could not refuse his offer, especially given Contenius's support, but he badly miscalculated. Warkentin had not won the allegiance of the majority of Molochnaia Mennonites solely by his opposition to Pietism; there was a broad, deep-rooted opposition among members of the Large Flemish Congregation to any outside interference in the settlement. Many Mennonites did not want to be told by the state how to run their agricultural affairs, and Cornies's efforts to portray the Saxony expedition as a Mennonite project could hardly deceive the Mennonites themselves. As Cornies described it, after Contenius left, some of "the current directors [tried] to arouse hatred toward me in the community, as though I wished to disrupt the peace in the community and destroy it."[85]

Cornies's description of the community's reaction against the project appears in a letter to Wilhelm Frank, a secretary in the Guardianship Committee bureau in Ekaterinoslav. In this period of political disputes in the Molochnaia, Cornies maintained a regular correspondence with Frank. The two men discussed religion and other personal concerns, and in addition, Cornies used Frank as a back channel into the committee through which to reinforce his own position and to learn about committee attitudes. By September 1826, when Cornies denounced the "current directors" to Frank, he was busily playing the committee and *Gebietsamt* against each other to secure his own position in relation to both.

Cornies's problem was that while the *Gebietsamt* had finally, reluctantly accepted the Saxony project, and along with it Cornies and Martens's 30,000-ruble loan, it had not accepted Cornies's refusal to lead the expedition. Instead, on 7 August the *Gebietsamt* notified Cornies that it had selected him to lead the expedition.[86] This decision, which the *Gebietsamt* relayed to the Guardianship Committee, showed that the *Gebietsamt* itself was not politically naive. As it well knew, Contenius had wanted Cornies to lead the expedition from the outset, and it was now going to be very difficult for Cornies to refuse. The proposal was also a good deal for the community: Cornies would front the money to buy the sheep and use his own time and resources to lead the expedition. While the community would eventually have to repay the loan, it expected to do so from future profits from the sheep it would acquire for the community breeding herd. Additionally, the proposal allowed the *Gebietsamt* to reclaim the political initiative by asserting its authority over Cornies.

Cornies was now at a political crossroads. His power within his community was based on his influence with the Guardianship Committee, while his power within the Guardianship Committee was based on his influence within his community. If he accepted Contenius's project on the *Gebietsamt*'s terms he would be bypassed by both. His pride, his personal ambition, and his ambitions for his community made that unacceptable. Realizing that appearances were important, Cornies scrambled for a way to respond to the *Gebietsamt*'s commission while convincing the Guardianship Committee that he retained his influence in the Molochnaia.

Cornies began by flatly rejecting the commission, telling the *Gebietsamt* that it had no right to assign him a task that he had already explicitly refused.[87] This took the *Gebietsamt* by surprise. It knew that news of this refusal would not be happily received in Ekaterinoslav. A personal delegation from the *Gebietsamt* visited Cornies and urged him to reconsider, but Cornies was adamant. On 3 September he wrote directly to Contenius, explaining that, while he was willing to do everything he could for the good of his community, he could not give in to the arbitrary decision of the *Gebietsamt* and still "uphold my position in the community in future."[88] The response to this letter is not extant, but Cornies's letter to Frank on 10 September included what was an obvious reaction to what must have been a very stormy letter from Contenius. It is clear that Contenius blamed the *Gebietsamt* for the problems, for Cornies wrote that he was "suffused with thankful feelings for the trust that" Contenius still placed in him.[89] Adopting the tone of a grateful supplicant, Cornies went on to write that it was "deeply painful for me that our benefactor and father [Contenius] is constantly burdened with sad news from us, when on the contrary we should concentrate on all the happy, sincere, positive actions his noble intellect plans for our benefit ... His faith is his guarantee that, before the seat of judgment, the fruits of his unselfish activity will gleam as genuine gold and will be seen as precious pearls. Our lack of recognition will, in contrast, be tossed aside as common dross and rotten fruit and our just reward and punishment earned as undeserving servants must be expected."[90]

Cornies laid the blame squarely at the *Gebietsamt*'s door. He wrote that it had "mounted a small attack on me ... Efforts here are to hang high anyone who speaks the truth to make him flee, but not everyone runs so easily. I am actually one of those who does not abandon something good just to maintain the peace. I consider that to be a sin."[91] Cornies spared no metaphors on the subject of sin, likening his efforts in the community to the building of Salem while accusing his opponents of building the Tower of Babel: "Granted the confusion is not that of many languages, but we cannot understand each other anymore even in one language ... I am not building with them and take no part in clearing stones. I do not depend on the multitude or on its majority, but on unity. Because I base myself on unity, I cannot sit quietly but must offer my few talents for the multitude, to profit the general well-being, even though ingratitude is my reward. Whatever is good, remains good and will bring its appropriate profit."[92]

Contenius may have blamed the *Gebietsamt*, but he did not let up his pressure on Cornies. In late September, again using Frank as his intermediary, Cornies took pains to assure Contenius of his desire to take the trip. However, he wrote, he could not "so easily" give in to the *Gebietsamt*.[93] The problem was that the community must take the initiative in order to show the state that it was willing to fulfil its role as a model colony. In this letter Cornies was reminding Contenius of the underlying political stakes. This was not just about buying sheep: regardless of the overwrought language of his letters, Cornies still had the final political prize in focus. The point was to prevent Warkentin and his supporters from blocking cooperation with the state's reform policies and thereby to preserve Mennonite privileges. Contenius had already gained the commitment of the *Gebietsamt* to retract its directive to Cornies and replace it with a polite request. Cornies assured Frank that should such a request come he would accept it, but he was sure that the *Gebietsamt* was intentionally dragging its feet in the hopes that the committee would grow frustrated and take the initiative, ordering Cornies to go. It was specifically this buck passing that Cornies wanted to avoid.

In October, Cornies travelled to Ekaterinoslav to make his case to Contenius and try to find an acceptable solution. After his return to the Molochnaia, at a meeting of 9 October, the *Gebietsamt* representatives appealed to Cornies to accept their directive. He again refused, saying that the offer had been made in such a grudging manner that it could not be accepted. The *Gebietsamt* wrote to Contenius that it had tried "repeatedly to persuade J. Cornies to undertake the proposed journey to Saxony for the general well-being of the community, [but] this was fruitless and J. Cornies totally renounced this business."[94] Contenius responded on 26 October with a strong official reprimand to the *Gebietsamt*: "Once the wrong way was chosen, contrary to my advice, and highly insulting slanders, disunity, hatred and envy were added, it does not seem at all strange that this matter has failed."[95] Unwilling to compromise with Cornies, the *Gebietsamt* told Contenius that it was now looking for someone else to lead the expedition, but Contenius told them that "this matter requires someone who is adroit, constantly active, indefatigable, with a penetrating glance. Should a man be found able to take the place of Cornies absolutely and perfectly in all respects, then I wish you good luck. If not, then I consider it better to postpone the undertaking … until more mature prudence is awakened."[96]

Although Contenius had taken Cornies's side, this was a Pyrrhic victory in Molochnaia politics. Cornies's actions had won him no friends, and in October elections Warkentin's brother-in-law Johann Klassen easily won the position of *Gebietsamt* mayor. Cornies's successful efforts to discredit the *Gebietsamt* with the Guardianship Committee had undercut his own influence in his community, and this endangered his value to the committee. Not only that, but by portraying the Molochnaia settlement as uncooperative with the committee, Cornies had potentially raised a challenge to Mennonite privileges, which is exactly what he wanted to avoid. With the "victory" won, it was time to find the least ignominious path of retreat.

Cornies's solution was to go to Saxony after all, but *not* as the settlement's appointed representative. In late December he informed Contenius that he would undertake the trip at his own expense, buy sheep for his own herds, and negotiate the sale of some of those sheep to his community after the fact.[97] The *Gebietsamt*, embarrassed by the entire episode, could hardly object, and in the end it bought sheep from Cornies on credit. Contenius, too, could not object, and when the *Gebietsamt* accepted Cornies's sheep it symbolically accepted his return to influence in community affairs, justifying Cornies's continued influence with the Guardianship Committee.

None of this was very satisfactory to Cornies. Politically he had made a mess. Rather than securing his position as middleman he barely avoided destroying it. In the midst of the dispute the October elections had given the Warkentin faction control of the *Gebietsamt*, a result that no doubt expressed the dissatisfaction of many Molochnaia Mennonites with Cornies. While the *Gebietsamt* still needed Cornies, his position in the community had been severely damaged. He had also undermined the Guardianship Committee's enthusiasm for the Mennonites by making it clear that they were deeply divided and could not be counted on to play their role as a model colony. As he departed for Saxony, Cornies had much to reflect upon. The trip would distance him from the day-to-day affairs of his community and give him a chance to regroup.

Sojourn in Saxony

Cornies left his home in Ohrloff on 15 February 1827. In Khortitsa he was joined by Jacob Penner, mayor of the Khortitsa Mennonite *Gebietsamt*, who was coming along to buy sheep for the Khortitsa Mennonite settlement. They arrived in Saxony on 16 April. They settled at a Dresden inn, and Penner and Cornies split up to inspect dozens of private herds around the region, ultimately buying 508 merino sheep. They headed home again, reaching the border between Prussian and Austrian Poland on 19 June, where Penner continued on to Khortitsa and Cornies travelled north to Heubuden and Danzig to visit friends. The sheep found their way to the Molochnaia at the start of September, and Cornies arrived home on 9 October.[98]

For Cornies and the rest of the travelling party, the journey provided an opportunity to see the West they had left behind more than two decades earlier. The journal kept for Cornies by his secretary reflects the wide-eyed enthusiasm of the rural tourists, who were awed by the beautiful architecture of the towns and noble estates and by the four-storey city buildings and grand castles they saw along the way.[99] In Lemberg (today Lviv), the secretary enthusiastically recorded how "we saw foreign animals such as ... two female lions, a leopard, various foreign snakes and similar things."[100] In Görlitz, Silesia, the party visited a re-creation of the Holy Land, and the journal breathlessly reports seeing "Christ's holy grave in a chapel on a hill outside the city, where the Lord Jesus is nailed to the cross. The pieces of silver for which Christ was sold lie on the table before the cross and Christ's prison is beside the cross."[101]

The West impressed Cornies but did not overawe him, for as he wrote to Frank, "one cannot clothe and feed oneself with sightseeing."[102] For all the sights, Cornies viewed Saxony and Prussia as places where there were few opportunities for people like him, self-made men who had risen to prosperity through hard work and talent. Russia was a land of opportunity, and Cornies told Frank that "it is this hope [of advancement] that fastens us to Russia's wise constitution and to our Christian duty."[103]

Perhaps the thing that impressed Cornies most in Saxony was the town of Herrnhut, the headquarters of the Moravian Brethren. Cornies travelled to Herrnhut at the invitation of Count Dohna, one of the Brethren's most important patrons.[104] Daniel Schlatter knew Dohna and had provided Cornies with an introduction, and Cornies consulted with Dohna about where to buy sheep in Saxony.[105] Yet for Cornies, Herrnhut had a significance that went far beyond business. He returned repeatedly to the village, which gave him "true pleasure and inner happiness."[106] When he wrote to Wilhelm Martens about the quiet, pious, industrious Moravian Brethren village, he implicitly contrasted it with the bitterly divided Molochnaia Mennonite settlement.[107]

Cornies's visits to Herrnhut allowed him the opportunity to continue his exploration of Pietism. The Moravians were aggressively evangelical, operating a missionary enterprise that reached into the Americas, Africa, and Eastern Europe. In contrast to Schlatter's eccentric religious beliefs, the Moravian Brethren had "warm" religion combined with strong community. Such a model balanced missionary zeal, modernization, and the community of faith. The Moravian belief in economic engagement with the world, which accepted that such engagement was a legitimate expression of evangelical mission, appealed strongly to Cornies.

The Saxony trip also permitted Cornies to visit Mennonite friends and relatives in the Vistula, and he took the opportunity to meet with David Epp, the minister of the Pietist Mennonite congregation in Heubuden, and Jacob van der Smissen, the Pietist Mennonite minister in Danzig. Years later he fondly recalled how the three had "climbed the Karlsberg in Oliva at daybreak to watch the sun rising majestically out of the Baltic Sea."[108] These meetings gave Cornies, who was already deeply engaged in his own exploration of religion, an opportunity to expand his understanding of contemporary Pietist religious thought, but they also had a practical side. Epp had been the leading Prussian organizer of the 1818–22 Mennonite immigration to the Molochnaia, so Cornies and he were old acquaintances. In 1825 Cornies, at the urging of the Guardianship Committee, had proposed to Epp that a new Mennonite settlement be established in Bessarabia, and Cornies undoubtedly used his visit to Heubuden to further these negotiations.[109] The Bessarabian plans would fizzle out, but Cornies and Epp would collaborate to organize further immigration to the Molochnaia in the 1830s.

Cornies arrived in Heubuden at a time when the Prussian Mennonite Church was deeply embroiled in controversy, and this too offered Cornies important lessons. The dispute revolved around a guest sermon preached in Epp's church, which Epp condemned for attributing "to man the good works he does with his own strength ... contrary to the gospel."[110] This had provoked a scandal in which Epp was forced to resign from the British and Foreign Bible Society and barely retained his position as minister.[111] Epp's position was worsened by his relationship to Theodor Horwitz, a Mennonite convert from Judaism and a friend of Daniel Schlatter, whom Cornies had personally recommended to Epp. Cornies corresponded with Horwitz in 1827, and he tried unsuccessfully to help Horwitz immigrate to the Molochnaia. In December 1828, Cornies told Schlatter that a letter from Horwitz to Epp had caused

Epp's community to turn against him.[112] Cornies came to this scandal as an outside observer, and it must have made him think hard about the disputes he had left behind in his own community. The Prussian state intruded far more into Mennonite affairs than the Russian state, and the danger of aggressive Prussian-style cameralism helped shape Cornies's new approach to community affairs after he returned home.

Illness and Reflection

Cornies returned to the Molochnaia full of new experiences, new religious ideas, and a new appreciation for the opportunities that Russia provided to him and his community. Arriving home at harvest time, he threw himself into the work the season demanded. Five weeks later he fell gravely ill and was confined to his home for four months. At the same time, Schlatter, only just returned from London, also fell severely ill, and he spent the following eight months convalescing at Cornies's home before returning to Switzerland for good in July 1828.

Cornies suffered from a recurring severe fever, dizziness, and weakness. Coming at the end of several years of turmoil and frantic activity, the illness prompted a series of letters almost unique within his surviving correspondence for their frankness and passion. Writing to friends and family in Prussia and Russia, he described his illness, but most importantly his faith, for he viewed his sickness as a religious calling: "I have often read that God's ways are marvellous but now, in part, I have experienced and understood them in practice ... I have learned to perceive that for the Christian simple recognition of the letter of God's word is not sufficient, but that one must experience it. The letter kills and the spirit alone gives life. I am happy to be alive and that God so obviously made me recognise many things that I did not know before."[113] This is Cornies's most explicit statement of his Pietist beliefs, his sense of a personal Christian calling that demanded his commitment.

Most important among the "many things" Cornies now recognized was that his Christian duty extended beyond his Mennonite community to the larger world: "Thank God that he has not limited our feelings of love to a tight circle but that they encompass the whole human race, that we may love everyone and be active on their behalf. The more we feel this impulse to love, the more we learn to comprehend that the whole world with all its millions of human inhabitants is bound together and the more we learn to comprehend this, the more energetically we become active and productive for everyone."[114] Cornies's 1828 letters often dwelt on the subject of love, and as he stressed, "to love meaningfully is to do so with deeds and not simply with words."[115] By spring 1828, recovered from his illness, Cornies had a sense of mission that he never abandoned. He never again questioned, as he had in 1826, whether or not to continue to serve his community. He was committed to the transformation of both the Mennonite settlement and the broader New Russian community that surrounded it. When he allied himself to the Guardianship Committee as the best available agent of change, he saw the alliance as God's will. Out of 1827 – both the trip west with its Herrnhut sojourn and the illness after his return home – emerged a growing sense of mission. Cornies became an activist, determinedly involved in community affairs, in the affairs of neighbouring peoples, and in the affairs of the Russian state. For him, progress was now essential to survival, and he would throw himself into transforming the Mennonite community and the world around it.

Conclusion

The period of 1824–8 was one of turmoil in the Molochnaia Mennonite settlement and in Cornies's personal life. The congregational dispute over Pietism and the role of the Russian state in Mennonite affairs had been amplified by the agricultural crisis of 1824–5, for on the one hand, it was no great stretch for Mennonites to interpret the crisis as God's punishment for their sins, including their dalliance with the secular world, and on the other, at the height of the crisis the *Gebietsamt* had no choice but to request outside aid from the Guardianship Committee.

The crisis had placed Cornies squarely in the Molochnaia community's spotlight. His wealth and generosity meant that community members turned to him for help, and he threw himself into relief efforts. At the same time, his relationship with Contenius and Fadeev made him the settlement's liaison to the Guardianship Committee, and he represented the Mennonites in their appeals for aid.

The crisis heightened religious tensions within the Molochnaia settlement and made Cornies a central figure in those tensions. Religious conservatives correctly viewed him as a Pietist and as a proponent of greater engagement with the larger world. When he withdrew from his community duties in response to accusations that he was a horse thief, he forced the *Gebietsamt* to take a public position on his status in the settlement by begging him to return. By directly engaging Contenius in the community's internal dispute, Cornies made himself the undisputed representative of state authority in the settlement.

The outcome of this clash was anything but a clear victory for Cornies, for he overestimated the influence of the Guardianship Committee and underestimated the willingness of the *Gebietsamt* to defy the committee. The settlement's refusal to follow Contenius's vigorous recommendations and send Cornies to Saxony to buy sheep was a major political blow to Cornies, and it damaged the settlement's reputation with both the committee and the state.

The politics of this crisis were inevitably coloured by religion, and for Cornies the mid-1820s were a period of intense religious reflection. Schlatter had exposed him to a personal, activist version of Christianity, influenced by romantic notions of individualism and heroism, that demanded that the true believer take action to change the world. This world view could not have reached Cornies at a better time. His prominence and success built in him a sense of mission, encouraging him to reach for greater influence in the Molochnaia. His intractable position toward the *Gebietsamt* in 1826 was influenced by this emerging religious philosophy.

Cornies's study of the Nogais reflects how his evolving religious beliefs intersected with his evolving attitude toward the practical demands of colonial administration. His understanding of the state's paternalistic mission to "civilize" the Nogais incorporates significant elements of his Pietist world view, including all of its racist and Islamophobic assumptions. That the state commissioned this report from Cornies is an indication that its attitude toward colonial subjects was changing – it was no longer so willing to accept diverse policies for diverse peoples. It is also evidence that the influence of Pietism in Russia had not ended with Tsar Alexander I's death in 1825. The coding of Pietism into Cornies's influential study of the Nogais, published in Moscow in 1836, is a reminder that many of its underlying assumptions did not simply fade away.

Cornies's trip to Saxony had given him time to reflect. The final stage in his religious journey in the 1820s came after his return home, during his illness, which lent urgency to his sense of mission, and the letters he wrote during his convalescence reflect a profound belief in his own Christian calling. His philosophical explorations were over. He was ready to move forward as a mature proponent of Mennonites as a progressive model community in service to the Russian state.

Chapter Five

Imposing Order, 1828–1834

Between 1828 and 1830 the Molochnaia Mennonite settlement experienced a welcome period of calm, prompting Johann Cornies to write to Daniel Schlatter that "everything is quiet in our community. The old prejudices seem to have retreated."[1] The congregational disputes brought on by the 1818 immigration had worked themselves out, and the state formally recognized Warkentin's Large Flemish Congregation in 1828. Although religious frictions still simmered beneath the surface, the Molochnaia Mennonites had accepted the new congregational realities. It helped that the community had recovered from the damage caused by the winter of 1825–6; record harvests in 1828 and 1829 reinvigorated the economy and kept everyone too busy to bicker. It must have helped, too, that Cornies, a lightning rod for community turmoil, spent much of 1827 in Saxony and the first half of 1828 in his sickbed. There was little opportunity for him to make trouble.

Cornies welcomed the calm and worked to maintain it, even though in that same 1830 letter he told Schlatter that trouble "may be waiting to appear anew."[2] By then Cornies was fully recovered from his illness and busily bringing order to his many business affairs. He was also getting ready to put his oar back into community waters by means of an important new administrative initiative, the Forestry Society. This society's goals were limited, its membership small, and its authority narrowly defined, and Cornies may have seen its creation as a way to avoid the controversy that had marked his earlier forays into public life.

The Forestry Society reflected significant changes in the state's approach to colonial administration. Under Tsar Alexander the Mennonites had been permitted to live relatively free of direct state interference, but Tsar Nicholas made far greater demands on his colonial subjects. He was about to activate the Mennonite laboratory of modernization, and to recruit Cornies as its chief laboratory technician.

Regime Change

In the second half of the 1820s circumstances in the Russian government were changing. When Tsar Alexander died suddenly in 1825 he left the question of succession in flux. His heir should have been his brother Konstantin, but in 1823 Alexander forced Konstantin to renounce his claim to the throne after he married a Polish woman of non-royal blood. The line of succession now fell to Alexander's younger brother Nicholas. Inexplicably, Alexander kept this change secret, and when he died most Russians assumed that Konstantin would become tsar. Konstantin, the unofficial governor of Congress Poland, was associated with the constitutional reforms that Alexander had implemented there, and many Russians hoped he would bring similar reforms to Russia. By comparison, Nicholas was widely disliked. He had no administrative training or aptitude and was regarded as a reactionary conservative martinet.[3]

The attempted revolution by a group of military officers that greeted Nicholas's ascension to the throne amplified the new tsar's conservative inclinations. The Decembrist Revolt was badly led and never seriously threatened Nicholas's rule, but it did confirm in him a lifelong hatred for liberalism and constitutions. Nicholas harshly suppressed the movement's leaders and shocked the Russian nobility by executing five young noble ringleaders. He dispatched another 124 noblemen to long exiles in Siberia, where many mouldered for his entire twenty-nine-year reign. The investigation lasted months and produced lengthy testimony from many participants. Over and over again they confirmed that they had been inspired by Western liberal ideals. They dreamed of constitutions, rights, and freedoms.[4]

Nicholas, both by personal inclination and in reaction to the Decembrists, devoted the early years of his reign to isolating Russia from the corrosive effects of Western liberalism and asserting tight control over his own empire.[5] This was a sharp reversal of Alexander's rule, for Alexander had always paid more attention to international than domestic affairs; he had dreamed big dreams for internal reform, although he had accomplished little for his own subjects. Nicholas, for all that his tenure is correctly identified with harsh autocratic repression, would do better in many ways.

What Nicholas feared most was the liberal inclinations of his own nobility, and consequently it was the elites who felt his restrictive policies most keenly. He restricted travel to the West, prohibited Russians from attending Western universities, and pruned Russian universities of "dangerous" subjects such as philosophy and politics. He created the Third Department of the Tsar's Own Chancery, his infamous secret police, and set it loose to keep a close eye on Russia's elites.

Mennonites reacted to Alexander's death with real sorrow. He had visited the Molochnaia settlement only weeks before he died, and Cornies, who had welcomed the tsar for tea in his own home, knew that Alexander had been a true friend to the Mennonites. As for the new tsar, the Mennonites were prepared to support him without question. Cornies described the Mennonites' understanding of the divine right of kings clearly in February 1826: "We praise God, our keeper and ruler. His exalted will is always most excellent for us and His decisions marvellous, even though we may find His ways incomprehensible. Yet His will is holy. May He grant that we also sanctify it. Praise be to God that Russia's throne is again occupied by a father. As good and loyal subjects, our wishes and prayers should try to support him."[6] The Mennonites had been shocked by the Decembrist Revolt and eagerly pursued news of the investigation. Cornies asked Blüher to send him a copy of the investigating committee's report on "the conspiracy against the life of the blessed monarch."[7]

The new tsar and his policies had little immediate impact on the Molochnaia Mennonites. Nicholas's hostility to Western ideas did not extend to the Mennonites or other foreign colonists in New Russia, who were, after all, peasant agriculturists and not elite intellectuals. The regional administration went largely untouched, for while Nicholas could pick and choose among his favourites to fill top spots in St. Petersburg, the paucity of competent bureaucrats on the frontier meant he could not afford to purge the existing ranks there. When Cornies returned from Saxony in 1827 there were few obvious indications that anything new was afoot.

At first the changes were subtle, only revealing themselves in the records assembled in the Ministry of Internal Affairs' offices in St. Petersburg. Before 1825 the ministry gathered records in a chaotic, inconsistent way. Sometimes it compiled astonishingly detailed accounts of village-by-village market prices or suicides, drownings, murders, and illegitimate births, but just as often entire broad regions of the empire went almost unaccounted for. By 1827 this recordkeeping had been transformed; there were now carefully compiled aggregate statistics for every region of the empire.[8] At the regional level, in the Ekaterinoslav bureau of the Guardianship Committee, Mennonites and other ethnocultural minorities remained sharply distinct after 1825, and their lives were often recorded in great detail. At the centre, however, the concern to document and control the *whole* population led to large aggregated statistical reports in which differences between groups were obscured. At the same time, the state implemented increasingly intrusive policies toward various religious sects and Jews.[9] It is not quite that the Mennonites lost their identity from the centre's point of view – they remained a recognized and important model community – but they were also now identified as part of a larger whole, with responsibilities to the whole.

This transition should not be overstated. In the post-Napoleonic period Tsar Alexander also had concerned himself with how to better administer his entire multi-ethnic empire. Indications that the administration expected more from the Mennonites had surfaced by 1818, when the second wave of Molochnaia immigration began. But Alexander's plans were haphazard, his focus distracted either inwardly on his personal religious life or outwardly on foreign affairs. Nicholas was subject to no such distractions; while the new focus would take a few years to settle closely upon the Mennonites, as of 1826 they were already in his peripheral vision.

In tandem with Nicholas's desire to better document and thereby control his subjects, a second policy had great significance for the Mennonites: the ideology of Official Nationality.[10] This ideology was an explicit reaction against the romantic nationalism of Western Europe, and particularly against the idea of national self-determination. Nicholas saw the revolutions in Italy, Spain, Greece, and Poland as the products of elite meddling and popular national aspirations. The danger to multi-ethnic Russia was plain, and Nicholas needed to snuff out any incipient national aspirations on his own turf. Official Nationality was defined by "orthodoxy, autocracy, and nationality." This concept was explicitly articulated in 1833, when Count Sergei Uvarov, Nicholas's Minister of Education, formally propounded it. However, it had been around in conservative circles since at least 1823, when the archconservative M.L. Magnitskii, a member of the Central School Administration and the overseer of the infamous purge of secular faculty at Kazan University (and, incidentally, a prominent member of the Russian Bible Society), wrote that "the national idea in our people's education consists of just two words: orthodoxy and autocracy."[11] The idea, implicit in Magnitskii's words and explicit in Uvarov's, was that the primary qualifications for full citizenship in Russia should be Orthodox faith and unquestioning allegiance to the tsar.

The danger that Official Nationality posed for Mennonites was not immediate. What Nicholas really feared was the disloyalty of his elites, and when he championed Orthodoxy it was mainly as an antidote to Catholicism, which enjoyed a certain vogue among the Russian nobility.[12] In the long term, though, an ideology that privileged Orthodoxy had to be dangerous for Mennonites, and anyone who was paying close attention had to recognize this.

Official Nationality was at its core contradictory to the administrative tendencies of Nicholas's reign, for the main thrust of his administrative policies seemed to be to aggregate and integrate his subjects and to cultivate their practical contributions to the empire.[13] Ideologically, Official Nationality tended to disaggregate, and to privilege Orthodox faith as the most trustworthy sign of loyalty to the Orthodox autocrat. Mennonites could not be Orthodox; if they were to defend their privileged status in the empire, they would need to emphasize their practical contributions.

When Johann Cornies returned home from Saxony in 1828, the new direction of Nicholas's regime was barely starting to show itself on the frontier. Still, it was already clear at every level of the empire that loyalty to the tsar would be vitally important. The investigation and punishment of the Decembrists had driven this message home with a vengeance, and Mennonites undoubtedly grasped as much. It would, however, be an error to suppose that the changes in Cornies's approach to public life were a direct response to the attitude and policies of the new tsar. Rather, they were a result of his own experiences and his reflections on the larger world, both East and West. To a degree, his goals and methods dovetailed with those of Nicholas. This coincidence of interests helps account for Cornies's rising power and prominence under the new tsar; even so, Cornies should not be viewed as a pragmatic opportunist who climbed onto Nicholas's bandwagon and betrayed the values of his community. Rather, he recognized and seized upon the opportunities that Nicholas's new policies offered, and he carefully negotiated the dangers that came along with them. The policies suited Cornies, whose talents and skills, shaped by his life and experiences in Tsar Alexander's "land of opportunity," found a perfect circumstance for achieving his ambitions in Nicholas's Russia.

As he returned to full health in 1828, Cornies found that the disputes that had divided his community before his departure had eased in his absence. This was good news, for the journey to Saxony had shown him the dangers of internal turmoil for the Russian Mennonites. The Prussian Mennonite Church had been embroiled in its own controversy during Cornies's visit, and that, coupled with the increasingly evident integration of Vistula Mennonites into the mainstream secular life of Prussia, gave Cornies much to think about. David Epp was a central figure in the Prussian controversy, and Cornies's correspondence with him after the Saxony trip reflects the serious concerns that had emerged in his mind. Since 1826, Cornies and Epp had been discussing the possibility of establishing a Mennonite settlement in Bessarabia; in 1828, Cornies told Epp that the outbreak of war between Russia and the Ottoman Empire made that project impossible.[14] Cornies added that he had leased land in the Mariupol region where a settlement might be created, but for the time being he was not willing to pursue the matter: "I am afraid of becoming involved with the dear Prussian Mennonites, because they are governed by indifference and nothing thorough can be attained by working with them. They are little concerned about their following generations and then, because of oppression and poverty, progress will no longer be possible even with the best will and lands will not be reserved for them forever. Generally, community spirit and sense of duty are missing."[15]

In February 1829, Cornies sent a long letter to Epp full of support and advice about dealing with the troubles facing the Prussian Mennonites. Epp, who was twenty years older than Cornies and had been an elder since 1817, must have been astonished at the tone of Cornies's letter, for it finds Cornies adopting the manner of an elder counselling his parishioner; he assured Epp that "it is the right of the Christian to do good and suffer evil, and with this, to experience such injustice, for if we experienced only justice, we would have plunged, long ago, into hell with body and soul."[16] Cornies wrote, too, that he was not surprised at the turmoil that had emerged among the Prussian Mennonites: "I knew that dissension had to arise among you when I visited there ... because, according to 1. Corinthians 11, 18, 19, Paul was also not surprised, but rather recognized it as a necessary requirement."[17]

Cornies's concern over the disunity in the Prussian Mennonite community reflected a new attitude. He remained a Pietist, but he had learned a lesson from both his Molochnaia entanglements in 1826 and the Prussian situation. If he wanted to be an agent of change, he would have to find ways to work within his community and build alliances with like-minded community leaders. By 1828 there seemed to be an opportunity to do just that, for the turmoil that had marked the settlement over the previous decade was abating.

The state's formal approval of the Large Flemish Congregation in 1828 was an important factor in the easing of community tensions. The two thirds of the Molochnaia population who comprised the congregation were now secure in their rights to places of worship, and Jacob Warkentin was confirmed in his position. As described in chapter 4, the dispute had involved the state in the internal religious affairs of the community. Its resolution lifted that scrutiny.[18]

In 1828, Cornies's first priority was to put his own affairs in order. His community obligations since 1817, his two long trips on community business, and his illness had all distracted him from his business interests. This did not prevent him from growing ever wealthier – by 1828 he was a rich man – but his business activities before 1828 are hard to trace accurately because of his chaotic bookkeeping. He rented land, kept large herds of sheep, sold wool, lent money, and partnered with Martens to run the regional brandy monopoly, but he did not carefully document any of this, and distinctions between community and personal affairs are almost impossible to discern. After Cornies recovered from his illness, his bookkeeping (mirroring the Russian state's) began taking the form of organized columns and rows, debits and credits, profits and losses. Also, he began paying closer attention to the details of his affairs; he apparently realized that to achieve his larger goals for his community, he would need to be far more focused and organized in all things.

The brandy distribution monopoly is the clearest example of this reorganization. It had been an important part of Cornies's business affairs since at least 1816. He and Wilhelm Martens leased the monopoly for successive four-year terms, paying the *Gebietsamt* a flat fee in exchange for control of all wholesale trade in distilled beverages in the district.[19]

Signs that the partners intended to pay more careful attention to the brandy business came in January 1829, when Cornies produced his first detailed report of income and expenses.[20] Around the same time, Cornies and Martens approached the Guardianship Committee with the complaint that smugglers were encroaching on their lease and affecting their profits. Their petition identified three offenders and asked that the committee take "stringent measures" to protect the monopoly.[21] In a second petition the partners complained that "for many years, publicans" in the Mennonite villages had failed to pay for the brandy they received and sold. This petition included a list of twenty-four of the "most negligent" debtors, who owed amounts ranging from 23 to 957 rubles, and asked the state to intervene and enforce payment. Clearly, the monopoly had been managed haphazardly, for the debts stretched back over almost a decade. The Guardianship Committee responded by ordering the arrest of the Mennonite smugglers and turning them over to the police.[22] This had the desired effect – the smugglers apologized, the debtors paid up, and Cornies and Martens agreed not to insist on prison sentences.[23]

None of this endeared Cornies and Martens to the *Gebietsamt*, and when the lease again came up for auction in December 1830, it tried to shut the two out of the bidding, hoping to retain the lease and profits for itself. It had no legal grounds to do so but tried to manipulate the bidding process by giving only one day's notice of the auction date and notifying village mayors only verbally. Martens got word of the ploy at the last minute, and at his urging Cornies sent Johann Neufeld, the manager of their brandy distribution business, to submit a bid. The *Gebietsamt* mayor refused to accept it, insisting that it had to be submitted by Cornies or Martens in person. This prompted an infuriated Cornies to write to Fadeev denouncing the "devious" officials in the *Gebietsamt*. He insisted that his denunciation was "not compelled by self-interest nor by envy, discord, or support for a faction," and he renounced any further interest in the lease. His letter, he said, was merely to inform Fadeev of the *Gebietsamt*'s "intrigues and actions counter to government directives," and he asked that Fadeev keep these remarks to himself.[24] In the end, Cornies and Martens retained the monopoly, but the ill will these events engendered festered.

The hostility between Cornies and the *Gebietsamt* was a continuation of the tensions that had first surfaced in 1826. Two thirds of the settlement's fullholders were members of Warkentin's Large Flemish Congregation, and because only fullholders voted in elections, Warkentin controlled the *Gebietsamt*. His brother-in-law, Johann Klassen, was mayor from 1826 to 1832, when he was succeeded by another Large Flemish Congregation member, Johann Regier. While there is no evidence that Warkentin intervened directly in the dispute over the brandy monopoly, that dispute inevitably contributed to the hostility between him and Cornies.

Moneylending, a second important element of Cornies's business affairs, became increasingly important to him in this period. Cornies had been lending money at interest since at least 1817, but as with his other business affairs, he paid more attention to it after 1828. This had particularly important implications for Mennonite economic development.[25] Credit plays a significant role in economic modernization. In Russia, modern banking institutions developed late, and the most important sources of credit, the Moscow and St. Petersburg Orphanages, lent only to the nobility.[26] Most accounts of Russian economic development claim that the Russian state kept an iron grip on banking, which created a significant impediment to modernization. However, as historian Sergei Antonov has shown, by the 1850s private lending was widespread, suggesting that the lack of credit was not as significant an obstacle as has long been supposed.[27] Cornies provides an example of large-scale private lending that in part supports Antonov's claims. However, Cornies's lending practices emphasized community interests, an important difference from the examples depicted by Antonov, and those practices offered unique advantages to his Mennonite community.

Mennonite economic successes in Russia have been attributed to a variety of factors, ranging from a religious and cultural predisposition to work hard, to the argument that state subsidies, tax privileges, and large land grants gave the Mennonites an unfair advantage over other Russian subjects.[28] The role of credit in their development should be added to this list.

Beginning in the 1820s, Cornies acted as his community's main moneylender, lending large sums to support commerce and industry and issuing small loans to help Mennonite families through hard times. Such unofficial lending practices were key to the rapid economic growth that sharply distinguished Mennonites from other Russian agricultural communities in the early nineteenth century. They also served as a vital precondition for their rise to industrial prominence in the second half of the century.

Moneylending was not new to Mennonites when Cornies began his private lending activities. In agricultural communities in Russia and the rest of Europe, the granting of small loans by relatives or neighbours was commonplace. According to Cornies's biographer David Epp, Cornies got his start in business with loans from an elderly Mennonite widow.[29] The Khortitsa preacher Jacob Epp recounts in his diary the role that small private loans played in permitting his relatively poor household to stay afloat in the mid-nineteenth century.[30] The tsarist Mennonites even had an institutionalized money-lending agency, the Orphan's Fund (*Waisenamt*), which held the estates of orphans in trust and used the money to make loans to community members. These loans were important to the community, but they were small, seldom exceeding 100 rubles. Because borrowers had to provide two guarantors from within the community, the loans were subject to constraints that prevented them from playing the developmental role of commercial credit. What distinguished Cornies's activities from this small lending was the size of his loans and his deliberate use of loans to promote Mennonite economic development.

Most of Cornies's lending was in support of the Molochnaia wool and grain trade, and those were the loans that had the greatest impact on Mennonite economic development. While he had begun lending money by 1817, his volume of lending expanded significantly after his 1824 trip to Moscow, where he had struck a business relationship with Blüher. As described in chapter 4, Blüher provided Cornies with the means to market wool in Moscow. This made sense for the wealthy Cornies; however, most Molochnaia Mennonites could not afford to send their wool to Moscow on speculation. Instead, needing ready cash to buy necessities, they sold at local fairs or to the travelling agents of foreign companies. Their wool trade was necessarily on a small scale, in part because there was no organized credit system but also because there was often an acute shortage of circulating currency in New Russia.[31] These problems meant that regional traders could not deal in large volumes.

Cornies, as chair of the Wool Improvement Society, was responsible for developing commercial wool production in the region. In 1824 he began offering loans to Mennonite wool merchants that enabled them to buy Molochnaia wool for resale by Blüher in Moscow. The first significant recipient was Gerhard Enns, a former chair of the *Gebietsamt* and the second-largest contributor to the Christian School Society after Cornies. He was one of Cornies's most important allies.[32] In 1825 alone, Enns used loans from Cornies to purchase 32,000 kilograms of Mennonite wool at a cost of more than 40,000 rubles.[33] By the early 1830s the demand for short-term loans by Enns and other Mennonite wool merchants during the June shearing season was so great that Cornies was sometimes left short of cash himself. In 1831 he apologetically refused to lend money to Fadeev because he had "loaned all my money not in use at the moment to the local wool merchants on monthly terms."[34] These loans met a critical economic need, for they provided both credit and currency, thus removing two of the chief disincentives to large-scale wool production. With the help of such loans, between 1825 and 1835 Mennonite sheep herds grew by 300 per cent, becoming the most important commercial activity in the Molochnaia.[35]

Cornies played an equally important role in financing commercial grain production in the Molochnaia in the 1830s. Grain became an important commercial crop in the region after the port of Berdiansk opened in 1836, providing easier access to markets.[36] As with wool, grain prices were volatile, and in order to convince Mennonites to shift their efforts from wool to grain, there had to be a secure local market.

Cornies financed the transition to grain production with large-scale loans to Mennonite grain merchants, the most prominent of whom were Abram Wieb and Peter Schmidt. With Cornies's help, Wieb emerged as the leading Molochnaia Mennonite grain merchant. Between 1840 and 1844 he borrowed tens of thousands of rubles for the purpose of establishing a permanent warehouse in Berdiansk and buying up and exporting Mennonite grain.[37] Like Enns, Wieb was among Cornies's inner circle of allies. His energy and Cornies's money helped underwrite the Mennonite shift from a wool to a grain economy that occurred in the 1840s, at a time when international wool markets were contracting and grain markets were expanding.[38]

Cornies's other important target for commercial loans was the Halbstadt cloth factory owned by Johann Klassen. Opened in 1815, the factory was the first significant industrial enterprise in the Molochnaia.

Klassen invested 20,000 rubles of his own money to establish the factory, but he never realized a profit. Cornies lent money to Klassen regularly beginning in 1817, and by 1827 he owed Cornies 33,758 rubles.[39] A drought in 1833–4 further damaged the factory's finances, and in 1836 Klassen asked the *Gebietsamt* to intervene and negotiate with his creditors for a five-year release from all debt repayments.[40] By then Klassen owed more than 72,000 rubles, the largest part to Cornies.[41]

Cornies consistently supported the Klassen factory with loans; he also used his Moscow contacts to keep track of markets and buy equipment for the factory. He became the factory's principal supporter in 1839 when the original factory burned down and had to be rebuilt (it reopened in 1842). Recognizing the important economic role of the factory, not just for making cloth but also for providing direct employment to landless Mennonites, Cornies arranged for the Agricultural Society to establish a commission to manage the factory's debts and oversee its rebuilding.[42] Cornies also continued to lend thousands of rubles to Klassen, even though there was little hope of such debts being repaid.

While large commercial loans were the greatest part of Cornies's lending business, he also provided small loans to a broad spectrum of Mennonites. These loans, usually of less than 1,000 rubles, are documented mainly in the dunning letters Cornies sent to defaulters and in the claims he made against the estates of deceased debtors.

A rare example where the original loan request survives indicates the nature of this small-loan business. In 1839, Mrs. Voth from Alexanderwohl wrote to Cornies asking urgently for a loan of 600 rubles. Her husband David, a wood merchant, was away from home buying wood, and in his absence she was unable to pay other suppliers for wood they were delivering.[43] This loan would not soon be repaid. In October 1840, Voth sent Cornies 46 rubles to cover the interest and pleaded for a further extension, and in December 1840 he wrote to say that he could "absolutely not scare up any money."[44] In May 1841, Cornies became insistent, writing to Voth, "Now, my dear friend, the time really has come for me to collect the debt you owe me ... You must devise the means. There's no other way."[45] This had no effect, and the loan remained unpaid as of December 1843, when Voth asked for a further extension. There is no record to show whether Cornies ever recovered his money.[46]

Loans of this type were a routine part of Cornies's business affairs from the early 1820s onward. The amounts were sometimes small – for example, he lent Heinrich Quiring 69 rubles in 1840. While Cornies normally charged the legal limit of 6 per cent annual interest, the Quiring loan demonstrates that he also routinely waived the interest when creditors struggled to repay him.[47] Collection of these debts was a constant source of irritation for Cornies, whose last recourse was to ask the *Gebietsamt* to intervene and exert community pressure on the debtors.[48] He nevertheless continued to make small loans, providing an essential service to the growing Molochnaia Mennonite economy.

It is not always clear what motivated Cornies to make loans. Certainly personal profit was a factor, but profit alone cannot explain the interest-free small loans he made to struggling families. Even his large commercial loans were made at a low interest rate (usually 6 per cent per annum), and those loans were far from secure in the conditions of high inflation that prevailed in Russia at the time; private lenders in Moscow and St. Petersburg often charged 6 per cent per *month* or more, and in 1879 the state deregulated interest rates in recognition that the 6 per cent limit was so low that it was an obstacle to economic development.[49] Cornies's loans to the Klassen cloth factory, which were always interest-free, continued long after there was any hope of repayment.

Cornies's correspondence provides important insights into his understanding of the role of wealth in Mennonite society. While he was not a typical Mennonite and there was no shortage of accusations and denunciations against him from his enemies, those attacks never mentioned his lending practices or criticized him for usury. The most critical account of Molochnaia Mennonite society in the 1830s, Heinrich Balzer's "Faith and Reason," does not list moneylending among the ills of Molochnaia society. It seems then that Cornies's role as moneylender and the general practice of lending at interest were accepted in the Mennonite community. Cornies's reflections on wealth and responsibility can thus be seen as important evidence of broader community attitudes.

Cornies was first forced to think seriously about the relationship between wealth and community responsibilities during the crisis of 1824–5. As recounted in chapter 4, he responded to the crisis by setting aside his personal business affairs and the demands of the Guardianship Committee and dedicating all his time and energy to his community. He assisted his neighbours as a private member of the community, using his personal wealth.

Cornies justified ignoring his responsibilities to the Guardianship Committee in a letter to Fadeev:

> Because, as a member of the community, I possess its confidence, I consider it to be my inescapable duty to employ it according to my best insights for the well-being of every single individual and for the whole community. This is even more so because the Lord, through His gentle hand, has blessed me with temporal riches to the extent that I have been freed of burdensome worries about survival and it is even more pertinent

for me than for many another upright men that I am obliged to carry out all responsibilities that can serve the purpose of the general well-being.[50]

Cornies described the drought to Blüher as "God's judgment," but this did not mean that its consequences should be accepted passively. It was a test, intended to benefit people by teaching them to seek solutions in "the Word of God, which is written down for us in the Bible."[51] As Cornies understood it, God had blessed him with wealth and ability, and with these blessings came obligations to his community. In December 1825, with the crisis finally over, he articulated this conclusion to his wealthy friend Diedrich Warkentin when he proposed that the two should create an emergency assistance fund for the Molochnaia settlement: "To the extent that we seek the general well-being and not our own self-interest, we do not have the right to bury our own capital. We must increase its value to the appropriate extent, so that on the great judgment day our capital will also be considered among the ordained."[52]

Cornies's belief in the responsibilities inherent in wealth clearly extended to lending money, for as he wrote in 1837, a loan "is a form of charity."[53] This statement was in a letter to the prominent educator Adrian Hausknecht, a longtime friend, and it came in the form of a stern admonishment. Hausknecht had borrowed 800 rubles from Cornies between 1828 and 1832 and had not repaid so much as a kopeck.[54] Cornies had never pursued his friend for the money, but when Hausknecht asked for a new loan, Cornies refused, saying bluntly that "whoever borrows with the assumption that the creditor can look after himself better and does not need what is borrowed as urgently as the debtor does, is in my opinion already not acting as a Christian and does not presume any Christian charity."[55]

Cornies lent money within his community for profit and as a way to subsidize the Molochnaia Mennonite economy. In both cases this amounted to a progressive economic policy that helped place Mennonites well in front of most Russian subjects on the road to modernization. But Cornies did not shy away from using his money for more old-fashioned purposes, lending or giving it to buy influence from important political figures in the Russian administrative system.

Cornies made loans to a number of influential officials in New Russia, ranging from Tavrida Civil Governor M.M. Muromtsev to Ekaterinoslav Police Chief Mikhail Lizovzov, but the clearest example of his use of credit to cement political patronage was his loans to Fadeev.[56] The relationship between Fadeev and Cornies was described earlier: Fadeev was Cornies's most important and well-connected patron, while Cornies was Fadeev's most important Mennonite client. As with most patronage networks the wheels sometimes needed to be greased. One of the best examples of this came in 1834, when the guardianship bureau was relocated from Ekaterinoslav to Odesa. When Fadeev wrote to Cornies to bemoan the high costs of setting up residence in the New Russian capital, Cornies wrote back to commiserate, and he and Martens sent along a gift of 1,300 rubles "as a small token of our affection."[57] A loan and other gifts to Fadeev would follow, and while Cornies may have seen them as a gesture of friendship, he did not make such gifts to his Mennonite friends.

Loans and gifts like those that Cornies made to Fadeev played a vital role in the Russian administrative world in the nineteenth century, and if Mennonites were to negotiate that world in a manner that preserved and promoted their own interests, it was important that they learn to properly engage in this system of influence-peddling.[58] This process was not new to Mennonites; they had experienced similar things in Poland. In New Russia, Mennonites needed to feel out the pressure points that would permit them to negotiate their rights in Russia, and Cornies was a central figure in this process.

Cornies's moneylending underscores the unique intermediary position he had come to occupy in his community. The Mennonites remained a rural community, and their attitude toward the urban world of commerce and industry was one of deep suspicion. Agriculture remained for them the most genuinely Christian way of life; cities, with their secular ways, threatened only "desolation," to use the famous description of Heinrich Balzer.[59]

Balzer provides a useful comparative perspective on Cornies's moneylending activities, for he is usually seen as the conservative antithesis of the progressive Cornies. There is good reason for this characterization: Balzer's "Faith and Reason" directly challenged many of the reforms that Cornies championed and funded. According to Balzer it was clear where his Molochnaia community was headed: "First, great wealth, then a disposition unto worldly knowledge. And then a focus and refinement of the senses for comedy and theatre (drama) in novels and ostentatious displays. Then follow atrophied (legalistic) morals and practices without Jesus. And then big business and civil service (the magistracy) and finally the military and service in war."[60]

While Balzer was condemning Mennonites for developing a taste for "comedy and theatre (drama) in novels," Cornies was writing to booksellers in Prussia and Switzerland to order copies of popular current works like *Genovefa* and *Rosa von Tannenberg*.[61] As Balzer decried Mennonite "ostentation," Cornies told his son that the best way to treat a recurring fever was to "wash your body now and then with

French brandy."[62] Balzer criticized Mennonites for resorting to the civil courts; Cornies turned to the Guardianship Committee to help collect debts owed to the brandy monopoly. Balzer described newspapers as snares that entrapped Mennonites in worldly matters; Cornies eagerly awaited the newspapers in Moscow, Odesa, and Prussia, to which he subscribed. Balzer criticized worldly education; in 1832, Cornies sent his son Johann Jr. away to Ekaterinoslav to pursue advanced, explicitly secular studies. In 1834 he sent Johann Jr. on to Moscow to continue his education.

Balzer wrote "Faith and Reason" in 1833, shortly after a cholera epidemic and in a time of drought and famine, and Cornies shared Balzer's interpretation of these crises as lessons from God about Mennonite life in Russia. Cornies also shared in some measure Balzer's disapproval of people who, as Cornies critically observed, "indulge in frivolity, even during this depressed, discouraging time."[63] Where the two parted ways was over the relationship between faith and reason. Balzer distinguished between "understanding" or faith, which he called "reason of the heart," and "natural reason," by which he meant secular rationalism.[64] Where Cornies saw the crises as God's encouragement to carry out rational reforms and become more engaged in the Russian world, Balzer saw them as punishment for the changes Mennonites had undergone in Russia and for their involvement with the Russian world. Balzer wrote that originally natural reason was not inimical to understanding, for reason was also a gift of God, provided to people so that they could "see, judge, test, and decide upon" their own actions.[65] But reason had become corrupted by the fall from Eden and become "outright hostile to God and His will." Among the truly faithful, reason needed therefore to be "subordinated to the faith, and be brought under its obedience."[66] This was because reason led to doubt and ultimately to "conformity with the world" and to the misguided conclusion that belief in "salvation in and through Christ" was "nothing but folly."[67]

Balzer did not place this critique in the specific context of Molochnaia conditions in 1833 (indeed, he identified the worst of these failings with Prussian Mennonites), but it is worth remembering how desperate Molochnaia conditions were at the time: Mennonites were again stripping the thatch from their roofs to feed emaciated livestock, and no one was sure where seed grain would come from for the next year. Both Balzer and Cornies saw the crises as a sign from God, and it is likely that most Mennonites shared this view. The difference between the two was that Balzer saw the crises as punishment for the Mennonites' drift into worldliness, while Cornies interpreted them as a call to push forward with reforms. He understood his money to be an essential catalyst for his reform program, and as he told Hausknecht, this was an exercise in Christian charity, not self-interest. Like Balzer, Cornies was deeply committed to the welfare of his community, but unlike Balzer he viewed economic modernization as the mainspring of that welfare. He lent money from a sense of Christian duty to the Mennonite community.

Cornies's closer attention to his business affairs after his return from Saxony was mirrored in his changing approach to Molochnaia community affairs. In 1828 he turned his attention to falling enrolment at the Ohrloff secondary school. As secretary of the Christian School Society he had always taken a leading role in the school's administration, and, as noted in chapter 3, he personally contributed over half of the school's budget. As father of two of its students, he had a strong personal interest as well. Problems at the school centred around Tobias Voth, a Pietist whose devotion to a passionate evangelical Christianity infused his teaching and alienated conservative Mennonites. He used the Ohrloff school as his pulpit, holding evening meetings where he promoted missionary work and gave extemporaneous sermons.[68] Cornies and Voth had enjoyed a friendly relationship before the Saxony trip, but when Cornies returned to the Molochnaia he suddenly withdrew his support for Voth. In December 1828, Cornies wrote that Voth needed to teach in a "more orderly and punctual way,"[69] and at a January 1829 School Society meeting Cornies chastised Voth, instructing him to reform his teaching methods. He berated Voth for not behaving in a "manly" way, suggesting that the emotional, evangelical Voth was not behaving in the sober, paternal manner expected of Mennonite men. When Voth resigned at the end of the school year, Cornies was not sorry to see him go, and although the two remained on polite terms, Cornies's later letters to Schlatter, and Voth's own 1831 account of his departure from the Molochnaia, show that their private relations were strained.[70]

The Christian School Society hired Heinrich Heese to replace Voth. Cornies had known Heese for several years; in the mid-1820s Heese was secretary of the Khortitsa Mennonite *Gebietsamt*, and he and Cornies corresponded about selling Khortitsa wool through Blüher in Moscow. The two shared a friendship with Schlatter, and Heese was a member of the Bible Society in Khortitsa. In his teaching Heese was a serious, sober figure, a sharp change from Voth. Under his firm hand, as Cornies would report with pleasure in 1830, the Ohrloff school was soon back on track, with enrolment grown to thirty students, three of whom were "from the opposition" (presumably he meant the Large Flemish Congregation). By then the school also had a handful of Lutheran students from the German colonies across the Molochnaia River. The School Society even considered (but quickly rejected) accepting Doukhobor students.[71]

There is no clear indication of what precisely motivated Cornies to turn against Voth, but several factors likely played a role. On a personal level, Cornies's son Johann Jr. was performing badly in school – his grades were a dismal *"schlecht"* – and when the father of a failing student is also the secretary of the School Society, this never bodes well for the teacher.[72] Declining enrolment in the school must also have concerned Cornies, who believed strongly in the role of education in building a better future for all Mennonites. But beyond this it is possible to discern in Cornies a new understanding that the public controversy that Voth was at the centre of was harmful to all his larger goals. Cornies was not turning away from Pietism, but he was backing away from one of its most controversial expressions.

With Voth gone, Heese ensconced, and the School Society back on firm footing, Cornies turned his attention to bringing order to the Wool Improvement Society. In January 1829, Cornies wrote to the members of the society with a five-point reorganization plan. He insisted that if the society was to achieve its goals, it needed to become more careful about how it collected and spent money and its members needed to become more organized and take on more clearly defined administrative roles. Attendance at the society's meetings needed to be compulsory, the meetings needed to be formally documented, and where members had questions about their responsibilities, there needed to be special meetings to consult and take advice. Cornies served notice that if the society was not prepared to accept this plan, then he would be too busy to continue to waste his time with it and would resign.[73]

This effort to reorganize the Wool Improvement Society was short-lived: its role in the Molochnaia was about to be superseded by more significant agencies. Even so, both the tone of Cornies's letter to the society and the general tenor of his public activities by 1829 were significant. As he had shown most clearly during the dispute over the brandy monopoly, he was no longer willing to allow the *Gebietsamt* to define the scope of his activities. Between the horse theft scandal and the dispute over the Saxony expedition, Cornies was fed up with the *Gebietsamt*. No longer would he let it order him around.

The Forestry Society

In 1830, Cornies founded the administrative vehicle to carry forward his own agenda for the Molochnaia: the Forestry Society. Like Tsar Alexander had been, Tsar Nicholas was eager to promote forestry programs on the steppe.[74] During his 1825 visit to the Molochnaia, Alexander had applauded Mennonite tree planting and urged them to redouble their efforts. The Mennonites valued trees for both economic and aesthetic reasons and happily promised to oblige.[75] In 1828, Nicholas ordered the creation of societies to promote steppe afforestation across New Russia. The Molochnaia settlement was the ideal place to get the ball rolling.[76]

While the idea for the Molochnaia Forestry Society was taking shape, in Ekaterinoslav the elderly Contenius's health was failing. He died on 30 May 1830 at the age of eighty-two.[77] Fadeev, who since 1819 had been the official head of the guardianship bureau in Ekaterinoslav, now had to stand entirely on his own as the main colonial administrator in Ekaterinoslav province. An ambitious man, unhappy with life in a frontier outpost and constantly living at the limit of his financial resources, Fadeev needed a success story if he was to ingratiate himself with the new tsar and climb his way up the bureaucratic ladder. With Cornies looking for a new role in the Molochnaia and Fadeev looking for new ways to distinguish himself, the relationship between the two grew into both a strong working alliance and a genuine friendship. That relationship would have important long-term implications for both men.

Fadeev's memoirs reveal him to be an ambitious social climber, disdainful of the frontier bumpkins he worked with in Ekaterinoslav, embarrassed by an income that could not support the lifestyle he craved, and toadying up to anyone of high birth or influence he could find.[78] But there was more to him than this. His success as an administrator and his climb to high office suggest real competence, and his apparently genuine friendship with Cornies suggests a depth of character that his memoirs nowhere reveal. The friendship between Cornies and Fadeev was the most unlikely of things. Fadeev always was ambitious to move on to bigger and better things, and while he respected the Mennonites, or at least appreciated that their accomplishments made him look good, there is no sign that he really liked them. Indeed, for all that he praised them in his official reports, in a personal letter to the St. Petersburg official Petr Keppen in 1839 he described them as a "completely ignorant people."[79] By the time he wrote his memoirs in the 1860s he regarded the entire foreign colonist experiment as a failure and a waste of state resources, although he allowed that the Mennonites were an exception to this rule.[80] Still, his friendship with Cornies seems to have been genuine. Their correspondence extended to concerns about families, health, and mutual friends. The two were of a similar age, had children of similar ages, and shared a reverence for Contenius, and of course, for both of them the success of the Mennonite settlement was important. In a memoir full of self-aggrandizement that seldom even mentioned people below his own social strata, Fadeev paused to praise Cornies, allowing that he had "loved the man."[81]

The Forestry Society charter that Fadeev drafted is an excellent example of the new attitude that Tsar Nicholas brought to frontier administration. Tsar Alexander had visited the Molochnaia, sat down to tea with community leaders, and on his way out of town exhorted them to grow trees, but he had never enacted laws to achieve this goal. In contrast, Nicholas issued orders from St. Petersburg for forests, and by 1830 Fadeev had complied by creating a charter for a forestry society that would, by the 1850s, result in a commercial forestry industry in the once-treeless Molochnaia.[82]

In creating the Forestry Society, Fadeev explicitly activated the Mennonite colonial laboratory of modernization. Until this point in time, the expectation that the Mennonites would act as didactic model colonists was somewhat hazy. The Forestry Society envisioned a specific role, defined by a specific charter, and directed by a specific secular agency. It reflected an evolving state attitude toward the Mennonites that would be even more clearly articulated in 1833 with a plan for the "Reorganisation of the Administration of the Colonists."[83] This plan, which provided a framework for reorganizing the Guardianship Committee (see chapter 6), echoed the Privilegium's justification for Mennonite privileges, but where the 1800 document characterised the privileges as a reward for the Mennonites' "excellent industry and morality," the 1833 plan made the "justifiable demand" that the Mennonites "be zealous and industrious" in exchange for their privileges.[84] It also expanded the target audience of the Mennonite model, from foreign colonists to all settlers in the region. Political scientist James C. Scott describes scientific forestry in the nineteenth century as a tool to extend the authority of modernizing states, and the Molochnaia case reflects this process.[85] The 1833 plan, like the Privilegium, still characterized the Mennonites as a passive model of "order and industry," but the tone had changed. As historian Natalia Venger observes, in this plan the state had begun to envision the Mennonite community as a "creative model of economic modernization."[86]

The intent of the Forestry Society, that Mennonites should grow trees, was not revolutionary: there were already fruit trees dotted throughout the settlement, and many fullholders grew shrubs and shade trees to mark their property lines, to provide windbreaks, or simply to recreate in a small way the lush landscape they remembered from Poland. The new society called for systematizing tree growing by creating public tree nurseries (called "plantations") in every village and by requiring that all Mennonite fullholders set aside one *desiatina* behind their home plot for trees. On it they were to plant between ten and forty trees per year until the orchard area was completely planted.[87] The society supplied seeds and saplings and issued detailed instructions on soil preparation, appropriate spacing, and care for the saplings.

What was revolutionary about the society was the way it envisaged extending Guardianship Committee authority into the Mennonite community and exercising that authority over individual fullholders. The main agent of secular authority in the settlement was the *Gebietsamt*, and before Fadeev created the Forestry Society all direct local executive power lay in the *Gebietsamt*'s hands. The *Gebietsamt* was by no means a fully compliant tool of the Guardianship Committee, for as it had demonstrated in 1826 regarding the Saxony trip, it sometimes refused to cooperate with the committee's plans. By 1830 Fadeev knew that under Tsar Nicholas's rule a repeat of the 1826 fiasco would not be good for his career. He equally knew that he could not achieve anything in the Molochnaia without Mennonite help. While the Mennonites' refusal to cooperate might have had dire consequences for their long-term status in the empire – there were already those in St. Petersburg who questioned their privileged status – the elimination of Mennonite privileges could gain nothing for Fadeev. He needed a success story.

Fadeev's plan was to create a completely new secular agency in the Molochnaia Mennonite settlement. The Forestry Society was to operate independently of the *Gebietsamt*, in its own clearly defined arena. Symbolically its headquarters were located on the southeastern edge of the settlement at Cornies's Iushanle estate rather than in Halbstadt, the administrative and economic centre of Molochnaia Mennonite life. Fadeev was aware that he was departing from past practice, and he carefully justified his decision in the society charter, writing that "the extent of [the settlement] constantly keeps the district officials busy with affairs in respect to administration, settlement, collection of taxes, keeping of accounts, etc., and even with their best intentions it becomes impossible for them to conduct the exact supervision that is required for success."[88]

Fadeev also paid close attention to the new society's leadership. Cornies was his best ally in the Molochnaia and naturally would be chairperson of the society. It seems likely that Fadeev consulted closely with Cornies about the society's organization and goals; there is no direct evidence of this, but in the fall of 1830, before Fadeev issued the society's charter, Cornies conspicuously established a model forest plantation at Iushanle. As for other society members, one lesson of 1826 was that Cornies faced significant opposition within his own community. He needed the support of other prominent Mennonites, for without them the Forestry Society would surely fail. Consequently the charter named two leading members of the community, Gerhard Enns and Dierk Warkentin, as initial members.[89] It was left to Cornies to fill out the society with two additional members. He chose Martens and the manager of his sheep farm at Iushanle, Abram Wieb.[90] As described earlier, this small group was closely connected by its economic interests and in turn by Cornies's money.

The members of the Forestry Society constituted a wealthy merchant elite in the Molochnaia. They shared common economic interests, but they also shared another important characteristic: most of them relied heavily on Cornies to bankroll their operations. For them, as for Fadeev, Cornies's services as moneylender played the double role of stimulating the economy and cementing a political alliance – what might be called the "Cornies Party" – to promote Cornies's economic reform agenda.

Notably, neither the *Gebietsamt* nor the congregational elders were represented in the society. Indeed, the charter explicitly excluded serving *Gebietsamt* members. The lack of *Gebietsamt* representation was bound to be problematic, because the direct authority that Fadeev's charter gave to the Forestry Society was ambiguous. Fadeev seemed to intend the society to stand on equal footing with congregational elders and the *Gebietsamt*, and like them the society members received an exemption from various community duties. The charter ordered that "all arrangements made by [the society] will be executed in every village by the village offices and by every settler, in the same way as those issued by the *Gebietsamt*," but because it provided no instrument for the society to enforce its policies, in practice the society had to rely upon the cooperation of the *Gebietsamt*.[91] These orders were bound to become controversial, for although the society's principal task was only to "impart advice and instruction to settlers," the charter contained the ominous threat that "anyone who is disobedient and pays no attention to these suggestions, will eventually lose his household. It will then be given over to another dependable young householder, who must obligate himself to fulfil the government's demands for his own advantage."[92]

Fadeev viewed the congregational elders as hostile to the state's goals for the settlement. On the eve of announcing the creation of the society, Fadeev addressed a harsh reprimand to the *Kirchenconvent* (church leaders) for their "great imprudence, especially with respect to arrangements made for the brandy trade." He accused them, along with the *Gebietsamt*, of "showing visible proof of their contempt and disdain for legal authority," and he reminded them that in other colonial communities "the wicked morality of leaders, their refractory behaviour toward superiors, and arrangements arising out of this for the Ministry, have already caused some foreign settlers in Russia *to lose their privileges. They were transferred from the Guardianship administration to the jurisdiction of the civilian administration. After more than twenty years, children curse their fathers who are guilty of these results."*[93]

The fact that Fadeev addressed those words to congregational elders and not to the *Gebietsamt* is a telling indication of how he understood the political situation in the Molochnaia settlement: he assumed that the *Gebietsamt* danced to the church's tune. Cornies, his inside source on community matters, must have informed this assessment, demonstrating how strong Cornies's antipathy was for Warkentin. The new society, notwithstanding its narrowly defined official role of promoting afforestation, was to be the state's political beachhead in the Molochnaia Mennonite settlement. From the outset Fadeev expected it to be a foil to Warkentin's conservative influence.

Fadeev formally announced the creation of the Forestry Society on 20 October 1831. Cornies was aware of the potential for controversy that the society raised, and he cautioned Fadeev not to expect too much too soon: "We are supposed to be teachers and advisers and thus we must be learned and experienced. Otherwise we would be disgraced, or not be able to maintain the authority we must definitely have for this important occupation."[94] Cornies proposed to spend the winter months gathering and studying literature on forestry and planning for the society's first planting season in 1832. In February 1832, the society began circulating bulletins on proper procedures for planting trees, and in April, Cornies and Enns toured the settlement to see how the society's plans were proceeding.[95] Their reports show that villages across the settlement were complying with society directives; there was no indication of resistance or complaint. In its first year the society seemed set to accomplish its goals without any great controversy.

While Fadeev laid out plans for the Forestry Society in 1830, Cornies was involving himself deeply in other state affairs. The cholera pandemic that swept across Europe in 1830–1 arrived in the Molochnaia in 1830, and with it came deep-seated fear and equally deep religious reflection. Close on the pandemic's heels came the Great Drought of 1832–3, which magnified the sense of crisis in the Molochnaia. These crises, and Cornies's official role in dealing with them, had a ratcheting effect on tensions in the settlement. The crises, fear, and religious reflections came in close company with the Forestry Society. Without the crises, the controversy over that society (described below) might never have arisen; but the crises did come, and the ensuing controversy had an impact on the Mennonites' future far more profound than it might have had otherwise.

The cholera pandemic killed almost a quarter of a million Russians.[96] Poorly equipped to confront so great a crisis, the state at first did nothing, but in the fall of 1830, as outbreaks of the disease came dangerously close to Moscow and St. Petersburg and panic set in, Nicholas imposed harsh quarantine measures, closing off infected regions and bringing trade to a standstill throughout much of the empire. Riots and rebellions followed before the disease receded and order was restored in 1832.[97]

The first reported cholera in the Molochnaia was in the Nogai village of Kakbas in the fall of 1830.[98] The Nogais feared a quarantine, which would not only isolate the disease but also isolate them from food supplies and prevent them from fleeing the affected area, so at first they concealed the outbreak. By mid-December, however, cholera was raging throughout the Nogai district, and nothing could be done to hide it.[99] The state imposed a tight quarantine, thus limiting the outbreak to the Nogai district, and by January it had died out. A second outbreak was reported on 14 July 1832, this time in the large state peasant village of Bol'shoi Tokmak. Within two weeks Orthodox and Nogai villages throughout the Molochnaia were recording deaths, and again the state imposed a quarantine. In neither case were deaths reported in colonist villages.[100]

Cornies served as Fadeev's eyes and ears in the Molochnaia, and it was he who first reported the outbreak, writing to Fadeev in mid-October 1830 that he did not think the Kakbas deaths were from cholera.[101] According to Cornies, he had received the report from the guardian of the Nogai Horde.[102] It is noteworthy that the report came first to Cornies, and not through normal administrative channels to the Ministry of Internal Affairs, which directly supervised the Nogais. Clearly, the Nogai guardian was aware of the most direct channel for raising concerns with higher authorities. In early December, Cornies reported that the deaths *were* from cholera and that the disease was spreading rapidly to other Nogai villages.[103] He urged the *Gebietsamt* to forbid unnecessary contact between Mennonites and Nogais. Reports of the outbreak brought official attention, and on 16 December, Prince Sakhar Chercheuslidsov, a member of the Central Committee for Cholera, visited Cornies to investigate.[104] He ordered a full quarantine.[105] This contained the disease but left the Nogais to a grim fate.

By early January the disease's grip was weakening, but Cornies still urged that a careful quarantine be maintained. He complained that the *Gebietsamt* was taking the enforcement of the quarantine too lightly, and he asked that Fadeev appoint Deputy Mayor Johann Regier to closely supervise prophylactic measures.[106] This was Cornies's first direct mention of Regier, the *Gebietsamt* official who eventually became his closest ally in the district administration. By the end of January the disease was fading away, leaving the Mennonites to contemplate its meaning.

Cornies was clear about what the cholera epidemic signified to him: just as with the crisis of 1824–5, it was a blunt reminder of the duty of all true Christians to serve God and His anointed rulers on earth. In December 1830, at the height of the outbreak, he had written to Johann Wiebe in Prussia that "with complete faith in our government we await the Almighty's ordinance without fear." After all, "everything that comes from God will serve our well-being."[107] Cornies stressed that this was not a call for passive inaction; indeed, he was sharply critical of what he interpreted as Nogai fatalism as manifested in the Islamic clerical leadership's resistance to prophylactic measures. He saw the same fatalism among some Mennonites, and in rejecting it he told Wiebe, "we are not simply striving against God's will if we use the power of thought to take precautionary measures against sickness and to battle against disruptive natural forces. We use the talents given us from above and submit them to His wise counsels. In using them, we praise his divine name."[108] Showing plainly that Pietist universalism remained a strong current in his personal beliefs, he wrote to Blüher in Moscow, asking worriedly for news of Blüher's own family and insisting that "the Lord intends our salvation and will gloriously guide this punitive judgment to our advantage. Many people are being reminded about death who would ordinarily not think about it and are being drawn to God."[109]

Cornies thus took on the task of running the Forestry Society at a time when his own sense of divine guidance was already particularly acute. The recurrence of cholera in the summer of 1832 re-emphasized this, and further emphasis came in the autumn when the Great Drought set in.[110] Rain stopped falling in the Molochnaia and the rest of southwestern Russia on 1 September 1832, and no rain or snow fell for seven months. With the prolonged drought came harvest failures and, in 1833, starvation in Slavic and Nogai villages, despite famine relief efforts that cost the state more than 8 million rubles.[111] Led by Cornies, the Mennonites established a community fund to buy grain and fodder, sending representatives to surrounding districts to purchase provisions.[112] Mennonites and German colonists sold off one quarter of their horses at low prices, keeping only what they absolutely needed for fieldwork in the coming year.[113] In the winter of 1833–4 those who could afford it moved their livestock to regions that were less severely affected, paying rack rent for pasture; poorer colonists could only wait and watch as their livestock died. By January the only fodder available to most Molochnaia settlers was a local weed called *kurrei*, which sometimes caused fatal diarrhoea in sheep.[114] By February even the *kurrei* was gone and the colonists began to feed their livestock thatch from the roofs of their homes.[115] Some desperate Nogais, facing starvation, raided colonists' cattle herds, and colonists began posting guards.[116] Disease swept through livestock, and thousands of head, already weakened by hunger, died.[117] Only the state's emergency famine relief efforts prevented similar massive fatalities in the human population before rain and warm weather returned in April 1834.[118]

As with the cholera outbreak, Cornies interpreted the drought and famine as divine guidance. He said as much to Fadeev (though in purely secular terms), writing that "this is a year of testing in many respects. The total crop failure this year will set the settlers back for several years but it will make us consider many things in advance, dealing with them more appropriately to prevent similar disasters in future."[119] To Blüher he interpreted events in religious terms, writing that "the Lord is revealing his justice to us. It will be well for the person who pays attention and recognises that God considers not only our possessions but us as individuals. We must give thanks that He deals with us so kindly and wisely drawing us to him in this way."[120]

The apparent equanimity with which Cornies greeted the cholera epidemic, drought, and famine was not universal in his community. His own correspondence only hinted at this when he wrote to Johann Wiebe "that some people here consider precautionary measures to be sinful."[121] Balzer's religious reflections show that some Mennonites in the Molochnaia reacted much more strongly.

Balzer's "Faith and Reason" reflected the most conservative views in the settlement. He had been an elder of the Pietist Frisian congregation that immigrated to the Molochnaia in 1819. He and Cornies worked together on the Settlement Commission, and Balzer joined the moderate Old Flemish Congregation in Ohrloff in the 1820s.[122] Balzer was known for his preaching style, which Cornies described in 1829 as "unctuous and fiery, without much thought," but at the same time Cornies observed a moderation in Balzer, writing that "he no longer improvises as he preaches."[123] In January 1833, Balzer left the Ohrloff congregation to join the conservative Kleine Gemeinde. He justified his departure on the grounds that the Ohrloff congregation – and the Molochnaia Mennonite population more broadly – had become too worldly, having abandoned "the single-minded following of [Jesus's] teachings and commandments."[124] In a letter to the elder of his old congregation explaining his departure he described the dangers he saw, of materialism and worldly knowledge.[125] Balzer's critique of Mennonite society is not necessarily representative of mainstream Mennonite opinion in the period, and there is no evidence that it was taken very seriously by the majority of Molochnaia Mennonites, who were used to Balzer's hyperbole. Still, it reveals one extreme of Mennonite reactions to the crises of the period and offers a more nuanced picture of the society as a whole.

Balzer placed strong emphasis on faith, writing that the "mind becomes illuminated in a reborn person through the divine power of the Holy Spirit, and the more a man opens his heart to the working of the Spirit of God, the more the mind will be illuminated and inspired."[126] Although "Faith and Reason" is usually upheld as a definitive rejection of Pietism in favour of traditional conservative Mennonite theology, Balzer's Pietist background is discernible in both the language and the meaning of these sentences. Religion "of the heart" was central to Pietist belief, and the idea that the individual, by opening his heart to God, might understand the Bible in a way closed to those who simply read and obeyed its words suggests that Balzer's understanding of Christian faith was a good deal more Pietistic than some of his modern interpreters would allow.[127] Conservative Mennonite belief called for believers to live their lives in imitation of Christ as revealed in the Bible – not to open their hearts to illumination and be reborn. This may help explain how Cornies and the Kleine Gemeinde leadership were frequently able to find common ground in the disputes of the 1840s.

In 1833, however, Balzer's criticisms seemed squarely aimed at Cornies. One of the harshest – and the point where his views most closely coincided with the mainstream Mennonite conservatism of Warkentin's Large Flemish Congregation – related to innovations in education that Cornies championed. Balzer accepted that reading and writing were necessary as "a useful training for the propagation of the Gospel," but he saw higher learning, characterized by "observation, analysis, experimentation, and logical deduction," as the snare of the devil.[128] He urged elders of all Molochnaia congregations to "sever our people from their apostasy to the world ... As soon as our young people will be educated (brainwashed) and enlightened in the fashion of the world, and after these polished worldlings have been in control of the rudder for the second and third generation! Suddenly they will have departed from the yoke of simplicity and brought great inertia to such power so that it will continually increase in strength with time and eventually stagger unto the great universal ruination."[129] Because Balzer thought that youth were particularly susceptible to the snares of reason, he urged that children be closely supervised to prevent them from falling "into all kinds of pleasure and company at an early age."[130] The "selection of one's reading material" was vitally important, for "that which is externally tasteful easily undermines the taste for the simple things, and for the Word of God."[131] Most of all, youth should not be exposed to newspapers, "for it is the intention of Satan to condition these young people for the doings of this world, and they will be captured by this fabric of truth and falsehood which is so pleasing to the senses."[132]

This critique of education was undoubtedly directed at Cornies, who was the leading proponent of secular education in the Molochnaia. "Faith and Reason" went further in its attack on the reforms that Cornies championed:

> Infatuated by reason and the riches and good things of this world, members of the church began to consider these things as no longer harmful for salvation, and therefore tried to obtain them by every possible means. One became enmeshed in big business and thus assumed duties and responsibilities which made worldly learning unavoidable. One necessity engendered another, and one need gave rise to a next one. The big trading connections made it absolutely necessary to study business administration, geography and political science. Reading of daily newspapers became a necessary and tempting habit, and made people familiar with the great politics of this world. They thoroughly enjoyed observing revolutions and overthrow of kings and states. Thus many of our good Mennonites gradually became conditioned to the doings of this world without even noticing it.[133]

Cornies's reaction to the crises of 1830–4 and to the criticisms levelled by Balzer and others echoed his reaction during the crisis of 1825 – he threw himself into community relief efforts and used his own money to provide aid where it was needed, both within the Mennonite community and beyond. But also as in 1825, he seemed to have little sense of how other members of his community would react to the crisis and his role in managing it. When it came to public opinion, Cornies was always tone deaf, and rather than backing away from his most aggressive reform plans until the crisis was over, he pressed forward even at the height of the harvest failure and famine, prompting hostility both to reforms and to himself as chief reformer. Such hostility was bound to make his reform efforts more difficult, and it is puzzling that Cornies, who seemed to learn so easily how to navigate the politics of Imperial Russia, had so much difficulty understanding the politics of his own community.

In 1833, Cornies began an aggressive push to enforce Forestry Society tree-planting targets. In January the society sent out stern letters to the mayors of villages that had not met their ploughing targets the previous year. In imperious tones the committee demanded "truthful" explanations for such negligence and issued detailed orders for mayors to report on the work of particularly negligent individuals.[134] The mayors were told they must sharply reprimand defaulters, and where negligence persisted, this must be reported to the society. Mayors and deputy mayors who failed to enforce society orders were threatened with monetary fines. In January 1833, in the middle of the drought, with not a flake of snow on the ground and the weather ominously warm and dry, the society wrote to the village offices with profound insensitivity that "since favourable weather conditions have arrived, village offices are hereby ordered to begin without delay and to continue operations in forest-tree plantations, such as ditch digging around plantations. Anyone not yet digging and planting or making enclosures must begin, without fail. Next week the society will make a tour to inspect what has been done and what else must be done without fail under the favourable weather conditions."[135] Only in September 1833 did the society grudgingly acknowledge that the weather was less "favourable" than it had earlier allowed, putting off ploughing in the tree lots because there were too few horses left to do the work.[136] Many of the saplings planted in the fall of 1832 and the spring of 1833 were by then dead, and as Cornies reported to Fadeev, "in this discouraging year, it will be enough of an effort for the settlers just to pull out dried trees and plant fresh ones in their place."[137] By then, the political damage was already done.

The Forestry Society bombarded the villages with demands and harassed them with detailed requirements that must have seemed intrusive at best and at times infuriating. In February 1833 it issued a circular to the village mayors admonishing them for allowing fullholders to dig the ditches around their tree lots four inches narrower and shallower than the required five-by-four Prussian feet.[138] When the mayors objected that the ditches had been dug according to the standard one-foot measure in use in the region, which was almost an inch shorter per foot than the Prussian standard, the committee reluctantly accepted this excuse, allowing that the existing ditches were acceptable – as long as they were expanded to the Prussian measure in the spring of 1834.[139]

This campaign to create orderly, perfectly uniform village tree lots and personal orchards across the settlement was intrusive and unwelcome, yet its reception in the Molochnaia was by no means completely negative. Most Mennonites wanted at least fruit trees, and the program came with a substantial incentive from the state in the form of tens of thousands of free saplings. One of the most distinguishing features of the Molochnaia settlement in later years – and a source of enormous pride and financial reward to the Mennonites – was the orchards, tree plantations, and tree-lined boulevards that set the settlement sharply apart from other regions of the southern steppe. Moreover, after the initial effort of deep-ploughing and trenching the tree lots, the annual demands on fullholders were not especially onerous: each was to plant one quarter-*desiatina* per year until one *desiatina* had been planted.[140] The society was controversial in part because it was making its demands during the depths of the Great Drought, but at least as controversial was *how* the society set out to enforce its orders.

As noted earlier, the Forestry Society charter threatened that fullholders who did not follow society orders could have their land confiscated and given to a "dependable young householder, who must obligate himself to fulfil the government's demands for his own advantage."[141] This was no empty threat: in the spring of 1833, on society orders, the village of Ladekopp confiscated a fullholding and handed it over to a younger, more energetic man, and by the end of the year the society had developed a model contract for "dependable young householders" that set out their tree-planting obligations on their new fullholdings.[142]

The confiscation and reallotment of land was not widespread – there is only one recorded example from 1833, and only a handful ever. In every case, the dispossessed fullholder was recognized by his village as incapable of supporting himself, and the new fullholder was someone whom the community saw as deserving and able to fulfil the community responsibilities that fell to fullholders. Notably, while tree planting stirred frequent and well-recorded protests, there is no record of a public outcry against reallotments of fullholdings. Still, the process did have grave significance for the Molochnaia Mennonite community, for at stake were basic issues of individual and community autonomy. In coming years, as Cornies's authority grew, his intrusion on individual rights would become central to his greatest political battle.

Conclusion

As Johann Cornies re-engaged with Molochnaia Mennonite affairs between 1828 and 1834, a set of converging forces revealed themselves. The state, now led by Nicholas I, was determined to play a more direct role in domestic affairs. Fadeev, the state's most important regional official, emerged from the shadow of Contenius, who died in 1830. Driven by the state's growing demands and by his own ambitions, Fadeev sought to distinguish himself with a success story in the Molochnaia settlement. Conservative Mennonites perceived the state's reform agenda as an unwarranted worldly intrusion into their quietist religious community and challenged its intrusive actions, as well as those of Cornies. The cholera pandemic and the Great Drought of 1833–4 contributed to a sense of crisis that Mennonites interpreted in religious terms.

As chair of the Forestry Society, Cornies represented the state's reform agenda. Fadeev was his most important patron and increasingly also his friend, and Cornies worked with him as an agent of the state's reform plans. But Fadeev's reform agenda was secular, and if Cornies accepted the state's reform plans as legitimate aspirations of the secular state, he also understood the reforms in religious terms, as reflections of God's will. He expressed this plainly in his reactions to the Great Drought, which both confirmed to him the necessity of change and drove him to push harder than he should have to achieve reforms in the midst of crisis.

Jacob Warkentin's voice is seemingly silent in all of this, but it is not hard to detect his influence behind the scenes. The *Gebietsamt*'s attempt to wrest control of the brandy monopoly from Cornies and Martens in 1830 was clearly credited by Fadeev to the baleful influence of the congregational leadership, and this principally meant Warkentin. In 1832 the *Gebietsamt* elections confirmed his political influence when Large Flemish Congregation member Johann Regier succeeded Warkentin's brother-in-law Johann Klassen as mayor.

For both Cornies and Fadeev the Forestry Society amounted to an end run around the authority of the *Gebietsamt* and, it follows, the Warkentin-led conservatives. This could only have been necessary if they saw the *Gebietsamt* as hostile to their reform plans. While the society was explicitly an economic reform agency, the decision to situate it physically and figuratively apart from the *Gebietsamt* gave it political significance. For Cornies, it was a vehicle for his re-entry into Molochnaia politics.

The Forestry Society expressed an evolving state policy that had critical implications for the Mennonites. On an empire-wide scale, Official Nationality expressed Tsar Nicholas's intent to reform and control his population. Regionally, the 1833 plan for the "Reorganisation of the Administration of the Colonists" reflected the influence of Official Nationality in that it envisioned a new role for colonist communities within the reorganized state. In the Molochnaia Mennonite settlement the Forestry Society was a local manifestation of tsarist policy, in that it formally established a laboratory of modernization with the potential to affect empire-wide policies. None of this boded well for conservative Mennonites.

Chapter Six

Mennonites and the Era of Small Reforms, 1834–1838

In 1833, Johann Cornies told Andrei Fadeev that the Great Drought was an opportunity for Mennonites to "look into the future and consider numerous issues that will need to be dealt with if we are to prevent similar disasters in the future."¹ The Forestry Society had provided a new vision for administration in the Molochnaia, but it was a limited vision, and by 1834, with the drought over, Cornies and Fadeev were scheming bigger schemes for an all-encompassing economic agency that would utterly transform the Mennonites' agricultural economy. The Agricultural Society they concocted was intended to supplant key functions of the *Gebietsamt* and hand Cornies much greater political power.

This plan came in the midst of, and as an implicit response to, major changes in the state administration. Historian Susan Smith-Peter has aptly labelled the 1830s the "era of small reforms," driven by a desire "to move the provinces and empire from feudalism to the next stage of a commercial or civil society marked by a flourishing economy and greater civility."² Smith-Peter describes how the reforms saw the state seek more and better information from its provinces. This resulted in more power being ceded to provincial elites, which led to the growth of distinct regional identities. In many ways the Mennonite experience confirms the process Smith-Peter describes, but for the Mennonites, who already possessed a strong sense of a distinct identity, the outcome was the opposite of what Smith-Peter documents in Vladimir *guberniia*. As the state reorganized peasant administration, it set out to bring the Mennonites more closely under its control in order to make them agents of its larger plans. If the era of small reforms heralded greater freedoms for Russian elites, for the empire's non-Russian population it signalled a declining tolerance for differences.

At the time, the Guardianship Committee was a division of the Department of State Domains within the Ministry of Internal Affairs. By 1834 Tsar Nicholas was planning a large-scale reorganization. The plan, implemented between 1836 and 1838, created a new Ministry of State Domains under the authority of Count Pavel Kiselev. Nicholas charged the new ministry with administering the state peasants, the first step toward a wholesale reform of peasant administration.

The Ministry of State Domains had ambitious economic reforms in mind. The Mennonites' Agricultural Society, created in 1836, may have been a reaction to this, or it may have been a happy case of very good timing; either way, the Agricultural Society sprang into being at a propitious moment to realize its creators' ambitions, and it would soon become the most powerful organization in the Molochnaia. This was an equally propitious moment for Cornies, because a reorganization of the Guardianship Committee saw new powers pass into his hands. In 1834 the Ekaterinoslav bureau of the committee closed and Fadeev was transferred to committee headquarters in Odesa. Two years later Fadeev was promoted and transferred to the Trans-Volga region as Guardian of the Kalmyk Horde. The departure of Cornies's powerful patron at first weakened Cornies, but in the long run it forced the state to rely on him more and allowed him to emerge as a major player in his own right. The main contest for authority in the Molochnaia would not be engaged until after 1838, but meanwhile, the Agricultural Society emerged in 1836 to challenge the traditional power structure in the Molochnaia and set the stage for the final battle.

Johann Jr. and Cornies's Reform Vision

The education of Johann Cornies Jr. offers insights into Cornies's personal and public views in the mid-1830s. The younger Cornies never achieved the success his father had. He performed poorly in the Ohrloff school, and by 1830 his father was hinting at his disappointment. Writing to friends in Ekaterinoslav to ask for help finding a new business secretary, Cornies felt compelled to explain why his eighteen-year-old son was not taking over the position. He explained that he didn't want to take Johann Jr. out of school yet, "before he understands what he has already learned thoroughly and well, and whatever he must still learn, so that his achievement in these respects progresses more easily than it does for someone who has only learned half of all this and only half understands it."[3] While this was a reasonable explanation for why Johann Jr. was to continue his education, it is tempting to read between the lines and wonder if he was really so "capable." In April 1832, Cornies sent his son to Ekaterinoslav, where the younger Cornies lived with an official named Kirilovsky, a senior translator in the Guardianship bureau who had been hired to teach him Russian. Cornies Jr. also received lessons in mathematics, surveying, and cartography from a bureau land surveyor. Cornies wrote to Kirilovsky to explain his goals:

> I am a father who has the well-being of his community, where he lives and belongs, at heart. I am concerned that I serve all its individual members to the limits of possibility and with all my powers, to achieve their well-being in every respect. My purpose is to have lived and worked with the calm knowledge of what was ordained as my holy duty in my life and work as man and Christian. This will enable you to understand the kind of education and knowledge I would like to give my son in order to develop his own personal worth, and to make him a useful and serving member of his community and of human society in general.[4]

Nowhere is there an indication that Johann Jr. wanted this arrangement; indeed, Cornies bluntly told Fadeev that land surveying was "the profession I have determined for [my son]."[5]

Cornies's decision to train Johann Jr. as a land surveyor probably had less to do with his son's interests and more to do with his own ambitions. After all, Cornies's first public role as the settlement's land surveyor had allowed him to impose order on the steppe, both functionally and symbolically. Land surveying was a lifelong passion for Cornies, but he never attempted to master its technical complexities; instead, he forced Johann Jr. to take up the profession. Johann Jr. showed little aptitude or desire for this career – he sent drawings of flowers home to his mother from Ekaterinoslav, and he left more drawings to adorn the walls of his Moscow host, Blüher, but his maps left no mark, and back home he disappeared into obscurity.[6] Perhaps by forcing Johann Jr. to become a map maker his father was trying to tame his artistic talent and make something useful of it. After all, Pietists were always suspicious of art for beauty's sake, and of the vanity of artists who presumed to interpret God's creation.[7] Cornies himself found beauty in the more prosaic form of ordering the world.[8]

Land surveying, however simple its original goal – the assignment of sixty-five-*desiatina* allotments to Mennonite immigrants – had forced Cornies to think seriously about the complexities of ordering life in New Russia. Land derived its value from its productive capacity, and Cornies devoted himself to understanding the environmental constraints that governed agriculture in his region. He investigated groundwater levels, he oversaw well digging across the region to determine which sites could support new villages, he paid close attention to precipitation, and he promoted dam projects to provide water for hay meadows. He also conducted detailed studies of native steppe plants and experimented with a number of different crops to find the most productive commercial varieties. By the late 1830s he had become an expert on crop rotation systems, attuned to both the limitations of the soil and the potential of fodder crops and fallow fields to preserve and increase productivity.[9]

Land surveying addressed the key importance of land allocation. This was a simple matter of wealth – in the 1830s in New Russia there were few ways to make money except from the land – but there was more to it than this. Cornies was keenly aware of the environmental and geographic conditions that made land economically viable, and from his experiences as settlement land surveyor he was equally aware of the political consequences of poor land allocation. He viewed land allocation and proper land use as vital to the economic development of his community, and his greatest political battles in the coming years would centre around these matters. Having his son trained as a land surveyor may have been his way to provide Johann Jr. with a profession, but the choice of profession suggests that Cornies was also concerned about this contentious issue.

Johann Jr. returned home briefly in 1834. Dissatisfied with the results of his two years of private schooling in Ekaterinoslav, Cornies decided that his son, now twenty years old, would continue his education as a surveyor in Moscow, where he would stay with Blüher. In September, Cornies wrote to Blüher there that "counting on your friendship, I do not hesitate to send [Johann Jr.] directly to you and commend him to your guardianship. As parents, this gives us great joy and relieves our worries knowing that our son will be well looked after."[10]

When Johann Jr. departed for Moscow, Cornies sent another letter to Blüher full of sincere thanks and hopeful expectations. The letter reveals the warmth of their friendship and the worries of parents whose son was travelling far from home: "Beloved friend … it would give us pleasure and comfort if our son could stay with you over the winter, but do not worry if that is impossible. In that case, he could naturally find lodgings nearby and visit you from time to time. I have taught him to get by on very little. I hope, in any case, that you might support him with advice and instruction in my stead. My son has learned to obey and, unless I am seriously mistaken, he will obey you as he does me."[11] Cornies also asked Blüher to hold on to the considerable sum of 5,173 rubles still owing from the previous winter's wool sales to cover Johann Jr.'s expenses, ensuring that the younger Cornies would not have to get by on *too* little.

In Ekaterinoslav and Moscow, far from the Mennonite settlement, Cornies provided his son with a decidedly secular education. The purpose of that education was to make Johann Jr. a "useful and serving member of the Mennonite community" and of "human society" as well.[12] Cornies insisted that Johann Jr. learn Russian, and in Ekaterinoslav he saw to it that his son took every opportunity to rub shoulders with high officials on the Guardianship Committee – though Cornies later grumbled that Johann Jr. had neglected his studies in Ekaterinoslav because he had "spent too many hours with persons of high rank."[13] Johann Jr. travelled with Fadeev on inspection trips in the Khortitsa Mennonite settlement, and Cornies thanked Fadeev effusively when the director took a personal interest in Johann Jr.'s education.[14]

Johann Jr.'s education reflects his father's understanding of the future direction of Mennonite life in Russia. It would not be enough to live an isolated existence within the community. Mennonite leaders (and he surely hoped his son would be one) needed to know the Russian language, and they needed strong contacts with the Russian administration. They also needed to have a strong understanding of the land itself. Cornies had acquired all of these things (except Russian) on his own, and now he was doing everything he could to provide his son with a head start.

Pietism in Practice

It is not obvious where religious belief fits into all of this. In the 1820s, Pietism had helped shape Cornies's world view, encouraging and legitimizing his engagement with the world beyond the Mennonite settlement. This is consistent with his decision to send Johann Jr. out into the Russian world for an education. In most of his correspondence in the 1830s Cornies shifted his tone away from religious exploration and limited himself to formulaic expressions of faith in the closing salutations of his letters. It might be concluded from this that as he grew older and more concerned with secular administration, he moderated his religious beliefs to fit his political ambitions. The alternative is to argue that Cornies's Pietism had evolved as he thought strategically about how to realize his goals – religious as well as secular – in the Russian colonial context. Johann Jr.'s departure for Moscow prompted Cornies to write his son a letter of advice that leads toward the latter interpretation.

Cornies offered Johann Jr. eleven precepts to guide his travels. Most have a delightfully timeless quality that rings familiar to any parent sending a child on a long trip alone: don't hang out with "jolly fellows" who might lead you astray; don't spend all your money on expensive clothes; and of course, "write often to your parents!" However, two of the precepts specifically address religion, and they are clear evidence, in this most personal of communications, that Cornies remained a Pietist.

The first was to "conduct your devotions quietly and do not neglect church attendance. Religious devotion is a spiritual state that can only be practised when we are so disposed. It can, for example, be awakened by contemplating a religious truth or by honouring God. Listen to your feelings that have an influence over you."[15] This statement plainly expressed a Pietist sensibility, stressing religion as a personal practice, dependent upon disposition and "feelings." By comparison, mainstream Mennonite religious practice in the Molochnaia settlement demanded public expression of faith through conformity with community practices. Cornies's belief that devotion could only be "practised when we are so disposed" would surely have shocked the Sunday crowd at the Ohrloff church! The second precept urged Johann Jr. to seek "out people who live and act in a Christian way. Allow them to teach you ... Examine everything and retain what is best." Here the Pietist ecumenism that Schlatter had introduced to Cornies is on display.

There were significant practical expressions of Cornies's continued allegiance to Pietism in the 1830s as well: his role in the 1834 immigration of the Gnadenfeld community, and his reform and expansion of secondary schooling in the settlement.[16] Both things increased Cornies's influence in the community but also contributed to growing opposition to his reforms.

Cornies helped negotiate the terms of the Gnadenfeld immigration through his Guardianship Committee connections, and despite the fact that he had resigned his position as settlement land surveyor seven years earlier, he personally helped survey the village site and lay out fullholdings.[17] Gnadenfeld would play a key role in the development of Pietism among the tsarist Mennonites, bringing about what is sometimes called the "Gnadenfeld Enlightenment."[18] The village became an important centre of education and administration, and it produced many of the leaders of the Mennonite Brethren congregation that formed in 1860.[19] Through Cornies and others, Pietism's influence was already evident in the Molochnaia in the 1820s, but in terms of its spread in the Mennonite community, Gnadenfeld was at the forefront.[20]

The Gnadenfeld immigrants had their roots in the Gröningen Old Flemish congregation. They were from the Prussian village of Brenkenhofswalde, where they were relatively isolated from the conservative Flemish congregations of the lower Vistula. Through interaction with their Lutheran neighbours they became open to the ideas of Pietism. Their elder, Wilhelm Lange, was a convert from Lutheranism who joined the Mennonite congregation in 1788, first serving as a teacher and, then, from 1810, as the community's elder and spiritual leader. When King Friedrich Wilhelm III introduced harsh restrictions on

Mennonite religious meetings in 1812, the Brenkenhofswalde Mennonites took advantage of the Moravian Brethren's exemption from the restriction, and from that year they met under the aegis of the Moravian Brethren. They adopted many of the Brethren's evangelical attitudes and brought these with them to the Molochnaia.

Cornies was well acquainted with the Moravian Brethren through Blüher and through his own visit to Herrnhut in 1827. He also knew something of Brenkenhofswalde, for the villagers of Alexanderwohl – one of the Pietist villages of the 1820 immigration – came from there. Tobias Voth, the Ohrloff school's first teacher, had been recruited from Brenkenhofswalde. It is possible that Cornies met Wilhelm Lange during his trip to Saxony, and whether or not they had met, he was certainly familiar enough with the elder to ask David Epp in 1830 how Lange and other "good friends" were doing.[21] Lange was an old man by the time he arrived in the Molochnaia in 1834, and Cornies treated him with a solicitous concern, even sending him a gift basket of apples. The elderly, distinguished religious leader thanked "Ohm Cornies" and his wife Anganetha for this sign of "love [that] has not only astonished me and my dear wife but has moved us to tears."[22] Lange's use of "Ohm" [uncle] – suggests the high regard the Gnadenfelders felt for Cornies, for it was a term of respect normally reserved for elders and other honoured persons.

One of the Gnadenfelders' first concerns after their arrival was to ensure that they would retain control of the education, and consequently the religious beliefs, of their children. Their efforts to establish a Gnadenfeld school were part of a broader expansion of secondary schooling in the settlement in the 1830s that contributed to rising tensions. Education had always been a flashpoint between Pietists and conservatives, and Cornies well understood that it was an important battleground within the settlement. In a January 1837 report he bragged about "measures to advance morality" brought about by improving the schools "through the hiring of better school teachers."[23] By that year there were three secondary schools in the settlement – the original one in Ohrloff, a second in Halbstadt, and a third in Steinbach – and planning was under way to open a fourth in Gnadenfeld. The Halbstadt school aimed to "train secretaries, bookkeepers and others for service in the community."[24] Its creation in 1835 was part of the state's efforts to use schooling to promote Russian-language training among foreign colonists. The other schools trained teachers for the settlement's elementary schools. They taught religion, German, Russian, history, geography, arithmetic, and drawing.

In 1837 the Ohrloff teacher was still Heinrich Heese, the Pietist hired to replace Voth, who had left the Molochnaia in 1829. Voth returned in

1836 to teach in the new Steinbach school. When Gnadenfeld first proposed its own school, Cornies suggested that the Gnadenfeld children could be taught in Steinbach by Voth, a surprising show of support for a man Cornies had played a key role in ousting eight years earlier, but the Gnadenfelders rejected this recommendation, arguing that the villages were too far apart.[25] Friedrich Wilhelm Lange, the nephew of Wilhelm Lange, taught briefly at the Steinbach school after Voth fell ill, before becoming the first teacher at the Gnadenfeld school. He would succeed his uncle as congregational elder in 1841 when Wilhelm died. Friedrich Wilhelm Lange was a noted Pietist preacher and, in the 1840s, a close friend of the famous Pietist evangelical Lutheran minister Eduard Wüst.[26]

In their description of their new school, the Gnadenfelders provided a good summary of precisely what Warkentin and his supporters feared: they intended "to mould [pupils] for life here on earth and especially for the kingdom of God."[27] The Gnadenfelders insisted that the school be in their own village in part because, if the students went to school in Steinbach, they would have to board there as well and would not have the chance to attend the Gnadenfeld church. At the Steinbach church they could only hear a sermon read from the pulpit, and, as the Gnadenfelders explained in explicitly Pietist terms, this "could never replace the living warmth and freshness of words from a believing heart" that they would hear in Gnadenfeld.[28]

The Gnadenfeld School Society met with Cornies, consulted about its plans, and sought approval. This points to Cornies's growing role in education in the 1830s: he led the rapid expansion of secondary schooling in the late 1830s, and that included finding and vetting teachers. Such schools, which provided an advanced education to train teachers for the settlement's elementary schools, offered a way for the Pietists – and for modernizers – to spread their influence widely. Little wonder they contributed to building tensions in the settlement.

The Expanding Authority of the Forestry Society

The attitudes Cornies revealed as he sought to prepare his son for service to his community and country, as he helped establish the Gnadenfeld immigrants in the Molochnaia, and as he expanded the secondary school system are reminders that his work as head of the Forestry Society was not motivated solely by personal ambition or the state's agenda. As noted in chapter 5, the Forestry Society's orders during the Great Drought were remarkably insensitive to community hardships. This was partly because Cornies was tone deaf to popular opinion, but it was also because he understood in ways that most of his community could not that old economic practices needed to change in response to new conditions. His community needed to adopt modern farming methods not only to satisfy the state's demands – although that was surely an imperative – but also to ensure its survival. The Great Drought lent urgency to the reform agenda, and the Forestry Society provided Cornies with an agency to help him press forward.

In its efforts to regulate the Molochnaia economy, the Forestry Society identified three main problems: (1) fullholdings were being sold without Guardianship Committee approval, (2) there were well-managed fullholdings whose owners were not complying with society regulations, and (3) some fullholdings were falling into disrepair. Only the second problem fell explicitly under the society's authority. It was the first, the unauthorized sale of fullholdings, that would enable it to expand that authority, and community tensions would rise as a consequence. Cornies would use the issue of unauthorized sales to gain control of land management at its most basic level – the right to own a fullholding.

The tsarist state placed conditions on the fullholdings it granted to Mennonite immigrants, which included the requirement that landowners have the economic means to build and maintain their homes, agricultural buildings, and equipment. That meant they needed to have wives, and if they were too old to do hard manual labour, they needed to have sons to do the work. Over time some fullholders fell ill, succumbed to alcoholism, or grew old and infirm. Some died, or their sons died or moved away, or they simply proved incapable of meeting the demands of frontier agriculture. The question of what then to do with their fullholdings was important for the economic health of the settlement and for its ability to uphold its role as a model community.

Several factors affected land transfers. By law, the fullholdings could not be subdivided, and this meant that landholdings remained large enough to be economically viable. By comparison, in other peasant villages in the region landholdings shrank as the population grew and the land was divided equally among a landowner's heirs. As individual holdings grew smaller, agriculture became less efficient, leading eventually to poverty. Meanwhile, the population in the Mennonite villages was growing, and by the 1830s there were increasing numbers of landless Mennonites. The efforts of Cornies and others to alleviate this problem are discussed in more detail in chapter 7.

A second important factor was Russian law, which dictated that the landholdings could not be subdivided and also insisted that all land transfers be approved by the Guardianship Committee. This ensured that whether Mennonites liked it or not, the state would play a role in the single most important economic issue in the settlement. The question was not *if* the state would regulate landholdings, but *how*.

A third factor was Mennonite tradition. In Poland, Mennonites were relatively free to use and dispose of land as they wished. This changed when Prussia expanded its authority into Poland in the late eighteenth century; indeed, many of the Mennonites who immigrated to Russia did so to escape the new restrictions in Prussia. Those who came to Russia to acquire land could hardly be happy to see their right to dispose of that land limited by the state.

One consequence of Nicholas I's reforms was that the state began to pay much closer attention to the disposition of agricultural land. This was not confined to the Mennonites: after the Great Drought the state was paying closer attention to *all* residents in the Molochnaia region, even to the extent of imposing land repartition on Slavic peasants, and similar efforts extended across the empire.[29] The policies being applied in the Mennonite settlement were consistent with broader state policies during this era of small reforms, from which no one was exempt. The difference was that Mennonites, unlike Slavic peasants, were allowed to have a say in the process.

When the Forestry Society began to inspect afforestation in the Mennonite settlement, it discovered that fullholdings had been sold without regard for the laws that required state approval. As long as the settlement had land to spare and the state's attention was focused elsewhere, the question of how land changed hands attracted little attention. When the Forestry Society did begin paying attention it discovered widespread unauthorized land transfers. Cornies reported to Fadeev in March 1833 that at least 100 fullholdings had changed hands without formal approval in the previous year alone.[30] This high turnover was probably a recent phenomenon: the first generation of immigrants was growing old and selling land to a younger generation; at the same time, the rapidly growing population was driving a high demand for fullholdings.[31]

At a March 1833 meeting the Forestry Society raised questions about unauthorized land sales, and the *Gebietsamt* responded that it assumed that it would satisfy legal requirements by reporting the transfers verbally to Fadeev the next time he visited the settlement. Cornies was unconvinced and sent a letter to Fadeev suggesting that the Forestry Society craft a standardized written contract that would define the obligations of people who acquired fullholdings. The contract the society developed and implemented in early 1834 with the support of the Guardianship Committee contained a generic commitment by new fullholders to fulfil all "conditions for takeovers in the regulations" as well as a more specific agreement to abide by "all prescribed rules and written orders issued by the Forestry Society ... On the hearth site I have taken over, I will increase plantings yearly until the whole area assigned for orchard and forest-tree cultivation is completely planted according to regulations, and the trees are growing well."[32]

This contract is a prime example of how the Forestry Society – and through it, the state – expanded its authority in the Mennonite settlement. While the contract was technically merely an affirmation of existing regulations, in truth it imposed controls where none had existed previously. Before 1834, Molochnaia fullholders had acted as landowners with apparently unconstrained rights to buy, sell, and transfer their fullholdings, at least to other Mennonites. With the new contract, the state had formalized its control of land transfers in a way that demanded explicit written approval. It had also made the Forestry Society the principal agent for approving land transfers. While the society's formal authority was over tree planting, where the contract specified "conditions for takeovers in the regulations" it was arrogating to itself much broader authority. In 1837, the local regulations created by the Forestry Society in 1834 were codified into new and more prescriptive Guardianship Committee regulations.[33]

The Forestry Society was also flexing its muscles in the area where it enjoyed explicit authority, tree planting. By 1834 the society's strict requirement that fullholders plant particular trees in particular ways to a particular schedule, combined with its general insensitivity to the hardships of the drought, was provoking open defiance from some fullholders. The most famous example, recounted by P.M. Friesen, is of a certain "Mayor T" from the "village of F" (almost certainly Dirk Thun of Fürstenwerder). Thun met the letter of Forestry Society orders, but in an act of defiance he planted his trees upside down. When Cornies and other society members inspected the village, they found the dead roots of Thun's trees waving in the air. The society reported Thun to his congregation, which banned him as punishment.[34]

Other famous reports of fullholder defiance describe an increasingly impatient Cornies imperiously demanding compliance with society policies. One oft-repeated instance is recounted by Heinrich Goerz: "The story is told of a lazy farmer who had not planted the prescribed number of trees on his farm. After a time, representatives of the society arrived to inspect the plantings. They went into the garden and when the farmer bent down to look for the trees among the weeds – trees which were not there because they had never been planted – the passing chairman gave him several sharp whacks across the seat of his trousers."[35]

Such colourful accounts have become part of Mennonite lore, and they undoubtedly reflect Cornies's domineering manner by the mid-1830s. Still, the scandalous reports of protest and defiance, and of Cornies's harsh response, leave an impression of revolt that is not supported by the records of the Forestry Society, at least before 1836. In fact, the surviving reports of annual society inspections suggest that the vast majority of fullholders were cooperating fully in the program. Some fullholders misunderstood either planting methods or the reporting requirements that went with them, but the Forestry Society's normal response in such instances was to educate rather than punish the fullholders.[36] In other cases, the society subjected fullholders to small monetary fines, and, in extreme instances, to extra communal duties such as dam or road maintenance. The vast majority of Forestry Society reports suggest that defiance of the type credited to Thun was a rare exception.

Equally rare – but probably far more contentious from the perspective of Cornies's opponents – were those occasions when the society identified fullholdings that had fallen into disrepair. Unlike afforestation, this was not explicitly part of the society's mandate. It had the right to insist that all fullholders plant trees, and when it identified failing fullholdings it was probably doing this, but the tone of the reports suggests a more substantial concern. From Cornies's perspective fullholders were obliged to be model farmers, and the Forestry Society reminded village and district mayors of their responsibility to ensure that fullholdings were properly maintained. The society was extending its influence beyond what its charter envisioned and toward the broad authority that the land transfer contracts hinted at.

Reports of failing fullholdings were never large in number, though the number increased over time. The record of an 1836 inspection of villages along the Kurushan Stream and Iushanle River demonstrates the expanding demands and insistent tone of the Forestry Society. It reported concerns about twenty-two fullholders, most of whom the society characterized as beyond redemption. Dirk Boldt of Neukirch was "a slacker ... addicted to drink"; Jacob Baerg of Marienthal was "unmotivated and [had] no prospects"; in Wernersdorf there was "no hope for improvement in the farming of three householders, Kaethler, Engbrecht and Giesbrecht."[37]

In all of these cases, Forestry Society concerns extended beyond trees, and its solution to the problems went far beyond the letter of the society charter: again and again it urged that the landowners be forced to give up their fullholdings. It asked, "Would it not be better if Franz Voht's and Klaas Ennz's hearth sites [in Rückenau] were assigned to others?" It urged that the property of one Dahlke in Alexanderwohl "be turned over to his son-in-law." It insisted that Jacob Nickel and Heinrich Quiring of Schardau "must give their fullholdings to others."[38]

The Forestry Society lacked the authority to compel fullholders to sell their property; it could only pressure village offices to take action. When those offices failed to do so, the society turned to the *Gebietsamt*.[39] Notably missing from this process was the congregational leadership, and this portended the political battle to come. The Forestry Society could neither force the transfer of fullholdings through civil authority nor bring pressure from the church to bear. It would need to expand its authority to do more, and that expansion was going to be controversial.

The Agricultural Society

The 1834 reorganization of the Guardianship Committee that closed the Ekaterinoslav office and transferred Fadeev to Odesa was described in a previous section. In early nineteenth-century Russia such a change could have a significant impact, for geographical distance slowed the pace of communications and left local authorities freer to exercise their arbitrary whims. Cornies felt the change keenly and complained about it to Fadeev, who counselled caution. As long as Fadeev was still at the Odesa bureau he continued to support Cornies, but in late 1835 word of a more momentous change reached the Mennonites: Fadeev was being transferred to Astrakhan as Guardian of the Kalmyk Tatars.[40]

Cornies immediately recognized the significance of this change. He relied on the power of the state to push through his plans, and that power was rooted in his personal relationship with Fadeev. Cornies now scrambled to prepare for a transfer of allegiance, asking Fadeev to do all in his power to ensure that he would have the ear of the authorities in Odesa. At the same time, he rushed to push through one last major project while Fadeev remained in Odesa.

In 1834 Fadeev and Cornies had begun discussing the creation of a Molochnaia organization modelled on the Forestry Society but with far broader scope and power. They envisioned an agency that would oversee the entire economic life of the Molochnaia Mennonites with authority to closely supervise all agricultural affairs. Fadeev wanted to press forward with the new plan in 1834, but Cornies convinced him that the Great Drought and the resulting Mennonite opposition to the Forestry Society made it unwise to move too quickly. When word came of Fadeev's imminent departure, both Cornies and Fadeev realized that it was now or never, for Fadeev told Cornies that he would "no longer be able, as before, to cooperate in advancing the well-being of the Molochnaia Mennonite District."[41]

Cornies's response to Fadeev's letter is lost, but some sense of its tenor is apparent from Fadeev's next letter: "Yes," the never-modest Fadeev agreed, his transfer imperilled "the future well-being of the Molochnaia Mennonite community and the giant strides made in its plantings ... But I will never cease to take an active interest in your community's well-being and will promote its arrangements with continued vigour."[42] The correspondence that followed reveals the complex interweaving of personal and public interests in tsarist frontier administration. The letters criss-crossed each other across the steppe between Odesa and Ohrloff, so it is difficult to clearly identify a chronology of requests and promises, but the general intent is apparent. Fadeev promised his continuing support for Cornies, the Forestry Society, and community interests, and at the same time he asked what he could do for Cornies personally. Cornies suggested that it might be helpful if General Ivan N. Inzov, head of the Guardianship Committee, "were to send a communication forcefully reminding all preachers that, being in possession of sixty-five desiatinas of land, they must serve in the orderly care of their plantations as examples to others in their community. And by admonishing community members to obey orders from the society in a timely fashion, they are required to support the society when difficulties occur."[43] In the same letter he asked whether Fadeev could advance his decade-long quest to acquire ownership of his 3,800 *desiatinas* of leased land at Iushanle.[44] Fadeev responded with a personal request of his own – could Cornies lend him 1,500 or 2,000 rubles to cover moving expenses?[45] Cornies agreed to the loan and also offered to hire horses and wagons for Fadeev's journey.[46] A few days later Fadeev reported to Cornies that Inzov was sending an "exhortation" to the church leaders; he added that efforts were under way to secure the Iushanle land for him and that he should be patient.[47] Cornies thanked Fadeev for his counsel, and at the end of February he turned to the big question regarding the Mennonites' future: "The time has perhaps arrived to establish a society with responsibilities for the improvement of field cultivation, pasture crops and farm implements ... I therefore respectfully submit for Yr. Honour's wise consideration my humble opinion that the existing [Forestry Society] pursue the improvement in all branches of field cultivation in this district."[48]

Fadeev took the proposal to Inzov, who approved it in March 1836. The new society, established on 1 May 1836, was an affirmation of Cornies's expanding authority and influence.[49] In 1824, Contenius had created the Wool Improvement Society, providing detailed instructions on its structure and activities. He then hand-picked Cornies as its chair-for-life and insisted that Cornies report extensively on his activities and successes. The Forestry Society was also Contenius's idea, although by the time it was established he was dead – it was Fadeev who would play the central role in formulating its charter. Again it was the state that laid out this society's mission and activities, although this time the Guardianship Committee consulted with Cornies and his closest associates about the society charter, signalling Cornies's growing role as political broker for his community.[50] The new Agricultural Society would have much greater authority than the Forestry Society, ultimately governing the economic activities of Molochnaia Mennonites. Inzov granted Cornies virtually free rein in defining the new society's authority in internal Mennonite economic affairs.[51]

Administrative Reforms and Molochnaia Politics

It was Fadeev's pending departure that triggered the creation of the Agricultural Society. Inzov played along in part because by now, in 1836, the Russian government was gripped by a desire for reform.[52] In that year Tsar Nicholas established the Fifth Department of the Tsar's Own Chancellery, which in 1838 became the Ministry of State Domains. Its mandate was to thoroughly reform the administration of the state peasants. Nicholas planned to extend tight state control down to the lowest levels of society, to the roughly 40 per cent of Russian peasants who fell into this legal category. For most state peasants this had no immediate impact; in practice the new department and then ministry focused on assessing the condition of the peasantry, which involved conducting surveys across the empire. These surveys were important – as historian W. Bruce Lincoln has shown, they provided both data about peasants and training for a generation of young "enlightened bureaucrats" who would help shape the Great Reforms of the 1860s. However, there is little evidence that the ministry had much impact on most peasants in the 1830s and 1840s.[53]

In the Molochnaia the story was different, for here was a group of people who were organized, literate, had a well-established and efficient local administration, and were responsive to state reform projects. Johann Cornies, his allies, and his community were poised to become the showcase of the new reform agenda – the Russian Empire's most important laboratory of modernization, a beachhead in the emerging effort to reshape and standardize imperial policy. Of course such great successes were still in the future, and in 1836 they were far from certain. First came a fierce contest for leadership in the community between Cornies and Warkentin.

This political battle was a continuation of the contest that had begun in the early 1820s. Politics were part of life in the Molochnaia: the

Mennonites had an electoral system, a *Gebietsamt* with a meaningful role in local administration, and two meaningful political alliances. Jacob Warkentin led the conservative alliance. Warkentin has long been directly equated with the Large Flemish Congregation, and that congregation was certainly his power base. However, even though more than half the Molochnaia Mennonite fullholders were members of the Large Flemish Congregation, the elected leaders in the *Gebietsamt* were sometimes *not* members of that congregation, and election results indicate that some members of the Large Flemish Congregation did not vote for Warkentin's candidates. Warkentin was powerful, and his power was based in the Large Flemish Congregation, but the two things were not coterminous. In terms of his political activities, it is more apt to think of a smaller Warkentin Party.

Despite what Cornies would eventually claim, the Warkentin Party's conservatism mainly pertained to religion, and they did not really oppose all state intervention in Mennonite affairs. Like all Molochnaia Mennonites, they recognized the tsar's sovereignty over worldly affairs. This is evident in their attitude toward the Privilegium, the symbolic centrepiece of Molochnaia Mennonite politics. The Warkentin Party argued that the tsar had clearly established the privileges and obligations of Mennonites, and they attempted to employ the Privilegium – and hence the tsar's authority – as a bulwark against the changes they opposed. In 1838 and 1842 the Warkentin Party approached the tsarist administration seeking state support for its position.

The Warkentin Party's primary concern was the right of the state and its agencies – among which it included the Forestry and Agricultural Societies – to interfere in the private affairs of Mennonite families. It argued that the Privilegium, in holding up Mennonites as a model for other state peasants, had certified their way of life and secured it from state intrusion. As long as the Mennonites remained stable and productive they were fulfilling their part of the bargain and should be free to live their private lives free of state interference.[54]

The crux of the matter was the relationship between the economic activities of Mennonite families and their religious lives. The state was willing to allow Mennonites their eccentric religious practices as long as the Mennonites performed as economic models. However, in the 1830s the state was aggressively reforming the state peasantry's economy. When Tsar Nicholas turned his back on the West and its revolutionary fervour, he also turned his back on the emerging Western industrial economic model. Instead he looked to agriculture as a bastion of social stability. If that agricultural economy was going to support a powerful, modern authoritarian state, it would need to become far more productive. Thus the drive for agricultural productivity was central to Nicholas's reform agenda.[55] He would honour his father's bargain with the Mennonites to permit them religious freedom so long – but only so long – as the Mennonites honoured the bargain by modelling progressive agricultural methods.

The Warkentin Party argued that the economic activities of Mennonite families were a reflection of their religious beliefs. The very justification for Mennonite immigration to Russia was, they claimed, rooted in this idea. Mennonite communities were meant to echo early Christian communities, separated from "the world." The communities, in their orderly lives, offered no threat to the tsar, but they were only models insofar as their quiet, industrious, independent activities were desirable for all Russian state peasants. The state had no right to demand change from such communities.

Warkentin's supporters were not demanding a rejection of modern technology. Many of them were prosperous farmers who happily invested in modern farming equipment and adopted modern farming techniques. The issue was not technology – it was the right of families to decide on their own how and when to change. They wanted independence from intrusive state economic policies, and in the context of the crises of the 1830s, this was perfectly understandable. The Great Drought had placed enormous strains on the Molochnaia economy, and this was hardly a propitious time for wholesale change. Cornies's lack of sensitivity to those strains only made matters worse. The result was strong support for Warkentin just at the time when the state was becoming more insistent on change, and just at the time when the state's strongest Mennonite ally, Cornies, was weakened by the departure of Fadeev.

The second key political alliance in the Molochnaia was the Cornies Party. Its most prominent members were prosperous merchants and business owners, who included Wilhelm Martens; Johann Klassen, who owned the Halbstadt cloth mill; and Cornies's brother-in-law Johann Neufeld, who managed Cornies's and Martens' brandy distribution business (in which he later became a partner) and also provided important currency exchange services to the community. All of the members of the Forestry Society and Agricultural Society were members of the Cornies Party.

The hostility between Cornies and Warkentin dated back to the founding of the Christian School Society and the Molochnaia branch of the Russian Bible Society in the early 1820s. Its renewal in the 1830s can be seen as a direct response to the interference of the Forestry Society and Agricultural Society in the affairs of fullholders. As described earlier, that interference focused on the allocation and use of land.

Both Warkentin and Cornies identified the Privilegium as central to the dispute. For Mennonites it had a quasi-constitutional character, being a legal document that defined their relationship to the state. To justify his reforms, Cornies invoked the Privilegium's requirement that Mennonites act as models. In 1837, Warkentin travelled to the Khortitsa Mennonite settlement to examine the original copy of the document, apparently seeking support for his opposition to reforms.[56] It would be an error, however, to suppose that either Warkentin or Cornies naively believed that the Privilegium could constrain the tsar's arbitrary authority to dictate and change policy toward the Mennonites. Rather, both saw it as the basis of a negotiated relationship between the Mennonites and the tsarist state, and what they fought over was the right to represent the Mennonites in that negotiation.

When Tsar Nicholas travelled to Crimea in 1837, Cornies pursued an audience with him with the express purpose of asking him to reconfirm the Privilegium. He would "present the monarch with a humble submission of thanks from the whole Mennonite brotherhood and ... petition him for a confirmation of our privileges."[57] Cornies, along with congregational elders Bernhard Fast and Wilhelm Lange, comprised the delegation. Warkentin, elder of the community's largest congregation, was notably absent, as were any representatives of the Khortitsa Mennonite settlement.

On 15 September 1837, Cornies wrote to Fadeev with evident pride about the meeting: "His Majesty kindly accepted our community's written expression of gratitude and its request that its [Privilegium] be confirmed. He graciously condescended to ask us a number of questions. Turning to me, he expressed himself in these words: 'I must thank you in particular. You have become useful to the state.'"[58]

This stress on Cornies's *usefulness* indicates that his interpretation of the Privilegium was in tune with the tsar's. The point was driven home on 16–17 October 1837, when Crown Prince Alexander – the future Tsar Alexander II – visited the Molochnaia Mennonite settlement. At Iushanle he deigned to meet Cornies's children (Aganetha was sick at home in Ohrloff) before asking Cornies to give him a personal tour of the model farm. Alexander was scheduled to breakfast at Iushanle and then move on to Steinbach, but as Cornies proudly reported to Fadeev, "a complete midday meal developed out of the breakfast, and hardly an hour was spent at the dinner table in Steinbach."[59]

Cornies also gave Alexander a tour of the Nogai village of Akkerman. This village was a clear expression of Cornies's plans to "civilize" the Nogais that he first described in his 1826 report. By 1833 he had begun working to improve Nogai agriculture through a program of lending merino sheep to some Nogai householders in what amounted to a sharecropping arrangement, albeit on terms that were very generous to the Nogais. His intention was to slowly improve the quality of Nogai herds on the assumption that Nogai leaders would become enmeshed in wool markets and thereby "civilize" themselves. At the same time he hatched a more elaborate plan, of transforming the Nogai village of Akkerman into a model village.[60]

Akkerman was Cornies's vision of an orderly peasant village, intended to erase the physical manifestations of Nogai culture in the region. He helped select the village site, planned the layout of the home plots, streets, and fields, and offered systematic instruction on the proper balance between grain crops and livestock. The assumption was that people forced to order their lives within "civilized" boundaries would become "civilized," and that, as the obvious merits of civilization became evident, other Nogais would imitate Akkerman.[61] Cornies's plan for Akkerman amounts to a depiction of what he understood to be the aesthetics of civilization. It was not enough that the Nogais grow grain and raise fine-wooled sheep – it was also necessary that their homes and villages take on the appearance of their "civilized" counterparts. Cornies described precisely what a "civilized," orderly village and its individual homes should look like, from the dimensions of front porches to a requirement that doors, shutters, and window-frames be properly painted.[62] Cornies used Akkerman as a showcase for the Mennonite laboratory of modernization, and the crown prince was exactly the audience Cornies had in mind. Alexander visited a Nogai home in the village, praised it warmly, and awarded the Nogai homeowner 100 rubles as a show of approval. In coming years a stop in Akkerman would become standard fare for official visitors to the Mennonite settlement.

While Cornies courted Russian leaders, Warkentin focused his political efforts closer to home. By 1837 the resistance of individual Mennonites to the Agricultural Society's orders began to grow and become more organized. Cornies's opponents spread rumours about the society and its allies in the *Gebietsamt*, claiming that they "no longer care about the foundation of their confession of faith and are therefore tyrants, forsaken by God."[63] Some Mennonite fullholders defied society orders on the grounds that the society had no right to tell them how to manage their personal affairs. They apparently received support in this from congregational elders, for in February 1837 the society and the *Gebietsamt* jointly sent an angry remonstration to Benjamin Ratzlaff, Wilhelm Lange, Peter Wedel, and Bernhard Fast – usually supporters of Cornies – reminding them of their responsibility to ensure that their congregations complied with society orders.[64] This was soon followed by fence-mending and a circular from the society claiming that Warkentin and his supporters had spread false rumours about Lange's position. The circular denounced the spreaders of "insults or fabrications" and threatened that if such malicious lies continued, the perpetrators would be punished.[65]

The Warkentin Party's attacks focused not only on Cornies and the Agricultural Society but also on the *Gebietsamt*. Cornies had learned from his political failures in 1826 and was working hard to forge an alliance with *Gebietsamt* leaders. The Agricultural Society charter differed from the Forestry Society charter, which barred *Gebietsamt* officials from membership. Cornies successfully lobbied Inzov to have the district chair, Johann Regier, appointed as a founding member of the Agricultural Society. By 1836, Regier and his deputy Abram Toews were important members of the Cornies Party.

By this point Cornies had found another important political ally, this time of much higher status, a senior state official named Petr Keppen, who would have a strong impact on Cornies's future successes. Keppen worked in Crimea in the 1820s, where he became a close friend of Christian Steven, the famous botanist who was instrumental in documenting Crimean flora and fauna. He was fascinated by the prehistoric burial mounds that dotted southern Russia and Ukraine, and while in Crimea he pursued his passion for archaeology, travelling throughout the peninsula and sketching dozens of burial sites. It is probable that during this period he made the acquaintance of Fadeev, with whom he corresponded in the 1830s and 1840s.

Keppen returned to St. Petersburg to work in the Ministry of Internal Affairs' Department of State Domains. In 1834 he received a prestigious appointment as editor of the capital's main German-language newspaper, *Sankt-Peterburgische Zeitung*. In 1838 he became head of the Learned Committee of the Ministry of State Domains, where he helped collect and publish studies of the Russian peasantry that would influence the Great Reforms of the 1860s.[66] From the mid-1830s until his death in 1864, Keppen was an important figure in the intellectual world of Russia. His articles on archaeology and history appeared in leading journals in Russia and abroad. He helped create the Russian Imperial Geographical Society in 1846, and his ethnographic and demographic studies, particularly of the Russian census of 1851, remain important tools for historians today.[67]

Keppen's return to St. Petersburg in 1832 coincided with the formal promulgation of the policy of Official Nationality by his old acquaintance and fellow Rumiantsev protégé, Count Sergei Uvarov. For Keppen, the new policy could only spell trouble, for he was neither Slavic nor Orthodox. His academic pursuits of the 1830s can be construed as a systematic, strategic response to the challenge of Official Nationality. That response, by the sheerest coincidence, drew Cornies into Keppen's circle of friends and provided Cornies with a pathway to empire-wide recognition.

Official Nationality was conceived as a response to the dangers of romantic nationalism. While Greeks, Poles, and Spaniards were defining their national ideals along ethnocultural lines, Nicholas sought an alternative definition of Russianness, rooted primarily in loyalty to the tsar. Keppen carved out his own unique position in this debate. In articles in the *Sankt-Petersburgische Zeitung* and another St. Petersburg newspaper, *Severnaia Pchela (The Northern Bee)*, he promoted a territorial version of Russian identity. He delineated his agenda most clearly in 1837 in three articles in *Severnaia Pchela* in which he insisted that it was vital to Russia's national interests to investigate the burial mounds of prehistoric peoples, who were, Keppen argued, "Russian" by virtue of living on "Russian" territory. Understanding the history of these ancients was essential to understanding modern Russians, and indeed it was a patriotic duty to pursue their study.[68] This sharply contrasted with the Orthodox Church's increasing focus on Orthodoxy as the unifying core of Russian identity, a position that found particular prominence in Crimea, where the study of ancient Christian ruins was of growing importance to Russian nationalists.[69]

If this version of Russian national identity was self-serving for the non-Slavic, non-Orthodox, German-speaking Keppen, it was also in service to a genuine scholarly agenda. In 1834, as part of his campaign to promote the study of burial mounds, Keppen published notices in several newspapers and journals asking readers to send him information about undisturbed burial mounds in their districts. He had been carefully documenting known sites for well over a decade, but like all scholars, he wanted his own original find.

It was in 1836 that Keppen first heard of the burial mounds that lined the ridge west of the Molochnaia River. He may have learned of the mounds from his friend Fadeev, who had seen them himself on visits to the Molochnaia. Cornies had reported finds of ancient coins in the region, and this too may have piqued Keppen's interest. He had already been recruited to tour Crimea in 1837 with the royal family. He seems to have been drafted for the trip because of his deep knowledge of the region's history. Excited by the reports of burial mounds in the Molochnaia, Keppen arranged for a side trip. He arrived in Halbstadt in November, where Cornies took him in hand.[70]

Keppen's notes from his visit to the Molochnaia reveal his keen interest in Cornies's accomplishments. He visited the Iushanle estate and gushed with praise at its arrangements. After visiting the model Nogai village of Akkerman, he concluded that Cornies had struck upon the key to "civilizing" the Tatar peoples. As for the ancient burial mounds, he provided Cornies with detailed instructions for their excavation and documentation. By the time Keppen left the Molochnaia several days later, he and Cornies had struck up a lasting friendship.[71]

It is perhaps this friendship that was the most important – and surprising – result of Keppen's visit. The St. Petersburg academician and the frontier Mennonite had little in common, yet Keppen's affection for Cornies, and his subsequent loyalty to and promotion of his new friend, brought Cornies far broader influence than was otherwise likely. When Keppen returned to St. Petersburg in 1838 he recruited Cornies as a corresponding member of the Learned Committee of the Ministry of State Domains, which was charged with "considering matters that required special scholarly attention."[72] This appointment gave Cornies new status, for most corresponding members were high-ranking provincial bureaucrats, and some were prestigious academics from Russia and Western Europe.[73] Keppen's arrival could not have come at a better moment for Cornies, for in 1837 he badly needed a patron to replace Fadeev. It did not hurt that, with the Guardianship Committee in decline, he had found his new patron in the influential Fifth Department, soon to become the Ministry of State Domains.

Cornies demonstrated his understanding of the importance of such patronage in a December 1837 letter to Fadeev, in which he reported that he had presented Keppen with his "heartfelt requests for changes in our administration," and Keppen had proven willing to take up the cause, asking Cornies to lay out the issues in writing. Cornies now asked Fadeev for help, for he

> feared that we were not knowledgeable enough about the relationship of the Mennonites to the state and about the views of the state regarding the citizenship of our local Mennonites. We therefore feared that we might raise points that could not possibly be approved or that would show us to be so biased in our wishes that we might be deemed unthankful inhabitants. Collectively, Mennonites are fortunate to be able to enjoy advantages greater than those accorded to other settlers in the empire. You, Yr. Honour and State Councillor, know our conditions concretely. Equally, you know the manner and extent to which Mennonites are useful to the state, and thus worthy of exceptions from the general principles governing the status of settlers. Mennonites are keen in spirit and zealous to demonstrate

through deeds that the state did not act in vain in granting them such great advantages over other settlers.[74]

By the end of 1837, Cornies had marshalled allies at every level of the administration to back his reform plans. Warkentin had no similar allies, but he had important support in the Mennonite settlement, and it was there that a key contest was played out in the *Gebietsamt* elections of 1838. The energy that Cornies and Warkentin invested in those elections serves as a reminder of how important local administrative offices were on the frontier. Regardless of the autocratic authority of the tsar and his officials, in the Molochnaia, elected *Gebietsamt* officials were essential agents of tsarist authority without whom no real reform was possible.

The reason the position of district mayor was so important lies in the office's administrative function. Mayors were not policy-makers, and the elections were consequently not about controlling the creation of policy, which came from the state. However, a district mayor who did *not* actively carry out state policy could be a roadblock to state plans. For evidence of this one need look no further than the non-Mennonite peasant villages in the Molochnaia, where state policies foundered on the lack of active local leadership. Cornies described such peasants as "unenlightened, indolent and too attached to tradition to achieve [state goals]. They reject everything new with loathing and prejudice."[75] While peasant agricultural practices were likely more rational than Cornies allowed, there is little doubt of the peasants' persistent resistance to state reform plans. The tsarist state, with its ineffective bureaucracy, could not provide good local administration, and village and district mayors offered no substitute. That is why, despite his efforts to bring about large-scale reforms through his Ministry of State Domains, Tsar Nicholas's plans led almost nowhere.

The Mennonites had no desire to become just another bunch of intransigent state peasants. Even their most conservative members – the Warkentin Party – were in agreement that they needed to retain the distinct status granted them under the Privilegium. That is what made the Privilegium so central to Molochnaia politics for all parties. What Warkentin and his supporters failed to recognize, and what Cornies recognized very clearly, was that the Nicholaevan state was unhappy with exceptions like the Mennonites. The entire bureaucratic thrust of Nicholas's reforms was to impose uniformity. If Mennonites were going to keep their privileges they were going to have to earn them.

In this context, it might be fair to say that by 1838 the Warkentin Party faced a no-win situation. If they won the *Gebietsamt* elections, they would use the mayoral office to block reform, making state intervention and a loss of Mennonite privileges likely; if they lost the elections, Cornies would use the mayoral office to impose the reforms they opposed.

Cornies's correspondence provides what little we know about the 1838 elections. In April he told Fadeev that Warkentin was employing "underhanded means" to oust District Mayor Johann Regier and Senior Deputy Mayor Abram Toews, both stalwart Cornies Party members, and replace them with Warkentin's "close relative" and loyal supporter, Second Deputy Mayor Driedger. Cornies warned that this would be "detrimental to all aspects of the community's well-being. You, Yr. Honour and esteemed State Councillor, are quite well acquainted with the attitudes of church Elder Warkentin. You know that Gebietsamt affairs cannot proceed in accordance with his attitudes and must not be allowed to do so if our morality and well-being are to be advanced."[76]

Cornies asked Fadeev to use his influence to have the Guardianship Committee cancel the elections and reappoint Friesen and Toews for another three years. He assured Fadeev that this move would be supported in the settlement, for all the congregational elders except Warkentin wanted Regier and Toews retain their posts.[77]

Fadeev advised Cornies to take up the matter directly with the Chief Guardian, General Inzov, and promised his support.[78] Cornies wrote to Inzov in July, telling him that "the firm measures and sense of orderliness of [Regier and Toews] are repugnant to" Warkentin. He urged Inzov to cancel the elections and reappoint Regier and Toews for a further three-year term.

Warkentin also appealed to Inzov, offering a starkly different version of the situation. He claimed that Regier was an alcoholic who, in violation of Mennonite beliefs and customs, was employing corporal punishment to enforce Cornies's orders. He said that Regier was no longer competent to fill his post and asked Inzov to permit his replacement.[79] Whether Warkentin's accusations were true is difficult to ascertain. There are other accounts that confirm Regier's excessive drinking, but there is no explicit evidence that it affected his administrative duties. Still other accounts confirm that some Mennonites who defied Agricultural Society orders were subject to corporal punishment, but according to P.M. Friesen, such punishments were ordered by the state and not Regier, who relied on fines and normal congregational disciplinary practices such as the ban to enforce society orders.[80]

Inzov backed Cornies and issued a stern letter to the leaders of the five Molochnaia congregations reminding them of their duties. As Cornies phrased it, "this had a salutary effect on the whole community."[81] Inzov did not cancel the elections, but he did give a strong indication of the results he expected, and in the end the settlement re-elected Regier and Toews with large majorities.[82]

This was a major political victory for Cornies. Warkentin's candidates had won every mayoral election since 1826, but now Cornies had emerged as a strong challenger to Warkentin's political dominance. The contest was by no means settled, for Cornies would not have needed to invoke Guardianship Committee authority had he been fully confident of his ability to win a straightforward election. On the other hand – as the settlement would prove three years later – Molochnaia Mennonite fullholders were prepared to defy Guardianship Committee wishes if they felt strongly enough about the issues, so by the time of the 1838 elections, Cornies had accrued significant support among the fullholders.

Conclusion

Changes in state policy and administrative structures had a strong ripple effect in the Molochnaia Mennonite settlement in the 1830s. Scholarly accounts of Official Nationality have focused mainly on its impact on Russian elites, but the Mennonite case shows that it had broader consequences. Tsar Nicholas's desire to gain a firm grip on his colonial communities as part of a broader policy of small reforms provides context to the reorganization of the Guardianship Committee in 1834. Fadeev's transfer to Odesa threatened to weaken Cornies, and that spurred him to press for an expansion of his authority through the creation of the Agricultural Society in 1836. The Fifth Department, the forerunner of the Ministry of State Domains, was created in 1836 for the purpose of addressing peasant issues more broadly; its founding signalled major shifts in the state's colonial goals and strategies that also affected the Mennonites. The state's desire to transform the peasant economy, in tandem with the consolidating impetus of Official Nationality, posed a fundamental challenge to the passive Mennonite model as a tool to promote modernization. Nicholas and his enlightened bureaucrats were poised to abandon the passive model and activate the Mennonites as a laboratory of modernization.

Cornies welcomed the change and wedded himself to the state's reformist agenda with the creation of the Agricultural Society in 1836. This does not mean he was prepared to abandon the Mennonites' religious beliefs or cultural identity; indeed, he believed that cooperation with the state was the only way to defend the Mennonite community's identity and privileges.

External threats were not the only challenge to Mennonite identity, however. Internally, the community's core religious values were being fiercely contested. When Warkentin fought against state intervention, he was defending what he saw as a central tenet of Mennonite faith, their conscious imitation of early Christian communities. Cornies's reforms impinged on the authority of the congregational elders, and from Warkentin's perspective this amounted to an attack on the Mennonites' religious identity.

In 1838 Warkentin responded to Cornies by attempting to wrest back control of the community through *Gebietsamt* elections. Cornies won this confrontation, but in doing so he invoked the authority of the Guardianship Committee. For the time being this satisfied the state by ensuring that Cornies's reforms continued, but it had the effect of driving an even deeper wedge into the community. Cornies was now empowered to pursue reforms with all of his energy. Warkentin would be no less energetic in defending Mennonite tradition.

Chapter Seven

"A Useful Man," 1838–1842

The creation of the Agricultural Society in 1836 and the victory of the pro-Cornies mayor Johann Regier in 1838 gave Cornies the power to aggressively pursue his economic reform agenda. One consequence was the bitter political battle of 1841–2 known as the "Warkentin Affair," which is described in chapter 8. The economic reforms discussed in the present chapter helped foment the political crisis, so the treatment of the Warkentin Affair separately imposes an artificial distinction between the two, but the complexities of both subjects demand such an approach.

This was a period of intense activity for Cornies: the state recognized his potential and placed enormous demands on his time and energy. Cornies rose to the occasion in ways that had far-reaching implications for both the Mennonite community and the state. In the Molochnaia he pressed forward with a transformation to market-oriented crop agriculture, and at Iushanle he experimented with a wide variety of new crops. Recognizing the looming problem of landlessness in his community, he advocated for a diversification of the Molochnaia economy through the creation of a crafts village beside Halbstadt. He also became the state's local watchdog over events in the soon-to-be-exiled Doukhobor community, trying to act as an intermediary. He continued to work to "civilize" his Nogai neighbours, and he offered his expert advice on efforts to reform the Kalmyk Tatar community that Fadeev now oversaw. Farther afield, he began a long correspondence with the Moravian Brethren community at Sarepta, offering advice and aid to its floundering economy.

All of this came at a cost for Cornies and for his community. The state's growing demands absorbed more and more of his time, isolating him and giving credence to his critics' claims that he had become an agent of the state. Cornies believed – probably correctly – that Mennonites could only preserve their privileges if they cooperated with the state, and he struggled to find the balance between cooperation and co-option.

Personal Challenges

Cornies's difficult personal life in this period must have contributed to the ways that he dealt with public controversies. In April 1839 his wife Aganetha fell seriously ill. Cornies's letters to friends and family through that summer and fall reported on her poor health and slow recovery. This was the beginning of a long decline that saw her bedridden for months at a time, near death in November 1841, and by 1843 afflicted with a cough that never fully left her.

Cornies's relationship with his wife is almost wholly unknown to us; their communication was mostly in their own home, and the letters he wrote to her while travelling are lost. Clearly he loved her deeply, and the general attitude he expressed about romantic love, described in chapter 2, undoubtedly reflected his feelings toward her. After Aganetha died in 1847, he told a friend that he was "terribly isolated and downcast."[1]

Aganetha's was not the only illness that preoccupied Cornies. His close friend Wilhelm Martens was also slipping away from him. Martens suffered from what Cornies called "hypochondria," a condition that, in early nineteenth-century parlance, probably meant bouts of severe depression, accompanied by manic periods of irrational anger and indecision.[2] The earliest known manifestation of Martens's illness came in 1830 when he sold his iron mill in Bol'shoi Tokmak to a Russian merchant, then immediately demanded the return of the mill.[3] Martens succeeded in repurchasing his mill, but when a similar incident happened in 1840 – this time, regarding the sale of a water mill to a German colonist named Schellenberg – despite the intercession of friends and family, the new owner would not sell the mill back. Cornies counselled Martens that any effort to force Schellenberg would be "a great injustice," and he urged his friend to "try to dismiss the mill from your thoughts."[4]

In January 1837, Cornies reported to Fadeev that Martens had suffered another severe attack of hypochondria.[5] He never fully recovered. In May, Cornies wrote that Martens was becoming "an indescribable burden to himself and his whole house," and Fadeev urged Cornies to send Martens to Piatigorsk in the Caucasus, where the mineral waters were reputed to have miraculous healing powers.[6] At first Martens refused, and for months he would not leave his home. When Crown Prince Alexander visited the Molochnaia in October, Martens briefly emerged to meet the future tsar at Iushanle. Alexander's personal physician examined him and recommended as well that Martens try the Piatigorsk waters, but it was only the following April that Cornies finally convinced his friend to take the cure.[7] Martens spent the summer and early fall there, returning in September temporarily recovered, but by spring he was again acting impulsively. Over the following seven years Martens was more often ill than well, and Cornies did his best to help his friend and his family cope. On 11 June 1845, Martens hanged himself.

Martens was Cornies's closest friend and ally and an important member of the Cornies Party. He was a member of the Agricultural Society, and while he did not play a significant administrative role, he lent his influence – backed by his enormous wealth – to society initiatives. However, as the society and Cornies headed into the years of their greatest influence and controversy, Martens could no longer offer Cornies either personal or public support. By 1838, Martens's son Jacob had replaced him in the Agricultural Society. Jacob was a much more active member of the society than Wilhelm had ever been, but he could hardly be a substitute for Cornies's oldest friend.

If the illnesses of his wife and of his best friend were Cornies's most difficult personal burdens after 1837, his son's failure to show aptitude for business and community affairs also weighed heavily upon him. Johann Jr. returned from Moscow in the late summer of 1836. On the way home, he spent three months in the Moravian Brethren community of Sarepta, then travelled on to Astrakhan to visit Fadeev.[8] That fall Cornies put him to work surveying orchard sites for the Agricultural Society, but the results of his work go unmentioned in surviving society correspondence.[9] Over the next two years he did odd jobs for his father, none of them particularly significant. In 1838, he was twenty-six and still not married – a fact sufficiently unusual that Cornies saw fit to comment on it in a letter to Fadeev.[10] In October 1839, Johann Jr. travelled to Prussia to study the benefits of barn-feeding sheep.[11] Apparently, Cornies by then had given up on making a leader of his son, for there is no indication after 1839 that Johann Jr. played any meaningful role in either community affairs or his father's business affairs. Johann Jr. married Justina Willms, a stepdaughter of Wilhelm Martens, in 1841; the couple had two children, Johann, born 31 December 1843, and Justina, born 7 May 1846. Justina died shortly after giving birth to their daughter.[12] The couple lived at Tashchenak, apparently disengaged from the affairs of the Mennonite settlement.

Cornies's daughter Agnes was made of sterner stuff. Her life is even harder to trace than Johann Jr.'s, for there is no father–daughter correspondence apart from a handful of very brief letters. There are hints, however, that Agnes played an important role in family life. While Johann Jr. floundered at the Ohrloff school in the late 1820s, Agnes shone.[13] At fourteen she went off for an extended stay in Ekaterinoslav to help out her uncle Heinrich when his son fell seriously ill.[14] Remarkably, in 1835, when she was just seventeen, Cornies sent her to Moscow to visit her brother and the Blüher family.[15]

If Johann's education in Ekaterinoslav and Moscow was unusual, Agnes' travels are unique in accounts of Mennonite life from this period. Mennonite men necessarily interacted with the broader world, at markets, during travels back to Prussia, when dealing with non-Mennonite employees, and in other ways. Mennonite women lived far more constrained lives in their own communities, where their duties lay primarily within their households. Agnes's trip to Ekaterinoslav to nurse her young cousin strayed only slightly from this pattern, but her trip to Moscow was something altogether different. It suggests that Cornies genuinely meant what he wrote in 1826 regarding the mistreatment of Nogai women, as well as what he implied about the nature of women in general. This does not mean that he imagined for Agnes the worldly responsibilities of the sort he so clearly intended for Johann Jr. When he sent instructions for his children's travel home from Moscow via Sarepta, he made his views in this regard quite plain. He instructed Johann Jr. to visit all of Sarepta's institutions, travel the region and take note of its agricultural potential, and perhaps travel to Astrakhan to visit Fadeev. As for Agnes, she "might use this time to occupy herself doing something useful in the Sisters' House in Sarepta."[16]

Back in the Molochnaia in 1837, Agnes largely disappeared from Cornies's correspondence, apart from occasional reports on her health and on her role looking after the household during her mother's many illnesses. There are, however, two fragmentary notes that suggest she played an important role: in July 1837, Cornies told Daniel Schlatter that Agnes – still just nineteen – was an assistant in his "agricultural establishments," and in a letter to Fadeev in August 1838 he reported that Johann Jr. was in Tashchenak while Agnes was in Iushanle. "Both," Cornies wrote, "give me much help in managing my estates."[17] Precisely what role Agnes played is impossible to say, but it can hardly be ignored that the headquarters of all of Cornies's activities was Iushanle, not Tashchenak.

One other important figure made his appearance at Iushanle in 1838: in June, Philip Wiebe became Cornies's new personal secretary. Wiebe was young and inexperienced, and at first his role in Cornies's affairs was minor, but at a time when the roles of Cornies's wife, his best friend, and his son were all diminishing or disappointing, Wiebe would come to play a major role – and not just in the business affairs of his boss, for on 3 October 1846, he married Agnes.

Modernizing Molochnaia Agriculture

In 1836 the state opened a port at the city of Berdiansk on the Azov coast, 65 kilometres east of the Molochnaia. This transformed the regional economy by making commercial grain production viable. Until that year, transportation costs to Crimea or Mariupol made the grain trade too risky, with the result that wool, which was more valuable by weight and easier to transport, was the principal commercial product of the region. As international competition drove wool prices down in the 1840s, grain took over as the driving force of the regional economy.[18]

This change made access to the Mennonites' finite supply of viable agricultural land all the more important, and land allocation and use became the central issue for the Agricultural Society. In 1838 the society issued new, stringent conditions on land transfers, advising fullholders that it would

> not agree to the transfer of a fullholding unless ... the owner has planted a considerable number of fruit trees in the orchard according to rules and regulations, and has maintained the orchard so that it is growing well ... The fullholder's cultivated fields should be well worked and in good condition. His buildings must be in an orderly state of repair ... and cleanliness and order should be observed in and around them at all times. He must pursue potato and flax cultivation ... and his livestock should be ... kept in good condition. In general, order and diligence must be recognisable in all parts of his fullholding.[19]

In an important departure, the society's regulations for the first time explicitly addressed the phenomenon of "halfholdings." Guardianship Committee regulations forbade the subdivision of fullholdings, but demographic pressures and the lack of opportunity to acquire new land meant that Mennonites were finding ways around the rules and creating shared two-family fullholdings: one family held the formal title to the land, but two families, living in two separate houses, shared the labour and profits. The society legitimized the practice by requiring that both halfholders sign formal contracts to uphold society regulations.[20] Twenty years later, when landlessness became a political crisis in the Mennonite community, halfholdings were offered as one solution, but in fact the practice was in place by the end of 1838.[21]

By 1839 almost 60 per cent of Molochnaia Mennonite families were landless, and there were too few shared fullholdings to provide a solution for the problem.[22] Cornies's solution was to promote trades and commerce as alternative employment for the landless. As early as 1828 he warned of the "shortages produced by a lack of trade," and in 1833 he urged Fadeev to take into account the contribution of crafts and trade to the well-being of the Mennonite community.[23] He frequently made loans to small traders and artisans, and he constantly promoted Mennonite-manufactured agricultural equipment to state officials. In 1835 the Forestry Society, looking far beyond its official role, demanded that each village in the settlement set aside four or five small cottage sites for artisans.[24] There were already "cottagers" in the settlements, usually agricultural workers who lived in cottages on the home sites of fullholders; what Cornies now envisioned was permanent craft and trade sites in each village.

In 1836, Cornies expanded his vision when he proposed the creation of an entire crafts village beside Halbstadt, the settlement's administrative centre. The project struggled to gain official support until P.D. Kiselev, the Minister of State Domains, visited the Molochnaia in 1840. Before Kiselev arrived, Cornies consulted with Keppen, who encouraged him to pitch the plan to Kiselev. The minister threw his influence behind it, and by November 1841 planning and construction were under way. In the summer of 1842, Neu-Halbstadt sprang into existence. It would become the commercial hub of the settlement and ultimately of the entire region.[25]

Cornies was also centrally involved in supporting the oldest manufacturing enterprise in the Molochnaia, Johann Klassen's Halbstadt cloth factory. Established in 1818, the factory had always struggled to turn a profit, making cloth that was too poor to attract Mennonite buyers and too expensive to sell to others in the region. The factory was hit hard by the Great Drought of 1833, which devastated the region's sheep flocks and caused shortages of wool. To keep afloat, Klassen borrowed heavily, and by 1839 he owed more than 72,000 rubles to various Mennonites, including Cornies, who was his largest creditor.[26] On 1 August 1839, Klassen's troubles went from bad to worse when a fire destroyed the mill.[27]

Cornies's support of the mill had little to do with business profits – it was a marginal venture, and after the fire it was clear that he was unlikely to ever recover his money. Apart from his friendship with Klassen and Klassen's reciprocal political support, Cornies funded the mill for two reasons. First, it was part of the Mennonite model, something to be shown with pride to visitors who toured the Molochnaia. The mill was well enough known that when it burned down in 1839 the fire was reported in St. Petersburg newspapers.[28] More importantly, the factory employed landless Mennonites, an increasing concern for Cornies by the late 1830s. Cornies said that the fire threw 236 people out of work. The mill directly employed only about sixty people, so Cornies was probably including suppliers, carters, and others who relied on it less directly for their livelihood.[29] Restoring their jobs was a main reason Cornies continued to fund the mill.

Rebuilding the factory did not depend solely on Cornies; Klassen had many other creditors, and the *Gebietsamt* established a committee to deal with their claims. The factory controlled 3,000 *desiatinas* of pastureland, and part of the solution to its problems was to give the use of half of that land to creditors for several years, until their profits retired the debt.[30] While this got rid of the old debt, Klassen also needed to borrow new money. He planned to raise it within the community, but to succeed he needed Cornies's support, and he variously badgered and pleaded with Cornies to endorse the project and provide loans.[31] It was only in October 1842 that the mill reopened.

Cornies saw artisans as vital to the Molochnaia agricultural economy, but, as always, agriculture remained his central concern. He had made his money raising sheep, but by the late 1830s he regarded crop agriculture as the future. In part this was a product of experience – both the harsh winter of 1824–5 and the Great Drought of 1833–4 had decimated livestock in the region, and crop agriculture was a more reliable source of income. He was also attuned to international markets, where wool prices were falling because of rising supplies from Australia, New Zealand, and North America. A third concern was the growing population in New Russia, which was making pastureland scarcer and more expensive. None of this meant that Cornies himself was getting out of the sheep business – he owned and leased thousands of *desiatinas* of land that was only suited for pasturage, and his wealth meant he could comfortably survive shifting markets and bad weather. However, he recognized that for most Mennonite fullholders grain was a better economic bet.

A key factor in this conclusion was the opening of the port at Berdiansk in 1836. Before this, the nearest port was in Crimea, too far away to permit profitable grain exports. By comparison, wool could be cheaply and easily transported to distant markets, as Cornies had proven with his annual shipment to Moscow. As soon as Berdiansk opened, graingrowing acquired a central place in Mennonite agricultural activities, leading Cornies to write in 1839 that "the previous exaggerated interest in sheep breeding has waned. Employment in field cultivation, on the other hand, now ties everyone down to his house and his soil. As the many easy days of sheep breeding are significantly reduced we embrace a way of life in which man must literally eat his bread by the sweat of his brow."[32]

Commercial grain-growing demanded new methods and new discipline, and the Agricultural Society was ready to provide both. Its most important innovation – perhaps its single most significant contribution to Mennonite economic development ever – was the introduction of a four-field crop rotation. Cornies informed Fadeev of the decision to impose four-field agriculture in 1837, writing that the society would insist that all fullholders adopt the system within two years.[33] As long as crop agriculture was a secondary activity in the Molochnaia, fullholders either used a three-field system or simply planted a single field until the soil was exhausted and then moved to a different section of land and started over. In a semi-arid region like the Molochnaia, this approach meant less effort but also low yields. The four-field system allowed three-quarters of a fullholder's arable land to be cropped each year. The rotation ensured that the entire arable area retained enough moisture and nutrients to ensure sustainable commercial agriculture. Once combined with new technologies, over the next decade it led to a tripling of agricultural production.[34]

The transition to crop agriculture greatly benefited the Mennonites; even so, the Agricultural Society's insistence on it was just one more example of interference in the affairs of fullholders. Cornies hinted indirectly at community attitudes when he wrote to Fadeev that "the plough, once the tool of the lowest classes, has risen in the estimation of many to become an honourable implement."[35] While Cornies framed the transition in a positive light, the notion that ploughing was the pursuit of the "lowest classes" provides a surprising insight into the early Molochnaia community, given that later perceptions of Mennonite life, coloured by accounts of a grain-growing economy, place crop agriculture at the centre of prosperity and identity. Yet Cornies had made his fortune raising sheep, and before the late 1830s the state encouraged sheep raising as the natural economic endeavour of isolated communities on the southern grasslands. The transition to the hard manual labour of crop agriculture would pay off, but before it did, it is not surprising that at first some Mennonite fullholders were disgruntled by the society's demands.

The combination of increasing the amount of land planted with grain and increasing the average yield from that land meant that by the end of the 1840s the Molochnaia Mennonites were some of the most productive farmers in the empire. A secondary benefit was that the transportation and sale of grain provided jobs. Nogais became the main grain haulers, but Mennonite merchants were the most significant beneficiaries.[36] In 1838 several Molochnaia Mennonite families built homes and warehouses in Berdiansk, where they became grain merchants. Abram Wiebe of Rudenerweide was the leading figure in this trade. An important member of the Cornies Party and one of the four members of the Agricultural Society, Wiebe borrowed large sums from Cornies to buy community wheat, which he then exported through Berdiansk.[37] Wiebe also established a trading firm that supplied the Molochnaia Mennonites with luxuries from abroad in addition to exporting Mennonite wool and grain.[38] In the 1840s he was among the first in the community to experiment with silk manufacture.

As chair of the Agricultural Society, Cornies experimented with a wide variety of new crops at his Iushanle estate, thus expanding its role in the laboratory of modernization. Historian Alison Smith recounts the state's efforts to improve and diversify its agricultural economy in response to the Great Drought, and Cornies was an important agent of this effort.[39] In close consultation with Christian Steven, the renowned botanist and the Ministry of State Domains' Chief Inspector of Silk Production and Agriculture in Crimea, he experimented with British wheat, Turkish tobacco, Crimean barley, and countless other crops. The most important was potatoes, which Tsar Nicholas promoted as a miracle crop that might prevent famines. Cornies became a leading figure in the project, planting potatoes himself, demanding that other Mennonites do likewise, and offering advice on the results. Unlike most of Russia's state peasants, Mennonites already grew potatoes, although only in their kitchen gardens. In 1838, Cornies added the requirement to grow "a considerable number of potatoes" to the standard Agricultural Society contract for purchasing a fullholding.[40]

The promotion of potatoes reflects a subtle but important process that was taking place in New Russia: the Ministry of State Domains was beginning to eclipse the Guardianship Committee in the Mennonite settlement. Technically, the administrative reorganization of the mid-1830s had placed the Guardianship Committee under the authority of the new ministry, but the committee was narrowly focused on New Russian colonists while the Ministry of State Domains had an empire-wide purview, and as a result, the two entities competed for Cornies's attention. At a time when the Guardianship Committee's senior leadership was weak and the new ministry was attracting a bright young generation of reform-minded bureaucrats, Cornies increasingly found himself answering to two separate agencies, which multiplied the demands on his time.

As the ministry ramped up potato production in 1840, Georg von Bradke, director of the Ministry's Third Department, wrote to Cornies directly, calling upon him to help develop the program. Bradke visited the Molochnaia in June 1840 and came away with a clear sense of Mennonite accomplishments.[41] He wanted very specific information: how much land, and how many seed potatoes, were needed to feed a peasant family of four? Cornies's response suggests why his importance to the ministry was increasing. He did more than carefully answer Bradke about local conditions; he went on to provide a learned description of potato cultivation in Prussia, demonstrating a broad expertise and knowledge and justifying his growing reputation as an agricultural expert.[42]

In correspondence with Steven in Crimea, Cornies displayed a growing self-confidence and assertiveness. In the early 1830s his letters to state officials had been couched in subservient terms; in 1840, responding to a report relayed by Steven, Cornies offered a clear, dismissive correction, ridiculing that report's false claims.[43] Cornies's tone was reminiscent of the rising confidence he showed in correspondence with David Epp about Prussian religious disputes after his trip to the Vistula in 1827. In 1828, Cornies had begun to assert himself in internal Mennonite matters; by 1840, he was asserting himself in broader Russian affairs.

Meanwhile, Cornies took seriously the state's expectation that Mennonites serve as a model for neighbouring peasants. The Agricultural Society was formally a Mennonite institution, but Cornies's role as its chair and his separate role as a corresponding member of the Learned Committee intersected, and there is little sign that he drew any distinction between the two. For the Learned Committee he experimented with agricultural methods and crops, using his Iushanle estate as an experimental farm; meanwhile the headquarters of the Agricultural Society were located at Iushanle, and he used the society's authority to demand that Mennonites adopt crops and methods tested at Iushanle for the ministry. This intersection of activities and authority reinforced Cornies's power within his community. It also had a second significant consequence – it engaged Cornies in affairs beyond the Mennonite settlement.

Cornies's first major involvement in state business outside the Molochnaia came at Fadeev's urging. In 1837, Fadeev, now Chief Guardian of the Kalmyk Horde, was ordered to conduct a general survey of peasant conditions in the Caucasus, Astrakhan *guberniia*, and the Sarepta Moravian Brethren settlement. He asked Cornies to accompany him and provide expert insights about the Kalmyk Horde based on his work with the Nogais.

One thing that distinguished the Russian Empire from overseas empires is that it had no separate colonial administration.[44] Fadeev's career trajectory and his recruitment of Cornies as an adviser on Kalmyk affairs together suggest that the Guardianship Committee, although ostensibly a regional body, played a broad role in the evolution of empire-wide policies, albeit an indirect one. After all, Fadeev's credentials for promotion to Chief Guardian of the Kalmyk Horde were his work with the Mennonites and, in particular, the alleged success of the Mennonite model in "civilizing" the Nogais. In a sense, Fadeev was himself a product of the Mennonite model, and he now recruited Cornies in an explicit attempt to expand that model.[45]

Cornies was already in touch with the Sarepta community. Encouraged by Fadeev, he had been corresponding with them for a year about the possibility of buying pastureland in Sarepta and establishing a model sheep farm there to help the Brethren revitalize their economic affairs. The inspection trip with Fadeev gave him the chance to look over the community and region and decide if this plan was viable.

Cornies left home at the end of June 1837 and spent six weeks travelling with Fadeev. It was his first long journey since Saxony a decade earlier and would be the last time he left New Russia. His correspondence reveals a sense of wonder at his encounter with the wider world. Perhaps recalling the excitement of the Saxony trip, he wrote vividly from the Piatigorsk Spa in the Caucasus to David Epp in Huebuden: "I am here at the foot of beautiful Mount Bisten [probably Mount Beshtau] in the Caucasus, located in a romantic region with glorious views of the Caucasus Mountains that are covered with eternal snow. Elbrus, the highest of these mountains, rises majestically far above the clouds."[46]

The celebrated Russian poet Mikhail Lermontov, exiled from St. Petersburg, arrived in Piatigorsk just days after Cornies, and his description of the hazy blue "amphitheatre of mountains," the "silver chain of snowy peaks," and the air "pure and fresh, as the kiss of a child" captures the region's breathtaking beauty.[47] Unfortunately, Cornies says nothing of the social scene that Lermontov so powerfully depicts. Beyond its reputed healing powers, Piatigorsk was a playground for the rich and famous, a "hotbed of high-class intrigue" and sexual tensions.[48] Lermontov's fictional account of high society at the spa depicts the very archetype of the "superfluous man," a class of people that the great Russian literary critic Vissarion Belinsky said was "characterised either by decisive inaction, or else by futile activity."[49] This was the polar opposite of Cornies, who soon moved on from Piatigorsk to continue his life of decisive action and fruitful activity.

Before leaving the Caucasus, Cornies visited the nearby settlement of Karass, first established by the Scottish Missionary Society in 1802 and, by the late 1830s, mainly occupied by German Pietists. He reported with dismay that it was a "miserable settlement, and so are its inhabitants, rent by dissension and quarrelling."[50] In 1835 the settlement deposed its querulous Scottish elder Alexander Patterson and replaced him with Jakob Lang.[51] Cornies called this political battle a "terrible business, with few traces of Christian spirit."[52] In the coming years he corresponded with Lang and did what he could to help the struggling settlement. Karass was yet another object lesson for Cornies about the dangers of divided loyalties in frontier colonies.

Cornies concluded his travels at Sarepta on the Volga River not far from Tsaritsyn (later Stalingrad, today Volgograd). Cornies was well if indirectly acquainted with Sarepta. This was Blüher's home town, and Johann Jr. and Agnes had visited there the previous summer. Cornies's respect for the Moravian Brethren dated back to the 1820s when he visited Herrnhut, and he had long been eager to visit Sarepta. Fadeev hoped that Cornies could help the community reverse its decline, and he urged Cornies to establish a sheep farm in the region and even to explore the possibility of transplanting a Mennonite village there.[53] Cornies at first looked on the prospect positively, and he even proposed to his brother Heinrich that he partner in the venture and move to Sarepta to manage the farm.[54]

Rising Mennonite landlessness would lead to the creation of "daughter" settlements as offshoots of the "mother" settlements. The possibility of establishing a daughter settlement on leased Kalmyk land near Sarepta was already on Cornies's mind when he visited in 1837. Fadeev wanted an extension of the Mennonite laboratory, including model colonists to show the Moravian Brethren how to make the best use of their land, but as Cornies wrote to his friend Johann Wiebe, his personal objective was "to assess whether it might eventually be of use to our brethren in faith."[55]

Cornies found Sarepta much as Herrnhut – peaceful and friendly – but while he thought Sarepta had good enough pastureland to raise sheep, he saw few prospects for the Kalmyk land. He concluded that the climate would not support large-scale sheep raising, and he gave up on his plan to lease nearby land. However, he promised to provide the Sarepta community with advice on establishing small private herds, which he assured Fadeev would soon "produce great advantages for the owners and community alike."[56] As soon as he returned to the Molochnaia he began corresponding with Daniel Doehring about selling merino sheep to Sarepta, and in 1838 he oversaw the selection, purchase, and delivery of breeding stock from his own herds to the Moravian Brethren.[57] He also actively pursued other ways to help Sarepta, offering advice on all aspects of agriculture, and in 1839 he hosted a delegation that came to see how the Molochnaia Mennonites managed their affairs.[58]

The 1837 inspection trip was an important step outward into the tsarist administrative world for Cornies. Back home he found himself entangled in other state projects beyond the Mennonite settlement. He took charge of regional efforts to promote potatoes, hiring Mennonites to supervise the state program in Slavic and Nogai peasant villages in the Molochnaia (see chapter 9). He also began training Slavic and Nogai peasants as agricultural apprentices at Iushanle. All of these activities came at the behest of the Ministry of State Domains and not the Guardianship Committee.

The apprenticeship program demonstrates the Ministry of State Domains' efforts to activate the Mennonite laboratory as a tool for reforming the state peasants. Cornies had always hired apprentices for his own agricultural affairs, and a number of his long-term employees served three-year apprenticeships before being promoted to more responsible positions. At Fadeev's request, in 1835 Cornies took on two apprentices from the Mariupol district, but this informal first stab at a regional training program went no further.[59] In December 1838, the ministry asked him to train peasants in modern agricultural methods and then send them back to their villages. The plan was not just to provide basic skills; the apprentices were to be taught to read and write and do basic math so that they could eventually provide training to other peasants in their own villages.[60] This was a way to transform the system of modelling progressive policies into a program of direct instruction extending down to the lowest levels of society.

Cornies responded to the ministry's request in his usual thorough, practical manner. Yes, he would take on sixteen apprentices, but there were limits to what he could do for them. Most importantly, he had neither the facilities nor the personnel to offer formal schooling. Iushanle was too far from Ohrloff to send the apprentices to school there, and at any rate the Ohrloff school was for Mennonites. Clearly, the language of instruction would have to be Russian, and the Mennonite settlement could not spare any of its Russian speakers for the task, because they were too important to settlement interests. Cornies added that he could not provide instruction in veterinary medicine, though he would of course ensure that they learned what amounted to basic first aid for livestock.[61]

The apprenticeship program raised complicated religious challenges. Cornies assured Steven that he already employed both Orthodox Christians and Muslims and was aware of their requirements. "I pledge," he wrote, "to insist that each one follow his religion eagerly ... All of my servants of the Russian religion ... must observe fasts properly ... They are given leave when necessary to go to confession and communion ... Though only three Muslims are presently in my service, they too are encouraged to be scrupulous in their choice of foods and in their other religious duties. On religious holidays, they attend the Mosque in Akkerman."[62]

The apprenticeship program became a tremendous nuisance to Cornies, for while he received a handful of very good apprentices and did his best to provide them with training, many of the peasants sent to him were far from satisfactory. Cornies's reports and complaints about the apprentices hint of the challenges the Russian state faced in its efforts to improve peasant agriculture. One example illustrates the point. The ministry recruited a literate Ukrainian peasant and former village scribe, Stepan Efimenko, both to become an agricultural apprentice and to teach reading and writing to the other apprentices. Efimenko almost immediately ran away from Iushanle, complaining to the other apprentices before he left that he was a teacher and not a field labourer. The police tracked down the unhappy Efimenko and returned him to Cornies under armed guard, at which point Cornies sent inquiries to Efimenko's home village of Chernigovka, asking after the young man's conduct. He learned that Chernigovka peasants could not say anything good about Efimenko's conduct, so he sent Efimenko back to the Chernigovka District Office with a letter stating that he would not be accepted back at Iushanle.[63]

Efimenko's was not an isolated case. Villages sent Cornies children too young to work, and he sent them back. They sent him alcoholics and criminals, apparently seeing the apprenticeship program as an opportunity to rid themselves of troublemakers, and he sent these back too.[64] District officials failed to explain the program to peasants, and rumours spread that, like military conscripts, the apprentices might "be sent abroad and never see their families again."[65] At first Cornies offered explanations to the ministry when he rejected apprentices, but before long he began sending them back without comment, for as he told Steven, the qualifications were clearly laid out in the original agreement, and the regional offices could read them for themselves.[66]

Stage Managing the Mennonite Model

By the end of the 1830s, Cornies's many activities had an *ad hoc* character. Administrative officials in Odesa, Simferopol, and St. Petersburg bombarded him with requests for advice, and he did his best to help all of them. Underlying all of this was a clear vision for the development of the Mennonite settlement and its role within the empire. Cornies had always insisted that Mennonites serve as role models, and the dimensions of the modelling project were clear to him: Mennonites were to be the standard-bearers of modern economic practices, from field rotations and agricultural equipment to trade and industry.

This vision contained a problematic ambiguity, to which Cornies contributed and which in turn contributed to tensions in his community. The Mennonite model was originally intended to produce change by consequence of its very appearance. The conservative version of the model insisted that it was a fixed, natural order of things, rooted in a fixed vision of early Christian life. Cornies's version of the model was a conscious construct, subject to change rooted in the changing values of its intended audience. According to the Priviligeum the model was intended for an audience of other colonists, but Cornies knew it had a second important audience: the state officials who controlled Mennonite privileges. He wrote that "individuals and statesmen who travel through our villages and honour us with their visits, judge entire regions by their appearance."[67]

Cornies was highly attuned to this state audience, and he carefully staged a Mennonite performance of "civilization" for official visitors. He anxiously sought news of planned visits and prepared careful itineraries for the visitors. Village mayors were given orders to ensure that villagers behaved "politely and decently to distinguished visitors," and Mennonites were admonished about proper clothing and behaviour.[68]

The Molochnaia performances of "civilization" that Cornies staged in 1837, first for Keppen and later for Crown Prince Alexander, had two key "acts": the Nogai model village of Akkerman, followed by Cornies's estate at Iushanle. Akkerman was on Nogai territory, which meant that as visitors approached the model village they first observed the Nogais in their natural, "uncivilized" state. On arriving at Akkerman, they found the Nogais transformed into "civilized" people, with proper homes and painted window frames, their own culture erased. At the climax of the performance the audiences were invited to enter a Nogai home and observe real live Nogais *in situ*.[69]

The larger Mennonite settlement provided the setting for the second act, the Iushanle estate. The settlement, with its bustling agricultural economy, was already an impressive sight to visitors. Its trees, so rare on the steppe, drew particular praise, and visitors often called the settlement an oasis. But on the tours that Cornies staged, Iushanle was the centrepiece of the performance, a 3,800-*desiatina* estate with a home, office, barns, corrals, orchards, and tree nurseries. It was a quintessential laboratory of modernity, where Cornies grew new crops, experimented with livestock breeding, tried out new barn feeding methods, and trained peasant apprentices.

Keppen described the Molochnaia Mennonite tour after his first visit in 1837. He arrived at Halbstadt, the settlement's administrative centre, and was taken in hand by Cornies, who swept him away to Iushanle.[70] What followed was a whirlwind tour of the settlement, which left Keppen overwhelmed by the fineness of Iushanle (he described in detail its interior walls painted in "various colours"), and by Akkerman, the shining example of Cornies's success in "civilizing" the Nogais.[71] Accounts of Crown Prince Alexander's 1837 visit, and other official visits in the 1840s, describe similarly staged tours.

The Iushanle performance helped establish an image of the Mennonites as model subjects in official minds, thus making an argument for preserving Mennonite privileges. In the 1840s the Mennonites became an empire-wide marvel, held up in journals, newspapers, and ministry circulars as a model of peasant progress to which all Russian officials should aspire for the peasants they administered. Cornies gained a reputation as an architect of civilizational reform, a status recognized with his prestigious appointment to the Learned Committee of the Ministry of State Domains.[72] His reputation spread as he wrote articles that appeared in major newspapers and journals, further burnishing the Mennonites' repute.

However, this performed identity raised expectations that would have to be met. By introducing Russian officials to his Iushanle laboratory of modernization, Cornies was strongly suggesting that the entire Mennonite settlement would equally act as a laboratory. Indeed, he staked his own status in official circles on the continuing successful performance. Yet the image he presented was part of a carefully constructed aesthetics of civilization that did not accurately reflect the Mennonite settlement as a whole. Cornies well knew this – the Agricultural Society's village inspections revealed the weak performances of bit players, and meanwhile, mounting political challenges from leading actors, described in chapter 8, threatened to close down the theatre.

Keppen and Fadeev undoubtedly understood that they were being fed an idealized version of the Molochnaia, but they had no desire to question it. The Molochnaia became their own success story, and for Fadeev in particular it helped to advance his career. His promotions, to Guardian of the Kalmyk Horde, and eventually to Civil Governor of Saratov *guberniia*, were also erected on the Mennonite model. Fadeev and Keppen conspired in this idealization of the Mennonites, even promoting it internationally.

Two important international visitors played significant roles in this process. The first was Auguste de Marmont, friend and aide-de-camp of Napoleon and an instrumental figure in the French surrender in 1814. After Napoleon's defeat Marmont loyally served Louis XVIII and Charles X, following the latter into exile in 1830. In the 1830s he travelled in Eastern Europe.[73] Marmont, accompanied by General Vorontsov, Prince Golitsyn, and Tavrida Civil Governor Muromtsev, spent two days in the Molochnaia in June 1834, visiting Iushanle and spending the night at Cornies's Ohrloff home.[74] The visit resulted in Marmont's glowing report of Cornies and the Mennonites. When Cornies received a copy of Marmont's description, he wrote to Fadeev to question unspecified inaccuracies, but he never challenged the report at higher levels. After all, glowing praise from a luminary like Marmont was not to be scoffed at.

A second important visitor arrived in 1843: Baron August von Haxthausen, a Westphalian landed nobleman. Educated at the University of Göttingen, he was a student of folklore and good friend of his famous fellow students, the brothers Grimm. He was trained in *Statistik,* "the detailed study of economic and social institutions," and devoted himself to legal history, in particular Prussian systems of land tenure.[75] His work gained the attention of the heir to the Prussian throne, the future Friedrich Wilhelm IV, and, funded generously by the Prussian crown, he spent the 1820s and 1830s gathering information about land tenure, intending to propose legislation that would protect peasants from unnecessary state interference in traditional practices.[76]

By the early 1840s, rising opposition from Prussian landowning elites cost Haxthausen his royal patronage and ended his Prussian research, but by then he had attracted the attention of Russian officialdom. Many of his conclusions about the Prussian peasantry suggested that his world view closely coincided with Nicholas I's Official Nationality, in particular his belief that legal systems ought to be rooted in traditional practices. In 1843 he accepted a commission to write an ethnographic and legal study of the Russian peasantry. His chief sponsor was the Minister of State Domains, P.D. Kiselev, who provided him with mountains of data that had been collected during the ministry's surveys of the state peasantry. Kiselev also ordered the ministry to facilitate Haxthausen's 1843 tour of Russia.[77]

Haxthausen's *Studies on the Interior of Russia* was a landmark publication that interpreted the Russian political and social scene in exactly the terms that Nicholas had hoped for. Haxthausen argued that the hierarchical Russian social system, rooted in the peasant commune, the Orthodox religion, and the despotic power of the nobility and tsars, permitted a unified state unhampered by the destructive revolutionary forces plaguing the West. The *Studies*, published in German, French, and English, offered an approving interpretation of Nicholas I's conservative regime.

Critics of *Studies on the Interior of Russia* point out that Haxthausen's conclusions were limited by his objectives. He was not interested in politics or high culture, and even his focus on the peasants was heavily influenced by his concerns about Prussian land-tenure practices. Yet within these constraints Haxthausen has generally been credited with being a reliable observer who, as historian S. Frederick Starr suggests, wrote "one of the best travel accounts of its era."[78] While Haxthausen's interpretation of the Russian social system and his admiration for the peasant commune are often challenged, his direct observations are seldom questioned.

It is not surprising that Haxthausen's travels brought him to the Molochnaia and to Cornies. After all, the Mennonite settlement was on the standard tour, and moreover Keppen served as a liaison to Haxthausen, providing him with ministry records and corresponding with provincial ministry officials about travel arrangements. Haxthausen spent just two days in the Molochnaia, but that brief visit left a powerful impact. He wrote that "in no district of Russia is there so high a state of civilization, or of the culture of the soil. The Mennonites may serve as a model, to the government and the people, of what may be affected by industry, morality, and order."[79] He was no less glowing in his assessment of Cornies:

> He ... went with his parents, in the beginning of the present century, to settle on the [Molochnaia]; he had received no school instruction, but possessed a clear and ingenious mind, an earnest character, an acute and practical understanding and loving heart; by his self-education he has unquestionably attained the highest degree of spiritual culture ... By his mental superiority, his upright and tried character, he has become one of the most influential men in Southern Russia ... The noble Prince Vorontsov would hardly take any step in the internal government of this district without asking the advice of Cornies.[80]

Haxthausen devoted two long passages to the Molochnaia, one singing the praises of the Mennonites, the other describing the Russian government's success in "civilizing" the Nogais. Given how brief Haxthausen's sojourn in the Molochnaia was, there is little doubt where the information for these descriptions came from. Cornies had provided the baron with the usual, carefully managed tour of the Molochnaia, and after Haxthausen returned to Westphalia he requested and received additional information from him.[81]

Cornies's management of Haxthausen's visit suggests something important about the entirety of *Studies on the Interior of Russia*: Just as the Russian state was using the Mennonite settlement as a model to promote the economic modernization of the peasantry, it intended Haxthausen's study to provide a model version of Russian society. What Haxthausen saw in the Molochnaia was what the state, working through its local agent Cornies, wanted him to see. There is no doubt that Haxthausen's view of the rest of the country was similarly rose-coloured. Indeed, when Fadeev, by now civil governor of Saratov *guberniia*, wrote anxiously to Keppen about Haxthausen's looming visit, Keppen reassured his friend that he should not worry. After Haxthausen's visit, Fadeev wrote to thank Keppen for his advice: "Baron Haxthausen ... was here just twelve hours, and passed through like a dispatch rider. It seems that your prediction was accurate: he could not have learned anything about the region."[82]

The most elaborate and important example of a carefully idealized representation of the Molochnaia settlement is Cornies's lengthy 1841 description of the Mennonite administrative system. Kiselev requested the description after he visited the settlement in 1841. He had done the Molochnaia tour too, and he was deeply impressed, writing to Cornies that "I viewed your settlements with sincere pleasure and especially the progress you have made in your own establishments. I brought this to His Majesty's attention and his Imperial Majesty deigned to remark that the name Cornies was familiar to him as a worthy and useful man."[83] While he was in the Molochnaia, Kiselev had asked Cornies to provide an "accurate description of the organisation and arrangements in our Mennonite villages and to offer suggestions about additional arrangements that might enable our industry and crafts to continue their progress more effectively."[84] This request, coming from the official whom Tsar Nicholas called his "chief of staff for peasant affairs," points to the prominence the Mennonite laboratory of modernity had attained. The resulting report is the quintessential example of how the Mennonite model became an idealized representation, in that it provided a vision of the settlement for the ministry to distribute across the empire as an administrative model.

This description of the Molochnaia Mennonites is among Cornies's most influential written works.[85] It reflected Cornies's vision of what constituted an orderly, efficiently run peasant society. It described the Mennonite administrative system in idealized terms, and promoted that system as a model for all peasant administration in Russia. It described the Agricultural Society as the central administrative office overseeing every aspect of Molochnaia Mennonite life. It claimed that the society's authority, once based on the authority of the Mennonite *Gebietsamt* and congregational elders, was now explicitly based on the authority of the Guardianship Committee, and it characterized *Gebietsamt* officials as little more than liaisons between the Agricultural Society and individual householders. Even village and district elections, it claimed, were vetted by the society.

This grandiose claim of Agricultural Society authority was part of Cornies's broader construction of an ideal version of the Molochnaia settlement for official consumption. Just as with Iushanle and Akkerman, it had more to do with Cornies's aspirations than with reality. But it was not just a matter of aspirations – Cornies continued to be profoundly aware that Mennonites were in danger of losing their status as model colonists. The 1833 plan for the "Reorganisation of the Administration of the Colonists," the creation of the Ministry of State Domains, and the creation of the Mennonite Agricultural Society all pointed to a fundamental shift in the state's attitude toward modernization.

The state's desire to change the role of the Mennonites was born of a growing understanding that the model, as originally constructed, had failed. The Mennonites were remarkably prosperous, but there was slim evidence that they had served any didactic role for other foreign settlers as the Privilegium had intended. The recurring observation of travellers that the Mennonite settlement was an oasis was as much a condemnation of the model paradigm as it was an affirmation of Mennonite accomplishments, for the oasis showed no sign of expanding into the desert. The plan for the "Reorganisation of the Administration of the Colonists" was one of the first signs that the state was dissatisfied with this failure. Although it continued to characterize the Mennonites as a passive model for surrounding peoples, it clearly envisioned a larger, more active role for them.[86]

In 1840, Fadeev privately characterized the use of didactic models as a failure, writing to Keppen that progress could only be achieved in New Russia with the benefit of "systematic supervision."[87] Here Fadeev reflected the state's growing dissatisfaction with inconsistent policies and results – it was beginning to look for universal, "systematic" policies. Cornies could hardly have objected to Fadeev's conclusions about the model's failure. Fourteen years earlier he had concluded that what was necessary to "civilize" the Nogais was the firm paternal hand of a competent administrator; the question was what role the Mennonites would play in the process. The increasing demands on Cornies to provide leadership beyond his community – establishing model

Nogai villages, training peasant apprentices, and overseeing potato cultivation – show the state's efforts to redeploy the Mennonites as direct administrators of other settlers. No longer were they to be simply passive models. This was not just a plan to make use of Cornies's well-established administrative talents; the state believed it was time to make the Mennonites work for their privileges.

In 1838, Keppen proposed a dramatic new use for Mennonites when he queried Cornies about the possibility of moving three Mennonite families to each of the government stations along the two roads from Simferopol to Perekop and Evpatoria in Crimea.[88] Keppen apparently envisioned an expansion of the model paradigm in which the Crimean settlers would serve as models to the mainly Tatar populations surrounding the stations. This shows that assumptions about the didactic utility of the paradigm still survived. At the same time, it suggested a more direct and active role for Mennonites, who would be asked to move away from the model settlement, out into the broader Russian world. Cornies's Nogai programs provided the impetus for Keppen's proposal, and their success was understood to be a product of Cornies's direct administrative role.

Cornies's dismayed response to Keppen's proposal reveals his ongoing allegiance to the model paradigm but also that program's underlying weakness. He stressed to Keppen that Mennonites required their community; few would be willing to take up such an isolated outpost existence, for

> a life lived in isolation is also not in keeping with Mennonite customs and would be too lonely. Mennonites like to visit back and forth, sharing joys and sorrows. This is a principle of their religion. This is the way in which they help one another with brotherly support, edifying themselves spiritually and comforting and encouraging one another. Their children must be provided with enough schooling that would allow them, at the very minimum, to learn to read and write. [At the time of their baptism,] they must be able to deliver their confession of faith orally in order to be accepted into the community and must convince the community of the propriety of their behaviour.[89]

Cornies allowed that the Mennonite model might work in Crimea, but only if a full Mennonite settlement was established. In this way, "leadership and protection could originate from the settlement."[90]

Cornies's response to Keppen closely echoed Fadeev's 1840 letter to Keppen criticizing the Mennonites, in that he concluded that the Mennonite model was a function of leadership rather than the Mennonites' inherent "industry and morality." When the Guardianship Committee proposed a similar scheme in 1841 – this time to move groups of three or four Molochnaia Mennonite families into various villages in Bessarabia – Cornies was even clearer about the situation. In a letter to Evgenii von Hahn, the committee's new deputy chair, he bluntly stated that most Molochnaia Mennonites were "accustomed to direct supervision and ... leadership" and that "if the ordinary agriculturalist is left to manage his establishment himself, he will remain what he was, a peasant." Mennonite families left on their own in Bessarabia, he warned Hahn, would "eventually revert to the old ways."[91]

The Price of Failure: The Doukhobor Exile

One example of the failure of the Mennonite model was the crisis besetting the Doukhobors, who were among the Mennonites' closest neighbours. This crisis appears to have largely been manufactured by enemies of the Doukhobors, who in 1835–6 accused them of a litany of crimes, including twenty-four murders. These accusations were driven by myriad factors, ranging from religious prejudices and the Orthodox Church's efforts to force the Doukhobors and other sectarians to convert to Orthodoxy, to new attitudes motivated by the policy of Official Nationality, to efforts by some corrupt local officials to acquire Doukhobor land.[92] The only extant copy of the report on this investigation is preserved in Cornies's papers. It is mainly a collection of rumours, reinforced by lurid accounts of a handful of alleged crimes. It found its way into Haxthausen's account of the region, and some of its allegations remain part of modern Doukhobor historiography.[93]

Cornies had written a report on the Doukhobors in the early 1830s.[94] He was sharply critical of Doukhobor religious beliefs, concluding that they were "true heathens, who deny the genuine worship and reverence of the Trinity and blaspheme the holy Word of God."[95] However, he allowed that "simplicity, sobriety, and a sense of honour are present" and that "they are a hard-working, business-like people."[96] Consistent with his general approach to modernization, he implicitly assumed that the Doukhobors' distinctive culture and beliefs could be erased and that they could be moulded into productive tsarist subjects.

The allegations of Doukhobor crimes in the 1835–6 report shocked Cornies, who wrote to Fadeev in 1836: "I am done with [them], crime upon crime, it makes your skin crawl."[97] Yet when the state ordered the exile of the first cohort of Doukhobors in February 1841, it was apparent that he was not really "done": he reported to Tavrida Civil Governor Muromtsev that until the exile decree was publicized the previous week, "the small stream that marks the boundary between the Mennonite and Doukhobor districts, was easily crossed, and lively interaction had characterised our relations."[98]

Muromtsev, who had himself visited the Doukhobors and announced the exile decree on 16 February, still held out hope that the Doukhbors would convert to Orthodoxy so that the wholesale exodus could be averted. He asked Cornies to use his influence to convince the Doukhobors to accept the state's conditions, but Cornies replied that he no longer held their trust: "Since learning about the Imperial decision, they have been uncommunicative, suspicious and refuse to maintain contacts with Mennonites as they once did."[99] Cornies counselled patience, suggesting that once the Doukhobors' initial anger subsided they would probably reconsider their decision. He added that "dependable people tell me that individual Doukhobors, when no one else is present, are known to say that it would better for them to remain here than move to regions where they could expect nothing of benefit for themselves."[100]

On 22 February, Cornies received a Doukhobor delegation asking if he thought that the state would carry through with the threatened exile. The delegation claimed no official capacity, but Cornies assumed that they represented the entire Doukhobor community. On 24 February, Fatei Zhikharev, the most important lieutenant of the Doukhobor hereditary leader Ilarion Kalmykov, visited Cornies and insisted that the Doukhobors would remain faithful to their beliefs and accept exile. Zhikharev warned that few Doukhobors could afford the journey, saying that "my greatest regret is that the great majority is poor and will starve on the road." He added that many Doukhobors "were frightened that even if they converted to the Orthodox faith, they would still not be allowed to remain here. The old would be scattered among the Russian villages and the young would be sent off as soldiers."[101]

Cornies toured the Doukhobor villages on 25 February to try to dispel these rumours. He reported to Muromtsev with cautious optimism that "it seems to me that the great majority of these people are fighting a great inner battle, and do not know what to do ... They have begun to communicate with Mennonites. They have also become more trusting. In contrast, they are more suspicious of their old conservative leaders who attempt to draw them in with excessive lies and falsehoods."[102] This optimism soon waned: on 6 March he reported that the Doukhobors were selling their property in preparation for leaving. He blamed Zhikarev, who he claimed controlled Kalmykov and was feared by the rest of the Doukhobors. Showing his willingness to use harsh measures to achieve state goals, he recommended the arrest of Zhikarev and Kalmykov as the best bet for winning over the Doukhobors.[103] In the end, none of Cornies's efforts had much effect. Between 1841 and 1844, 4,992 Doukhobors departed for the Caucasus, while only 248 converted to Orthodoxy and stayed.[104]

For Cornies the Doukhobor story held important lessons. The most direct had to do with the arbitrary power of the state to punish its subjects. The Doukhobors – whom New Russian Governor General Vorontsov characterized in 1839 as "an extremely useful community [which can] even serve as model agriculturists" – were being forced from their homes on spurious charges, without appeal or recourse.[105] Being useful model agriculturists was by itself no guarantee that privileges would be retained. A more subtle lesson, perhaps not yet fully articulated, was that Official Nationality had significant implications for frontier communities. The pressure to convert was a manifestation of Nicholas's ideology, which placed a premium on Orthodoxy as evidence of loyalty. As historian Mara Kozelsky has shown, while Orthodox Church policies focused particularly on Russian sectarians, the Church saw other sectarians, including the Mennonites, as harmful influences on Orthodox peasants.[106] These lessons had dangerous implications for Mennonites, which Cornies had to weigh as he responded to the Ministry of State Domains' demands.

Conclusion

In a sense, Cornies's response to the Ministry of State Domains' proposals to move Mennonite families to Crimea or Bessarabia as local models aligned him with Mennonite conservatives. The Mennonites could provide a model of modernization, but he insisted that they could do little to initiate modernization beyond their own settlement. This was not what the Guardianship Committee and the ministry wanted to hear, but Cornies offered a sop to the state: he personally was willing and able to be its agent, both within his community and beyond. Because the state sought his opinions and took him seriously, he was in a position to push back against state demands that he viewed as dangerous to his community and its religious values. This satisfied the state for now but did nothing to quiet conservative opposition within his community led by Warkentin.

The efforts to extend the Mennonite model beyond the Molochnaia were a sign of shifting state attitudes toward its colonial subjects: it was beginning to seek a one-size-fits-all administrative model. This shift away from what Willard Sunderland labels laissez-faire imperialism toward a more intrusive, centralized model would only gain steam in the late nineteenth century, but the Mennonite story shows that it was already in process by the 1830s.[107] When the Nicholaevan state began the investigation of the state peasants that would lead to the Great Reforms of the 1860s, it also set in motion a reconsideration of colonial policies. The Mennonite laboratory was foundational to that process.

Chapter Eight

The Warkentin Affair, 1841–1842

In 1841, Johann Warkentin led a rebellion against the Agricultural Society, encouraging his congregation to defy society directives and challenging Cornies's power in the settlement through the *Gebietsamt* elections. The Guardianship Committee stepped in and ordered new elections, mandating the choice of a reform-friendly mayor. When Warkentin continued to resist, the committee deposed him and dissolved the Large Flemish Congregation, forcing the creation of three smaller congregations in its place.

These events were scandalous at the time and provoked a wave of outrage and recriminations in the tsarist and Prussian Mennonite communities, but their long-term significance has never been clear. Cornies enjoyed virtually unchallenged authority from 1842 until his death in 1848, but after that the power of the Agricultural Society waned, so the affair had only temporary political significance. As for religious significance, direct state interference in Mennonite religious affairs prompted apocalyptic language from Warkentin's supporters, but religious upheavals brought on by the creation of the Mennonite Brethren in 1860 relegated the Warkentin Affair to minor status in the larger Mennonite story.

This chapter will argue that the Warkentin Affair deserves closer attention. It is conventional to regard the affair as a conflict between secular and religious authority, but if Cornies's reforms are understood as explicitly reflecting Pietist beliefs, then the Warkentin Affair must be seen as an important event in the emergence of Pietism in the Molochnaia that helped lay the foundations for the formation of the Mennonite Brethren. Beyond the settlement, the Mennonite case sheds light on the evolving relationship between the Russian state and its colonial laboratory of modernization. The state's intervention in the affair was an inevitable product of the era of small reforms, designed to reshape the imperial project.

The Bricks and Mortar of Revolt

The economic and educational reforms that stoked tensions in the Molochnaia in the late 1830s and early 1840s were at the heart of the Warkentin Affair, but the tipping point in the crisis was a seemingly trivial matter. In Cornies's account of the Warkentin Affair, he wrote that the Warkentin Party was "particularly offended by the new, attractive and more appropriate building style using fired brick for houses and barns. This style was strongly supported by the society because it gave our villages a more cheerful and beautiful appearance."[1]

Cornies had begun building with bricks and tile at Iushanle and Tashchenak in 1837, and he was soon pushing for all new construction in the Molochnaia to follow suit. In 1837 he insisted that the new Ohrloff church be built with bricks in a "new, tasteful design," and in 1839 he required brick construction for the entire village of Landskrone.[2] In 1842 the Agricultural Society mandated brick and tile for all new construction in the settlement.[3] There were economic justifications for these regulations. For one thing they helped limit damage from fires, such as the ones that destroyed nine houses in Sparrau and the Klassen cloth mill in Halbstadt in 1839.[4] They also provided jobs for the landless, in that bricks had to be manufactured and bricklaying was labour-intensive work. But as Cornies made clear in 1842, bricks were first and foremost about aesthetics, an important expression of his concern with the aesthetics of order and morality.

From land surveying to village planning to ordering that trees be planted along Molochnaia's roads, Cornies consistently tied together order, beauty, and morality. This was fundamental to his world view and an important motivation for all his reforms. As described in chapter 4, this understanding was informed by Lavater's pernicious racial theories. Cornies, confronted by what he perceived as the disorder of a frontier populated by "wild" and "immoral" nomads, was seeking to correct the world's natural flaws. In his vivid 1837 account of the Caucasus, Cornies provided one of his clearest statements of this vision: the mountains were awesome and beautiful, but the Russian subjects lived in constant fear of the "Circassians on fleet-footed horses bent on kidnapping [them] and dragging them off to the mountains"; the valleys and forests were luxuriant, but they also served "as secret hiding places for the Circassians."[5] In this account, Cornies either ignored or was ignorant of the genocidal tsarist campaign that had prompted the Circassians' response.[6] On the same trip, as he left behind the mountains for the steppe, he described the Kalmyks living "in great darkness on a colossal, 600 verst stretch of desert."[7] Such Kalmyks, he said, were simple children of nature, in need of the civilizing influence of the state.

In the Caucasus, far from home and confronted by such natural "disorder," Cornies wrote about his feelings to his key Pietist confidants, Daniel Schlatter and David Epp. The letters show that for Cornies there was a clear connection between his Pietist religious views and his project of imposing order on nature. This is hardly surprising: the missionary impulse that brought Schlatter and other Pietists to the Molochnaia in the early nineteenth century employed exactly the same language of darkness and light that Cornies used in these letters. As noted in chapter 5, Pietism claimed for itself a civilizing role that frequently adopted the modernizing agenda (with all of its racial and religious prejudices) of the Enlightenment even as it rejected the secularizing tendencies of that agenda. Cornies's political defeats in the 1820s had taught him to be cautious about using such language in public, but his private letters show that they remained vital to his sense of mission in the late 1830s.

The Warkentin Affair reveals that if Cornies understood brick and tile as part of a moral aesthetic, so did the Molochnaia conservatives. Opposition to ostentatious clothing and buildings was deeply rooted in Mennonite religious belief, and Cornies's aim to beautify the Molochnaia through brick construction was controversial on this ground alone. Building the Ohrloff church – Cornies's home church – of bricks in 1837 poured fuel on an already burning fire. Cornies viewed brick buildings as part of a larger aesthetic of order and morality; conservatives like Warkentin viewed them as an unacceptable extension of Cornies's reordering of the world. Warkentin insisted that the Mennonite model remain static because he and other conservatives understood the Mennonite way of life as a survival of the early Christian community. It was not an economic model in a laboratory of modernization – it was a model of God's kingdom on earth. This is why, among the economic reforms and political challenges that Cornies championed in the late 1830s, his aesthetic reforms emerged as a key concern for conservatives.

Accounts written years after the Warkentin Affair have fostered the perception that Cornies's reforms in the 1830s led to open revolt, but there is very little evidence to support this. Even Khortitsa elder Jacob Dyck, a strong ally of Warkentin, acknowledged that things looked "very much better" in the Molochnaia than in Khortitsa, although he claimed this prosperity masked underlying problems.[8] In January 1840, Cornies characterized the disputes in his community as healthy political debate and not civil disobedience, telling a Prussian friend that "we are in a constant battle here in our community because people are alive. If they were dead, there would be no struggle nor would anything positive be achieved ... What the English parliament is on a large scale, the Molochnaia Mennonites are on a small scale ... Should you ever hear that the Molochnaia Mennonite community is calm, you can safely conclude that it is in a state of advanced decay."[9]

Had there been open defiance, the most likely place to find evidence of it would be the internal records of the Agricultural Society. However, while these records describe a small number of failing fullholdings, they trace the failures to old age, alcoholism, or illness, never to open disobedience. There is just one famous case of open rebellion, when Dirk Thun planted his trees upside down, and there is no doubt that Thun was a vocal opponent of Cornies and his reforms. Cornies's own accounts of the Warkentin Affair make Thun a leading figure in the opposition – but only after September 1840.

The event that transformed this "English parliament" into open rebellion came in the summer of 1840, when Johann Klassen, mayor of the village of Münsterberg and son of the former *Gebietsamt* mayor Johann Klassen, disobeyed Agricultural Society orders.[10] Heinrich Neufeld, a village preacher in the Warkentin congregation who authored the most influential account of the Warkentin Affair, referred to this incident as "the case of a certain [Klassen] from Münsterberg, a [village mayor who] committed an offence against Joh. Cornies."[11] Neither Neufeld's account nor any other reveals what order Klassen disobeyed, though it certainly pertained to Agricultural Society regulations regarding new buildings, so when Cornies placed bricks and tiles at the centre of the rebellion he identified a logical candidate.[12] Neufeld said that Klassen was unjustly sentenced to five days of "punishment labour."[13] Klassen, a member of the Large Flemish Congregation, appealed to Warkentin, who concluded that Klassen had done nothing wrong and appealed on his behalf to the *Gebietsamt*. Warkentin told Klassen not to carry out the sentence until the appeal was adjudicated. The *Gebietsamt* rejected the appeal and ordered that Klassen serve an additional two days of labour for failing to comply with the original sentence. Warkentin took responsibility for Klassen's failure to serve the sentence on time and offered to complete the additional two days of labour in Klassen's place, but the *Gebietsamt* insisted that Klassen carry out the full sentence.

In this account, Neufeld implied that Warkentin, representing congregational authority, should have been free to rule on a dispute between two Mennonites, and that neither the *Gebietsamt* nor the Agricultural Society nor the state had the right to interfere in the matter. He suggested that this was a personal dispute between Klassen and Cornies, having nothing at all to do with the Agricultural Society's reform program.

Other accounts tell a different story, showing that Neufeld was being disingenuous. This "certain Klassen" was Warkentin's nephew and close ally. According to Colonial Inspector Khariton Pelekh, it was he [Pelekh] and not Cornies who ordered the punishment "for [Klassen's] failure to carry out directives on various subjects of the [Agricultural Society] and by the *Gebietsamt*."[14] When the mayor and deputy mayor of Münsterberg refused to enforce the sentence, it was Pelekh who tacked on an additional two days of community labour. He also levied a fine of 5 paper rubles against the two for not carrying out his orders. An incensed Pelekh wrote to the *Gebietsamt* that "the Münsterberg village office has been apprised of this matter and ordered to publicise it in the villages, namely that the mayor has received a severe punishment for not carrying out administrative orders plus a further two days of punitive work. This is done lest other Mennonites think that, on grounds of their religious rights, governmental authorities are not entitled to punish them."[15]

Pelekh's version of events confirms Neufeld's claim that the Warkentin Party saw the central issue as congregational authority to punish Mennonites. Pelekh said the Münsterberg village office refused to carry out his orders because, "according to the Mennonite faith, one brother cannot punish another. When someone transgresses, he must be reported to the spiritual leadership. It will then, before [further] steps are taken, consult [with the civil authority] about the reprimand and instruction to be given the offender."[16] Although Pelekh said nothing of Warkentin, Neufeld's account makes it clear that Warkentin was behind this claim.

Pelekh's account confirms the underlying issue of congregational authority but also directly contradicts other elements of Neufeld's account. Most importantly, Neufeld characterized the dispute as a personal one between Cornies and Klassen, thus justifying the authority of the congregational elders to resolve it as a matter between Mennonites. There is a considerable distance between Neufeld's account of "a certain [Klassen] … [who] committed an offence against Joh. Cornies" and Pelekh's account of the nephew of Warkentin who refused to obey the orders of the Agricultural Society, the *Gebietsamt*, and the colonial inspector. Neufeld insisted that the Warkentin Party did not oppose the Agricultural Society's reform agenda, only its methods. He also acknowledged that Mennonites were "subject unto [the government] if they would want to punish anyone physically, provided that only individuals may be ordered to carry this out who have freedom of conscience in that regard."[17] Klassen's offence was his refusal to carry out Agricultural Society orders, and his punishment was ordered by a non-Mennonite representative of the Russian state, so on Neufeld's own terms, this would seem to justify Klassen's punishment.

In the final analysis, Neufeld, as Warkentin's proxy, was arguing that only the Mennonite religious establishment had the authority to punish Klassen. But of course, Warkentin had objected to Klassen's punishment and tried to prevent it. If Neufeld's arguments were accepted, it would mean that if a Mennonite refused to carry out reforms ordered by the Agricultural Society, then as long as Warkentin or any other Mennonite elder concluded that the orders were not justified, the state had no legitimate means to enforce the orders. This would have left the entire reform program subject to the authority of the religious establishment, and because Warkentin was the elder of the largest congregation, in practice he would have gained final say on all state reforms. Such an outcome was clearly unacceptable for the state.

The Klassen dispute unsettled the Molochnaia in the fall of 1840. In 1841 other events, most of them completely outside of the community's control, amplified the unease. Wool prices collapsed in a time of worldwide recession, and high Russian tariffs made things worse for Russian exporters.[18] The usual parade of Odesa wool buyers never appeared in the Molochnaia, and by mid-summer wool was selling for just 15 rubles per *pud* (16 kg), half the price of a year earlier. This slump contributed to general disquiet in the settlement. It was particularly hard on those fullholders who had been slow to transition from sheep rearing to crop agriculture. To make matters worse, Cornies, who needed ready cash for his own enterprises and to back local merchants who were dependent on him, began to ramp up pressure on delinquent debtors, many of whom were unable to pay as a result of the bad economy.

The summer of 1841 also saw an outbreak of illness in the community. In August Cornies reported to Steven that his wife, daughter, and daughter-in-law were all sick in bed, and virtually every household in the settlement was equally afflicted.[19] The epidemic continued on into the fall. The unnamed disease was not fatal, but for a population accustomed to thinking of their afflictions as reflections of God's will, the epidemic could only contribute to tensions.

Further troubling news set the settlement on edge. The state was contemplating closing the Guardianship Committee, and if it did, Mennonite affairs would be placed under the direct authority of the Ministry of State Domains. This had serious implications for Molochnaia politics, for most Mennonites saw the Guardianship Committee as an agency that not only regulated but also protected them. The Privilegium had been issued by the tsar, but it was the Guardianship Committee that implemented it. Few Mennonites had any direct contact with the ministry, while all had met representatives of the Guardianship Committee, if only its lowly district inspector Pelekh. The Ministry of State Domains, by comparison, was well outside of the experience of most Mennonites, with the singular exception of Cornies.

Kiselev's 1841 visit was particularly ominous for conservatives, for it was then that Kiselev commissioned Cornies to write the detailed description of the Mennonite administrative system described in chapter 7. In November 1841, Cornies wrote to Fadeev describing Kiselev's visit and the report the minister had requested; he went on to say that Rosen, the chair of the ministry's Simferopol office, "would like to ensure that the progress made by the Molochnaia villages in their economic arrangements might not be disturbed by this transfer [to the ministry's control] in any way. We are happy that we will soon receive a constitution that will permit the best and highest degree of development of our economic arrangements."[20] Cornies did not say how this "constitution" would relate to the Privilegium, but there was every reason for Warkentin to fear that Cornies was taking a further step in cementing his control of the settlement.

Fadeev responded to Cornies that he thought the Guardianship Committee would survive. On 23 December he sent first word of the appointment of a new assistant for the aging and increasingly ineffective Chief Guardian Inzov. Inzov had allowed Guardianship Committee affairs to drift aimlessly for years, and the expectation that the committee was about to be eliminated added to the malaise. Hahn's appointment signalled the state's decision to retain the committee, and along with it the special status of the colonists. He would soon play a dramatic role in the Molochnaia settlement.[21]

Young and energetic, Hahn had been sent to Odesa to straighten out the mess and get the New Russian laboratory back on its feet. He was thirty-four in 1841, the son of a privy councillor from St. Petersburg. He had graduated from the prestigious Tsarskoe Selo Lycée in 1826, worked for the Ministry of Internal Affairs, and served briefly in the court of Grand Prince Mikhail Pavlovich. From 1838 to 1840 he worked for the Ministry of State Domains, where he oversaw a series of provincial surveys of state peasant conditions. This was the same program that had brought Keppen to Tavrida in 1838 and meant that Hahn was well acquainted with both peasant conditions and the Ministry of State Domains' mission. Hahn's appointment to the Guardianship Committee was a further stepping stone in a career that would see him rise to become a senator and play a prominent role in the Great Reforms of the 1860s. He was ambitious and eager to make his mark in his new position.[22] He was Inzov's deputy in name only – in practice he now oversaw all Guardianship Committee affairs.

In the midst of the various tensions in the Molochnaia, the settlement held its regularly scheduled *Gebietsamt* and village elections in fall 1841.[23]

As in 1837, Warkentin attempted to use the elections to reassert his own authority. His candidate was Tiege fullholder Peter Toews. He was fifty-seven, elderly by the standards of his time. In a political atmosphere that was about to grow very bitter, even Cornies never directly criticized him.[24]

Little is known about the 1841 elections, although Cornies's correspondence provides a few details. Regier was terminally ill and did not stand for re-election.[25] The candidate whom Cornies supported to replace Regier was Jacob Penner, mayor of the Khortitsa settlement from 1826 to 1829 and chair of the Khortitsa Agricultural Society in the 1830s. Cornies and Penner were old friends, and Penner had accompanied Cornies on his trip to Saxony in 1827. A third candidate was Halbstadt mayor David Friesen, who as district mayor from 1848 to 1865 would distinguish himself mainly as a conservative defender of the landowning elites. In 1841 Cornies opposed his candidacy because of his inexperience.

Warkentin's opposition to Cornies focused on what he saw as Cornies's intrusion upon ministerial authority, with the punishment of Johann Klassen a year earlier as the most important example. Warkentin argued that Cornies was using the *Gebietsamt*'s secular authority to punish Mennonite offences that properly fell under the authority of the congregational elders. He claimed that the Privilegium, in granting Mennonites religious freedoms, implicitly recognized the authority of the elders to adjudicate internal matters. His solution was to ensure that the office of *Gebietsamt* mayor be filled by a Mennonite who acknowledged ministerial authority.[26]

According to Cornies, in the run-up to the elections Dirk Thun "was so unscrupulous that he allowed himself to be used for Warkentin's purposes. Travelling through our villages spreading this delusion on the pretext that his journey was intended to unite the congregations, this village mayor tried to criticise the actions of members of the *Gebietsamt* and to arouse hatred against them."[27] Warkentin also looked to the powerful Khortitsa elder Jacob Dyck for support. He and Warkentin were friends and allies, and as the senior Flemish elder in Russia he had substantial influence.[28] There is no evidence that Cornies – as he had in the 1837 elections – tried to invoke Guardianship Committee influence to affect the outcome of this election. Given the disarray on the Guardianship Committee in 1841, it may be that that there was little influence to be invoked. When the dust settled, Peter Toews had won the election with just 395 votes.[29] Jacob Penner came second and David Friesen third, but their vote totals are unknown.

There is no record of the total number of votes cast in this election. There were approximately 1,500 fullholdings in the settlement that year, meaning 1,500 eligible voters, but only 955 fullholders had voted in 1838 and only 1,024 would vote in 1847, so not everyone voted.[30] If the 1841 numbers were comparable to those of 1837 and 1847, then Toews won with less than 40 per cent of the votes cast in the settlement – hardly a strong showing given Warkentin's supposed tight control of his congregation. Indeed, a striking thing about the election is that neither Warkentin nor Cornies succeeded in controlling the outcome: Molochnaia fullholders had their own minds when they went to the polls.

Cornies could not accept the election of Peter Toews, and he asserted his authority as Agricultural Society chair to refuse to ratify the vote. Toews should have taken office on 1 January 1842, but on 17 December the Guardianship Committee blocked his appointment "because his advanced age makes it impossible for him to discharge the responsibilities of this office adequately."[31] There is no record that Cornies influenced this decision, but it is unimaginable that he did not play a role. In his own account of the events Cornies gave a more honest appraisal of Toews – the problem was not that he was too old, but rather that he was too loyal to Warkentin.[32] The Guardianship Committee blocked Toews's appointment, but it also refused to appoint Cornies's candidate Penner, who was ineligible because he was not registered as a Molochnaia resident. Penner had moved to the Molochnaia at some point in the late 1830s, but he was still registered in Khortitsa, and his new registration could not be processed before September.[33] The Guardianship Committee left the position of *Gebietsamt* mayor in limbo awaiting a "special decision" at an undefined future date.

According to Neufeld's account, Regier remained in office pending the Guardianship Committee's decision.[34] This was technically true, but Regier was on his deathbed and his senior deputy, Abraham Toews, was actually filling the position, closely supported by Cornies. This was not a long-term solution, so with Warkentin's candidate Peter Toews already rejected and Penner ruled ineligible, Cornies and the other members of the Agricultural Society met with Pelekh on 5 January to discuss their options.[35] The Guardianship Committee favoured appointing the third-place candidate David Friesen, but Cornies objected that Friesen, the newly elected Halbstadt mayor, was too young and inexperienced to run the *Gebietsamt*. This may have been an honest appraisal – relations between Cornies and Friesen were good, and Freisen was not a Warkentin supporter – but it also served Cornies's desire to have his own candidate in office. Cornies recommended that Abraham Toews serve as interim mayor until a final decision came from the Guardianship Committee. If Toews served as interim mayor, someone would have to fill his role as deputy mayor, and Cornies's recommendation suggests some effort to find an intermediary with Warkentin: he proposed Johann Neufeld. Neufeld was a respected member of the community who had been Halbstadt mayor in the 1830s. He was the brother of Warkentin's close ally Heinrich Neufeld and a member of the Large Flemish Congregation, but he was also Cornies's brother-in-law.[36] More importantly, he was Cornies's business partner (along with Wilhelm Martens) in the brewery in Halbstadt. He was also the settlement's principal currency exchanger, a vital role in the frontier economy.

While Pelekh and Cornies discussed strategies, in late January Warkentin assembled a conference of congregational elders and preachers in the village of Margenau.[37] Cornies later claimed that this conference was held in secret and that, apart from the four elders, Warkentin only invited a small group of his own supporters. The only record of what was said at the conference comes from Cornies, and clearly this must be taken with a grain of salt. He wrote that Warkentin was trying to rally the settlement's entire religious leadership in support of the appointment of Peter Toews. Cornies claimed that the conference also sought to reassert congregational authority over community discipline, the key issue in the elections. He suggested that Warkentin's goal was to reinforce the right of congregational elders to discipline members of their own congregations.[38]

According to both Cornies and Heinrich Neufeld, Warkentin drew surprising support from the Frisian congregation's elder Peter Wedel as well as from Wilhelm Lange, the Gnadenfeld elder. Only Bernhard Fast, elder of the Old Flemish Congregation and a long-time Cornies ally, opposed Warkentin.[39] On 2 February, Warkentin, armed with this support and accompanied by Johann Klassen, set out for Odesa to seek an audience with Hahn, who had only been in office for a month and was still acclimating himself to his role as Deputy Chief Guardian.[40] He was an unknown quantity to the Mennonites, and the politically savvy Warkentin was making sure he got to Hahn first.

Cornies's response to the Margenau Conference is the first sign that he was rattled by the Warkentin-aligned opposition. Until this point he seemed to believe that he had the situation under control. After all, he enjoyed official support at every level, from local Colonial Inspector Pelekh all the way to Minister of State Domains Kiselev. While Cornies's candidate Penner had lost the election, Peter Toews had won only a small plurality, and Cornies had every reason to suppose that he could manipulate the results of this election just as he had the 1837 election. Certainly this was the tenor of his early January meeting with Pelekh.

When Cornies got wind of the Margenau Conference he sent a furious letter to Elder Bernhard Fast, co-signed by Agricultural Society members Gerhard Enns and Jacob Martens and by fifty-two other members of the Old Flemish Congregation.[41] The letter denounced the Lichtenau, Rudnerweide, Gnadenfeld, and Alexanderwohl congregations for promoting "disobedience against state directives."[42] The letter framed Warkentin's position in dangerous terms, as "rebelling against our authorities," which could only "deserve punishment by the government."[43] Mennonites of Cornies's and Warkentin's generation had seen two rebellions against tsarist authority – the Decembrist Revolt of 1825 and the Polish Rebellion of 1830 – and they knew how harshly the rebels had been punished. While it is far-fetched to suppose that Cornies saw Warkentin's opposition in such stark terms, he certainly feared that the state's response could gravely harm Mennonite interests. Cornies and his supporters distanced themselves from the supposed rebellion: "We declare and give our holy assurance that, according to our voluntarily given solemn confession of faith, we not only love our authorities, treasure them highly and strive to follow their directives punctually, but pray for them, that God might keep them and arm them with wisdom and understanding. This would enable us to stand under the authorities' protection and leadership, lead us to peaceful and quiet lives lived in piety and honesty and demonstrate through our work and words that they have not wasted their efforts on those who are unworthy of this favour."[44]

In this critically important letter, Cornies for the first time characterized his own position in the political crisis in explicitly religious terms. Cornies wrote that Warkentin and his supporters, by promoting disobedience to "our legal authorities" and blocking economic reforms that were intended to promote "the country's welfare and the community's success," were turning "God's blessings away from us, [keeping] the land from producing its fruits and [causing] our livestock to die of hunger."[45] In his 1842 summary of the affair, Cornies made religion the central issue, writing that "Warkentin's basic beliefs [were] contrary both to the Bible and to Mennonite beliefs."[46] These statements echo a recurring theme in all of Cornies's justifications of his reforming role in the settlement: as he had written during the agricultural crises in 1825 and 1833, God used hardships to promote change; by corollary, God would send hardships to punish the failure to change.

This letter took on a major role in the growing crisis. Cornies hoped that Mennonites would come to their senses and abandon the "rebellion," but the letter had the opposite effect. Before this, Cornies had always maintained that his reforms were a legitimate expression of state authority over the Mennonites' secular economic role as a model colony, and he had claimed that Warkentin was attempting to extend his religious authority into secular matters. In truth, Warkentin acknowledged a legitimate role for secular authority, but he also argued that where Mennonites found themselves in disputes with one another about how secular authority was exercised, the elders needed to be the court of last resort. He claimed that Cornies's assertion that the Agricultural Society had the authority to punish recalcitrant fullholders violated the religious rights of the Mennonites by bypassing ministerial authority.[47] On these terms, Cornies had been winning the political battle: most Mennonite fullholders were benefiting from the reforms, and in the 1841 elections Warkentin had been unable to rally a majority even within his own congregation. But in the 27 January letter, Cornies accepted Warkentin's terms of debate. By characterizing Agricultural Society reforms – and implicitly his own authority – as an expression of God's will and not of the state's secular will, he accepted that the reforms themselves were not the core issue; the key was God's will, and that could only mean that the elders, and not Cornies, had the final say. Cornies implicitly if unintentionally acknowledged this by asking Fast, his elder, to take up the cause. By accepting religion as the issue, Cornies had opened the door to a political disaster. For all of his successes in the 1830s, he now found himself threatened with a political defeat even more serious than the one he had suffered in 1826.

In a sense, it is Warkentin who offered Cornies a way out of this predicament. Even as Cornies acknowledged religious authority, Warkentin set off for Odesa to make his case to Hahn, thus acknowledging secular authority. He also forced Cornies to respond, and in the arena of Guardianship Committee politics, Cornies had the upper hand.

Hahn had not yet visited the Molochnaia, nor had he had any communication with Cornies. He undoubtedly had been briefed on the Mennonites and their key role in New Russian development, but his initial fumbling of Mennonite affairs suggests that he was not well briefed. According to Heinrich Neufeld, Warkentin received a cordial reception from Hahn.[48] However, Hahn did not agree to Warkentin's request that Peter Toews, the winner of the 1841 election, be appointed *Gebietsamt* mayor. In December Inzov had ruled that Toews was too old to fill the office, and the newly arrived Hahn did not choose to overrule the general. Instead, on 27 January he sent an order to Pelekh to conduct new elections.[49] Neufeld claimed that Hahn told Warkentin he would accept the results of that election, even if Peter Toews again won.

Pelekh informed Cornies of the decision to hold new elections, and on 7 February, Cornies – fully aware that Warkentin was already in Odesa to meet with Hahn in person – sent a letter to Hahn stating the Agricultural Society's case. Cornies told Hahn that "everyone to whom the well-being of the community is not a matter of indifference has heard of this decision [to hold a new election] with great astonishment," and he urged Hahn to reconsider.[50] Cornies cautioned Hahn that it was "an open question" who might win such an election, and he offered his own introduction to the Molochnaia Mennonite situation:

> The [Agricultural Society] has been assigned the obligation of functioning as the principal means of promoting our well-being and morality. Through its regulations, the society reaches into every branch of agriculture and even into home and family life. The head of this office must discuss many subjects with the Gebietsamt mayor and reach conclusions that ensure a united voice that would help to achieve our goals. The promotion of the community's well-being must be unambiguous. It must be established step by step, with continuity and permanence and without disruption. A Gebietsamt mayor must be serious, understanding, and loving. He must feel a sense of duty and have the community's well-being more at heart than even his own. He must feel a sense for order and justice and take pleasure in both.[51]

Cornies did not directly attack Warkentin, saying only that the community might not elect the right type of mayor because the majority of Mennonites were naive, simple religious folk, who would "try to elect quiet, pious and righteous persons to these offices. In such an election, many think little … about … whether such persons have any desire, inclination or ability to promote everything that is in the best interests of the community, and if they show the requisite prudence and zeal to establish it for succeeding generations."[52]

Cornies was attempting to strike a delicate balance. He knew better than anyone that Mennonites owed their privileges to their conduct as model colonists. He likewise knew that the state had no patience for schisms within its religious confessions – it expected the Mennonites to act as the state's agents, and it did not want to have to deal with a divided community.[53] By admitting that the community was divided, he exposed the Mennonites to the possibility that they might lose their privileges. Rather than characterizing the divide as a fundamental political split, he argued that Mennonites, like all peasants, needed good leadership. Even this seemed to challenge the premise of the model colony, for if the key was good leadership, then how were the Mennonites different from any other peasant community? Cornies also faced a second serious problem: Hahn, newly arrived from St. Petersburg and unfamiliar with the New Russian scene, needed to get a grip on Mennonite affairs. If, as Cornies seemed to admit, the majority of Mennonites backed Warkentin, then the quickest resolution to the problem was for Hahn to also back Warkentin.

In his letter to Hahn, Cornies repeated his recommendation that Abraham Toews be appointed interim mayor and Johann Neufeld interim deputy mayor. He dropped his suggestion that Penner be appointed mayor as soon as his residency status permitted it and instead suggested that if Toews and Neufeld proved competent, their appointments could be made permanent.[54]

Hahn rejected these recommendations and ordered a new election. Regier died on 26 February, and from then until the elections, Abraham Toews was interim mayor. He was also Cornies's candidate to hold the office permanently in what was the most contentious election ever staged in the Molochnaia under tsarist rule.[55]

Armed with Hahn's promise that the Guardianship Committee would accept the results of the election regardless of the outcome, Warkentin, Klassen, and Thun toured the Molochnaia in the spring of 1842 attacking Cornies and Abraham Toews.[56] They accused Cornies of acting "harshly and dictatorially" and interfering in religious affairs, and to this they added the accusation that Regier had been guilty of financial improprieties. According to Neufeld the books could not be balanced and Wilhelm Martens contributed money to make up the shortfall.[57] There is a hint from Cornies that there were indeed difficulties balancing the books – in late February he urged the *Gebietsamt* to see to the "final completion of community accounts" so that there would be "no confusion" when the Guardianship Committee reviewed them – but there is no evidence that this was a consequence of anything other than bad bookkeeping. What it did reflect was the bitterness of the campaign.

Cornies's January letter to Fast denouncing the other congregational elders became a *cause célèbre* during this second election. Neufeld said that the letter was intended to "divide the [settlement] into two factions."[58] If so, it succeeded. By late March the Molochnaia was divided into two hostile camps, the majority clearly aligned with Warkentin. The letter to Fast had eroded the middle ground of fullholders who accepted Cornies's economic leadership but Warkentin's religious leadership. They had been forced to choose sides, and in the end they chose their congregational elder.

Neufeld's account of the elections claims that Hahn assured Warkentin that the Guardianship Committee would accept the results of the election and appoint Peter Toews as mayor if he were elected. Cornies's account insists that the directive from the Guardianship Committee that announced the new elections plainly ordered the community not to choose Peter Toews."[59] The truth probably lies somewhere between the two versions. The Guardianship Committee's 27 January directive to Pelekh to hold a new election – sent before Warkentin met with Hahn – said nothing about who was eligible to run. Hahn simply charged Pelekh with ordering the new election, and while there is no record of what Pelekh's directive to the *Gebietsamt* said, given that the Guardianship Committee had ruled Peter Toews ineligible in December it is quite possible that Pelekh repeated this conclusion in his own directive. Hahn was unfamiliar with the political situation in the Molochnaia, and it is possible that he assured Warkentin that Peter Toews would be appointed if elected, not knowing that Pelekh would order differently. Whatever the source of the confusion, Peter Toews' eligibility became a contentious issue. Cornies recorded that while campaigning for Toews, "Warkentin and Klaasen dismissed [the Guardianship Committee directive] as a fabrication on the part of the Gebietsamt and the inspector. Most inhabitants ignored the directive."[60] If Hahn had told Warkentin that Peter Toews was eligible, then Warkentin may have honestly believed this, but Pelekh was the official representative of the Guardianship Committee in the Molochnaia, and Warkentin's defiance of his orders would later be used by Cornies to argue that Warkentin had rebelled against state authority.[61] This served as an important justification for the severity of the punishment that awaited Warkentin.

There is no record of when the new election took place, although it was probably in late March or early April, and certainly before 27 April.[62] Warkentin's candidate Peter Toews won the election with at least eight hundred votes, an overwhelming victory for Warkentin and a crushing defeat for Cornies.[63]

In late April Hahn finally made his first appearance in the Molochnaia. He stopped for one night at Pelekh's home in Prishchib, met briefly with Cornies, and then travelled through the German settlement and on to Mariupol. The meeting with Cornies was apparently intended to bring an end to the community disputes and broker a peace between Cornies and Warkentin. It must have been a grim affair for Cornies, who met Hahn for the first time having failed to manage the *Gebietsamt* elections, in the process alienating a majority of the community. If Hahn's first priority was to restore order, then Warkentin must have seemed a better ally than Cornies. There is every indication that the message Cornies took away from this meeting was that it was up to him to restore the peace.

On 27 April, Cornies offered an olive branch to Warkentin. He, Gerhard Enns, and Jacob Martens – the three principal authors of the inflammatory letter to Bernhard Fast in January – sent an abject apology to Warkentin: "We regret our actions from the bottom of our hearts. Yet since it is impossible to undo what has once been done, we do not hesitate, beloved elders, with complete honesty, to ask your forgiveness and that of every member of your congregations for the unjust accusations contained in that letter that have offended you."[64] They quickly qualified this apology, writing that "we might of course reasonably excuse ourselves, pointing to the sad dissension among the church teachers that has continued for many years to your pain, ours and to the pain of all true lovers of mankind."[65] This letter was the first real attempt to end a conflict that had simmered and sometimes boiled for two decades. It must have galled Cornies deeply to ask Warkentin and his congregation to "forgive us in your hearts, even as we join you in the hope and desire to be forgiven for all our sins before God, our heavenly Father in Christ."[66] When Warkentin rejected this overture and Cornies regained his authority, Cornies would show no signs of forgiveness.

The apology was followed by two meetings between Cornies and Warkentin. According to Neufeld, at these meetings Cornies offered Warkentin his help in setting "everything right."[67] Cornies's version is different, and in its characterization of Warkentin as a rebellious conspirator it again evokes the language of the January letter. According to Cornies, at the first meeting Warkentin complained to him about "unfair activities during the elections."[68] Cornies responded that the unrest in the community was in nobody's interest, and that Warkentin could "make peace ... if he wished to do so."[69] This much of Cornies's account is compatible with the letter of apology, but Cornies went on to threaten Warkentin with punishment if the elder was not willing to make peace. He claimed that Warkentin replied: "I can restore peace in my congregation but I will first consult my fellow servants." Then he added: "I do comprehend that nothing good can come from such an uproar, which will be shameful for our descendants for a hundred years."[70]

The next day Warkentin invited Cornies to meet with him again. Cornies later recalled that he immediately suspected that something was amiss. Warkentin greeted him outside his house "in an unusually friendly manner," and Cornies

> began to suspect him of being cunning ... I became aware of two persons sitting near the window in the house. It seemed to me that Warkentin wanted to start a discussion outside, but I decided that I would not do so without witnesses. I therefore hurried through the door ahead of Warkentin and stepped into the room. In the presence of the two men from Warkentin's congregation waiting there, I said that I had responded to his

invitation and now wanted him to explain what he expected of me. With the gravity of a Haman sitting on his divan, he made gestures indicating he did not know anything about having invited me to his house. I referred to the letter in my pocket, which had been written by one of his members at his request. Then he remembered, acting in a manner that seemed to indicate that the Seven Year's War had meanwhile occurred. Yes, he now remembered having invited me.[71]

Cornies claimed that Warkentin used "trickery and reproach … [and] criticised everything built up over the last twenty years and derided everything in which he had not been allowed to have his own way."[72] Warkentin claimed that he could not calm his congregation, which was only pursuing justice; his nephew Klassen had been unjustly punished, and his ally Thun had been acting "with the best intentions to promote the community's well-being."[73] The only solution to the conflict that Warkentin offered was that Cornies retract his opposition to Warkentin's and Klassen's actions. Cornies told Warkentin that "this could never be," and left.[74]

Cornies accused Warkentin of spreading the story that Cornies had requested forgiveness for the "injustices" he had committed and that he had agreed to follow orders from Warkentin in the future. Cornies wrote that the ensuing events "resembled the dark ages, the times of the Vandals." His attempts to "maintain the community's respectable image were misinterpreted and maliciously depicted" as arising from his "fear of punishment." He was "almost completely overwhelmed by anguish."[75]

Other accounts of Warkentin's response to the election confirm that the elder celebrated Cornies's apology as a decisive victory. According to Abraham Friesen, leader of the Kleine Gemeinde and a Cornies supporter, Warkentin even claimed that Hahn was going to deport Cornies to Siberia.[76] Neufeld wrote that after the election everyone in the settlement "rejoiced, that peace and calm would … again be restored."[77] In early May, Warkentin assembled another conference of congregational elders and village preachers, apparently confident that he had wrested control of the settlement back from Cornies.[78]

Warkentin's victory celebration was short-lived. On 16 May, Hahn arrived back in the Molochnaia and spent two days with Cornies at Iushanle. On 18 May he moved on to Halbstadt, where he stayed with Johann Neufeld, the new deputy mayor. On 19 May, Hahn summoned Warkentin and the other elders to a meeting at Neufeld's house. He instructed Warkentin to arrive early for a private meeting, and Warkentin apparently anticipated that Hahn wanted to discuss community affairs with the *de facto* new community leader. Instead, Hahn summarily dismissed Warkentin from his position as elder and ordered him to "keep silent and no longer participate" in community affairs.[79] After the stunned Warkentin departed, Hahn met with the rest of the elders and informed them of what had transpired. According to Heinrich Neufeld, the elders were shocked, with the exception of Fast, who apparently had advance warning of what was to come.[80]

There is no clear explanation for Hahn's dramatic about-face. It seems apparent that at the end of April he was prepared to accept the outcome of the election and the reality of Warkentin's political dominance. Three weeks later he deposed Warkentin, disallowed Peter Toews's election, and ordered a third election, this time with clear instructions that the Mennonites should elect Cornies's candidate, Abraham Toews. In part this must have been a consequence of what he encountered during his first visit to the region. The Molochnaia oasis was a New Russian marvel, and as Hahn visited the surrounding settlements the contrast would have been driven home. During his inspection tour Hahn had the opportunity to ask lots of questions about how the Mennonite settlement had achieved its remarkable condition. There is no doubt what answer he would have received: Cornies was the driving force.

Among the most striking things about the conclusion of the Warkentin Affair is how quickly and completely Warkentin disappeared from public affairs. He was fifty-six in 1842 and had been a preacher since 1817, an elder since he formed the Large Flemish Congregation in 1824. Now, threatened with arrest and exile, he withdrew completely from public affairs. There is not a single indication that he meddled in Molochnaia politics, or even provided advice to his former supporters, between May 1842 and his death in 1852.

Warkentin's silence left the Large Flemish Congregation leaderless. Thun had never been part of the congregational leadership – his support as village mayor was important to Warkentin, but he could not replace the elder. As for Johann Klassen, while his 1840 punishment had been a key symbolic event initiating the crisis, he was just an adjunct to his powerful uncle. After 1842 he also quietly dropped from view.

When Hahn dismissed Warkentin, he also ordered the Large Flemish Congregation disbanded. He deputized Cornies to oversee the process and report the results back to the Guardianship Committee.[81] Cornies chose his brother-in-law Heinrich Neufeld, whom he viewed as a moderate and responsible figure within the Large Flemish Congregation, as his liaison to the congregational leaders.[82] Neufeld, a village preacher with no apparent ambition to fill the job of elder, reluctantly complied. On 24 May, five days after Warkentin's dismissal, he presided over a congregational meeting where it was decided to create two new congregations. He reported back to Cornies, explaining the decision and asking time for the preachers to fast and pray before electing the new elders.[83] Cornies insisted that the Large Flemish Congregation comply with Hahn's orders and split into three smaller congregations, but he granted the congregation until January to form the third. The first two congregations would still have to be established by the end of June.[84] On 18 June the Large Flemish Congregation preachers elected Heinrich Wiens of Gnadenheim village as the elder of the new Margenau Congregation. Neufeld asked for an extension until after harvest season to elect a second elder. At the same time, Neufeld asked Cornies to free him from his liaison role and deal directly with Wiens.[85] Cornies was apparently not impressed – he sent Heinrich's brother, the settlement's new deputy mayor Johann Neufeld, to deliver a warning that if the Large Flemish Congregation did not quickly comply with orders, Warkentin and Thun would be punished.[86]

The last gasp of Large Flemish Congregation opposition came in August and September. The preachers of the dissolved congregation met in Margenau on 13 August and discussed sending Toews and Thun to Odesa to plead their case directly with Hahn. Over the next three days Neufeld, Toews, Wiens, and Thun met with the elders of the other Molochnaia congregations in a final effort to rally support. This failed, according to Neufeld's hyperbolic account, because the elders feared "the Neronian government of Cornies."[87] The leaders of the Large Flemish Congregation met three more times, on 31 August, 7 September, and 8 September. They debated sending a letter to Russia's Department of Spiritual Affairs and meeting with Hahn, who was back in the Molochnaia to check up on affairs, but without Warkentin's leadership this rump of the Large Flemish Congregation did not carry through any of its plans.[88]

On 10 September, Hahn summoned Heinrich Neufeld to a meeting in Halbstadt and demanded that he account for the delay in establishing the new congregations. Neufeld bravely protested that the congregation wanted an explanation for Warkentin's dismissal before it complied, and this may confirm Cornies's claim that the congregation still held out hope that Warkentin would be permitted to return as the elder of the third congregation.[89] Hahn offered three justifications, but Neufeld detailed just one in his account of the meeting – Johann Klassen's disobedience of orders in 1840, and Warkentin's defence of Klassen.[90]

Hahn now called Heinrich Wiens, as well as the members of the Agricultural Society and representatives of the *Gebietsamt*, into the meeting. He issued stern orders that the Large Flemish Congregation create two more congregations and elect their elders by the end of the month.[91]

A follow-up letter from Cornies confirmed this order and added that conspiratorial meetings of the sort that the Large Flemish Congregation leaders had held in August and early September to "hatch plots against our regulations and laws" would no longer be permitted.[92] If they continued, Warkentin, as the presumed instigator, would be exiled. The congregational elections followed on 22 September, when Dirk Warkentin of Petershagen was chosen to lead the Lichtenau Congregation, and 29 September, when Heinrich Toews was chosen to lead the Pordenau congregation.[93]

When the *Gebietsamt* election was held for a third time, in August 1842, Cornies's candidate Abraham Toews won easily, but seventy defiant members of the Large Flemish Congregation again voted for Peter Toews.[94] Hahn punished the seventy with community service, and, in a move that particularly shocked the pacifist Mennonites, during his September visit to the settlement he had their leader publicly flogged. Neufeld provided the only report of this flogging, identifying the victim as "a village mayor."[95] It was almost certainly Thun, although there are no records to confirm this. In July, Cornies had told Hahn that Thun was trying to "stir up rebellion" and urged that "stern action" be taken; in late August, Hahn had concluded that Thun had taken "highly illegal and punishable actions" and resolved to return to the Molochnaia and personally "take the sternest measures ... to halt this evil and to reduce the guilty persons to a position in which they are completely harmless in future."[96]

The flogging shocked the Mennonites. It also had significant implications for their privileged status in the empire. As historian Abby Schrader writes, public flogging was used by the Russian state to demarcate "boundaries between elite and lower-estate subjects."[97] It was a form of punishment reserved "for the lower estates which [the state believed] lacked the ability to understand the laws and the moral sense to be corrected by less extreme forms of punishment."[98] While the Mennonites enjoyed no formal exemption from flogging, their Privilegium-defined status as model colonists offered them unwritten but meaningful protection from such symbolic degradation. Tsar Nicholas had initiated a thorough review of Russia's penal codes in 1826, and by the time Thun was flogged in 1842 the 1845 Penal Code was nearing completion. Its provisions would more clearly define the status of all tsarist subjects, and there was a clear danger that the Mennonites were being written into the wrong side of this ledger.[99]

With Hahn's departure and the election of the three new congregational elders, the main events of the Warkentin Affair were over. On 18 October 1842, Cornies reported on the "calm, peace and obedience" of the new congregations.[100] Warkentin was keeping to himself at his home in Altona, as was Thun in Fürstenwerder. As for the rest of the dissolved congregation, Cornies claimed that "many members find the actions of these men abhorrent and are remorseful about them. They seem ashamed."[101]

The Aftermath

While the resolution of the Warkentin Affair saw Cornies's political opponents crushed, a strong undercurrent of bitterness survived. The next *Gebietsamt* elections in 1845 provide interesting – if somewhat ambiguous – hints about the character of the settlement's religious and political divides in the wake of the affair. The elections brought none of the fireworks of the previous two contests, and there is no sign that they particularly troubled Cornies. For the first time since the 1832 elections, no one in the community appealed the outcome to the Guardianship Committee, although perhaps after the events of 1842 there was no point – Hahn's support of Cornies was unambiguous. Cornies barely noted the elections at all in his correspondence.

The two main candidates for mayor in 1845 were Johann Neufeld and David Friesen, both of Halbstadt. Neufeld was the Cornies Party candidate. David Friesen was the Halbstadt mayor who had been rejected as a replacement for Peter Toews in 1841 because of his inexperience. By 1845 he was clearly aligned against Cornies as the Warkentin Party candidate. Neufeld won the election with 608 of the 1,024 votes cast (59 per cent). Friesen received 216 votes (21 per cent), while Peter Toews, the Warkentin Party candidate in 1842, received 62 votes. The support for Toews was clearly a protest vote.

A fourth candidate made a surprise appearance in the results: 13 votes were cast for Peter Cornies, Johann's brother and a former mayor of Ohrloff. It is hard to know what to make of Peter's candidacy. He almost never appeared in Cornies's correspondence after 1828, when Johann sharply criticized him for mismanaging his (Johann's) affairs while he was away in Saxony. Even when Peter died in 1847, it barely received a passing comment from Johann.[102] There are grounds, then, for suspecting that relations between the brothers were not warm. Perhaps this too was a sort of protest vote? These elections show that Cornies was firmly in control of the settlement, but they also show that the 1842 elections had not fully suppressed opposition to Cornies: many Molochnaia Mennonites remained willing to openly oppose his candidate.

There are interesting patterns buried in the results that show other dynamics within the community. Neufeld, Cornies's candidate, received overwhelming support (82 per cent) from the villages established after

1824, while Friesen, the Warkentin candidate, received his strongest support – though still just 44 per cent – from the villages established before 1825. This suggests that the newer immigrants, accustomed to the changing religious and secular world of Prussia, were an important constituency for Cornies within the settlement. Surprisingly, the Frisian Pietists of the 1818–24 immigration split their support between the Cornies and Warkentin parties. As they established themselves as prosperous, established fullholders, perhaps they had come to resent Cornies's interference in their affairs.

Among the more recently established villages, 100 per cent of Gnadenfeld (est. 1836) and Hutterthal (est. 1842) residents voted for Neufeld, and 78 per cent followed suit in Waldheim (est. 1836), and Landskrone (est. 1839). The latter two villages were populated by formerly landless Mennonites from within the existing settlement, rather than new immigrants, and this raises an important question about the attitude of the landless toward the settlement's disputes. By 1839 there were about 3,000 families in the Molochnaia, of which half were landless. In 1842, when the Warkentin congregation was divided into three, Heinrich Neufeld listed 1,000 families as members. This suggests that the claim that the majority of Molochnaia Mennonites were members of the Warkentin congregation may not be accurate – the majority of the *fullholders* were surely Warkentin congregants, but there is reason to suspect that the landless, who depended on Cornies's policies for jobs, and equally depended on his oversight of land allocation for their future prospects to buy land, preferred Cornies. This foreshadows the landlessness crisis of the 1860s, when merchant and estate-owning elites sided with the landless against the fullholders.[103]

If the 1845 elections offer only general implications about attitudes in the Molochnaia settlement, other post-1842 events clearly document the bitterness of some members of the Warkentin Party. In 1843 this bitterness flared up in a letter-writing campaign, as Molochnaia Mennonites contacted their relatives in Prussia denouncing Cornies and seeking support. Responses from Prussia brought renewed controversies. Most notably, a letter from the conservative Prussian Mennonite elder Abraham Regier asserted that the removal of Warkentin "is unheard of since freedom of religious practice has always been allowed in Russia. The situation cannot be allowed to remain this way without the reinstatement of Warkentin."[104] In March 1843 Cornies wrote to David Epp that Regier's letters were "highly damaging" to the Molochnaia Mennonites. Cornies asked Epp to intercede and warn Regier that his continued rabble-rousing would be harmful to the entire Russian Mennonite community. Epp's response offered little help – while he supported

Cornies's views, he saw no harm in Prussian Mennonites asking for information about the Warkentin Affair or discussing its significance.[105]

Epp's response prompted an angry letter from Cornies's secretary Wiebe. The fact that Cornies did not himself write this letter to his old friend suggests the extent of his anger. Wiebe's letter was stilted and officious and said that Cornies thought it best to leave Epp's most recent letter "completely unanswered, above all because Mr. Epp seeks to excuse Elder Regier's impure influence." Wiebe went on: "It is no small matter that Mr. Epp meant to blame Mr. Cornies, who holds the true well-being of our local Mennonites close to his heart, even though many in our area and some in Prussia lack the insight to understand his selfless endeavours."[106]

Regier's interference in Molochnaia affairs had attracted Hahn's attention, prompting the deputy director of the Guardianship Committee to visit the settlement. Wiebe claimed that Regier was not just challenging Cornies – he was trying to "instil mistrust in Russia's high administration and its most wise enactments."[107] During his visit Hahn confronted Elder Heinrich Wiens and told him that further congregational interference in administrative affairs would not be tolerated; according to Wiebe, it was "only because of Mr. Cornies's intercession that the highly detrimental matter involving Elder Regier's interference had not been considered at further levels."[108] Wiebe concluded with a stern message to Epp – he should advise Regier to keep out of Molochnaia business.

Cornies's role in the dispute over Regier's letter points to a significant outcome of the Warkentin Affair: Hahn was now asking him to take a direct role in religious disputes in the settlement. An important example of this came in 1844, when the troublesome relationships of the Lange family in Gnadenfeld forced him to act as a mediator between Molochnaia congregations. While the matter had no direct relationship to the Warkentin Affair, Cornies's role in it vividly depicts how the affair had changed his position in the religious affairs of the community.

Wilhelm Lange, the revered elder of the Gnadenfeld congregation, died in 1841, and the congregation elected his nephew Friedrich Wilhelm Lange to replace him. In 1838, Friedrich Wilhelm's wife Henriette (née Kluge) inherited a large sum of money from her Prussian family, and she and her husband travelled back to Prussia to take possession of the inheritance. Friedrich Wilhelm insisted on leaving his children with relatives in Gnadenfeld because he feared that Henriette would leave him and stay in Prussia with the children.[109] While the cause of the dispute is not clear – Cornies blamed it on Henriette's vanity and pride – several sources hint that Friedrich Wilhelm was a controlling, perhaps abusive figure. Lange was having an affair with a young woman in his congregation, and he was forced out of Gnadenfeld in 1849 for this infidelity.[110]

After the Langes returned from Prussia, their dispute became a public scandal. They brought some of the inheritance back with them, but they left 10,000 thalers in Prussia, lent out as an investment. Friedrich Wilhelm signed a document that required that he have written permission from Henriette before he could withdraw money from this fund, an arrangement that he later claimed he had only agreed to as a result of lies told by agents of his wife's family.[111]

In 1844, Friedrich Wilhelm received word from friends in Prussia that Henriette had secretly sent instructions to have money from the fund issued to her relatives.[112] This prompted a major dispute. Henriette, supported by Wilhelm Lange – also a preacher and Friedrich Wilhelm's cousin – demanded a divorce and the right to return to Prussia.[113] At this point Cornies intervened, in the process showing that the concern he sometimes expressed about the treatment of women could be quickly set aside when the interests of his political allies were threatened. On Friedrich Wilhelm's behalf, Cornies wrote to Hahn, asking for advice about how the remainder of the 10,000 thalers could be transferred to Russia, where Friedrich Wilhelm could presumably control both the money and Henriette.[114] Hahn responded with regret that he could do nothing about the money – under Russian law a woman had the legal right to control her own inheritance – but added that Russian law prohibited Henriette from obtaining a divorce and leaving the country while she still had minor children.[115] The unhappy marriage continued, despite Friedrich Wilhelm's adultery and his move to a Lutheran community on the Dnieper River in 1849.[116]

The marital scandal provoked a serious problem for the Molochnaia congregations. Wilhelm Lange, Henriette's supporter, took up her cause in Gnadenfeld and in letters back to Prussia. His attacks on Friedrich Wilhelm disrupted the community, and in July 1844 the Gnadenfeld congregation banned Wilhelm Lange and his wife. The congregation justified the ban on the grounds that these Langes had "been behaving improperly since winter, acting as though all of our church teachers are worthy only of being tied to a millstone and thrown into the sea. [Wilhelm Lange] has treated the whole congregation worse than a secretive thief and written deceitful perjuries to Prussia."[117]

The response of the other Molochnaia congregations to this punishment shows that in the broader settlement there was sympathy for Henriette Lange's plight. The banned Langes refused to submit to congregational authority, instead applying for and receiving admission into the Waldheim congregation.[118] This was inevitably controversial.

The ban served a key function in maintaining community discipline and social cohesion. If Mennonites could avoid congregational discipline by changing congregations, the authority of the congregations would be undermined, necessitating the intrusion of secular authority. The Gnadenfeld congregation approached Cornies for help, and he convinced the Waldheim congregation to reverse its decision.[119] Then, at a ministerial conference in September 1844, the Waldheim congregation again reversed course – apparently supported by the other congregations – and said it would accept the Langes.[120] The Gnadenfeld congregation again turned to Cornies, asking for his advice and assistance. What could they do, they asked? From a Gnadenfeld perspective, the Langes were banned. From a Waldheim perspective, they were in good standing. The Gnadenfeld congregational leaders wrote to Cornies in frustration, saying that they were at their wits' end and probably "large numbers of [the Gnadenfeld] congregation will act contrary to [the ban] or join other congregations."[121]

The Gnadenfeld congregation's informal request to Cornies for advice was followed by a formal appeal to Cornies and the Agricultural Society for intervention.[122] On 15 October 1844 the Agricultural Society sent a letter to the other congregations laying out Gnadenfeld's concerns and urging the elders to either justify their actions with specific reference to relevant biblical texts or enforce the Gnadenfeld ban. The society acknowledged that it had no authority to intercede but added that it was required to relay complaints to the Guardianship Committee. It gave the elders fourteen days to reply, saying that if nothing happened, it would "reluctantly" send the complaint to Odesa, "conscious of the fact that it would redound to the community's shame."[123]

This letter had no effect, and when Hahn visited in October the Gnadenfeld congregation appealed directly to him. Hahn sided with Gnadenfeld and issued orders that the ban be enforced. On 22 November, Cornies wrote to congregational elders Benjamin Ratzlaff and Peter Wedel, ordering them to enforce the ban and to advise their congregations to follow suit.[124]

Cornies's role in the Lange dispute is striking. Before 1842 he had taken no direct role in religious matters – he was clearly focused on economic policy. The Warkentin Affair changed this, and in 1844 the Gnadenfeld congregation asked him to intervene directly in an intra-congregational dispute. He was now understood to wield the authority of the state, and the Gnadenfelders, accepting this new reality, were prepared to invite the state's representative into congregational affairs when it suited their interests. This does not mean that Cornies personally possessed the authority to dictate solutions in religious squabbles, for the Waldheim congregation rejected Cornies's strongly worded recommendation that they refuse to accept Wilhelm Lange. Hahn once again stepped in to impose a resolution, insisting that congregational bans be enforced. For Hahn, this was consistent with his resolution of the Warkentin Affair. His goal was to ensure that the Mennonites responded to state orders as a single coherent group. This required that the community maintain a coherent system of discipline.

Cornies faced one further religious controversy in 1846, and it would bring about the final resolution of the Warkentin Affair. After Hahn's decisive intervention in 1842 there was an uneasy truce between Cornies and Heinrich Weins, elder of the Margenau congregation and the leading figure among Warkentin's former adherents. Cornies worked to avoid controversy, addressing Wiens respectfully when it was necessary to address him at all.

The 1846 controversy began in June when a Hutterite villager got in a fight with a Russian servant (regarding the larger story of the Hutterites, see chapter 9). Heinrich Neufeld wrote that the Hutterite was "teased and hurt" by the Russian and in response hit him "on the shoulder," but Dirk Wiebe, the Lichtefeld village mayor, told *Gebietsamt* Deputy Mayor Johann Neufeld that the Russian servant's ribs were broken.[125] According to Heinrich Neufeld, the Russian servant filed a complaint with Cornies, who ordered that the Hutterite receive twelve lashes as punishment, to be administered by four local Mennonite landowners.[126] Johann Neufeld offered a different account of the event, suggesting that Cornies did not order the punishment; he wrote that the whole matter was "not the business of the *Gebietsamt* or the Agricultural Society. Local [Russian] authorities have responded with a punishment appropriate for the mistreatment of these Russians."[127]

Johann Neufeld's version of the event has a ring of truth to it. He was writing soon after the altercation occurred, before Wiens became involved in the matter, in a private note to Cornies apprising him of the situation. By comparison, Heinrich Neufeld's description was written three years later in a public condemnation of Cornies's treatment of Wiens. Another reason to prefer Johann Neufeld's account is that neither the *Gebietsamt* nor the Agricultural Society had jurisdiction in a dispute between a Hutterite and a Russian; as Johann Neufeld noted, the local Russian authorities were responsible for adjudicating such disputes and punishing wrongdoers. It is also noteworthy that Johann Neufeld assumed that he had to explain to Cornies what had happened. If Cornies had really ordered the punishment, Neufeld would presumably not have needed to tell him that the local authorities had dealt with the matter.

There is no disputing that the twelve lashes were administered by Mennonites, three of whom were members of Wiens's congregation. Wiens banned the three as punishment for this violation of the Mennonite principle of non-violence.[128] They repented to the congregation, which readmitted them, but for Cornies and the administration, Wiens's challenge of the secular authorities' right to order punishment was seen as a renewal of the Warkentin congregation's defiance of state authority. Heinrich Neufeld insisted that this was not true: the issue was not the right of the state to order the punishment of Mennonites, it was that Mennonites should not carry out such punishments. He wrote that any Mennonite who "considers himself as a government person and … adheres to the laws and ordinances of the worldly government which are in conflict with the teachings of Christ … is no Mennonite, and indeed, no true Christian."[129] While this was a justification for banning the congregational members, it was also clearly aimed at Cornies, whom Heinrich Neufeld – probably incorrectly – held accountable for ordering the punishment.

When Hahn made his annual tour of the settlement in July 1846, he called Wiens to account for meddling in government affairs. Hahn told Wiens that all Russian subjects, including the Mennonites, were obliged to obey official orders, and that if Wiens himself were ordered to carry out corporal punishment he would have to do so. Wiens responded that this he "would not do."[130] He argued that the Privilegium protected the Mennonites from such orders, which violated their religious principles. Hahn responded that "if the Privilegium [said] that the government no longer has the liberty to command disobedient subjects to be punished, then [he] would be the first to lobby the government to terminate such a Privilegium."[131] In December, Hahn repeated this public threat in a private letter that warned Cornies that "it seems as though the Mennonites are too privileged here in Russia and are getting restless. From this, evil consequences are sure to follow. Children will not be able to achieve as much as their fathers will lose through their own arrogance and stupidity."[132] Hahn's words echoed the symbolic threat of the 1842 flogging of Thun: the Mennonites' special status in Russia was hanging in the balance. This threat to Mennonite privileges was not an isolated phenomenon, for by the mid-1840s Nicholas was ramping up pressure on non-Slavic, non-Orthodox subjects across the empire. In 1844 he formally abolished the Kahal – the Jewish system of self-government – and that same year he sharply reduced the rights of the Lamaist Buriats in Siberia.[133] The changes to Russia's colonial compact that had begun in the 1820s were accelerating, and as Hahn made clear, the Mennonites were not exempt.

The Privilegium was again at the centre of Mennonite internal conflict, and Cornies again found himself defending Mennonite privileges. In September, Hahn dismissed Wiens from his position as congregational elder.[134] Cornies appealed to the other congregational elders, asking that they support this action, and elders Fast, Lange, and Ratzlaff wrote to Wiens supporting his dismissal and warning him that he should no longer carry out an elder's functions.[135] When Wiens's congregation refused to accept his dismissal, Cornies responded with a denunciation of what he characterized as "the complete disruption and destruction of all governmental authority [and an attempt to] arouse citizens against the government."[136] As in 1842, Cornies employed dangerous accusations of rebellion to get his way. At the end of November, Wiens's supporters sent a letter to Hahn asking for his protection; on 12 December they followed up with a request for an independent investigation of the matter.[137] Hahn did not reply to the congregation, instead writing the angry letter to Cornies that is quoted above.

Cornies now sought a resolution to the conflict. His first proposal – vetoed by Hahn – was to have Wiens declared insane and confined to an asylum.[138] This recommendation shows Cornies at his tyrannical worst and echoes his 1841 recommendation that the Doukhobor leaders, though innocent of any crime, be arrested to end their opposition to the state's coercive efforts to convert their community. Hahn suggested instead that Cornies ask the other congregational elders to make written complaints against Wiens. Armed with such letters Hahn could approach the Minister of State Domains and ask for an order deporting Wiens from Russia. Cornies followed this advice, requesting and receiving a denunciatory letter from a compliant Friedrich Wilhelm Lange on 10 March 1847.[139] On 12 March, Wiens was arrested and confined at the home of the colonial inspector in Prischib. The order for his deportation came on 16 April, and on 3 June, Wiens departed for Prussia.[140]

Unlike the Warkentin Affair, the events of 1846–7 never threatened Cornies's position in the community. By this point Hahn understood the lay of the land, and he was clearly committed to Cornies, whose relationship to the Mennonite congregations was now much more clearly defined. They understood that he represented state interests, and they looked to him as an arbitrator in intra-congregational disputes. They no doubt also understood that despite Heinrich Neufeld's claims, Cornies could not be blamed for a fight between a Hutterite villager and a Russian servant or for the punishment that had been ordered by a Russian official. When Abraham Friesen, elder of the conservative Kleine Gemeinde, assessed the entire affair after Wiens's departure, he revealed that some in the settlement sided with Cornies, and he chided

Wiens with words from Baruch 3:11: "How happeneth it that thou art in a foreign land? That is the reason, why you have forsaken the fountain of wisdom. For if thou hadst walked in the way of God, thou shouldest have dwelled in peace forever."[141]

Conclusion

The Warkentin Affair concluded a political battle in the Molochnaia Mennonite settlement that had spanned two decades. While many former members of Warkentin's congregation were unhappy with the outcome and some actively opposed Cornies again in 1846, in practical terms Cornies had won. From 1842 until his death in 1848 he was the unchallenged locus of authority in the settlement.

The Warkentin Affair was also significant for evolving religious attitudes in the Molochnaia. The Large Flemish Congregation had long dominated religious life in the community and had been an effective obstacle to significant changes. Dramatic religious transformations were still in the future, but many historians have argued that the arrival of the Gnadenfeld congregation in the Molochnaia in 1835 was an important first stimulus to the Pietist awakening that resulted in the creation of the Mennonite Brethren in the late 1850s.[142] The importance of the Gnadenfeld congregation is uncontested, but the defeat of Warkentin was also pivotal, for it undermined the power of conservative religious quietism to obstruct change.

The Warkentin Affair also signalled the end of an era in state administrative policy. The 1831 founding of the Forestry Society, which marked the beginning of Cornies's political comeback, was the first step in activating the Mennonite model. The 1834 reorganization of the Guardianship Committee, the 1836 creation of the Fifth Department – the forerunner of the Ministry of State Domains – and the creation of the Agricultural Society were all part of the same process. By the end of the 1830s the state had concluded that the static, didactic model had failed. The appointment of Hahn as Deputy Chief Guardian in 1842 marked the end of the transition: as a representative of the new state policy, he came into office determined to put the Mennonites to work, and the Warkentin Affair provided him with the impetus and opportunity to act.

For Cornies, the defeat of Warkentin was a qualified victory. The power it brought him came at a cost. He had defended the model paradigm and the privileges that accompanied it throughout his life, and he justified his role in the Warkentin Affair as a necessary act to prove that Mennonites deserved their special status. When he labelled Warkentin a rebel, he believed that it was as much a rebellion against Mennonite interests as against state interests. The problem was that the role Cornies played in suppressing the "rebellion" was as a direct agent of state interests. His correspondence with Hahn beginning in May 1842 makes this role explicit: Cornies was Hahn's agent, carrying out Hahn's orders, and reporting back to his boss. This was markedly different from Cornies's role in the 1830s, when the Guardianship Committee had charged him with creating the Agricultural Society and left him to decide for himself how it would function. At the height of the Warkentin Affair, Cornies lost the autonomy to make decisions about Mennonite interests; instead he acted as a direct agent of the state.

After the crisis Cornies regained some of his former autonomy and did his best to defend the Mennonites' status in the eyes of the state. As will be described in chapter 9, he used his accomplishments in the 1840s to continue to justify Mennonite privileges. But as Hahn had shown, Mennonite privilege went only as far as the state permitted, and while Cornies had more power than ever within the Mennonite settlement after the Warkentin Affair, it was power over a community in which many viewed him with bitter suspicion. His final years were marked by increasing alienation and isolation.

Chapter Nine

An Agent of the State, 1842–1847

After Fadeev's departure in 1836 the Guardianship Committee had become distant and disengaged from Molochnaia affairs, and the Ministry of State Domains eclipsed its influence. While Johann Cornies continued to pursue his Mennonite modernization agenda through the Agricultural Society, many of his initiatives served the broader state peasant goals of the new ministry. Ministry officials like Keppen, Steven, and Rosen monopolized his time with tasks that demanded his direct engagement in regional administration. Cornies's political victory in 1842 had positioned him as an agent of the state and opened a floodgate of new demands on his time and energy.

That same year Hahn's appointment revitalized the Guardianship Committee, and under his leadership the committee powerfully reasserted its role in the New Russian colonial world. The partnership that emerged between Cornies and Hahn was perhaps even stronger than the one that Cornies had enjoyed with Fadeev. By Hahn's own admission he did not know much about agriculture, and he leaned heavily on Cornies's knowledge.[1] The Guardianship Committee was part of the Ministry of State Domains. The two institutions had clearly defined areas of authority and did not compete with each other; however, they did compete for Cornies's time and energy, and by 1844 he wrote wearily of the "interruptions by gentlemen from Petersburg or Odesa" that constantly burdened him.[2] A Russian peasant proverb holds that "God is high above and the tsar is far away." It means that local demands always come first, and for Cornies, this meant that Hahn and the Guardianship Committee would have to take precedence. Still, the demands of the ministry could not simply be ignored.

Redefining Priorities

Soon after the Warkentin Affair, Cornies attempted to pull back from his obligations to the ministry. Most notably, he tried to disengage from his role in Nogai affairs. Writing to Rosen in Simferopol, he explained that "for thirty-five years I have, in hope and generosity, sacrificed a large part of my life for the Nogais. Now that I am starting to get old and gray I had [sic] been looking forward to a little rest."[3]

"Civilizing" the Nogais had been one of Cornies's first causes, and his successes had helped cement his reputation with tsarist officialdom. This project always had an ambiguous relationship to Guardianship Committee authority, because the Nogais were not colonists and the committee had no authority over them. However, Cornies used his Nogai projects to demonstrate to the committee the success of the Mennonite model. Some of his Nogai projects were essentially philanthropic. In particular, the sheep-sharing program he pioneered in the 1820s and promoted among other Mennonites in the 1830s and 1840s was mainly intended to improve the quality of Nogai sheep and draw the Nogais into the market economy. It had done little for the Nogais, though, and by the 1840s, with wool prices falling, the benefits were dwindling.

The model Nogai village of Akkerman was a much more important venture. It was Cornies's personal project, although it enjoyed the direct support of the ministry. It was a way to show that the Mennonite model could be transferred to the Nogais and that the Mennonites could overwrite the Nogais' distinct identity and be instrumental in their "civilization." The underlying idea was a product of the 1820s, when Cornies's world view was coming to maturity, and its realization came in the 1830s, when Cornies's power was catching up with his ambitions. It was Akkerman that had captured the imagination of Keppen in 1837; it was a standard part of the Molochnaia tour, and Cornies's apparent ability to transform semi-nomadic Tatars into "civilized" peasants was symbolically central to his rise to prominence within the Ministry of State Domains.

The Nogais are also an important example of the failure of the didactic model. For all that Cornies had promoted his successes, there is little indication that he had achieved meaningful change among the Nogais and considerable evidence of serious Nogai resistance to Cornies's signature program. Afforestation provides a good illustration.

Cornies had tried to promote the establishment of tree nurseries in the Nogai settlements since the 1820s. His best pupil was Ali Pasha from the village of Edinochta. Pasha had been a protégé of de Maison, the Nogai guardian from 1808 to 1821. De Maison had Pasha trained in a state orchard and then assigned him land in the village of Edinochta to establish his own orchard. Pasha and his orchard were to be another didactic model, intended to convince the Nogais to grow trees. When de Maison retired and official patronage evaporated, two hundred Nogais attacked and destroyed Pasha's orchard in a clear expression of the general Nogai attitude toward the program. In 1834, when the state eliminated the position of Nogai guardian and the Nogais came under the direct authority of the Ministry of Internal Affairs, Pasha decided to try again. With the protection of the regional administrator he established a new orchard in Edinochta. By the end of the 1830s Cornies was promoting the new orchard – and Pasha – as models deserving of recognition and support. At Cornies's urging, in 1841 the ministry awarded Pasha a silver medal, imprinted with the words "for zeal," which he apparently wore proudly to the market where he sold saplings.[4]

This sounds like a success story, but even as Cornies trumpeted Pasha's accomplishments, he acknowledged that Pasha's "small plantation adorns the treeless region."[5] What made Pasha so deserving of rewards was that, like Cornies, he was exceptional; the anti-colonial attitudes that drove two hundred other Nogais to destroy his original orchard were more typical. As demands on Cornies's time grew in the 1840s, he backed away from his direct involvement in such failing afforestation programs. His solution was to delegate the work and the responsibility to other Mennonites through a single large project to create a model forestry plantation near Melitopol.[6]

The Ministry of State Domains proposed the model plantation in 1843.[7] Its purpose was to expand the apprenticeship program that Cornies had been involved with since 1838 by opening a school to teach forestry to Nogais and other state peasants. Rosen asked Cornies to create and oversee the plantation.[8] Reluctantly, he agreed to take on six forestry apprentices at Iushanle and convinced David Reimer, who had a large private orchard at his Felsenthal estate on the Tokmak River, to train an additional two.[9]

Rosen had envisaged something larger: a new model plantation in Berdiansk district to provide training and encouragement for the Nogais and other state peasants. In 1845 Cornies helped him achieve this goal, but he refused to directly manage the project. Instead he convinced the ministry to hire two Mennonites, Hermann Sudermann as supervisor and Peter Fast as chief forester.[10] Cornies had the site surveyed, and by late August he was urging the ministry to provide seeds before the fall planting season passed.[11] No trees were planted that year, but construction of the first buildings at the site began, intended for the new employees. In January 1846 Cornies sent plans for additional buildings to the ministry, and by the beginning of April, seven peasant apprentices had arrived and begun to prepare the soil for planting.[12] Soon an eighth joined them, and in spring 1847 another eight brought the total to sixteen.[13]

In this project Cornies mainly served as a ministry liaison. He was the local authority charged with ensuring that the plantation got off the ground, but he did his best to distance himself from its day-to-day operations.[14] The one element to which he paid close attention was the training of the apprentices, for he continued to believe strongly that education was critical for economic and moral reforms. He insisted that the apprentices be "of good character, intelligent, completely healthy, physically strong and no less than seventeen years old in every case."[15] Apprentices came from across the region, often from villages too distant to allow them to return home during their four-year apprenticeship. While they learned, they laboured, doing back-breaking agricultural work. For this they received no pay – just clothing, food, and accommodations.

For all Cornies's best intentions, living conditions for the apprentices were sometimes very harsh. In August 1847 Cornies inspected the forestry project and was furious at what he found. In a stern letter to Sudermann and Fast he wrote: "The crown apprentices live under extremely oppressive conditions. The food they are required to cook is so badly prepared and filthy as to endanger their health. Their clothes are extremely shabby, infrequently provided and dirty. Nor do they have boots. Not wanting to show themselves to me in this state, I found several of them slinking shyly away into the corners of their rooms, barefooted [and] discouraged ... I concluded that they had not been encouraged to maintain themselves in decency and order, but had simply been left to themselves." He upbraided Sudermann and Fast for "your excessive arrogance, lack of consideration and efforts to enrich yourselves at the expense of the apprentices," and he demanded a careful accounting of how the money allocated for the apprentices had been spent, promising that Sudermann and Fast would be required to make up any missing sum from their own salaries.[16]

This inspection shows that Cornies remained engaged in state projects; but it is also the case that in his last years he delegated more and more direct supervision to other Mennonites. This was evident in one of the Ministry of State Domains' signature programs in the 1840s, potato growing. It is a good example of how the ministry tried to get Cornies to take on a more direct role in regional administration. At first the ministry only asked Cornies, as a member of the Learned Committee, to report on Mennonite practices, and Cornies took up this task with his usual attention to detail. Soon, however, he was pressed into duty to hire Mennonites to oversee the planting, harvest, and storage of potatoes in a one-*desiatina* model plot in each of thirty-nine Slavic and Nogai state peasant villages.[17] In March 1841 Cornies accepted the task of "direction and leadership in the introduction of potato cultivation among state peasants."[18] He hired Heinrich Balzer to oversee the program.[19]

The potato program became a source of frustration for Cornies. He entered into it with his customary enthusiasm, personally inspecting the first potato plots in May 1841. His report on that inspection trip indicates how little had really been achieved in the Nogai and Slavic villages over the preceding decades. For the program to succeed, it would need the active support of village elders, but Cornies concluded that few of them, Nogais and Slavic peasants alike, were competent. One was "deceitful and greedy," another "a drunkard and ... disorderly," a third lacked "the intelligence to fill his position," and so on.[20] This dismal assessment was a sharp contrast to the reports Cornies had for years been making of his own supposed successes, particularly in "civilizing" the Nogais. In the same letter Cornies offered an equally dismal assessment of the model village of Akkerman. The villagers there had become "lazy," he wrote, and the village elder should be dismissed.[21]

One particularly vexing example of the difficulties the potato program faced arose in the Nogai village of Aul. The village had stored seed potatoes from its first potato harvest in a covered pit, a common and effective practice in the region. In December 1841 the district supervisor, a Russian official named Mitskevich, reported that the pit cover had collapsed and one third of the potatoes had rotted and been thrown out. Cornies sent Abraham Huebert, the Mennonite who had supervised potato planting in the district, to investigate. Huebert reported back that there was no sign of rot in the remaining potatoes and that Mitskevich could not produce any of the rotted potatoes as evidence. He concluded that Mitskevich had probably stolen and sold the potatoes. Cornies reported this to Rosen and asked him to send out a stern reminder to all district supervisors about their responsibility to oversee potatoes.[22]

This was not the end of the scandal. In February, Cornies reported that Mitskevich's deputy, Pavel Kalenitchenko, was part of the plot. Cornies alleged that Kalenitchenko, "through intrigue, cunning and deceit," had plundered the inhabitants of the region; as well, the deputy chief was particularly hostile to Cornies's role in Nogai affairs, which interfered with Kalenitchenko's ability to extort money from them.[23] According to Cornies, Kalenitchenko was conspiring to undermine his authority, and Cornies urged Rosen to replace him.[24] In a further investigation, the Aul village elder, who it seems was complicit in the theft of the potatoes, claimed that Huebert was drunk when he came to investigate in December and had misunderstood everything. He insisted that all that had happened was that a few rotten potatoes had been removed from the pit and fed to the pigs; there was no wrongdoing. Huebert vehemently denied the accusations, and with this the case disappears from the surviving records.[25]

Cornies's solution to the potato program was similar to his solution to the afforestation program – he could not altogether abandon it, so he delegated it to other Mennonites, whom the ministry hired as salaried supervisors. He reported on the results of the project and occasionally interceded in problems – as he had with the Aul potatoes – but beyond that, he devoted little attention to it. Perhaps this indicates that he was simply becoming a better manager, learning to delegate responsibility as his affairs became more complex. Equally, though, it is evidence that Cornies was attempting to disengage from one of his signature projects, the "civilization" of the Nogais. They had helped establish his reputation in Russia, and he owed his status in the Ministry of State Domains in part to his claimed accomplishments among them, but in the 1840s, he repeatedly expressed the opinion that the Nogai project had been a failure. When Grand Prince Konstantin Nikolaevich visited the region in 1844, Cornies dropped the Nogai district and the model village of Akkerman from his tour. There had been many fires in the Nogai district, Cornies reported, and they would present Konstantin with "very depressing sights."[26]

Refocusing on Mennonite Projects

As part of his efforts to back away from state demands, in the 1840s Cornies tailored his activities on behalf of the Ministry of State Domains in ways that more narrowly served the Mennonites. In particular he continued to carry out experiments with a wide variety of crops provided by Steven, the ministry's chief inspector of silk production and agriculture. Cornies planted crops ranging from tobacco to oil radishes, carefully documenting each experiment and reporting back to Steven. Such experiments had broad benefits for Russia, but they also had the potential to benefit the Mennonites, and Cornies constantly had this in mind.

From a Mennonite perspective, one of the most important of Cornies's 1840s projects for the ministry involved promoting Mennonite agricultural machinery. By the 1830s the Mennonites had developed a reputation for building high-quality wagons and carriages. In 1839 Steven asked Cornies to have a wagon built for him, and their correspondence indicates that Mennonite artisans had earned a sterling reputation, which Cornies took care to defend. Cornies was deeply embarrassed when the wagon arrived in Simferopol damaged. He assured Steven that he had personally inspected it before he sent it and that it was a new, sturdy, high-quality Mennonite product. The damage, he insisted, must have been the fault of the Nogai who delivered it.[27] Steven told Cornies not to worry: "For some time, people here have complained that wagons are not being built as solidly as in the past."[28] Cornies hastened to assure Steven that no such shoddy workmanship was happening in the Mennonite villages: "Wagons here are still built solidly by local wagon builders. Rivals, inferior artisans, can be found among the other settlers in the area and among neighbouring Russians. They build wagons and sell them as though they were Mennonite ones. Such wagons are not built of durable wood and are poorly crafted."[29]

Cornies's concern about the reputation of Mennonite artisans went hand in hand with his efforts to gain approval to establish the craft village of Neu-Halbstadt. More and more people in the settlement were landless, and he was keenly aware that there was not enough suitable land to permit them all to farm. Those people needed employment, and besides that, the Mennonite economy needed to diversify. So he promoted Mennonite agricultural equipment, sending model machines off to Simferopol and Odesa to demonstrate their value. In 1839 he bragged to Fadeev that the shift to crop agriculture in the Molochnaia had stimulated the production and improvement of agricultural implements; horse-powered threshing machines and three-tined ploughs were changing the face of agriculture in the community as well as providing work for the landless.[30] This transition to machine agriculture placed Mennonites at the leading edge of agricultural modernization and placed New Russia at the forefront of agricultural modernization throughout the empire.[31]

The potato program provided Cornies with an opportunity to develop Mennonite manufacturing on a larger scale. In September 1841 the ministry decided to expand the trial program in the Molochnaia settlement across New Russia. Kiselev had visited the settlement that summer and been particularly impressed with a specially developed mounding plough for potato planting. At his directive the ministry asked if the Mennonites could produce three hundred of those ploughs to distribute to other peasants.[32] It also asked if the Mennonites could produce row markers and potato diggers.[33] By 1842, Mennonite potato ploughs, at 11 rubles per plough, were being distributed across New Russia and as far away as Saratov and Nizhnii Novgorod – an example of the state's application of the results of experiments in the Mennonite laboratory of modernization.[34] Cornies also discussed with Steven the cost and effectiveness of other Mennonite agricultural equipment. He was sceptical that Slavic peasants could use or maintain the more sophisticated machinery; thus, he saw no point in providing expensive threshing machines, which cost more than 800 rubles. However, he was happy to recommend sturdy Mennonite ploughs and other equipment, and he sent a long price list to Steven detailing costs and availability.[35] The scale of such manufacturing in the 1840s is difficult to ascertain; clearly, though, the industry was still in its infancy, for it was not until the 1870s that it became a mainstay of the regional economy.[36] However, the industry's expansion is evidence of Cornies's careful attention to the issue of landlessness and the need to diversify the economy. It also shows how Cornies made use of his ministry contacts to address internal Mennonite issues. Where the ministry's plans had a direct local benefit, he was happy to give them his full attention.

A Resurgent Guardianship Committee

Cornies's efforts to back away from Ministry of State Domains' demands came as the demands of the Guardianship Committee grew. After Fadeev's departure in 1836 the committee had neither asked much of Cornies nor offered him much support, and he had necessarily realigned himself with the ministry. Hahn's December 1841 appointment changed things dramatically.

Hahn's first steps in the Molochnaia reflected an assertive manner but little familiarity with conditions in the region. As described in chapter 8, on his arrival in April 1842 in the midst of the Warkentin Crisis he seemed ready to push Cornies aside and back Warkentin. It did not take him long to realize that Cornies was an essential ally, and a friendship between the two men developed. Hahn was eighteen years younger than Cornies, and as he admitted in a June 1842 letter, "I am personally a professional who understands nothing about agriculture, and have no adviser in regard to these matters."[37] He looked to Cornies to become his adviser, one who would take an active role in the administration of all foreign colonists in the region. This expanded Cornies's authority but also made him more directly subservient to the Guardianship Committee; at times he almost functioned as an unofficial and unpaid state employee.

One consequence of this new relationship is that after 1842 the authority of the Agricultural Society and Cornies's personal authority blurred. Between 1836 and 1842, the Guardianship Committee was weak and ineffective, and Cornies relied upon the other members of the Agricultural Society to help promote his reform plans in the Mennonite community. After 1842 the Agricultural Society was the official agency through which Cornies's authority was asserted, but in practice Cornies relied less and less on other members of the society and more and more on his own personal authority, strongly backed by Hahn. When Hahn had Thun flogged in September 1842, he was sending a message to all Mennonites regarding what the Guardianship Committee expected of them, and this meant that Cornies could spend less time worrying about how to gain local cooperation.

Cornies's growing power allowed him to take up a project he had first proposed in 1836: the relocation of the Hutterites to the Molochnaia. Hutterites, like Mennonites, are Anabaptists, though they embrace a distinct religious doctrine – for example, their community holds almost all goods in common. In the early sixteenth century, Anabaptists from various German states fled to Moravia to escape persecution. Jakob Hutter united the fugitives into one congregation.[38]

After being driven out of Moravia during the Thirty Years' War, the Hutterites spent time in Upper Hungary and Transylvania before immigrating to the Russian Empire in the 1760s, where they established a community at Radishchev in Chernigov *guberniia*, northeast of Kyiv. There they faced religious and economic challenges similar to those faced by the Mennonites. Their leader, Johannes Waldner, was heavily influenced by his contacts with the Moravian Brethren, and he began to champion a more open relationship to other religious confessions. He faced strong opposition from conservative Hutterites, who insisted on strict separation.

The Hutterites were a small community – a single village – so they lacked the broad mutual support network that the Mennonites enjoyed. They struggled economically as well as doctrinally, and in 1818 a split in the community almost destroyed it. Jacob Walther, a Hutterite leader who wanted to end the practice of community of goods, led a splinter group out of Radishchev to the Khortitsa Mennonite Settlement. Soon after, a fire destroyed Radishchev, and the Walther group returned to help rebuild the community. This helped the Radishchev Hutterite settlement survive, although it did not prosper.

The Hutterites were well known in Mennonite circles. Cornies heard first-hand accounts of them from his friend Peter Reimer, a Molochnaia Mennonite who became the Radishchev village secretary in the early 1830s.[39] Reimer sought advice and aid for Radishchev from Cornies, and Cornies did what he could to help.

Cornies saw the Hutterites as backward and impoverished Mennonites (he usually called them either the Radishchev Mennonites or the Hutterite Mennonites). He described them as "good, healthy, and industrious people."[40] He believed that "their Christian morality has not deteriorated much," but he fretted that "externally, in dress and economic arrangements, they are almost Russian peasants."[41] He made their rescue a personal project.

In late 1835, while Fadeev was preparing his move to the Kalmyk steppe, Cornies asked him to intercede with Inzov and request permission for the Hutterites to move to the Molochnaia.[42] The idea apparently originated with the Hutterites themselves, who had asked Cornies to arrange the transfer. Cornies was willing to help, but from the outset he laid down conditions. The Hutterites would not receive Mennonite reserve land – instead, they were to settle on four thousand *desiatinas* of land provided by the state, along the Tashchenak River not far from Cornies's Tashchenak estate. Cornies cautioned them that they would not be permitted to settle on his land, as some Hutterites apparently expected. He stressed that they must found an orderly settlement and insisted that they end their community of goods and adopt Mennonite landowning practices. He would help them with advice, but he promised nothing more.[43]

In the 1830s, after Fadeev's transfer, the plan to relocate the Hutterites fell victim to the Guardianship Committee's general malaise. The Hutterites drafted petitions and sent them to Cornies for advice and editing, but the petitions disappeared into the Odesa bureaucracy.[44] Cornies never abandoned the idea, however, and in 1841, when Kiselev visited the Molochnaia, Cornies raised it again. Kiselev was hesitant – he thought it better to leave the Hutterites in Chernigov and give them more land to solve their economic problems.[45]

Hahn's arrival in 1842 gave Cornies new hope, and he took up the Hutterite cause yet again. On 2 February he wrote to Fadeev for advice, telling his old friend that the Hutterites remained close to his heart. He worried that their "moral status continues to deteriorate," and although giving them more land was part of the solution, the bigger issue was that "they live isolated from the fatherly care of the administration and their brethren in faith. They have few examples of good order nearby and are unable to benefit from the administration's encouragement to improve their farms and raise their general well-being."[46] As usual, Cornies saw the solution in good leadership – implicitly, his own.

By February 1842 Cornies had received assurances that approval for the move was imminent.[47] He wrote to the Hutterite leaders telling them to make preparations – they should expect to spend the next winter in the Molochnaia with host families, then build their new homes on the Tashchenak River in the summer of 1843. These assurances came at a time when the Warkentin Affair was roiling the Molochnaia, and

Cornies warned the Hutterites that they should not bring their own dissension with them to their new homes. "God's blessing," he wrote, "is present only where harmony and love reign."[48] If some Hutterites did not want to move, Cornies suggested that the village leaders "exclude him from your midst as one who is insubordinate and allow him to follow his own wishes and register among the local Russians."[49] Perhaps he was wishing he could do the same with the most recalcitrant of Warkentin's supporters.

The first twelve Hutterite families arrived in June 1842, sent ahead to mow hay as winter feed for their community's livestock. By then someone had already mowed and harvested the hay on their new land, so Cornies gave them hay from his Tashchenak estate. He also gave the Hutterites use of forty *desiatinas* of ploughed land on his estate to plant winter rye so that they would have grain to harvest and carry them through the next summer, until their own summer crops could be harvested.[50] The seed grain came from community reserves. For food the billeting families were asked to give grain to the Hutterites, to be repaid the following year, also from community reserves.[51] The Hutterite immigration was Cornies's personal project, and he quickly took them in hand. He asked Hahn to issue a directive to the Mennonite *Gebietsamt* and Colonial Inspector Pelekh, letting them know he was in charge and urging their cooperation.[52]

The Hutterites arrived in the Molochnaia as impoverished newcomers to a prosperous community. Poor to begin with, they had been forced to accept fire-sale prices for their homes and belongings in Radishchev and were unable to sell community buildings such as their church and mill.[53] To make matters worse, the summer of 1842 brought poor harvests in the Molochnaia.[54] While this did not endanger the well-off Molochnaia community, it did mean that the Mennonites were cash-poor that year. Cornies had hoped that the Hutterites might find local employment over the winter to help pay their way, but this was not to be.

Cornies's solution to all this foreshadowed future Mennonite methods of financing daughter settlements. The Hutterites needed money to build their new village, and the Mennonites had community reserves; in particular, the Khortitsa settlement had a large surplus in its treasury. Cornies asked Hahn to authorize a loan of 15,000 rubles on generous terms to the Hutterites. This loan needed Guardianship Committee approval because the money was designated for other purposes and only the committee could authorize its reallocation. Cornies personally guaranteed the loan.[55]

Cornies also selected the new Hutterite village site and ensured that the village was laid out in an orderly manner. In his typically officious way he insisted that the Hutterites abandon their traditional village layout and build their houses in a manner that he deemed would be both "more comfortable" and better looking. He named the village Hutterthal.[56]

The relationship of the Hutterites to the Molochnaia Mennonite settlement was ill-defined. Cornies clearly intended that they be integrated into the settlement. However, they did not live on settlement land, they were poor, and they spoke a Tyrolian German dialect that marked them as outsiders. Their relationship to local authorities was especially ambiguous. At first Cornies saw them almost as his personal wards, and he urged the Guardianship Committee to endorse this and allow him to oversee their settlement independent from either the *Gebietstamt* or the colonial inspector. For the Hutterite village mayor and deputy mayors he endorsed candidates whom he believed would serve the Hutterites' best interests as he saw them.[57]

Cornies saw his role in the Hutterite community as extending to basic issues of morality. He went so far as to question the marriage of the daughter of a Hutterite. Cornies called the marriage "frivolous" and "untimely" and suggested that the couple would be unable to support themselves and would become a burden on the community. He strictly forbade the Hutterite village office from approving marriages "for people still under guardianship or in service." In future, he wrote, any such engagements would require his personal approval."[58]

Cornies's insistence on personal control over the Hutterites brought him into conflict with his long-time ally Pelekh, the district inspector. As recently as 1841 Cornies had used his influence to help gain Pelekh recognition for his service by appointment to the Holy Order of Stanislas, but in 1844 the two had a falling out over Pelekh's interference in Hutterite affairs.[59] It is not clear what Pelekh did to offend Cornies, but whatever it was, it was so egregious that Cornies asked Hahn to fire the inspector.[60] For Hahn, Cornies was a more important asset than Pelekh, but Hahn diplomatically noted that he could hardly just dismiss the inspector, who had served the committee loyally for twenty years. He promised to look around for a new position for Pelekh, although the committee's budget was so tight that he doubted that a transfer would come soon.[61] In 1847, Pelekh was reassigned to Odesa.[62]

Probably the Hutterites were glad at first to have Cornies as their protector. An influential patron, he tried to arrange several tax-free years for them to help them pay for their resettlement, and when this failed he secured them loans on generous terms. In 1843 he solicited donations from the Mennonites of grain and money, as well as loans of draft animals to help the Hutterites get their first crops in the ground.[63] Even the

Wiens congregation chipped in 10 rubles, and Cornies donated bricks from his brickworks at Tashchenak to help with the construction of their homes.[64] For Cornies, the Hutterites were a humanitarian mission, and he did all in his power to look after them.

Historian Astrid von Schlachta writes that Cornies's long-term impact on the Hutterites was both positive and negative.[65] The Radishchev community had been on the verge of total collapse, and it may not be hyperbole to say that Cornies rescued the Hutterites from extinction. But he also introduced fundamental challenges to their core beliefs. The ensuing internal disputes echoed those of the larger Molochnaia settlement, and some Hutterites were deeply concerned about the intrusion of Russian civil authority into the community. The Mennonites at the time of their own arrival had accepted that their members could fill secular positions like mayor and deputy mayor, but for the Hutterites, this remained an unresolved issue, as was Cornies's assertion of secular authority in their village. An anonymous Hutterite wrote an account titled "The Decline of the church in Russia and whose fault it is" that defiantly concluded that "God has departed from the [village office]."[66] Support for community of goods survived, and two Hutterites petitioned the Guardianship Committee for its restoration in 1848.[67] They would achieve this goal in the 1850s. Schlachta concludes that the turmoil that struck the Hutterites in the later nineteenth century had been seeded in part by Cornies's policies.

As for the Hutterites' impact on Cornies, that group blended in with his broader concerns in the 1840s, as one more project to exhaust and exasperate him. It is clear that Cornies saw in Hahn's arrival an opportunity to take up the cause of these desperately poor and struggling settlers. Clear as well is that his goals were shaped not only by state policies but also by an enduring dedication to the welfare of the Mennonites. For him, the Hutterite project was a matter of principle and morality.

The Bergthal Mennonite Daughter Settlement

Hahn's arrival placed new demands on Cornies's time. For example, Hahn ordered him to come to the aid of the Bergthal Mennonite settlement, located 60 kilometres east of the Molochnaia. Bergthal was the first Mennonite daughter settlement and had been established to provide an outlet for landless Mennonites from the overcrowded Khortitsa mother settlement. It consisted of four villages: Bergthal (est. 1836), Schönfeld (est. 1837), Schönthal (est. 1838), and Heubuden (est. 1839). A fifth village, Friedrichstal, would follow in 1852.[68]

Hahn inspected the Bergthal settlement in May 1842 and was not impressed. In June he ordered that Cornies and the Molochnaia Agricultural Society take over supervision of Bergthal's economic affairs. Hahn appointed a colonial inspector, Carl Stempel, as the official voice of the Guardianship Committee in the region, but it was clear that Cornies was to be the real driving force in Bergthal affairs.[69]

Cornies was already familiar with the Bergthal land because it had been carved out of his Mariupol leased land, and he still leased nineteen thousand *desiatinas* of neighbouring land.[70] He inspected the settlement in October 1842 and was dismayed by what he found. He reported that the Khortitsa settlement had used Bergthal as a dumping ground for poor and "indolent" Mennonites, many of whom had neither the means nor the desire to bring Bergthal up to speed.[71] To make matters worse, wealthy Mennonite merchants from Khortitsa and Molochnaia were trying to take advantage of the Bergthalers by buying up prime properties in the villages at bargain prices. Cornies suggested to Hahn that he forbid such purchases and permit only short-term leases at fair prices.[72]

Cornies had established the parameters for orderly economic development in the Molochnaia in the 1830s. Now, in October 1842, he issued a brusque seventeen-point memorandum to the Bergthal *Gebietsamt*, setting out his expectations for them to bring the new settlement into alignment.[73] This memorandum suggests how little had been done in the settlement over the preceding six years. Many of the fullholders had still not properly laid out their hearthsites, and they were living in homes built of rough-hewn logs and stone. Cornies ordered that the villages properly demarcate hearth sites and construct regulation homes and outbuildings of brick or stone. He also insisted that the Bergthalers begin to lay out forest and orchard tree lots according to Forestry Society guidelines, and he ordered the proper regulation of pasturage and watering holes. He was particularly dismayed by the unregulated dumping of manure and ash in the villages, and he insisted that this be addressed immediately. In November he hired a Khortitsa Mennonite, Wilhelm Penner, as Bergthal district secretary.[74] An efficient secretary was needed because Cornies, who lived 60 kilometres away, intended to issue a lot of orders, and the accurate, quick transmission of orders, along with clear recordkeeping of the results, was essential.

As Cornies investigated the problems in Bergthal more closely he came to realize that one of the settlement's key problems was that the cash deposits that all Bergthal fullholders were supposed to have made to the settlement treasury to defray construction costs had never materialized. Khortitsa Mennonites who moved to Bergthal were supposed to have produced a deposit of 2,500 rubles to show that they were capable of setting up their own fullholdings. Many of them were poor and did not have the deposit money, and they had been required to find guarantors – usually their parents – who would help them. Among Cornies's first actions was to ask Hahn to direct the Khortitsa *Gebietsamt* to forcefully remind the guarantors of their responsibilities.[75]

In the ensuing years, Cornies inspected the Bergthal settlement annually and closely managed the progress of its villages, its forestry plantations, and its school. Bergthal soon conformed to the orderly pattern of the Molochnaia settlement, and its rich agricultural land soon added to Mennonite grain exports from regional ports.[76] Cornies's intervention won him no friends in the Khortitsa settlement, upon which he had placed most of the blame for Bergthal's troubles, but it further built his reputation with Hahn and forged a new alliance with Colonial Inspector Stempel.[77]

The Württemberg Settlement

The alliance with Stempel strengthened when Cornies became involved in the affairs of a colonist settlement that lay between the Molochnaia and Bergthal settlements. Sometimes known as the Brüdergemeinde Colony, and usually referred to by Cornies as the Württemberg Colony, the settlement on the Berda River a few kilometres east of the Molochnaia consisted of four villages founded between 1816 and 1819. The colonists had immigrated from the Württemberg region and were Pietists.[78]

Because of their proximity to the Molochnaia and their German language, the Württembergers were known to the Molochnaia Mennonites, but they were far enough away that they seem to have had no close interactions. Cornies occasionally corresponded with one of the community leaders, District Mayor Oppenländer, and in 1837 Cornies tried to help Oppenländer submit a petition to Keppen regarding undisclosed community disputes.[79]

Cornies became directly involved in the community in the 1840s as the result of religious disputes. Some Württembergers, disgruntled with their church leadership, sought to leave their Pietist congregation and join the Lutheran Church. The exact nature of the dispute is unclear, although there is a hint in Cornies's correspondence that the community's minister, one Hekel, was part of the problem. In 1843 members of the settlement objected to having to contribute to his upkeep, and Friedrich Prinz, Oppenländer's successor as mayor, asked Cornies for advice. Prinz told Cornies that the breakaway settlers were questioning Hahn's authority, and he asked Cornies to review a petition to Hahn that he had drafted.[80] Thus began a regular correspondence between

Cornies and Prinz, who routinely asked his powerful neighbour for advice and assistance. Prinz took no enjoyment from his stressful position, and at the end of 1843 he attempted to resign as mayor, but on Cornies's advice Hahn refused to allow it.[81]

Cornies consulted with Stempel about the Württemberg settlement's problems, and Stempel suggested that Cornies visit the settlement and see if he could resolve the matter.[82] Stempel's intervention created a problem, because Pelekh was the colonial inspector for the Württemberg settlement. Cornies was angry about Pelekh's interference in Hutterite affairs and was trying to bypass his authority. Pelekh sided with the breakaway Lutheran group, and in November 1844 Cornies complained to Hahn that "since Mr. Stempel investigated the local matter in question, the Pietists have collectively drawn down upon themselves Inspector Pelekh's undeserved and irreconcilable hatred and my work among them suffers from a decided prejudice."[83] He added that Pelekh's actions were bringing his own efforts at reform "to a complete halt." Cornies's solution, enacted by Hahn in November 1844, was to transfer administrative authority over the settlement to Stempel and commission Cornies to directly oversee reforms there.[84] This further worsened Cornies's relationship with Pelekh and strengthened his growing bond with Stempel.

Cornies helped organize the Württemberg settlement's agricultural economy and worked with its Forestry Society in his normal efficient manner. The more interesting problem the community faced was the need to recruit a new minister for the Pietist congregation. The disputes had driven the previous minister, Hekel, to resign, leaving the community without a spiritual leader. Prinz asked Cornies for advice, and Cornies did his best to help.[85] A Lutheran minister applied for the job, saying he wished to leave his congregation and become a Pietist, but Cornies counselled caution, questioning whether an "ordinary Lutheran pastor" would have the necessary qualities for the position, which he described at length:

> The spiritual leader of a Pietist congregation should not only be a good preacher, but also a man of solid character, possessing quiet, peaceable and loving qualities. The desire simply to lead the congregation to Christ must be close to his heart, since this is the only means of creating good citizens for human society. He must accept Pietist principles out of pure conviction and not only for the sake of a salary and his own employment. In social dealings, he should not try to present himself as being too far above members of his congregation. As a cultured man, he should lead the congregation as an example in his daily conduct and in the way he lives at a higher level.[86]

The Württembergers considered two candidates, rejected them, and then contemplated choosing an elder from among their own congregation.

After more than a year of uncertainty, in October 1845 a delighted Prinz sent a letter to Cornies to let him know that the settlement had finally found a new minister: Eduard Hugo Otto Wüst. Prinz urged Cornies to honour the settlement with a visit to Wüst to confirm his support for the choice.[87] Prinz could not have known it, but in Wüst he had found a dynamic and transformative figure who would profoundly affect both the Württemberg settlement and the broader New Russian religious world. By the 1850s his revival meetings and ecumenical Pietist appeals were attracting huge audiences, including some Mennonites. Wüst had a profound influence on the creation of the Mennonite Brethren in 1860 and thus on modern Mennonite beliefs and practices. He was equally influential in the growth of the Ukrainian Baptist movement.[88]

Hahn's initial response to Wüst's hiring was to forbid it on the grounds that he was not a Russian subject.[89] This probably reflected concerns that extended far beyond the Württemberg settlement. The millennialist Sect of Nazareth, led by Johan Strolle, had created turmoil in the Bessarabian colonist settlements in the early 1840s, and the Guardianship Committee was anxious to prevent further religious upheavals in its jurisdiction.[90] When Stempel was ordered to investigate the Pietists in the Württemberg settlement in December, Cornies wrote to Prinz warning him of the investigation and suggesting what kinds of questions he ought to be prepared to answer.[91] Cornies told Stempel that he had primed Prinz and that the investigation would likely turn up nothing harmful to the Württembergers, who were law-abiding, obedient subjects. He did, however, ask Stempel to allow him to "run my eyes over the Pietist's explanations before they are sent on."[92] This effort to support Wüst's hiring implies that Cornies approved of the controversial minister. The results of Stempel's investigation apparently satisfied Hahn, for Wüst was soon confirmed as the settlement's minister.

The Professionalization of Education

Within the Molochnaia settlement Cornies's last significant initiative, and one of his most important long-term contributions to the Mennonites, was the professionalization of the Mennonite education system. This is a further example of how state demands on Cornies grew, but in this case, it was a project that he willingly took up, for education had always been one of his great passions.

For Mennonites, education was closely linked to religion, so Cornies's work to bring order to Mennonite education by professionalizing teaching in the Molochnaia settlement, and eventually in the Khortitsa Mennonite settlement, was an important extension of his authority. Because elementary education was traditionally a religious function, all education was understood to have an explicitly moral function. Cornies stressed education's role in economic modernization and demanded that children learn more than their Bible verses, but as always, he closely associated prosperity with morality. When Hahn asked him to take control of Molochnaia education, he took the task to heart.

Education was one of Cornies's first and greatest passions. He was a founder of the Ohrloff school in 1822, and he and the Agricultural Society had taken a close interest in the creation of the Gnadenfeld and Steinbach schools in the late 1830s. Graduates of these schools often worked as teachers in village elementary schools; however, once they went off to the villages, they fell under the control of the local residents. Village teachers were poorly paid and had low standing in the Mennonite villages, where landownership was the most important marker of status.[93]

Cornies was never very happy with the quality of teaching in the settlement, and he took a personal interest in improving it. In early 1841 he paid tuition for and a monthly stipend to a young landless Molochnaia Mennonite, Martin Riediger, to attend St. Paul's Evangelical Lutheran Church School in Odesa.[94] The school was supervised by Karl Friedrich Wilhelm Fletnitzer, the pastor of the Odesa Lutheran congregation. Fletnitzer, a graduate of the Basel Missionary Society, had come to Russia in 1825 intending to do missionary work in the Caucasus, but after a brief stint in Karrass he ended up in Odesa, first as the director of the school, and then also as pastor of St. Paul's. He also played a leading role in Protestant Bible Society activities in the region. His school provided the best German-language education in New Russia, offering its students training in religion, German, Russian, French, arithmetic, geography, calligraphy, drawing, singing, and basic bookkeeping.[95] After Riediger graduated he became the teacher at the Ohrloff school in the fall of 1843, and held that post for four years before illness forced him to give it up.

Riediger's education reflected Cornies's priorities. He considered it vitally important that Mennonites expand their education to include the Russian language. Arithmetic, geography, and drawing were basic tools for one of his other passions, land surveying. It is also revealing that Cornies paid to have the Ohrloff teacher educated at a school founded by a product of the Pietist missionary establishment. Fletnitzer would be an important source for Cornies's broader school reforms in the 1840s.

In January 1843 the *Gebietsamt* sent Cornies what amounted to a to-do list. The sixteenth of the twenty-three tasks on that list was "put village schools under the [Agricultural] Society's direction."[96] Cornies appended point-by-point notes to this list. Regarding schools, he wrote: "The society to develop a draft about the way in which the [Guardianship] Committee should dispense directives on this matter."[97] Cornies was thinking strategically about how the Guardianship Committee could best go about introducing reforms to the broader community. He knew that if he and the Agricultural Society were seen as initiators of the reforms, they would provoke a hostile reaction from their enemies; the orders needed to come from above.

The exchange between the *Gebietsamt* and Cornies reveals an ongoing dialogue about education in the Molochnaia. Hahn was part of this dialogue, for the decision to change the system had been prompted by his 1842 tour of the settlement at the height of the Warkentin Affair.[98] Given the Russian Ministry of Education's use of education as a tool for Russification of national minorities, it seems likely that Hahn saw these reforms as a way to address the dissent he had encountered in the Molochnaia.[99] The Mennonite settlement was now to become a laboratory for experiments in Russification as well as agriculture. Here again the state's emerging goal of standardization was evident.

On 10 July 1843 Hahn issued a directive ordering the Agricultural Society "to take responsibility for all schools in the district." In this order he explicitly adopted the language of the Privilegium: the Mennonite schools were to become "a model for other foreign settlers."[100] However, Hahn's description of the purpose of the reforms made it clear that the main intent was to continue to develop the utility of Mennonites themselves in state projects: the goal was to make schools "orderly" and "useful."[101] He directed Cornies to take responsibility for every aspect of schooling, from the condition of schoolhouses to the quality of teaching. As for religion, he allowed that "the church preachers should carefully supervise the schools to ensure that no lessons injurious to the Mennonite confession of faith are taught."[102] Hahn gave his full backing to this project, ordering Cornies to file "periodic, detailed and careful reports" and to immediately report any "obstacles" that got in his way.[103]

In the 1840s Cornies frequently delegated the supervision of major projects to trusted associates, but the school reforms were close to his heart and he gave them his personal attention. He made it his first priority to improve and standardize the quality of instruction in all village schools. In April 1845 he wrote and distributed to the schools what amounted to a pedagogical primer for teachers. It had two sections: "In the School in A" and "In the School in X."[104] It was a simple document, intended to train teachers by example. In village X the teacher in his nightgown works from a grubby room in his home, his "instruments for punishment" near to hand and chickens pecking at the floor; he "scolds, curses, and screams" at his students.[105] Education in the school at X consists of rote memory work, soon forgotten by the students. In the school at A the teacher is a model of comportment, the schoolroom a "warm, bright" space where students are ordered by age, ability, and gender. The teacher is "austere but friendly," conscientiously preparing his lessons from the professional handbooks he buys from his own salary (the teacher in village X spends his money on beer!).[106] A teacher in the school at A seldom has to mete out corporal punishment, "which might damage the child emotionally." Instead, he relies on winning the "respect and love" of his students.[107] Rather than rote memory, the teacher in village A "questions his students as though he would learn from them, leading them from the familiar to the unfamiliar ... It is not the memory but the understanding that is taught."[108]

This teaching primer was based on contemporary Prussian pedagogy. Cornies had been closely involved with the Ohrloff school since its founding. By the 1840s the Molochnaia had a number of Prussian-trained teachers, including Friedrich Wilhelm Lange, Heinrich Franz, and Adrian Hausknecht, all of whom would have influenced his thinking. He was also acquainted with the teaching methods of Fletnitzer in Odesa. Through them, the progressive ideas of Johann Heinrich Pestalozzi and Friedrich Froebel found their way into Cornies's model for schools. Their ideas found particularly clear expression in Cornies's emphasis on the psychological development of children. He also embraced Pestalozzi's emphasis on physical education.[109]

In November 1845 the Agricultural Society expanded its efforts at school reform when it ordered that the forty-four schools in the settlement be divided into six school districts. The teachers in each district were instructed to meet and discuss best teaching practices and to establish a standardized school curriculum. They were to report the results to the society by the end of December. The outcome of this exercise was the "General Rules on the Instruction and Treatment of School Children: A Manual for Teachers in Molochnaia School Districts."[110] If Cornies's "School at X" was a caricature of bad teaching and his "School at A" was an unattainable ideal, the eighty-seven points in the "General Rules" were an attempt at practical guidelines.

Cornies's educational reforms and their centrepiece "General Rules" were critical to the professionalization of Mennonite education. The results would be realized in future generations, as Mennonites led the way in Ukrainian economic development in the latter half of the nineteenth century. But the "General Rules" offer something more: they are a window onto Cornies's broader world view at the height of – and near the end of – his power. They were drafted at a time when his personal life gave him much reason for reflection. By then he had a grandson – another Johann, born on 31 December 1843 – and his daughter-in-law Justina was expecting a second child in May 1846. The arrival of these grandchildren gave him additional impetus to think about education.

The "General Rules" expressed values and beliefs that went well beyond mere pedagogy. Indeed, they can be read as a direct continuation of a dialogue with Balzer's 1832 reflections on faith and reason. Balzer had feared that reason, as acquired from secular sources, was an affront to faith. This led him to question education. The Large Flemish Congregation shared this concern, and this had made the Ohrloff school a flashpoint in community tensions. The "General Rules" were not secular, for they insisted that "religious principles must underlie all other principles" and they held up Jesus Christ as the ultimate model of a teacher, the "one who is most worthy of love and emulation."[111] But if the "General Rules" stressed God as creator, it was God's creation – the natural world – that was to be the real subject in Molochnaia schools.

The "General Rules" told teachers that "Godliness should be the aim of a true education," but those rules also stressed in clearly Baconian terms that "all knowledge and understanding is the result of our observation of nature ... Human knowledge always begins with observation, proceeds from there to understanding and finally to judgments and conclusions."[112] Cornies was telling Mennonite teachers to focus their lessons on the natural world and the creative role of humans within it so as to inculcate "a love of order and meaningful activity."[113] This expressed Cornies's own world view quite succinctly: he had dedicated his life to reshaping the world in orderly, productive ways, and he now sought to educate a new generation of Mennonites to follow his example.

Cornies equally emphasized the importance of emotional development, particularly among younger children. Education, he wrote, ought to promote a love of learning; the study of writing ought to "develop aesthetic sensibilities," and the study of singing ought to arouse "pious feelings."[114] He believed that humans could be moulded, and he viewed emotional education as a developmental process. Young children were "more responsive to emotional appeals," older children more responsive to a "rational approach."[115] Rationality was thus equated with maturity. Education would train children to control their tempers, because "too much emphasis on the emotions can destroy all joy and contentment."[116] Yet this was not a rejection of emotions – indeed,

Cornies emphasized that good teaching was passionate teaching and that its goal was to "inspire" students.[117] What he sought was passion regulated by purpose.

This emphasis on emotional response to the created world, and consequently to the creator, is a defining characteristic of Pietism. When Cornies called for students to engage in discussion and interpretation of the Bible, he was promoting a religious view that was antithetical to traditional Mennonite beliefs. In conservative congregations, elders conducted religious services by reading from the Bible and the role of congregants was to accept the Bible as God's revealed word, not to interpret it. In the context of Molochnaia religious disputes in the 1840s, the "General Rules" might fairly be seen as a Pietist manifesto. When Cornies wrote that a teacher inspired by religion could "ignite the divine spark in the child's soul," he was directly evoking Pietists' emphasis on a "warm" religion of the heart.[118]

The "General Rules" also offer an important reflection on discipline and punishment at a time when these were hotly contested issues. Cornies was excoriated in the 1840s for his arbitrary, authoritarian manner and in particular for his support of corporal punishment during the Warkentin Affair. The "General Rules" governed the treatment of children by adults, but in a similar vein, the patriarchal relationship of individual subjects to the Russian state was never just metaphorical: Cornies consistently characterized Fadeev as a "father" to the Mennonites, and such language was routine in governmental correspondence. When Cornies described the correct relationship between a teacher and his students, he must surely have thought about his own relationship to his community. Was he a good teacher who naturally enjoyed the respect and obedience of his students, or was he one who resorted too quickly to punishment? He wrote that "no system will be successful if the students are merely forced to submit to it. They must have the feeling that they are active participants in it."[119] His "At the School of X" derided a teacher who had to keep the "instruments of punishment" near at hand, and the "General Rules" spoke of punishment as a last resort.[120] "Despotism," he wrote, "leads to the repression of noble sentiments, undermines trust and love and destroys free and open relationships ... Slavish obedience to authority should be discouraged so that the student may become aware of his worth as an individual."[121] The "General Rules" acknowledged that sometimes punishment was unavoidable, and "In the School at A" made it clear that this extended to corporal punishment. Yet those rules also implicitly characterized the resort to punishment as reflecting a failure on the teacher's part.

Expanding Authority: Khortitsa

In 1845 Hahn consulted Cornies on problems in the Khortitsa Central School, and this led to the direct extension of Cornies's authority into the Khortitsa settlement.[122] The teacher in Khortitsa was Heinrich Heese, who had taught at the Ohrloff school from 1829 to 1841. Heese abruptly resigned from the Ohrloff school in 1841 and later claimed that he had quit because Cornies demanded too much work from him outside of his teaching duties.[123] Jacob Neumann, the chair of the Christian School Society, said that Heese was teaching dancing at the school, and when the society demanded that he stop, he refused and resigned.[124] In Khortitsa, Heese allied himself with opponents of state authority in the settlement. Following a June 1845 inspection Hahn decided to remove Heese from his position, and he asked Cornies for advice about a replacement.[125] Cornies suggested Heinrich Franz, the former teacher in Gnadenfeld, who in 1845 was teaching at the Mennonite school in Ekaterinoslav while he studied Russian. However, Cornies cautioned Hahn that the Khortitsa Mennonites might not welcome anyone associated with the Molochnaia.[126] Hahn endorsed the selection, and in the summer of 1846 Franz replaced Heese. He went on to have a distinguished career in Khortitsa.[127]

Franz looked to Cornies for direction as he set out to reshape the Khortitsa school. In August he sent a detailed curriculum to Cornies, who had the newly created Molochnaia Society to Improve the School System review and annotate it.[128] Cornies returned the annotated version of the curriculum to Franz with instructions that he should increase Russian-language instruction to one third of the total instruction time. Cornies told Franz that this must be the main goal of the school.[129]

Cornies's intrusion into the Khortitsa school system foreshadowed a significant expansion of his authority. From 28 July to 7 August 1846 he toured the Khortitsa settlement with Hahn; he returned to Khortitsa on 14 August and spent the rest of the month conducting a detailed survey in preparation for a visit by Kiselev. Kiselev arrived in Khortitsa on 1 September, and Cornies travelled with him throughout the district.[130] Three months later, on 5 December, Cornies was placed in charge of the Khortitsa settlement's Agricultural Society.[131] Johann Siemens continued as chair, but he now took orders from Cornies.

Cornies described the tensions within the Khortitsa settlement in letters to Hahn. Siemens and Jacob Bartsch, the *Gebietsamt* mayor, were intensely hostile to each other. The problem was that "only prejudice motivates Gebietsamt Mayor Bartsch, causing him repeatedly to work in opposition to the society, possibly not always intentionally. In my opinion the Khortitsa society and its energetic members such as chair Siemens and member Epp should definitely be given more independence ... To achieve greater order and efficacy, all economic proposals should be subject to the society's examination. Necessary arrangements could be made to ensure that the Khortitsa society is not restricted or disturbed in the area of activity assigned to it, and even more, that it receive all possible help in this regard."[132] Cornies recommended that Bartsch be removed from office, but Bartsch would not be so easily gotten rid of, for he was popular in his community and a close ally of Jacob Dyck, elder of the main Khortitsa congregation.[133] Cornies's appointment to oversee the Khortitsa economy did give Siemens and the Agricultural Society the power to counter Bartsch's influence. With the help of a firm reprimand from Hahn, in May 1847 Bartsch and Dyck made peace with Siemens, promising to keep out of Agricultural Society affairs.[134]

The expansion of Cornies's authority to Khortitsa was controversial in that settlement, but it came too late in his life to have a major impact. By the end of 1847 Cornies's active public role was rapidly waning. His most significant and effective reforms had always relied on his direct supervision, and without strong allies in Khortitsa he could have little direct impact on the settlement's economic life. His educational reforms, which were backed by a strong state reform program, had far more impact on Khortitsa.

The educational reforms were one of Cornies's last significant projects to reshape the Molochnaia settlement. His description in the "General Instructions" of punishment as the product of failure reflects the increasingly discouraged tone that penetrated his correspondence in the last years of his life. It was implicitly a reflection on his own failings. It was not, however, an admission of defeat, for he remained heavily engaged in other projects.

The *Judenplan*

The last major demand that the state made of Cornies was for advice on creating mixed Jewish–Mennonite agricultural villages in New Russia. The so-called *Judenplan* was part of the tsarist state's efforts to solve the "Jewish question" by erasing the distinctive characteristics of Jews in the Pale of Settlement. It is a further example of how Nicholas I's policies increasingly characterized non-Slavic, non-Orthodox communities as occupying lower rungs on the scale of social evolution, and of how the imperial state was moving toward seeking a single, unifying policy for its diverse subjects.[135] It also provides a final glimpse of Cornies's reform vision at the end of his life.

In March 1846 Hahn approached Cornies for advice on Kiselev's proposal to establish *Judenplan* villages in Ekaterinoslav, Kherson, and Tavrida *guberniias*. Hahn hoped that the Mennonites would take the lead. This would ultimately result in the 1852 creation of the six-village *Judenplan* settlement in Kherson *guberniia*.[136]

The plan was to place ten Mennonite families in each village, where they would serve as models to the fifty or so Jewish families that made up the bulk of the population. A salaried Mennonite supervisor would oversee each village. The Jewish families would be drawn from the poor, landless Jewish population of the overcrowded shtetls in the Pale of Settlement. The state's hope was that, by teaching them to farm, it would turn them into "useful" peasants.[137]

The *Judenplan* villages were not created until after Cornies's death, and their troubled history is beyond the scope of this account.[138] Cornies was expected to advise on the project and promote it to the Mennonites, and he dutifully obliged, but the project never occupied much of his time. It does, however, provide an important insight into Cornies's view of the Mennonite laboratory of modernization and his larger understanding of the Mennonites' place in Russia. As he entered the last year of his life, he finally, firmly rejected the very idea of Mennonites as model colonists.

Hahn was frankly sceptical of the project, suggesting that "it would be very difficult" to turn Jews into agriculturists.[139] Cornies, convinced as always that good leadership could transform any people, assured him that the plan could work. However, echoing his rejection of earlier plans to move Mennonite families to Crimea, he told Hahn that it was unlikely any Mennonites would agree to move to such villages. Instead, it would be better to situate the villages close to the Molochnaia settlement and provide each with a salaried Mennonite supervisor who would live in the village, farm his own fullholding, and teach the Jewish population. The villages could be built by Mennonite artisans, who would at the same time teach their trades to the new Jewish inhabitants. The Jewish settlers, supervised by Mennonites, over time would adopt their ways.[140]

When Hahn asked for Cornies's help he pointed to the Nogai "success" story, but by 1846 Cornies had given up on the Nogais. He offered Hahn a highly qualified assessment of the value of the Mennonite model, writing that even the Mennonites' impact on neighbouring Slavic peasant villages was "barely perceptible." While he allowed that there had been some small change, he said that the Russian peasants "see the establishments of the [Mennonites] as too perfect and claim they are themselves too clumsy to ever achieve anything similar."[141] If the *Judenplan* project was going to succeed, it would require "special supervision combined with firm, step-by-step leadership."¹⁴²

Leadership, rather than a model, was the most important thing that Mennonites could provide. Leadership had been part of Cornies's vision dating back to his 1826 observations about the Nogais, and by 1846 supervision almost wholly replaced modelling in his view of how Mennonites could best serve the state and thereby justify their privileges. He had already implemented this new vision twice in the 1840s, using Mennonite supervisors to oversee Russian and Nogai potato growing and to direct the model forestry plantation.

The relationship Cornies was now proposing between the Mennonites and the state blurred the old, hard demarcation that distinguished the Mennonites from other tsarist subjects, for it would make Mennonite supervisors direct employees of the state. Mennonite potato and forestry supervisors already received state salaries, but the money passed through Cornies's hands and he oversaw the projects. He envisioned the same arrangement with the *Judenplan* villages, but the state rejected his proposal to locate the villages in the Molochnaia and assign them a single Mennonite supervisor. Instead, it proceeded with the original plan of locating the villages in Kherson and populating them with contingents of Mennonite families as well as Mennonite village supervisors. Cornies supported the final decision and even lobbied to place non-Mennonite friends in administrative positions as the direct bosses of the Mennonite village supervisors.¹⁴³

The *Judenplan* confronted Cornies with the fundamental problem of the Mennonite Privilegium and the model paradigm that justified it. Through his efforts at Iushanle, Akkerman, and elsewhere, Cornies had succeeded in satisfying the state that the Mennonites were earning the continuation of their privileges, but as he acknowledged, the model had limited utility. Sooner or later the state would notice what he already had – while the Mennonites were thriving, their neighbours were realizing almost no benefits from the model. Cornies remained committed to preserving Mennonite privileges, and his arguments against the original conception of the *Judenplan* explicitly objected to the danger it posed to Mennonites: "Separated from their own brethren," he wrote, "they could not possibly assure themselves and their descendants of an untroubled future."¹⁴⁴

Cornies now saw direct service, rather than passive modelling, as the solution to this conundrum. What he did not clearly articulate, though he seemed to sense it, was that this too held enormous dangers. After all, every Russian subject was bound in service to the tsar, so the obligation to serve was a questionable justification for special privileges.

He was fumbling toward the argument that Mennonites were particularly suited to serve by virtue of their membership in their distinctive community. Thus Mennonites could supervise local projects – potatoes, forestry, Jewish settlements – while living in the Mennonite settlement, but Mennonites who separated from the settlement were in danger of losing their value to serve. He held to this view when he first proposed establishing the *Judenplan* villages in the Molochnaia, but when he lent his support to the Kherson plan he opened the door to the wholesale challenges to Mennonite privileges that would emerge during the great reforms of the 1860s and 1870s. He justified this change on the grounds that the *Judenplan* villages would have large enough contingents of Mennonites to retain their community values. Even so, when Mennonites entered direct state employment as supervisors of Jewish villagers, they crossed a significant threshold in their relationship to the state.

Conclusion

The Warkentin Affair eliminated meaningful opposition to Cornies in the Molochnaia settlement, but this did not signal the start of dramatic new reforms. Cornies's key economic innovations came in the 1830s, and dramatic religious changes would come only in the 1860s. The period from 1842–7 saw Cornies turn his reform efforts outward to the surrounding community as he promoted afforestation and agricultural improvements in Slavic and Nogai villages.

Cornies's role in the 1840s reflects the Russian state's movement away from accommodation with its diverse population, and toward the policy of Russification that would fully take hold in the second half of the nineteenth century. The Mennonites continued to function as colonial agents, but the policies they implemented were more and more directly defined by the state. Their own agency, which had been so critical to their early successes in New Russia, was now tolerated rather than promoted as a model, and as Hahn had made clear during the Warkentin Affair, that tolerance had strict limits.

Within the Mennonite settlement Cornies still had one significant contribution to make: the professionalization of Mennonite schools. His concern with schooling extended back to the 1820s, but it was in the 1840s that he implemented a standardized curriculum and imposed new controls over teachers. This would have a lasting effect on Mennonites as they negotiated their position in the modernizing tsarist empire in coming decades.

As Cornies's authority and responsibilities expanded, his understanding of the relationship of Mennonites to the state evolved one last time. In the end he wholly rejected the idea of the Mennonites as model colonists, acknowledging that there was little sign that the model had produced meaningful change. He now argued that Mennonites needed to play a direct supervisory role over other tsarist subjects as educated, progressive agents of reform. He himself was the shining example of this vision of the new Mennonite citizen. Cornies implicitly argued that this was the only basis for preserving the Mennonite Privilegium.

The expansion of Cornies's responsibilities beyond the Molochnaia settlement to the Bergthal daughter settlement and the Khortitsa settlement, and into the Slavic, Nogai, and Jewish populations, had exhausted him. Already in 1845 he commented about the effects of such efforts on "people of my age." He assured Hahn he was still immune to those effects.[145] But they were catching up.

Chapter Ten

Conclusion: "Something for the Future," 1847–1848

In his final years, Johann Cornies often complained that his administrative responsibilities were exhausting him. Beginning in 1845 a series of deaths took an additional toll. On 11 June 1845 his oldest friend Wilhelm Martens committed suicide. Eleven months later, on 15 May 1846, his daughter-in-law Justina died a week after giving birth to a daughter, also named Justina. Aganetha, his beloved wife, died on 30 March 1847 after a long illness. His brother Peter died on 10 September 1847.

The death of his daughter-in-law had a double impact, for its effect on Johann Jr. left his parents deeply worried. Johann Jr. stayed on a while at Tashchenak after her death, but by 3 December 1846 his father was looking for an administrator to take over, someone "gifted with discretion and the ability to motivate himself."[1] Unspoken but implied was that Johann Jr. was neither of these things. Johann and Aganetha worried about his depression and sent him away to Prussia that December in the hopes that a change of scenery would help.[2] They would never see their son again. The children did not accompany him to Prussia; young Johann, now three, stayed with the Cornies family in the care of Agnes, and baby Justina was left in the care of her maternal grandmother. Cornies's brother Heinrich accompanied Johann Jr. to Prussia. Johann Jr. was now thirty-four and widely travelled, and he should not have needed a chaperone. Heinrich's presence is a further sign that his parents were worried about his state of mind; the spectre of Wilhelm Martens's recent suicide must have troubled them.

Aganetha's death left Cornies "deeply troubled by this separation forever from my friend, with whom I had lived for almost thirty-six years and with whom I had shared joy and sorrow. I must openly admit that at my advanced and considerable age, I feel terribly isolated and downcast."[3] In a consoling letter to Johann Jr. he wrote that "as painful as the passing of our beloved mother is, we must remember, to our own great comfort, that the departed had experienced long years of repeated illness and prepared herself for this release with a steadfast Christian belief and that she went to sleep with peace in her soul." He urged his son not to rush home, for "you know that Mother wanted you to make the journey to Prussia as much as I did. She encouraged me to write to you and grant you permission to travel even farther."[4] He also told Johann Jr. to "not give yourself up to continuing, irrational sorrow and grief."[5] This was advice that Cornies could not easily follow himself, for he was "shattered" and "bowed down by the resulting emptiness."[6]

There were times of joy as well as sorrow in Cornies's last years. In October 1846 Agnes married Philipp Wiebe, Cornies's personal secretary and trusted assistant. Meanwhile little Johann was a source of particular joy for his grandfather, who reported with obvious pride on the child's exploits. In letters to Johann Jr. in Prussia he recounted how "your son ... sings, jumps about, and often speaks about Papa."[7] In April 1847 he wrote that the youngest Johann was "already wearing pants. This gives him a great deal of pleasure," and the following January he reported on the boy "riding down mountains of snow" on his new sleigh, then regaling his grandfather with "long tales about his adventure."[8] Soon after, perhaps a bit sheepishly, Cornies wrote that the little boy was "eating fewer sweets on doctor's orders, [so] he has become much more active." In this last letter to his son, Cornies added that he would "very much" miss his grandson, who was soon setting off to Prussia with his aunt and uncle to attend his father's wedding: "He has raised the spirits of our entire household."[9]

Johann Jr. was supposed to come home in fall 1847, but in October he wrote to say that he would be delayed: he had proposed to a woman named Therese Thiessen, and he asked permission to stay in Prussia until April 1848 for the wedding.[10] Johann Jr.'s letter was followed by a letter from Cornies's Prussian friend Johann Wiebe, who assured Cornies that Therese was a respectable woman and a good match.[11] Cornies was overjoyed by the news, writing to his son that his mind was "completely at rest, especially since divine guidance has led you to find your heart's desire, your life's companion."[12]

Cornies considered attending the wedding himself, but in the end he decided to send Agnes and Philipp instead. He claimed that he could not risk the "total stagnation of my business matters while away," but it is likely his declining health played a part in the decision.[13] He wrote Johann Jr. that he was content to remain behind, for Agnes ought to be at the wedding, and "what else can I do to increase the joy of my children, what more can I sacrifice? The happiness of my children is my happiness, their joys are my joys. They are going out into the world and I am leaving it."[14] On this foreboding note, Agnes, Philipp, and little Johann took their last departure from Cornies and headed for Prussia on 5 February 1848.

Cornies was not alone at his home in Ohrloff – there were workers, servants, a maid to cook and clean, and a secretary to write his letters. It seems that some acquaintances hoped the maid might become more than just a common servant – in a letter to Wiebe, Cornies implied that his friends were trying to find him a new wife, but their first choice, a "little old woman from Peitzmerdorf," was not to his liking and he had sent her away: "Granted, she was not a hindrance, like the fifth wheel of a wagon, but still much like an old piece of furniture, out of style and useless. Without my doing, good friends are now trying to find me a household administrator. I do not object. I will thank them if they manage to find me a person with whom I can be content."[15]

Cornies kept busy in February, fielding correspondence and working long hours. He wrote to Wiebe that he had "enough to do from morning until ten at night."[16] Other accounts suggest that his energy and abilities were flagging. According to David Epp, that February Cornies could no longer concentrate on his work, and while he kept his secretary in the office late into the night he seldom accomplished much, for he was "unable to articulate his thoughts."[17] His correspondence shortened to brief letters, a few sentences of questions and orders, with little sign of the attention to detail that had always been his hallmark. On 29 February Cornies fell ill. Two weeks later, on 13 March, he died. He was buried on 16 March at the Ohrloff cemetery.[18] Wiebe described the death and funeral in a letter to Blüher after his return from Prussia:

> Then, at a great distance, we learned about the death of [our] unforgettably good father. More difficult, upon our return, was our entry into the desolate house of our father where we were welcomed by the stream of tears of many sympathetic and painfully grieving relatives and friends. This tore at our hearts and especially that of my dear wife who has, since then, kept mainly to her bed, and is only slowly regaining her strength. Only the Lord can and will comfort us and help us to bear what cannot be changed. May His will remain holy for us …
>
> The last service for the treasured body was on 16 March. On this day, many, very many people from near and far took their final leave of their lost benefactor and protector. Many a quiet tear flowed into his coffin as clear evidence of the sincere love and attachment they had borne him during his lifetime. The scene must have been a beautiful one, yet also painful, as Molochnaia Germans, Russians, Nogais and Hebrew colonists from distant places thronged past the coffin to say their final farewells. Many

a person's most beloved wishes were buried with him. After the Church Elder's final words, and since the church could naturally not accommodate everyone, the body was displayed in the church yard. The gathered crowd then joined in the procession to the cemetery. The most beautiful weather blessed the celebration of this burial. Death had not changed the facial features of the deceased in any way. The serious features we remembered from the past had come back fully. Only the now closed but once lively eyes betrayed the fact that his soul had departed its mortal frame. May his ashes rest gently.[19]

In St. Petersburg, Keppen heard rumours of Cornies's death and wrote anxiously to Fadeev for news. Fadeev told Keppen that he would be "very, very sad" if it were true, but Cornies's uncharacteristic failure to respond to his urgent letters suggested that it was.[20] On 1 June a letter from Steven in Crimea confirmed Cornies's death, and Keppen wondered who would take over the important affairs of the Mennonite settlement – surely not Johann Jr.? Steven reassured him that the far more able Wiebe would step in.[21]

That October the German-language Odesa newspaper *Unterhaltungsblatt für deutsche Ansiedler im südlichen Rußland* published a long obituary, written by a Guardianship Committee agronomist named Gavel. A Russian translation followed in the *Journal of the Ministry of State Domains*.[22] Gavel was an acquaintance of Cornies's who had visited Iushanle. He painted Cornies in the style of Great Man history, and he left no doubt about what constituted greatness: "The wellspring of his public career was an ardent desire, first of all, to secure the future well-being of the colonies, namely of the Mennonite settlements, and, secondly, to demonstrate the greatest devotion to his Monarch and to the new Fatherland."[23] This obituary provided the foundations of much of what was written about Cornies by Mennonite historians in the late nineteenth and early twentieth centuries, but as historian Harvey Dyck points out, there are grounds for believing that in 1848 many in the settlement were not so laudatory. That fall, at the Ministry of State Domains' direction, the settlement compiled village histories, and most of them were pointedly silent about Cornies.[24] In the 1848 settlement elections David Friesen became *Gebietsamt* Mayor, marking the beginning of a conservative reaction that returned the Warkentin Party (*sans* Warkentin) to power. Conservative fullholders would dominate the settlement into the 1860s. That same fall Hahn left the Guardianship Committee, having been promoted to Director of the First Department of the Ministry of State Domains.[25] With both Cornies and Hahn gone, the power of the Agricultural Society waned, despite Wiebe's best efforts as its new chair.

Cornies and the Tsarist Mennonites

If the power of the Agricultural Society did not survive, its reforms were more durable. The Molochnaia Mennonite settlement was at the cutting edge of tsarist economic development in 1848, and while a plethora of events, conditions, and individuals had influenced its transformation, Cornies was undoubtedly instrumental. The spread of sheep rearing, the development of field agriculture and forestry, and the growth of the nascent manufacturing sector were all important parts of his legacy. He also contributed to significant and controversial changes in Mennonite religious life, as a Pietist and promoter of Pietism, and equally as an opponent of religious conservatives.

Most of the economic reforms were initiated by the state through the Guardianship Committee and the Ministry of State Domains, so we cannot credit Cornies alone for their conception. Still, while the state promoted these reforms across New Russia and sometimes the entire empire, it was in Cornies's hands that they achieved their signal success. Afforestation is a case in point: planting trees on the steppe was a tsarist priority from 1825, when Tsar Alexander I exhorted the Mennonites to expand their efforts, and in 1828 Tsar Nicholas I decreed the creation of forestry societies throughout New Russia. Despite this, in 1848 many New Russian travellers still encountered the steppe as a desert, with the Molochnaia settlement its astonishing oasis. It was Fadeev who had written the charter for the Molochnaia Mennonite Forestry Society, and it was the state that had provided thousands of rubles and hundreds of thousands of saplings and seeds. But it was Cornies who had doggedly driven Mennonites to plant and nurture those trees, and after his disastrous and discouraging early forays into Molochnaia settlement administration and politics in the 1820s, they had renewed his resolve; in 1830 he wrote that "everyone, in my view, should leave behind something for the future ... I have decided that trees will be my purpose."[26] Trees took root in his imagination as a hallmark of civilization, for he believed that "as soon as people from time immemorial left their savage state and became cultivators of the soil, they developed orchards."[27] At the height of his power and influence in 1844 this forestry evangelism remained undiminished, and he wrote that "in my imagination, I see myself transported to a time when small forests, here and there, will shoot up and grow toward the sky on high steppe ridges. They will provide pleasure for travellers, draw in the air's moisture, increase the fruitfulness of the soils, and break the back of this region's damaging hurricanes."[28]

This passion reached into all of Cornies's reform efforts and helps account for the remarkable role played by the Molochnaia settlement in tsarist economic development. Historian Natalia Venger has shown that the Mennonites, a tiny minority, were "one of the critical factors in south Russian industrialisation" and served as a "gateway to innovation" for the entire country.[29] Their agricultural accomplishments were no less impressive; by the end of the nineteenth century Mennonites were among the most modern, productive, and profitable farmers in the empire.[30]

This account of Cornies's contributions to tsarist economic development is not new or controversial. My depiction of his role in Mennonite religious life is more contentious. Some scholars have characterized Cornies as a secular and secularizing figure who undermined the authority of the Mennonite congregational elders and served as a fifth column for the modernizing state. This interpretation pays little attention to religion as a modernizing force, beyond identifying Cornies's role in attacking religious conservatives. Others have insisted that Cornies was a Pietist forerunner who cleared the way for the religious revival that swept through the Russian Mennonite community in the 1860s and continues to exert a profound influence on international Mennonitism today.[31]

Foremost among the scholars who view Cornies as an agent of secularizing modernization is James Urry, whose seminal *None but Saints* labels Cornies the "prophet of progress."[32] Urry argues that for Cornies, "the interests of the government appear to have taken preceden[ce] over religious scruples," and that in practice Cornies functioned as a surrogate for the state's modernizing agenda.[33] Urry's influential account has coloured most secular academic assessments of Cornies since its publication in 1989, and for good reason. While the present study employs a wealth of archival information that was unavailable to Urry and focuses far more on the external Russian policies that affected Cornies's actions, it barely disputes the broad outlines of Mennonite economic development provided in *None but Saints*.

I differ from Urry regarding the role of religion in Mennonite economic modernization, and more specifically, the role of Pietism in Cornies's economic and personal agenda. The idea that Cornies was a Pietist is not new – late nineteenth- and early twentieth-century Mennonite accounts understood him in this light, as does Johannes Reimer's 2015 biography, *Johann Cornies: Der Sozialreformer aus den Steppen Südrusslands*.[34] I reinforce this characterization with a close examination of his religious views, which show him to be a Pietist whose beliefs directly influenced all of his actions and had a significant impact on the religious life of his community. Mennonite historiography has always identified the tension between Pietism and quietism as a central dynamic of the late nineteenth century, and the account of Cornies's religious beliefs provided here shows that this tension played a key role dating back to the Frisian immigration of 1818–22.

But if Cornies was a Pietist, this does not mean that his reforms did not also have the secularizing effect that Urry and others argue. In the early decades of the nineteenth century the Mennonites enjoyed a significant degree of independence from state interference in their religious, economic, and community life, and whatever Cornies's religious justifications, it is undoubtedly true that his reforms helped reduce that autonomy. Moreover, his arbitrary and authoritarian manner deeply divided his community and attacked important traditional Mennonite values. In his dealings with his political and religious opponents he was anything but a sympathetic figure; if he did not order Dirk Thun's flogging, he happily acquiesced to it, and his suggestion that Heinrich Wiens be confined to a mental asylum exceeded even Evgenii von Hahn's sense of propriety.

While Cornies deserves criticism, it is worth asking what the alternative was. An implicit assumption of such criticism is that there was a pathway for Mennonites to avoid state infringement on their rights. Close attention to the broader history of the Russian Empire suggests that there was not. As Russia entered the era of small reforms under Nicholas I, it was intent on changing its relationship to all of its subjects, and those who refused to cooperate would suffer. The Doukhobors are an extreme case, but when an angry Hahn ordered Thun flogged in 1842, and told Heinrich Wiens in 1846 that "if the Privilegium [said] that the government no longer has the liberty to command disobedient subjects to be punished, then [he] would be the first to lobby the government to terminate such a Privilegium,"[35] the spectre of the ongoing Doukhobor exile hovered in the air. Throughout his life Cornies consistently maintained that his reforms were intended to preserve Mennonite privileges, and while the state's shocking dissolution of Warkentin's Large Flemish Congregation was a staggering blow to those privileges, Cornies also helped ensure that Mennonites would retain far more control of their community than other colonists in New Russia in the second half of the nineteenth century. Whether this ought to be counted as a political success or a moral failing is purely subjective.

Cornies and the Tsarist Empire

Since the collapse of the Soviet Union, the "imperial turn" in Russian historiography has challenged traditional conceptions of how the empire related to its subjects. The new imperial history turns away from an older view that presented the empire as a "prison of nations" with a powerful central autocracy and powerless subject populations. In its place, recent scholarship has stressed the ways in which subject populations asserted their own agency so as to shape imperial policy and identity.[36] Within this new scholarship there is a growing focus on "place-based" history, "the history of a system of sites, relationships, and their meanings, and a productive way to uncover the spatial logic of the empire."[37]

Susan Smith-Peter coined the term "era of small reforms" that I have adopted in this study. She has documented the ways these reforms stimulated the formation of regional identity in Vladimir *guberniia* and provided foundations for the development of civil society in Russia. There are obvious similarities between the Vladimir and Molochnaia cases. The founding of the Sheep Society in 1824, the Forestry Society in 1831, and the Agricultural Society in 1836, as well as the recruitment of Cornies to the Learned Committee of the Ministry of State Domains in 1838, reflect the state's efforts to cultivate local knowledge and expertise. Yet there is a key difference between the Vladimir and Molochnaia cases, for in Vladimir there was a growing sense of regional identity between the 1830s and the 1860s, centred around civic institutions and encouraged by the state. The Mennonites' experience was the opposite: they entered the 1830s with a clearly defined identity and meaningful civic institutions. By the 1840s the state saw those institutions as impeding its goal of making the Mennonites more useful subjects, and its interference in elections and congregational structures was a direct attack on Mennonite identity. This shows that the Vladimir case was not universal and suggests that the difference centred on the nature of pre-existing identities. The Mennonites were not Slavic, Orthodox, or Russian-speaking, and the state's new policies challenged their identity, prompting Mennonite resistance to reforms. The Mennonite story bears a striking similarity to Kelly O'Neill's account of the experience of Crimean Tatars in the same period. It suggests that the era of small reforms and the policy of Official Nationality that took hold in the 1830s had different implications for colonial subjects than for Orthodox Slavs. The transition toward a policy of Russification for Russia's colonial subjects is commonly dated to the late nineteenth century, but the Mennonite case reveals its genesis in the first half of the century.

Russia had recruited Mennonite immigrants to model progressive agricultural practices, and while the Mennonites fulfilled their part of the bargain, neighbouring Slavic peasants and Nogai Tatars rejected their example. For Mennonites the era of small reforms amounted to the state's recognition of this failure and the emergence of a new vision of their role: they were pushed to transform themselves from a static model into an active laboratory of modernization. This still afforded them special status, but it also shifted their role to that of, at best, laboratory technicians; at worst they became laboratory test subjects. They were now expected to change their economic practices at the behest of the state, and such changes inevitably impinged on their cultural practices, most notably their religious beliefs. The more they resisted, the more the state threatened to wholly reclassify them from colonists to colonial subjects.

The Mennonite story addresses at ground level what O'Neill succinctly identifies as "one of the most fundamental, bedevilling questions in Russian history: where did 'interior Russia' ... end and the empire begin ... In this multi-ethnic, contiguous, dynastic entity, is it possible to discern static, or more or less stable, geographic or cultural boundaries?"[38] The fact that non-Slavic, non-Orthodox, German-speaking Mennonites served as colonial agents charged with modernizing Slavic, Orthodox peasants, all of them settled on land annexed from Nogai Tatars, argues that before the 1830s conventional understandings of centre and periphery had little meaning. However, during the era of small reforms the boundaries of centre and periphery were reifying. While there was still room for the Mennonites in the centre, the practices and values that gave them their unique identity were increasingly peripheral to the state's agenda; to survive they needed to either abandon key elements of their identity or else lose it altogether.

A Continuing Legacy

Although the presence and memory of the Mennonites was wiped from depictions of the region in the Soviet era, their existence is no longer forgotten, and neither is their influence. On a golden autumn day in 2016, local residents, schoolchildren from surrounding communities, representatives from district and regional governments, Ukrainian scholars from regional universities, and Mennonites from Germany and Canada gathered at the Staro-Berdiansk forest plantation near the Ukrainian city of Melitopol – the model forest plantation that Cornies created in 1846 – to unveil a monument to Cornies. It was a festive occasion, with music, booths selling local crafts and agricultural products, folk singers, and a children's dance recital. A bounce house distracted the youngest children from the tedium of the inevitable speeches.[39]

Cornies probably would have despised the statue, for he always shied away from official recognition of his accomplishments. He certainly would have condemned the dance recital as a shockingly immoral affront to his Mennonite sensibilities. But more importantly, the survival of the forest plantation and its continuing educational role in the Tavria State Agrotechnical University's forestry program, would have thrilled him, as would the presence of schoolchildren, attending (ostensibly) for educational purposes.

Most of all, Cornies would have understood and valued the forest plantation as a symbol of the role of Mennonites as both loyal servants and respected leaders in the creation of a modern state. Of course, it was the Russian state that he served, while the 2016 event was defiantly Ukrainian, carefully framed by regional officials as a patriotic celebration of Ukrainian accomplishments. Cornies, who spent his public life navigating the conflicting, constantly shifting demands of Mennonite congregations, the Molochnaia *Gebietsamt*, the Guardianship Committee, and the Ministry of State Domains, would have understood the new geographies of power without much trouble. But his first response to the celebration would certainly have been to ask, who was responsible for tending the trees, and why were they neglecting their work?

Notes

1. Introduction

1 Haxthausen, *Studien über die innern Zustände*, vol. 2, 430.
2 On the challenges of using imperial records to study colonial peoples, see Steinwedel, *Threads of Empire*, 15–16.
3 This study focuses closely on Russian colonialism from the Mennonite perspective. While it is also informed by central records, I have intentionally and consistently pushed those records to the periphery of the account. For a more extensive view of what the central archival records say about the Molochnaia story, see Staples, *Cross-Cultural Encounters*. On Russian colonial policy in New Russia, see Sunderland, *Taming the Wild Field*.
4 P.M. Friesen, *The Mennonite Brotherhood in Russia*, 199.
5 This study references four generations of the Johann Cornies family. For clarity I refer to the principal subject as Johann Cornies, his father as Johann Cornies Sr., his son as Johann Cornies Jr., and his grandson variously as "little Johann" and "grandson Johann."
6 Today the villages are Młynary (Mühlhausen), Drewnica (Schönbaum), and Niedźwiedzica (Bärwalde).
7 Several versions of this story survive. See David H. Epp, *Johann Cornies*, 1, and genealogies compiled at http://cornies-genealogy.blogspot.com. The earliest published account is Marmont, *Voyage de M. Le Maréchal Duc de Raguse*, vol. 1., 356–61. The family consisted of: Johann Cornies Sr. (1741–1814); his wife Maria Cornies, née Klassen (1761–1831); Johann (1789–1848); Peter (1791–1847); David (1794–1873); and Heinrich, who was born in New Russia (1806–??). Their first child, also Johann, died in infancy (1786–1787); their fifth, Heinrich, died at the age of three (1796–1799); their sixth, Katharina, died in New Russia at the age of eight (1800–1808).
8 Epp, *Johann Cornies*, 1.

9 Epp, *Johann Cornies*, 1–2.
10 Peter Rempel, *Mennonite Migration to Russia*, 78.
11 On Russia's use of migration as a tool of empire, see Randolph and Avrutin, *Russia in Motion*.
12 LeDonne, *Forging a Unitary State*, 4.
13 On military colonies, see Janet M. Hartley, *Russia*, 190–208; and Pipes, "The Russian Military Colonies." On the broader security concerns that shaped colonization along the Ottoman frontier, see Nicholas Breyfogle, *Heretics and Colonizers*, 17. On the relationship between security, economic exploitation, and other factors in colonization, see Schorkowitz et al., "The Shifting Forms of Continental Colonialism," 23–68.
14 On the Mennonite role in tsarist economic development, see Venger, *Mennonitskoe predprinimatel'stvo*.
15 For the Canadian case, see Loewen, *Family, Church, and Market*. For Latin America, see Valladeres, *Mission and Migration*. For the Latin American historiography, see Benjamin W. Goossen, "Mennonites in Latin America."
16 On Mennonites in Poland before the Russian emigration, see Klassen, *Mennonites in Early Modern Poland and Prussia*; and Jantzen, *Mennonite German Soldiers*.
17 Jantzen, *Mennonite German Soldiers*, 15–48.
18 Klassen, *Mennonites in Early Modern Poland*, 24.
19 Jantzen, *Mennonite German Soldiers*, 27.
20 Ibid., 16–17.
21 Ibid.
22 Ibid., 128–30.
23 On Pietism, see Ward, *The Protestant Evangelical Awakening*.
24 Historians such as Benjamin Marschke, Klaus Depperman, Mary Fulbrook, Carl Hinrichs, and, most emphatically, Richard L. Gawthrop place Pietism at the centre of the development of the cameralist Prussian state model: Depperman, *Der hallesche Pietismus*; Fulbrook, *Piety and Politics*; Hinrichs, *Preussentum und Pietismus*; Gawthrop, *Pietism and the Making of Eighteenth-Century Prussia*. On Prussia, see Raeff, *The Well-Ordered Police State*.
25 Quoted in Jantzen, *Mennonite German Soldiers*, 69.
26 On these concerns, see Sunderland, *Taming the Wild Field*, 112.
27 De Madariaga, *Russia in the Age of Catharine the Great*, 384.
28 Bartlett, *Human Capital*, 31–4. Eric Lohr describes Russia's recruitment policy as "attract and hold"; Lohr, *Russian Citizenship*, 5.
29 For a comparison of American and Russian colonization, see Sabol, "*The Touch of Civilization*." Faith Hillis shows that restricting migration, as well as encouraging it, was an important facet of tsarist governance; Hillis, "Human Mobility." See also Randolph and Avrutin, *Russia in Motion*, 25.

30 Bartlett, *Human Capital*. Sunderland calls it tutelary colonization and stresses the paternalist role of the state rather than the role of the foreign colonists: Sunderland, *Taming the Wild Field*, 115.
31 Quoted in Bartlett, *Human Capital*, 211. Patricia Herlihy offers similar conclusions; Herlihy, *Odessa*, 33. Richelieu's full name and title was Armand-Emmanuel du Plessis, duc de Richelieu.
32 A 5 August 1819 decree ended the period of rapid immigration. See Kabuzan, *Emigratsiia i Reemigratsiia v Rossii*, 59.
33 Cooper and Stoler, "Between Metropole and Colony," 5.
34 Young, *Empire*, 38–41. Young provides a useful recent overview of the concept and its application. In a similar vein, Alexander Martin calls New Russia a "space of social experimentation"; Martin, *From the Holy Roman Empire*, 258.
35 Visvanathan, *A Carnival for Science*, 17.
36 Barlow, "Debates over Colonial Modernity."
37 Sunderland, *Taming the Wild Field*, 88–9. On the historiography see Kivelson and Suny, *Russia's Empires*, 116–39.
38 O'Neill, *Claiming Crimea*, 4–5.
39 LeDonne, *Forging a Unitary State*, 6–10.
40 Jantzen, *German Mennonite Soldiers*, 19.
41 The committee was called the Guardianship Office for Foreign Settlers in New Russia from 1800 to 1801, the Guardianship Committee for Foreign Settlers in New Russia from 1801 to 1818, and the Guardianship Committee for Foreign Settlers in Southern Russia from 1818 until it was disbanded in 1871. Throughout this study I use its second title, the one most used in the documentary record during the period.
42 Environmental conditions are detailed in Staples, *Cross-Cultural Encounters*, 5–9.
43 The tsarist Mennonites are often labelled the "Mennonite Commonwealth," a term that I find problematic. See my "The Mennonite Commonwealth Paradigm"; and James Urry's critical response, "The Mennonite Commonwealth Revisited."
44 The Privilegium is reproduced in translation in Urry, *None but Saints*, 282–4. Its role in tsarist Mennonite society is detailed in Staples, "Religion, Politics, and the Mennonite Privilegium." On the larger history of Privilegiums, see Urry, *Mennonites, Politics, and Peoplehood*.
45 Urry, *None but Saints*, 282–4.
46 Ibid.
47 Venger characterizes the attitude of the Mennonite immigrants as "pragmatic" and focused on economic opportunities; *Mennonitskoe Predpinimatel'stvo*, 98–9.
48 Jantzen, *German Mennonite Soldiers*, 21–2.

49 Mennonite terms were laid out in a 1787 petition; see David G. Rempel, "From Danzig to Russia."
50 Eck, "Diarium."
51 On the insider–outsider dichotomy in settler colonialism, see Young, *Empire*, 34. The Mennonite case is unusual due to their transition from insiders to outsiders.
52 On the challenge of finding non-state sources, see Steinwedel, *Threads of Empire*, 15–16.
53 Similarly, Mark Gamsa writes of the "cognitive richness of exceptions." Gamsa, "Biography and (Global) Microhistory," 238.
54 "Opisanie Menonitskikh kolonii v Rossii: Proizkhozhdenie Menonistov i vodverenie ikh v Rossii," *ZhMGI* 4 (1842): 1–42; Cornies, "Po otnosheniiu Departmenta Sel'skago Khoziaistva o vvedenii u russkikh pereselentsev khoziastva i poriadka upravleniia menonitov," RGIA f. 383, o. 10, d. 7164.
55 Two valuable recent examples of the rich potential of microhistory are Martin, *From the Holy Roman Empire*; and Sunderland, *The Baron's Cloak*.

2. Land of Opportunity, 1804–1817

1 For a similar assessment of the opportunities that Russia provided to German immigrants, see Martin, *From the Holy Roman* Empire, 163–4. Some of Cornies's journal entries from the journey are reproduced in Dyck et al., eds., *Transformation on the South Ukrainian Steppe* (hereafter *Transformation*), vol. 1, 96–155. The entire journal is located in DAOO *f*. 89, *o*. 1, *d*. 103.
2 Martin reaches similar conclusions in his microhistory of another German immigrant to Russia, Johannes Ambrosius Rosenstrauch; *From the Holy Roman Empire*, 164.
3 Detlef Brandes describes the administration of the New Russian colonies in this period as "more improvisation than planning"; Brandes, *Von den Zaren adoptiert*, 147.
4 On the economic circumstances of the Khortitsa Mennonites, see Jantzen, *Mennonite German Soldiers*, 46. On the broader struggles of New Russian immigrants, see Herlihy, *Odessa*, 30.
5 The value of the guilder in Russia is difficult to establish. In 1804 it exchanged at 3.3 rubles per guilder. Thus, 300 guilder amounted to approximately one year's wages for a Russian peasant agricultural labourer. In 1804 a paper rouble (correctly called a "rouble assignat") was worth 0.8 silver roubles, but the exchange rate climbed sharply during the Napoleonic Wars, peaking in 1815, when the value of the paper rouble fell to below 0.24 silver roubles. It then stabilized between 0.25 and 0.29 paper roubles until the currency reforms of 1839. See Owen, "A Standard Ruble." The Dutch guilder exchanged for an average of 3.57 silver roubles in the

first decades of the nineteenth century, but the rate fluctuated widely; see Marmefelt, *The History of Money*, 48.
6 Venger, *Mennonitskoe predprinimatel'stvo*, 11.
7 Rempel, *Mennonite Migration*, 78.
8 Huebert, *Molotschna Historical Atlas*, 167. On the hardships that immigrants experienced in their first year in New Russia, see Herlihy, *Odessa*, 30–1.
9 On environmental conditions in the Molochnaia, see Staples, *Cross-Cultural Encounters*, 5–9.
10 Ibid.
11 Ibid., 29–32.
12 Ibid., 32–7.
13 Breyfogle, *Heretics and Colonizers*, 11.
14 Ibid., 37–41.
15 Ibid., 41–4.
16 B.H. Unruh, *Die niederländisch-niederdeutschen Hintergründe*, 324.
17 The housebarn style dated to the sixteenth-century Netherlands. See Dyck, "Introduction and Analysis," 15.
18 Eck, "Diarium."
19 Report of the Department of Agriculture of the Department of State Domains to the Ministry of Internal Affairs, 26 July 1813, DAOO *f.* 134, *o.* 1, *d.* 343.
20 On Russian recruitment and subsidies, see Bartlett, *Human Capital*, 23–30; Urry, *None but Saints*, 282–4; Staples, *Cross-Cultural Encounters*, 41–2; and Venger, *Mennonitskoe predprinimatel'stvo*, 111–12.
21 Regarding the Smolensk peasants, see Sunderland, *Taming the Wild Field*, 123–5. An example of the argument over the role of subsidies in colonist development, which incorrectly asserts that internal migrants did not receive subsidies, is Kabuzan, *Emigratsiia*, 59.
22 On the system of subsidies, see Venger, *Mennonitskoe predprinimatel'stvo*, 11–13; on the significance of subsidies and privileges, see Staples, *Cross-Cultural Encounters*, 182.
23 See the 1806 settlement census, DAOO *f.* 134, *o.* 1, *d.* 158. Genealogist Tim Janzen has transcribed and published the census; http://www.mennonitegenealogy.com/russia/Molotschna_Mennonite_Settlement_Census_27_October_1806.pdf. The total population was 1,749. The census lists age but not birthdate: Johann Sr. was one of four sixty-five-year-olds; twelve people were older. Anna Wiens (78) was the oldest person in the settlement. The oldest person in Ohrloff was Wilhelm Wiens (69).
24 Epp, *Johann Cornies*, 5.
25 Ibid., 7–9.
26 Ibid., 7.

27 Epp claims that Cornies pioneered this trade, but the 1806 Moravian Brethren description referenced earlier shows otherwise. Ibid., 8–9.
28 Ibid., 9.
29 For Marmont's description of the Molochnaia, see his *Voyage*, vol. 1, 354–61.
30 Cornies to Fadeev, 26 April 1838, *Transformation*, vol. 2, 120; Cornies to Fadeev, 15 August 1838, *Transformation*, vol. 2, 133–5.
31 Epp, *Johann Cornies*, 8–9.
32 Ibid., 1.
33 On Cornies's mother's death, see Cornies to Fadeev, 17 July 1833, *Transformation*, vol. 1, 330–1. Regarding his grandson, see Cornies to Johann Cornies Jr., 5 April 1847, DAOO *f.* 89, *o.* 1, *d.* 1260, l. 39.
34 Goerz, *The Molotschna Settlement*, 30.
35 Cornies to Jacob Wiebe, 5 November 1847, DAOO *f.* 89, *o.* 1, *d.* 1260, l. 108.
36 Staples, "Romance, Marriage, Sex."
37 Ibid., 305.
38 The three children (1814, 1816, 1818) were never named, suggesting they were either stillborn or died soon after birth.
39 Gehrmann, "Infant Mortality in Germany," 849. Regarding infant death and grieving, see Woods, *Children Remembered*.
40 Branca, *Women in Europe*, 89–91; Rachel G. Fuchs, *Gender and Poverty*, 23.
41 Ibid., 23.
42 Johann Cornies to Traugott Blüher 29 June 1847, DAOO *f.* 89, *o.* 1, *d.* 1260, l. 67.
43 Cornies, "The Nogai Tatars in Russia," *Transformation*, vol. 1, 481.
44 Ibid., vol. 1, 482.
45 Cornies to Fadeev, 29 November 1840, *Transformation*, vol. 2, 310–13.
46 Johann Cornies to Johann Wiebe, 5 November 1847, DAOO *f.* 89, *o.* 1, *d.* 1260, l. 107.
47 Molochnaia Colonial Inspector Sieter to Johann Cornies, 1 January 1812, *Transformation*, vol. 1, 3–4. When the lease was signed the amount and dimensions of the land were still in flux.
48 Cornies identified the author of the pamphlet, titled *Encouragement for the Improvement and Refining of Sheep Breeding in Russia*, as M.L. Friebe. See Cornies to Ivan N. Inzov, 24 June 1820, *Transformation*, vol. 1, 6–7. On the economic rationale for sheep-raising rather than grain farming, see Herlihy, *Odessa*, 49–50.
49 Herlihy describes the broader state effort to introduce and interbreed merino sheep in *Odessa*, 49–50.
50 Goerz, *The Molotschna Settlement*, 63.
51 Regarding the Crimean Armenians, see Mikaelian, *Istoriia Krymskikh Armian*, 148–9. On the general application of Catherine's decree and

the Mennonite exception, see Myeshkov, *Die Schwarzmeerdeutschen*, 357. Venger calls the Privilegium "unprecedented" and writes that Mennonites occupied a "special niche" in the tsarist social system; *Mennonitskoe predprinimatel'stvo*, 1.
52 Plett, *The Golden Years*, 165.
53 Jantzen, *Mennonite German Soldiers*, 16–20.
54 Goerz, *The Molotschna Settlement*, 63.
55 Krahn and Sawatsky, "Russia."
56 D. Schlatter, *Bruchstücke aus einigen Reisen*, 15. See also Schlatter's letter to the *Baptist Magazine and Literary Review* 17 (1825) and his letter to Angas in the *Baptist Magazine and Literary Review* 16 (1824).
57 Reimer, "Ein Kleines Aufsatz."
58 Regarding the application of the ban, see Dyck, "Introduction and Analysis," 22–4.
59 Quoted in Plett, *The Golden Years*, 184.
60 Staples, "Romance, Marriage, Sex," 314–16.
61 Plett, *The Golden Years*, 180–1; Staples, "Romance, Marriage, Sex," 311–12. The last record of Anna Thiessen is a letter to a Kleine Gemeinde elder sent from Siberia in 1828; see Plett, *Golden Years*, 181.
62 Ibid., 172–4.
63 In 1813 Johann Sr.'s household, including wife Aganetha and son Johann Jr., owned seven horses (the village average), twenty-eight head of cattle (the average was twelve), and twenty-two sheep (the average was eight). After 1813 there are no detailed family statistics, but scattered settlement statistics show that by 1817, Ohrloff village, with a population of 126 (4.8 per cent of the settlement population), owned 811 sheep (10 per cent of all sheep in the settlement). Ohrloff had the largest sheep herds in the settlement, and most of these additional sheep undoubtedly belonged to Cornies.
64 Cornies account books, 1812–17, DAOO *f.* 89, *o.* 1, *d.* 7.
65 Epp, *Johann Cornies*, 7–8.
66 Cornies account books, 1812–17, DAOO *f.* 89, *o.* 1, *d.* 7.
67 The date of the purchase is not extant – the first reference to it is in Cornies's 1816 account books; see Cornies account books, 1812–17, DAOO *f.* 89, *o.* 1, *d.* 7.
68 Contenius claimed that its profits were 15,000 roubles in 1826 (Contenius to Cornies, 4 January 1826, *Transformation*, vol. 1, 51–2). Detailed records from 1828 and 1829 show profits of 12,311 roubles and 10,705 roubles respectively; DAOO *f.* 89, *o.* 1, *d.* 130 (1828); DAOO *f.* 89, *o.* 1, *d.* 153 (1829).
69 Martens's wealth is not documented; by his death he reputedly owned more than 100,000 *desiatinas* of land. See Loewen and Prieb, "The Abuse of Power."

70 Grellet, *Memoirs*, 404.
71 Ibid., 405–6.
72 On colonial inspectors, see Myeshkov, *Die Schwarzmeerdeutschen*, 384–96.
73 Raeff, *The Decembrist Movement*, 10. On the significance of the Decembrist Movement in the Russian Imperial context see Kivelson and Suny, *Russia's Empires*, 154–7.
74 On Doukhobor origins and early history, see Breyfogle, *Heretics and Colonizers*, 23–46; Woodcock and Avakumovic, *The Doukhobors*, 17–34; Fry, "Doukhobors 1801–1855," 30–78; and Klibanov, *Istoriia religioznogo sektantstva*, 85–121.
75 Breyfogle, *Heretics and Colonizers*, 10–11; Woodcock and Avakumovic, *The Doukhobors*, 20.
76 On shifting state attitudes toward the Doukhobors and the 1840s exile, see Breyfogle, *Heretics and Colonizers*, 17–46.
77 On the accusations and investigation, see Staples, *Cross-Cultural Encounters*, 37–41; and Woodcock and Avakumovic, *The Doukhobors*, 49–52. For a full record of the investigation see DAOO, *f.* 1, *o.* 219, *d.* 3.
78 Staples, *Cross-Cultural Encounters*, 37–41, Woodcock and Avakumovic, *The Doukhobors*, 49–51.
79 Grellet, *Memoirs*, 399.
80 Grellet, *Memoirs*, 405.
81 Breyfogle identifies similar freedoms in the Caucasus; see *Heretics and Colonizers*, 50.
82 See chapter 1, page 16 and note 43.

3. A Public Life, 1818–1824

1 Quoted in Goerz, *The Molotschna Settlement*, 20–1.
2 On military colonies, see Hartley, *Russia, 1762–1825*, 190–208; and Pipes, "The Russian Military Colonies."
3 Regarding the impact of the Napoleonic Wars, see Jantzen, *Mennonite German Soldiers*, 79–106.
4 Staples, *Cross-Cultural Encounters*, 42–3.
5 Urry, *Mennonites, Politics, and Peoplehood*, 90.
6 Gebietsamt to Cornies, 11 November 1817, *Transformation*, vol. 1, 4–5.
7 There is no record of the membership of the Settlement Commission. In 1825 it included, in addition to Cornies, Heinrich Balzer Sr. and Salomon Ediger. Given Balzer's status in the community he probably headed the commission. See Gebietsamt to Cornies, 29 July 1825, *Transformation*, vol. 1, 31. On Balzer's status, see Urry, "Ohm Heinrich Balzer 1800–46."
8 The first such reference appears in the "Zhurnal registratsii iskhodiashchikh dokumentov," 20 May 1821, DADO *f.* 134, *o.* 1, *d.* 692.

9 Seegel, *Mapping Europe's Borderlands*, 34. On the significance of land surveying in the colonial process, see also O'Neill, *Claiming Crimea*, 164–218. On mapping and state power, see Scott, *Seeing Like a State*, 37–9.
10 Alexanderwohl did not have enough water. See *Transformation*, vol. 1, 30–1, 35–6, 114–15.
11 Fadeev, *Vospominaniia*, bk. 3, 388.
12 On Alexander's religious views after the Napoleonic invasion see Menger, *Die Heilige Allianz*, 213–49. See also Werth, *The Tsar's Foreign Faiths*, 53–4. On Golitsyn see Walter William Sawatsky, "Prince Alexander N. Golitsyn (1773–1844)."
13 Werth, *The Tsar's Foreign Faiths*, 53. On the Russian Bible Society see Cohen Zacek, "The Russian Bible Society"; Zacek, "The Russian Bible Society and the Catholic Church"; and Zacek, "The Russian Bible Society and the Orthodox Church." Menger describes Tsar Alexander's attitude toward the Bible Society in *Die Heilige Allianz*, 240–9. Stephen Batalden has published extensively on the activities and significance of the BFBS; see his publications "The BFBS Petersburg Agency"; "Printing the Bible in the Reign of Alexander I"; and "Musul'manskii i evreiskii voprosy." The standard Russian-language account is Pypin, *Religiozniia dvizheniia pri Aleksandre I*. Regarding the society's political influence, see Vishlenkova, *Zabotias' o dushakh poddannykh*; and Menger, *Die Heilige Allianz*. The society's main British agents published accounts of their work; see Paterson, *The Book of Every Land*; Henderson, *Biblical Researches*; and Pinkerton, *Russia*. The best introduction to the history of the BFBS is Batalden et al., *Sowing the Word*. George Brown provides a detailed narrative account in *British and Foreign Bible Society*. On the BFBS's place in the British evangelical movement, see R.H. Martin, *Evangelicals United*.
14 James Urry summarizes the Russian Bible Society's contacts with Molochnaia Mennonites but describes no lasting effect. Urry, "'Servants from Far.'"
15 This was a core element of the BFBS strategy. See *Reports of the British and Foreign Bible Society*, 24.
16 Quoted in Menger, *Die Heilige Allianz*, 224. Menger addresses the concept of conversion and Alexander's experience. See also Sawatsky, "Prince Alexander N. Golitsyn," 194.
17 Vishlenkova, *Zabotias' o dushakh*, 135–7. Menger says that the society's influence was not "insignificant" (*Die Heilige Allianz*, 245). See also Werth, *The Tsar's Foreign Faiths*, 43–5.
18 Vishlenkova, *Zabotias' o dushakh*, 397.
19 On Langeron, see Zacek, "The Russian Bible Society, 1812–1826," 73. On Inzov, see Pypin, *Religiozniia dvizheniia*, 131–2.

20 Zacek, "The Russian Bible Society, 1812–1826," 65; Menger, *Die Heilige Allianz*, 244. On Bible Society membership, see Zacek, "The Russian Bible Society, 1812–1826," 42–65.
21 Lothe, "La 'British and Foreign Bible Society,'" 73.
22 Batalden, in "Printing the Bible," writes that the Russian Bible Society was an agent of modernization in Russia; Vishlenkova, in *Zabotias' o dushakh*, 398–9, suggests that it promoted discussion and renewal within the Orthodox Church.
23 Andrey V. Ivanov describes this as a conservative "coup" led by Archimandrite Fotii; Ivanov, *A Spiritual Revolution*, 271–2. In a critical 1824 memo to Tsar Alexander, Fotii labelled the society "revolutionary"; Menger, *Die Heilige Allianz*, 248.
24 On the role of the Bible Society for Slavic peasants, see Nikitenko, *Up from Serfdom*, 177–85. Golitsyn intervened directly to help Nikitenko gain his freedom from serfdom.
25 Membership records are not extant, but regional officials routinely joined the Russian Bible Society. Contenius's relations with BFBS members Grellet and Allen makes his membership likely. Fadeev issued a lengthy endorsement of the Russian Bible Society's activities in the Molochnaia in the name of the Guradianship Committee in 1818: Fadeev to the Gebietsamt, 26 July 2018, DAOO *f.* 89, *o.* 1, *d.* 38.
26 Friedmann, *Mennonite Piety*, 88.
27 Hughes, *The Excellency of the Holy Scriptures*, quoted in Batalden, *Sowing the Word*, 2.
28 Henderson, *Biblical Researches*, 386. Missionaries from the Basle Mission Society described Odessa as a "strong and fertile" base for missionary work, noting "the possibility of grounding an expansion of Evangelical work from the scattered German colonies." Quoted in W. Schlatter, *Geschichte der Basler Mission*, vol. 1, 96, 100.
29 On the relationship between Evangelical Christian missions and the Enlightenment, see Stanley, "Christian Missions and the Enlightenment"; and Menger, *Die Heilige Allianz*, 241.
30 Comaroff, "Images of Empire," 175.
31 Matthew 5:14.
32 La Vopa, *Grace, Talent, and Merit*, 139–41.
33 Allen, *Life*, vol. 1, 440.
34 Ibid., 439. Ivanov describes debates regarding the dangers of educating peasants in *A Spiritual Revolution*, 216.
35 Allen, *Life*, vol. 1, 466–7.
36 Henderson, *Biblical Researches*, 386.
37 Ibid., 390; Schlatter, *Geschichte der Basler Mission*, vol. 1, 66–9. Henderson calls Schlatter a member of the Basle Society, but the society rejected him.

38 Urry, *None but Saints*, 105. The society raised money and built its school between 1820 and 1822. Regarding the school's construction, see Contributions of Material and Labour … in 1820, 7 October 1822, DAOO *f.* 89, *o.* 1, *d.* 126.
39 No other association member contributed more than 153 roubles; the average contribution – excluding Cornies's – was 15 roubles. School Society Accounts 1820–1827, n.d., DAOO *f.* 89, *o.* 1, *d.* 126.
40 John Friesen, "Education, Pietism, and Change"; Klassen, "Faith and Culture in Conflict"; Friedmann, "Anabaptism and Pietism."
41 On the Christian response to capitalism, see Hilton, *The Age of Atonement*.
42 Urry, *None but Saints*, 101.
43 Urry, "'Servants from Far,'" 219.
44 Urry, *None but Saints*, 102.
45 John B. Toews summarizes the religious position of the conservative Flemish congregation in the Molochnaia as quietist, formalistic, and liturgically rigid. See Toews, *Czars, Soviets and Mennonites*, 18–21.
46 Warkentin to Fadeev, 7 May 1827, in Isaac, *Die Molotschnaer Mennoniten*, 104.
47 "Memorandum of Tobias Voth," in Friesen, *The Mennonite Brotherhood*, 694.
48 Raeff, *Understanding Imperial Russia*, 24–31.
49 Fadeev, *Vospominaniia*, bk. 2, 321–2.
50 "Zhurnal registratsii iskhodiashchikh dokumentov," 20 May 1821, DADO, *f.* 134, *o.* 1, *d.* 692.
51 Konovalova, *Pis'ma gertsoga Armana*, 5–20.
52 Contenius's background before he arrived in Russia is mysterious. Some sources say he was born in Silesia, but most say Westphalia. See Eisfeld, "Introduction," in *Samuil Khristianovich Kontenius*, 5–6.
53 Fadeev describes appointments in *Vospominaniia*, bk. 3.
54 Even this number is inflated because a handful of fullholders, including Cornies, had very large herds. The median was much lower.
55 On patronage see Lincoln, *In the Vanguard of Reform*, 15–18.
56 See, for example, O'Neill's account of attempts to co-opt the Crimean elites; *Claiming Crimea*, 84–124.
57 On Richelieu's background and service in Russia, see Herlihy, *Odessa*, 21–2. The career of De Maison ("Demaison" in Russian sources) is described in Staples, *Cross-Cultural Encounters*, 32–7. LeDonne describes the tenures of Richelieu, Langeron, and other New Russian governors general in *Forging a Unitary State*, 298–302.
58 Fadeev, *Vospominaniia*, bk. 3, 421–2. The journal editor added a footnote saying that Contenius had fled a mysterious past life in the West but providing no details. On the mystery of Contenius's early life see Eisfeld, "Introduction," in *Samuil Khristianovich Kontenius*, 5–6.

59 Cornies's copy of the order is undated but clearly dates from April 1824 (Guardianship Committee to Cornies, n.d., *Transformation*, vol. 1, 13–15). The letters from the two Gebietsamts are: Khortitsa Gebietsamt to Cornies, 8 April 1824, *Transformation*, vol. 1, 15–16; and Molochnaia Gebietsamt to Cornies, 9 April 1824, *Transformation*, vol. 1, 16.
60 Guardianship Committee to Cornies, 16 April 1824, *Transformation*, vol. 1, 16–17.
61 Fadeev, *Vospominaniia*, bk. 3, 319.
62 Guardianship Committee to Cornies, n.d., DAOO *f.* 89, *o.* 1, *d.* 58, l. 52.
63 Their departure date is not known. Cornies was in Ekaterinoslav on 17 April, when he received the 1,000 roubles to buy stationary.
64 Fadeev to Petr Keppen, 3 May 1839, ARAN, *f.* 30, *o.* 3, *d.* 302, l. 6–7.
65 Cornies to David Epp, 25 November 1826, *Transformation*, vol. 1, 102–5.
66 Cornies to Blüher, 20 September 1834, *Transformation*, vol. 1, 375.
67 Blüher to Cornies, 21 April 1844, DAOO, *f.* 89, *o.* 1, *d.* 1094, l. 99.
68 On Moravian Brethren history, see Hutton, *History of the Moravian Church*.

4. Awakening, 1824–1828

1 Fadeev, *Vospominaniia*, bk. 2: 405.
2 Ibid., 403.
3 Cornies to Contenius, 30 January 1825, *Transformation*, vol. 1, 24–5.
4 Daniel Schlatter, August 1824 letter to the *Baptist Magazine*, printed in the *Baptist Magazine*, 1825, 410.
5 Cornies to Fadeev, 4 March 1825, *Transformation*, vol. 1, 26.
6 Regarding the 12,000 *desiatina* lease, see Wilhelm Frank to Cornies, 9 January 1825, DAOO *f.* 89, *o.* 1, *d.* 77, l. 10. For the Mariupol lease, see DAOO *f.* 6, *o.* 1, *d.* 2464, l. 1; and Cornies to Semenov, 29 October 1825, *Transformation*, vol. 1, 37.
7 Cornies to Contenius, 30 January 1825, *Transformation*, vol. 1, 24.
8 Cornies to David Epp, 10 March 1826, *Transformation*, vol. 1, 61–2; Cornies to Fadeev, 27 January 1825, *Transformation*, vol. 1, 22–3.
9 Matthew 19:23–24.
10 See Sprunger, "Dutch Mennonites," 30.
11 Cornies to Fadeev, 27 January 1825, *Transformation*, vol. 1, 22–3.
12 Cornies to Blüher, December 1824, *Transformation*, vol. 1, 19–20.
13 Cornies to Fadeev, 5 February 1825, *Transformation*, vol. 1, 25–6.
14 Cornies to Fadeev, 5 February 1825, *Transformation*, vol. 1, 25–6. Regarding modes of address in official correspondence, see L. E. Shepelev, *Chinovnyi mir Rossii*, 48.
15 Cornies to Blüher, 25 June 1825, *Transformation*, vol. 1, 26–30.
16 Fadeev to Cornies, 16 January 1825, *Transformation*, vol. 1, 21–2.

17 Contenius to Cornies, 24 January 1825, *Transformation*, vol. 1, 24–5.
18 The original petition is not extant, but Cornies refers to it in a letter to Contenius, 17 October 1828, *Transformation*, vol. 1, 159–60.
19 Cornies to Fadeev, 27 January 1825, *Transformation*, vol. 1, 22–3. See also Cornies to Contenius, 30 January 1825, *Transformation*, vol. 1, 24–5.
20 On the New Russian wool trade and the role of purchasing agents, see Herlihy, *Odessa*, 83–7.
21 Cornies to Blüher, 27 August 1825, *Transformation*, vol. 1, 32–4.
22 Cornies to Blüher, 15 February 1826, *Transformation*, vol. 1, 56–7.
23 See the official report on the murder investigation, DAOO *f.* 6, *o.* 1, d. 1834 (8 August 1825). Cornies to Blüher, 24 November 1826, DAOO *f.* 89, *o.* 1, *d.* 82: l. 64–5.
24 Official report on the murder investigation, 3 August 1825, DAOO *f.* 6, *o.* 1, d. 1834.
25 David Moon, "Agriculture and the Environment," 87–8.
26 Mark Bassin, "Russia Between Europe and Asia."
27 Ibid.
28 Tempest, "Madman or Criminal."
29 On the relationship between Islamophobia, racism, and European colonialism in the nineteenth century, see Kumar, *Islamophobia*, 30–3.
30 Cornies, "The Nogai Tatars in Russia," *Transformation*, vol. 1, 457.
31 Kivelson and Suny, *Russia's Empires*, 130. Sunderland describes the eighteenth-century genesis of this civilizational mission in *Taming the Wild Field*, 55–95; Steinwedel describes similar developments in Bashkiria in *Threads of Empire*, 106. See also Kumar, *Islamophobia*, 33.
32 Cornies, "The Nogai Tatars in Russia," *Transformation*, vol. 1, 459.
33 Ibid., 483.
34 Ibid.
35 Ibid.
36 Ibid., 484.
37 Ibid., 489.
38 Ibid., 491.
39 Ibid., 486.
40 Ibid., 459.
41 Ibid., 461.
42 Ibid., 461–2.
43 On the challenges of undergovernment, see Sunderland, *Taming the Wild Field*, 107.
44 The accusations are described in Staples, *Cross-Cultural Encounters*, 36.
45 See O'Neill, *Claiming Crimea*, 49–56; and Kivelson and Suny, *Russia's Empires*, 128–30, 174–7.

46 On the significance of differentiated local and regional policies, see Kivelson and Suny, *Russia's Empires*, 128–9.
47 On the relationship between nomadism, sedentary farming, and civility in state perceptions, see Sunderland, *Taming the Wild Field*, 62–3.
48 Cornies, "The Nogai Tatars in Russia," *Transformation*, vol. 1, 463.
49 Ibid., 491.
50 Jehle, *Anna Schlatter-Bernet*.
51 Lavater, *Essays on Physiognomy*. Originally published as *Physiognomische Fragmente zur Befoerderung der Menschenkenntniss und Menschenliebe* (Leipzig: Weidmanns Erben und Reich, 1776).
52 Ibid., 15–16.
53 Graham, "Lavater's Physiognomy in England," 563.
54 Lavater, *Essays on Physiognomy*, 90, 168ff.
55 Gray, *German Physiognomic Thought*.
56 Graham, "Lavater's Physiognomy in England," 563.
57 Ibid., 461.
58 Cornies to David Epp, 14 August 1826, *Transformation*, vol. 1, 78–9.
59 Ibid.
60 On Schlatter's association with the Basel Institute, see Schlatter, *Bruchstücke*, 421. The Basel Institute's proper name was the Institut zur Bildung junger Leute zum Missionsdienste. On his rejection by the Basel Institute, see Angas, letter dated 24 September 1823, printed in the *Baptist Magazine*, 1824, 490–1. On his rejection by the British Baptists, see *Baptist Magazine*, 1827, 344.
61 Angas, letter dated 24 September 1823, *Baptist Magazine*, 1824, 490–1.
62 Ibid.
63 Ibid.
64 Schlatter to Cornies, 20 September 1828, *Transformation*, vol. 1, 158–9.
65 Schlatter, *Bruchstücke*, ix–x.
66 Ibid.
67 Ibid., xiii.
68 Ibid., 66.
69 Cornies to Blüher, 27 August 1825, *Transformation*, vol. 1, 32–4.
70 Schlatter, *Bruchstücke*, 15.
71 Schlatter, letter to Angas, 27 April 1824, printed in the *American Baptist Magazine* 7 (1827), 83–5.
72 Ibid.
73 Cornies's letter to the Gebietsamt is not extant, but the Gebietsamt's response makes the nature of the inquiry clear. Gebietsamt to Cornies, 29 July 1825, *Transformation*, vol. 1, 31.
74 Cornies to Gebietsamt, 10 September 1825, *Transformation*, vol. 1, 34–5.
75 Cornies to Gebietsamt, 26 April 1826, *Transformation*, vol. 1, 65. The four men were Abram Klassen, Johann Klassen, Jacob Klassen, and Peter Reimer.

76 Cornies to Wilhelm Frank, 31 October 1826, *Transformation*, vol. 1, 90–1.
77 Werth, *The Tsar's Foreign Faiths*, 53.
78 The threat was explicit – see the 9 December 1827 letter from the Guardianship Committee to the Mennonite Community ("Mennonitenkonvent") reproduced in Franz Isaac, *Die Molotschnaer Mennoniten*, 107–9. Schlatter attested to the general understanding of this threat – see his letter to Angas, 27 April 1824, printed in the *American Baptist Magazine* 7 (1827), 83–5.
79 Johann Cornies to David Epp, 10 March 1826, *Transformation*, vol. 1, 61–2.
80 Gebietsamt to village offices, 15 May 1826, *Transformation*, vol. 1, 67.
81 Gebietsamt to Cornies, 15 May 1826, *Transformation*, vol. 1, 67.
82 Contenius to Cornies, 4 January 1826, *Transformation*, vol. 1, 51–3.
83 Cornies to Schlatter, 5 August 1826, *Transformation*, vol. 1, 72–4.
84 Cornies to Klaas Dyck, 14 August 1826, *Transformation*, vol. 1, 79–81.
85 Cornies to Wilhem Frank, 28 September 1826, *Transformation*, vol. 1, 86. Frank's name sometimes appears as "Franke" in the correspondence.
86 The letter from the Gebietsamt to Cornies is not extant. It came between 8 August, when he told Schlatter that he did not know whether the Gebietsamt would approve the Saxony project at all, and 14 August, when he grumbled to Klaas Dyck that he had been drafted to lead it. Cornies to Schlatter, 5 August 1826, *Transformation*, vol. 1, 72–4; Cornies to Dyck, 14 August 1826, *Transformation*, vol. 1, 79–81.
87 Cornies to Gebietsamt, 18 August 1826, *Transformation*, vol. 1, 82.
88 Cornies to Contenius, 3 September 1826, *Transformation*, vol. 1, 82.
89 Cornies to Frank, 10 September 1826, *Transformation*, vol. 1, 83–4.
90 Ibid.
91 Ibid.
92 Ibid.
93 Cornies to Frank, 28 September, *Transformation*, vol. 1, 86.
94 Contenius to Cornies, 11 November 1826, *Transformation*, vol. 1, 100–1.
95 Contenius to Gebietsamt, 26 October 1826, *Transformation*, vol. 1, 89–90.
96 Ibid.
97 Cornies to Contenius, 28 December 1826, *Transformation*, vol. 1, 109–10.
98 The details of the trip are described in Cornies's Saxony travel journal, DAOO *f.* 89, *o.* 1, *d.* 103. For selected entries see *Transformation*, vol. 1, 115–46.
99 Ibid.
100 Ibid., 122.
101 Ibid, 125–6.
102 Cornies to Frank, 15 May 1827, *Transformation*, vol. 1, 135–6.
103 Ibid.
104 Regarding the Dohna family, see Treitschke, *Historische und politische Aufsatze*, vol. 4, 317.

105 Count Dohna to Cornies, 2 January 1827, *Transformation*, vol. 1, 113.
106 Cornies to David Epp, 2 May 1827, *Transformation*, vol. 1, 130–1.
107 Cornies to Martens, 2 May 1827, *Transformation*, vol. 1, 131–2.
108 Cornies to van der Smissen, 18 September 1831, *Transformation*, vol. 1, 243–5.
109 Cornies to Epp, 13 December 1825, *Transformation*, vol. 1, 41–2.
110 Cornies describes the dispute in a letter to Schlatter, 22 December 1828, DAOO *f.* 89, *o.* 1, *d.* 1.
111 Ibid.
112 Ibid.
113 Ibid.
114 Cornies to Jacob Penner and Heinrich Heese, 31 July 1828, *Transformation*, vol. 1, 156–7.
115 Cornies to Abraham Dueck, 9 July 1828, DAOO *f.* 89, *o.* 1, *d.* 129.

5. Imposing Order, 1828–1834

1 Cornies to Schlatter, 12 March 1830, *Transformation*, vol. 1, 187–90.
2 Ibid.
3 Raeff, *The Decembrist Movement*, 3–5.
4 Ibid., 17–24.
5 The literature on the Decembrists and Nicholas's response is summarized in Kivelson and Suny, *Russia's Empires*, 154–61.
6 Cornies to Blüher, 15 February 1826, *Transformation*, vol. 1, 56–7.
7 Ibid.
8 This transition is clear in records pertaining to New Russia. Based on a small sampling of records from other regions there is evidence to suggest that the phenomenon extended broadly to the empire. See "Otchety Tavricheskikh Gubernatorov," RGIA, *f.* 1281, *o.* 11, *dela* 131–3. The transition emerges clearly in *d.* 133 (1825–7). Martin observes a similar pattern in *From the Holy Roman Empire*, 269, as does Steinwedel in *Threads of Empire*, 92. On the evolution of the Russian bureaucracy and recordkeeping, see Shepelev, *Chinovnyi mir*, 47–55. On shifting Jewish policies, see Klier, "State Policies" 98–9. On sectarians, see Breyfogle, *Heretics and Colonizers*, 18.
9 On the conflicting forces of integration and differentiation under Nicholas, see Kivelson and Suny, *Russia's Empires*, 175.
10 The standard study of Official Nationality is Riasanovsky, *Nicholas I and Official Nationality*. For a recent summary in the context of imperial policy, see Kivelson and Suny, *Russia's Empires*, 157–61.
11 Quoted in Vishlenkova, *Zabotias' o dushakh*, 160–1. On Magnitskii's role in the university purges, see Menger, *Die Heilige Allianz*, 247. Barbara Skinner traces the genesis of Official Nationality's religious attitudes back to the reign of Catherine the Great; see her *The Western Front*, 232.

12 Elites' conversion to Catholicism particularly worried Nicholas; see Zorin and Schönle, *On the Periphery of Europe*, 108. On broader suspicions of Catholicism, see Skinner, *The Western Front*.
13 Nicholas's policies toward the Jews demonstrate a similar concern with utility rather than religion; see Klier, "State Policies," 98.
14 Cornies to Epp, 7 July 1828, *Transformation*, vol. 1, 155–6.
15 Ibid. Cornies called his Mariupol lease land "Beschtasch."
16 Cornies to Epp, 26 February 1829, *Transformation*, vol. 1, 167–9.
17 Ibid.
18 Urry, *Mennonites, Politics, and Peoplehood*, 90–1.
19 The first explicit indication of the profits says that it turned an annual profit of 15,000 roubles: Contenius to Cornies, 4 January 1826, *Transformation*, vol. 1, 51–3.
20 Account of Brandy Sales, 1 January 1829, DAOO *f.* 89, *o.* 1, *d.* 130. In 1828 profits totalled 12,311 roubles, 66 kopecks.
21 Martens and Cornies to Guardianship Committee, 30 January 1829, *Transformation*, vol. 1, 165–6.
22 Guardianship Committee to Molochnaia Mennonite Gebietsamt, 12 February 1829, *Transformation*, vol. 1, 166.
23 Cornies and Martens to Gebietsamt, 20 April 1829, *Transformation*, vol. 1, 173–4.
24 Cornies to Fadeev, 22 December 1830, *Transformation*, vol. 1, 201–3.
25 On moneylending, see Staples, "Johann Cornies, Money-Lending, and Modernization."
26 Antonov, *Bankrupts and Usurers*, 28. On the historiography of the relationship of credit to economic development, see Lindgren, "The Modernization of Swedish Credit Markets." On credit in early nineteenth-century Russia, see Pintner, "Government and Industry."
27 For an overview of the historiography, see Antonov, *Bankrupts and Usurers*, 7–10.
28 For an assessment of this historiography see Staples, *Cross-Cultural Encounters*, 181–3.
29 D.H. Epp, *Johann Cornies*, 8.
30 Borrowing money, and the difficulty of repaying it, are a constant refrain in Epp's memoir. J.D. Epp, *A Mennonite in Russia*.
31 Cornies frequently mentioned the shortage of circulating currency. See, for, example, Cornies to Frank, 9 June 1831, *Transformation*, vol. 1, 226. On the role of foreign agents, see Herlihy, *Odessa*, 83–8.
32 Christian School Society Accounts 1820–1827, n.d., DAOO *f.* 89, *o.* 1, *d.* 126.
33 Cornies to Blüher, 25 June 1825, *Transformation*, vol. 1, 26–9.
34 Cornies to Frank, 9 June 1831, *Transformation*, vol. 1, 226.

35 On the development of sheep farming in the Molochnaia, see Staples, *Cross-Cultural Encounters*, 72–84.
36 On grain production, see Staples, *Cross-Cultural Encounters*, 124.
37 A series of letters from Wieb to Cornies document this: *Transformation*, 4 September 1840, vol. 2, 283; 31 May 1841, vol. 2, 368; 1 March 1844, DAOO *f.* 89, *o.* 1, *d.* 1094: l. 41; 13 May 1844, DAOO *f.* 89, *o.* 1, *d.* 1094: l. 44; and 21 February 1845, DAOO *f.* 89, *o.* 1, *d.* 1132: l. 58. Regarding Peter Schmidt, see Schmidt to Cornies, 4 Sept. 1840, *Transformation*, vol. 2, 283.
38 On the growth of grain exports, see *Cross-Cultural Encounters*, 132–7.
39 Account of lending to Johann Klassen, 8 February 1827, DAOO *f.* 89, *o.* 1, *d.* 151. Between 1817 and 1827, Klassen borrowed 37487.16 roubles and repaid 3729.09. See also Meshkov, "K istorii sukonnoi fabriki Ioganna Klassena." Meshkov summarises his findings in Myeshkov, *Die Schwarzmeerdeutschen*, 96–9.
40 Cornies to Fadeev, 2 September 1836, DAOO *f.* 89, *o.* 1, *d.* 388, l. 36.
41 In 1841 Klassen proposed repaying his creditors by giving them use of land belonging to the factory, which he estimated would generate an income of 72,000 paper roubles, an amount that would "not cover the old debt totally." Klassen to Cornies, 18 January 1841, *Transformation*, vol. 2, 325–7.
42 Regarding the establishment of the commission, see Cornies to Fadeev, 12 August 1839, *Transformation*, vol. 2, 191–2. Klassen claimed that the factory employed 236 Mennonites (Cornies to Keppen, 12 August 1839, *Transformation*, vol. 2, 193–4). This figure is probably inflated – between 1821 and 1833 it never employed more than seventy people. Klassen may have included the families of his workers, who were dependent on factory wages (Meshkov, "K istorii sukonnoi fabriki Ioganna Klassena," 161–2). Elsewhere Klassen wrote that the factory supported forty Mennonite families; Klassen to Cornies and Regier, 4 August 1838, *Transformation*, vol. 2, 190–1).
43 Mrs. David Voth to Cornies, 27 May 1839, *Transformation*, vol. 2, 176.
44 Voth to Cornies, 30 October 1840, *Transformation*, vol. 2, 299; Voth to Cornies, 20 December 1840, *Transformation*, vol. 2, 316.
45 Cornies to Voth, 20 May 1841, *Transformation*, vol. 2, 367.
46 Voth to Cornies, 3 December 1843, DAOO, *f.* 89, *o.* 1, *d.* 923, l. 44.
47 Cornies to Gebietsamt, 2 October 1840, *Transformation*, vol. 2, 287. Cornies offered to waive the interest. The interest rate – 6 per cent – was far below typical private lending rates documented by Antonov in *Bankrupts and Usurers*, which routinely exceeded 6 per cent per month.
48 In December 1840 Cornies resorted to the Gebietsamt to collect his debt from Quiring, along with a number of other defaulters. Gebietsamt to Cornies, 11 December 1840, *Transformation*, vol. 2, 315.

49 Antonov, *Bankrupts and Usurers*, 70–1. Antonov documents interest rates as high as 300 per cent per annum, but none at the low legal rate of 6 per cent.
50 Cornies to Fadeev, 27 January 1825, *Transformation*, 1:22–3.
51 Cornies to Blüher, December 1824, *Transformation*, vol. 2, 19–20.
52 Cornies to Warkentin, 27 December 1825, *Transformation*, vol. 2, 43–4.
53 Ibid.
54 The 800 rubles came in a series of loans, the most recent of which was in 1832. See Hausknecht to Johann Cornies, 24 October 1832, *Transformation*, vol. 1, 288.
55 Cornies to Warkentin, 27 December 1825, *Transformation*, vol. 1, 43–4.
56 Cornies lent 5,000 roubles to Muromtzev in May 1841; Cornies to Muromtzev, 17 May 1841, *Transformation*, vol. 2, 364; he lent 1,000 roubles to the Ekaterinoslav police chief Mikhail Lizovzov in 1839; Cornies to Heinrich Cornies, 1 October 1839, *Transformation*, vol. 2, 199.
57 Cornies to Fadeev, 18 September 1834, *Transformation*, vol. 1, 372–5.
58 On gift-giving, bribery, and the exchange of favours in Russian society, see Lovell et al., *Bribery and Blat in Russia*. On the role of lending in creating connections across social boundaries, see Antonov, *Bankrupts and Usurers*, 89–104.
59 Balzer, "Epistle to the Aeltesten," in Plett, *The Golden Years*, 319.
60 Ibid.
61 Schmidt, *Genovefa*; Schmidt, *Rosa von Tannenburg*. Schmidt, a Catholic priest, wrote Pietistic children's stories.
62 Cornies to Johann Cornies Jr., 22 December 1832, *Transformation*, vol. 1, 295–6.
63 Cornies to Johann Wieb, 30 December 1830, *Transformation*, vol. 1, 203–7.
64 Balzer, "Faith and Reason," 82.
65 Ibid., 84.
66 Ibid.
67 Ibid., 86.
68 P.M. Friesen, *The Mennonite Brotherhood*, 97.
69 Quoted in ibid., 695.
70 Cornies to Schlatter, 6 June 1829, *Transformation*, vol. 1, 176–7. See also Voth's parting letter to Cornies, 30 August 1829, *Transformation*, vol. 1, 180–1; Voth's 1831 account of his departure from the Molochnaia in P.M. Friesen, *The Mennonite Brotherhood*, 695; and Cornies's letter to Schlatter about Voth's "hypocrisy," 12 March 1830, *Transformation*, vol. 1, 187–90.
71 Cornies to Schlatter, 12 March 1830, *Transformation*, vol. 1, 187–90.
72 Report on student performance, 1 November 1828, DAOO, *f.* 89, *o.* 1, *d.* 126.
73 Cornies to Wool Improvement Society, 9 January 1829, *Transformation*, vol. 1, 163–4.

274   Notes to pages 123–8

74 On evolving tsarist attitudes and policies toward steppe forestry, see Moon, *The Plough That Broke the Steppes*, 173–205.
75 On colonist desires to recreate the treed landscapes of their homelands, see ibid., 173.
76 Senate decree on the creation of forestry societies, 14 September 1828, DAOO *f.* 1, *o.* 192, *d.* 1. On the state's afforestation project see Moon, *The Plough That Broke the Steppes*, 173–205.
77 Contenius was eighty-two, according to Fadeev, but his age and date of birth are disputed. See Eisfeld, "Introduction," in *Samuil Khristianovich Kontenius*, 5–6.
78 Fadeev, *Vospominaniia, passim*.
79 Fadeev to Keppen, 3 May 1839, *ARAN, f.* 30, *o.* 3, *d.* 302, l. 6–7.
80 Fadeev, *Vospominaniia*, bk. 2, 324, and bk. 3, 116.
81 Fadeev, *Vospominaniia*, bk. 2, 481.
82 Regarding Alexander's exhortation to the Mennonites to grow trees, see Fadeev, *Vospominaniia*, bk. 2, 405.
83 "Ob organizatsii upravleniia kolonistov" (1833), RGIA *f.* 383, *o.* 29, *d.* 609, 12. Cited in Venger, *Mennonitskoe predprinimatel'stvo*, 143. Steinwedel recounts a similar process in Bashkiria in *Threads of Empire*, 106–10.
84 Ibid.
85 Scott, *Seeing Like a State*, 11–22.
86 Venger, *Mennonitskoe predprinimatel'stvo*, 143.
87 The charter is contained in Fadeev to Cornies, 13 July 1831, *Transformation*, vol. 1, 227–35.
88 Ibid.
89 Ibid.
90 Cornies to Warkentin and Enns, *Transformation*, vol. 1, 235–6.
91 Fadeev to Cornies, 13 July 1831, *Transformation*, vol. 1, 227–35.
92 Ibid.
93 Fadeev to Molochnaia Mennonite church leadership, 12 January 1831, *Transformation*, vol. 1, 211. Emphasis in the original.
94 Cornies to Fadeev, 1 November 1831, *Transformation*, vol. 1, 246–7.
95 For an example of these circulars, see Cornies, Enns, and Warkentin to village offices, 25 February 1832, *Transformation*, vol. 1, 265–6. Regarding the inspection tours, see Forestry Inspection of Ohrloff Plantation, *Transformation*, vol. 1, 270–1.
96 On the impact of the cholera epidemic in the Molochnaia, see "Sravnenie neurozhaev 1833/34 i 1839/40, RGIA *f.* 1589, *o.* 1, *d.* 693, *ll.* 1–7ob. These data are summarized in Staples, *Cross-Cultural Encounters*, 88. For a detailed account, see Roderick E. McGrew, *Russia and the Cholera*. The official death toll was 234,604, but the real number was probably much higher; ibid., 98.

97 McGrew, *Russia and the Cholera*, 67.
98 Cornies to Fadeev, 15 October 1830, *Transformation*, vol. 1, 194–5.
99 Cornies to Fadeev, 22 December 1830, *Transformation*, vol. 1, 201–3. Cornies implies that the Nogais paid their supervisor (*nachal'nik*) a bribe to file an October report denying the outbreak.
100 Cornies to Fadeev, 29 July 1831, *Transformation*, vol. 1, 239.
101 Cornies to Fadeev, 15 October 1830, *Transformation*, vol. 1, 194–5.
102 Cornies to Gebietsamt, 19 October 1830, *Transformation*, vol. 1, 195.
103 Cornies to Gebietsamt, 6 December 1830, *Transformation*, vol. 1, 198.
104 Cornies to Fadeev, 22 December 1830, *Transformation*, vol. 1, 201–2.
105 Ibid.
106 Cornies to Fadeev, 7 January 1831, *Transformation*, vol. 1, 210.
107 Cornies to Wiebe, 30 December 1830, *Transformation*, vol. 1, 203–7.
108 Ibid.
109 Cornies to Blüher, 10 June 1833, *Transformation*, vol. 1, 327–8.
110 The drought is described in Staples, *Cross-Cultural Encounters*, 87–106.
111 Cornies to Blüher, 10 June 1833, *Transformation*, vol. 1, 327–8.
112 Cornies to Fadeev, 17 July 1833, *Transformation*, vol. 1, 330–1.
113 Cornies to Blüher, 15 February 1834, *Transformation*, vol. 1, 357–8.
114 Ibid.
115 Cornies to Blüher, 22 June 1834, *Transformation*, vol. 1, 365–7.
116 Cornies to Johann Regier, 12 February 1834, *Transformation*, vol. 1, 355–6.
117 Cornies to Blüher, 15 February 1834, *Transformation*, vol. 1, 357–8.
118 "Sravnenie neurozhaev 1833/34 i 1839/40," 1840, RGIA, *f.* 1589, *o.* 1, *d.* 693, l. 1–7.
119 Cornies to Fadeev, 13 September 1833, *Transformation*, vol. 1, 338–9.
120 Cornies to Blüher, 15 February 1834, *Transformation*, vol. 1, 357–8.
121 Cornies to Wiebe, 30 December 1830, *Transformation*, vol. 1, 203–7.
122 Heinrich Balzer, "Epistle to the Aeltesten," in Plett, *The Golden Years*, 314. For a summary of Balzer's philosophy, see Urry, "Ohm Heinrich Balzer."
123 Cornies to Schlatter, *Transformation*, vol. 1, 187–90.
124 Balzer, "Epistle to the Aeltesten," 319.
125 Ibid.
126 Balzer, "Faith and Reason," 84.
127 See, for example, Robert Friedmann's introduction to his translation of Balzer, "Faith and Reason," 80.
128 Balzer, "Faith and Reason," 87.
129 Balzer, "Epistle to the Aeltesten," 319.
130 Balzer, "Faith and Reason," 92.
131 Ibid, 93.
132 Ibid.
133 Ibid., 90.

134 Forestry Society to village offices, 23 January 1833, *Transformation*, vol. 1, 304.
135 Ibid.
136 Forestry Society to Guardianship Committee, 13 September 1833, *Transformation*, vol. 1, 337–8.
137 Forestry Society to Guardianship Committee, 13 September 1833, *Transformation*, vol. 1, 337–8.
138 Forestry Society to Village Offices, 22 February 1833, *Transformation*, vol. 1, 310.
139 Forestry Society to Village Offices, 24 February 1833, *Transformation*, vol. 1, 312.
140 Described in Cornies to Fadeev, 25 October 1834, *Transformation*, vol. 1, 380–2.
141 Cornies to Fadeev, 13 July 1831, *Transformation*, vol. 1, 227–35.
142 Regarding Ladekopp, see Cornies to Fadeev, 10 March 1833, *Transformation*, vol. 1, 315. "Model for written undertaking" n.d. (1833), *Transformation*, vol. 1, 347.

6. Mennonites and the Era of Small Reforms, 1834–1838

1 Cornies to Fadeev, 13 September 1833, *Transformation*, vol. 1, 338–9.
2 Smith-Peter, *Imagining Russian Regions*, 60.
3 Cornies to Casper Adrian Hausknecht, n.d. [November 1830], DAOO *f.* 45, *o.* 1, *d.* 169, l. 45.
4 Cornies to Kirilovsky, 19 April 1832, *Transformation*, vol. 1, 272.
5 Cornies to Fadeev, 18 September 1834, *Transformation*, vol. 1, 372–5.
6 His mother Aganetha had the drawing of flowers framed and hung; see Cornies to Cornies Jr., 27 November 1833, *Transformation*, vol. 1, 345. His drawings still hung on the walls of his Moscow host, Traugott Blüher, six years after he returned home; see Blüher to Cornies, 7 May 1843, DAOO *f.* 89, *o.* 1, *d.* 911.
7 Stephenson, *Veneration and Revolt*, 46–8.
8 Scott writes of the aesthetics of scientific forestry as a part of the state project of ordering the world in *Seeing Like a State*, 18–19.
9 Staples, *Cross-Cultural Encounters*, 118–23.
10 Cornies to Blüher, 20 September 1834, *Transformation*, vol. 1, 375.
11 Cornies to Blüher, 7 November 1834, *Transformation*, vol. 1, 383–4.
12 Cornies to Kirilovskii, 19 April 1832, *Transformation*, vol. 1, 272.
13 Cornies to Peter Neufeldt, 31 August 1834, *Transformation*, vol. 1, 371.
14 Johann Cornies Jr. to Cornies, 5 September 1832, *Transformation*, vol. 1, 283. In December 1832 Fadeev recommended that Johann Jr. take additional instruction in mathematics from Haustek; Fadeev to Cornies, 2 December 1832, *Transformation*, vol. 1, 292–3. Cornies responded with warm thanks; Cornies to Fadeev, 30 December 1832, *Transformation*, vol. 1, 296–8.

15 Cornies to Johann Cornies Jr., after 16 October 1834, *Transformation*, vol. 1, 378–9.
16 The Gnadenfelders arrived in the Molochnaia in autumn 1834, wintered with families in existing villages, and established their own village in 1835. See Schroeder, *Mennonite Historical Atlas*, 127.
17 On Cornies's role in surveying the site, see Forestry Society to Gebietsamt, 12 March 1835, *Transformation*, vol. 1, 409–10.
18 Toews, *Perilous Journey*, 17.
19 On Gnadenfeld's relationship to the Mennonite Brethren, see ibid., 16–17.
20 On Gnadenfeld's role in spreading Pietism among tsarist Mennonites, see Jantz, "Pietism's Gift."
21 Cornies to Epp, 7 January 1830, *Transformation*, vol. 1, 183–4.
22 Wilhelm Lange to Cornies, 18 August 1836, *Transformation*, vol. 2, 17–18.
23 Cornies to Fadeev, 28 January 1835, *Transformation*, vol. 1, 405–6.
24 Cherkazianova, "Mennonite Schools and the Russian Empire," 89–91.
25 Gnadenfeld Christian School Society to Agricultural Society, 1 February 1838, *Transformation*, vol. 2, 106–11.
26 Regarding Wüst, see Jantz, "A Pietist Pastor." See also Urry, *None but Saints*, 172–6; and Zhuk, *Russia's Lost Reformation*, 157–8. Lange officiated at Wüst's wedding.
27 Gnadenfeld Christian School Society to Agricultural Society, 1 February 1838, *Transformation*, vol. 2, 106–11.
28 Ibid.
29 Regarding the Molochnaia, see Staples, *Cross-Cultural Encounters*, 144–64. Regarding the broader trend, see Smith, *Recipes for Russia*, 22–3.
30 Cornies to Fadeev, 10 March 1833, *Transformation*, vol. 1, 315.
31 The Colonial Inspector said that it was mainly a product of elderly people transferring land to their children: Khariton Pelekh to Guardianship Committee, 27 February 1835, DAOO *f.* 6, *o.* 1, *d.* 3765.
32 Model form for a written undertaking, n.d. (probably December 1833), *Transformation*, vol. 1, 347.
33 The new Guardianship Committee regulation was issued on 5 February 1837. It is described in Pelekh to Guardianship Committee, 18 January 1843, DAOO *f.* 6, *o.* 1, *d.* 6890.
34 P.M. Friesen, *The Mennonite Brotherhood*, 197. Friesen implies that this occurred in the 1830s, but it may have been during the disputes of the early 1840s described in chapter 8. Friesen writes that Thun lived out the rest of his life under the ban, and if the event happened in the 1830s this cannot be true – he was elected village mayor again in the 1840s, which could not have happened if he were banned.
35 Goerz, *The Molotschna Settlement*, 36. Goerz bases his account on D.H. Epp, *Johann Cornies*, 45.

36 See, for example, the case of Johann Mierau: Forestry Society to Petershagen Village Office, 4 March 1835, *Transformation*, vol. 1, 409.
37 Forestry Society records, n.d. (February 1836), *Transformation*, vol. 1, 444–5.
38 Ibid.
39 See, for example, the case of Dirk Boldt, ibid.
40 Cornies to Fadeev, n.d. (December 1835), *Transformation*, vol. 1, 429. Steinwedel documents the appointment of guardians to the Bashkirs in the same period, suggesting that this might have been a broader trend; see *Threads of Empire*, 106.
41 Ibid.
42 Fadeev to Johann Cornies, 17 December 1835, *Transformation*, vol. 1, 430–1.
43 Cornies to Fadeev, 24 January 1836, *Transformation*, vol. 1, 439–41.
44 Ibid. Cornies refers to 4,500 *desiatinas* of land, but all other sources say the size of the land parcel was 3,800 *desiatinas*.
45 Fadeev to Cornies, 15 January 1836, *Transformation*, vol. 1, 438–9.
46 Cornies to Fadeev, 31 January 1836, *Transformation*, vol. 1, 441.
47 Fadeev to Cornies, 6 February 1836, *Transformation*, vol. 1, 443–4.
48 Cornies to Fadeev, 26 February 1826, *Transformation*, vol. 2, 3–4.
49 Agricultural Society to Inzov, 12 May 1836, DAOO *f*. 6, *o*. 1, *d*. 4389, l. 5.
50 Fadeev's request that Cornies offer advice is not extant, but Cornies's response refers to the request. Cornies to Fadeev, 24 July 1831, *Transformation*, vol. 1, 238.
51 On the role of these societies, see Staples, *Cross-Cultural Encounters*, 114.
52 The Great Drought provided impetus to this reform drive; see Smith, *Recipes for Russia*, 14. The 1837 reform of provincial administration was a landmark in the history of the internal Russian provinces, but for the Molochnaia the creation of the Ministry of State Domains was far more important. See ibid., 61.
53 Lincoln, *In the Vanguard of Reform*.
54 Urry, *Mennonites, Politics, and People*, 91–3.
55 Smith-Peters, *Imagining Russian Regions*, 60; A.A. Mironos, *Uchenye komitety*, 52.
56 Urry, *Mennonites, Politics, and Peoplehood*, 91–3.
57 Cornies to Fadeev, 6 August 1837, *Transformation*, vol. 2, 66–8.
58 Cornies to Fadeev, 15 September 1837, *Transformation*, vol. 2, 77.
59 Cornies to Fadeev, 20 October 1837, *Transformation*, vol. 2, 80–2.
60 The first mention of the plan is in Cornies to Schlatter, 11 March 1833, *Transformation*, vol. 1, 316–18. For a fuller description, see Staples, "'On Civilizing the Nogais.'"
61 This concern with the physical manifestation of civility was echoed in policies in Bashkiria in the 1840s; see Steinwedel, *Threads of Empire*, 107.
62 Staples, "'On Civilizing the Nogais.'"

63 Gebietsamt and Agricultural Society to Church Elders, 22 February 1837, *Transformation*, vol. 2, 41–2.
64 Ibid.
65 Gebietsamt and Forestry Society to village offices, n.d. (after 22 February 1837), *Transformation*, vol. 2, 42–3.
66 On the creation of this committee and Keppen's role, see Moronos, *Uchenye komitety*, 69–70.
67 Keppen, *Deviataia reviziia*.
68 Keppen, "Spisok izvestneishim," pt. 1, *Severnaia Pchela* (2 January 1837), 3–4; pt. 2, *Severnaia Pchela* (3 January 1837), 7–8; pt. 3, *Severnaia Pchela* (4 January 1837), 10–12.
69 Kozelsky, *Christianizing Crimea*, 19, 49–59.
70 Keppen, personal journal, n.d. (after 4 December 1837), ARAN, *f.* 30, *o.* 1, *d.* 226.
71 Ibid.
72 Druzhinin, *Gosudarstvennye krest'iane i reforma*, vol. 1, 525. See also Moronos, *Uchenye komitety*, 69–70.
73 On the social composition of the Learned Committees, see Mironos, *Uchenye komitety*, 126–30.
74 Cornies to Fadeev, 22 December 1837, *Transformation*, vol. 2, 93–4.
75 Cornies to Rosen, 30 April 1841, *Transformation*, vol. 2, 356–7.
76 Cornies to Fadeev, 26 April 1838, *Transformation*, vol. 2, 120–3.
77 Ibid.
78 Fadeev's response is not extant, but on 15 August 1838 Cornies thanked him for the advice and support; Cornies to Fadeev, 15 August 1838, *Transformation*, vol. 2, 133–5.
79 Described in Neufeld, "The Dismissal of Aeltester Jakob Warkentin."
80 P.M. Friesen, *The Mennonite Brotherhood*, 197.
81 Cornies to Fadeev, 15 November 1838, *Transformation*, vol. 2, 142–3.
82 Regier received 563 votes (59 per cent of the 955 votes cast). Pelekh to Guardianship Committee, n.d. [after 15 November 1838], DAOO *f.* 6, *o.* 1, *d. 4850*, l. 210–12.

7. "A Useful Man," 1838–1842

1 Cornies to Hahn, 9 April 1847, DAOO *f.* 89, *o.* 1, *d.* 1260, l. 42.
2 Regarding Martens's "hypochondria," see Cornies to Fadeev, 28 January 1837, *Transformation*, vol. 2, 34–9. Regarding the nineteenth-century meaning of the term, see Bauer, *Hypochondria*, 21–8.
3 Cornies to Fadeev, 12 January 1832, *Transformation*, vol. 1, 257–8.
4 Cornies to Martens, 16 July 1840, *Transformation*, vol. 2, 266–7.
5 Cornies to Fadeev, 28 January 1837, *Transformation*, vol. 2, 34–9.

6 Cornies to Fadeev, 19 May 1837, *Transformation*, vol. 2, 52–3.
7 Regarding Martens's consultation with Alexander's physician, see Cornies to Fadeev, 20 October 1837, *Transformation*, vol. 2, 80–2. Regarding Martens's April departure for Piatigorsk, see Cornies to Fadeev, 26 April 1838, *Transformation*, vol. 2, 120–3.
8 Detailed in several 1836 letters; see particularly Cornies to Johann Jr., 28 April 1836, *Transformation*, vol. 2, 11–12; and Cornies to Heinrich Cornies, 8 July 1836, *Transformation*, vol. 2, 16.
9 Cornies to Fadeev, 28 January 1837, *Transformation*, vol. 2, 34–9.
10 Ibid.
11 Cornies to Fadeev, 6 March 1840, *Transformation*, vol. 2, 232–5.
12 Regarding the birth of Justina see Johann Cornies Jr. to Cornies, 7 May 1846, DAOO *f.* 89, *o.* 1, *d.* 1230, l. 94. Regarding their son Johann and the death of Justina, see https://familienforschung-dick.de/index.php?id=108; and Braun and Thiessen, "Klatt, Johann Karl (1842–1918)."
13 Cornies to Schlatter, *Transformation*, vol. 1, 187–90.
14 Agnes's trip to Ekaterinoslav is mentioned in Cornies Jr. to Cornies, 5 September 1832, *Transformation*, vol. 1, 283.
15 The first mention of this trip comes from Blüher to Cornies, 6 August 1835, *Transformation*, vol. 1, 421–2.
16 Cornies to Johann Cornies Jr., 18 March 1836, *Transformation*, vol. 2, 8–9.
17 Cornies to Blüher, 29 August 1838, *Transformation*, vol. 2, 135–6.
18 On the transition to crop agriculture, see Staples, *Cross-Cultural Encounters*, 123–8. On high transportation costs in New Russia, see Herlihy, *Odessa*, 65–71.
19 Agricultural Society to Village Offices, n.d. [1838], *Transformation*, vol. 2, 182.
20 The Ministry of State Domains acknowledged this arrangement in 1846; "Po otnosheniuu Departamenta Sel'skago Khoziaistvo o vvedenii u russkikh pereselentsev khoziaistvo I poriadka upravleniia mennonitov," RGIA, *f.* 383, *op.* 10, *d.* 7164, *ll.* 92–127.
21 There was an important difference between the shared holdings created in 1838 and the half-holdings created in the 1860s; the latter were fully subdivided, meaning the holders could sell or cede them without the permission of another half-holder.
22 Staples, *Cross-Cultural Encounters*, 77.
23 Cornies to Jacob Penner and Heinrich Heese, 31 July 1828, *Transformation*, vol. 1, 156–7.
24 Forestry Society to Blumenort Village Office, 1835, *Transformation*, vol. 1, 416–7.
25 Regarding the establishment of Neuhalbstadt, see *Transformation*, vol. 2: Gebietsamt to Pelekh, 25 November 1836, 32–5; Cornies to Fadeev,

12 August 1839, 191–2; Fadeev to Cornies, 14 April 1840, 245; Cornies to Fadeev, 2 July 1840, 258–60; Fadeev to Cornies, 28 October 1840, 296–7; Cornies to Fadeev, 29 November 1840, 310–13; Fadeev to Cornies, 2 February 1841, 327; Cornies to Bradke, 24 March 1841, 346; Cornies to Keppen, 24 March 1841, 346–7; Cornies to Fadeev, 20 August 1841, 384–5; Cornies to Keppen, 17 November 1841, 408–10.
26 Klassen to Cornies, 18 January 1841, *Transformation*, vol. 2, 325–7.
27 The fire is reported in Johann Regier to Cornies, 4 August 1839, *Transformation*, vol. 2, 189–90.
28 Keppen to Cornies, 23 September 1839, *Transformation*, vol. 2, 199.
29 On cloth production, profits, and numbers of employees, see Myeshkov, *Die Schwarzmeerdeutschen*, 96–8.
30 Klassen to Cornies, 18 January 1841, *Transformation*, vol. 2, 325–7.
31 Klassen solicited money throughout the Molochnaia and Khortitsa settlements.
32 Cornies to Fadeev, 26 June 1839, *Transformation*, vol. 2, 180–3.
33 1838 Annual Report, 1 January 1839, *Transformation*, vol. 2, 151–6.
34 From 54,000 *chetverts* in 1836 to 180,000 in 1847. Staples, *Cross-Cultural Encounters*, 124. Elsewhere in New Russia yields averaged between 1:2 and 1:4.5. See Herlihy, *Odessa*, 58. On state efforts to improve steppe agriculture, including through new field rotations, see Moon, *The Plough That Broke the Steppe*, 242–78.
35 Cornies to Fadeev, 26 April 1838, *Transformation*, vol. 2, 120–3.
36 Ibid.
37 See, for example, his request for a loan of 10,000 rubles, Wiebe to Cornies, 4 September 1840, *Transformation*, vol. 2, 283; and his letter regarding loan payments, Wiebe to Cornies, 31 May 1841, *Transformation*, vol. 2, 368.
38 For example, Cornies's purchase of a barrel of wine, Cornies to Steven, 22 January 1842, *Transformation*, vol. 2, 454–5. Regarding the international export of wool, see Wiebe to Cornies, 1 March 1844, DAOO *f.* 89, *o.* 1, *d.* 1094, l. 41.
39 Smith, *Recipes for Russia*, 22.
40 Agricultural Society to Village Offices, n.d. [1838], *Transformation*, vol. 2, 147–8.
41 Cornies to Keppen, 10 July 1840, *Transformation*, vol. 2, 262–5. Bradke was accompanied by Julius Witte, a ministry agronomist, future son-in-law of Fadeev, and father of Sergei Witte.
42 Cornies to Bradke, 15 November 1840, *Transformation*, vol. 2, 303–4. This was part of a broader initiative to collect data about nutritional requirements; see Smith, *Recipes for Russia*, 52–6.
43 Cornies to Steven, 17 November 1840, *Transformation*, vol. 2, 305–8.
44 Schorkowitz, "Was Russia a Colonial Empire?," 121. On the Guardianship Committee as a colonial administration, see Sunderland, "The Ministry of Asiatic Russia."

282 Notes to pages 173–8

45 The Kalmyks were placed under the direct control of the Ministry of State Domains in 1838; see Schorkowitz, *Imperial Formations and Ethnic Diversity*, 7.
46 Cornies to Epp, 15 July 1837, *Transformation*, vol. 2, 60–1.
47 Lermontov, *A Hero of Our Time*, 91. Lermontov died after a dual in Piatigorsk in 1841.
48 Morgan, "Topographic Transmissions," 2.
49 Quoted in Foote, "Introduction," in Lermontov, *A Hero of Our Time*, 12.
50 Cornies to Schlatter, 22 July 1837, *Transformation*, vol. 2, 61–2.
51 On Patterson, see Haralampieva, "Scottish Missionaries in Karass." Regarding Lang, see the *Center For Volga German Studies Gazetteer*, s.v. "Karass," http://cvgs.cu-portland.edu/gazetteer/other_places/karras.cfm.
52 Cornies to Schlatter, 22 July 1837, *Transformation*, vol. 2, 61–2.
53 Fadeev to Cornies, June 1837, *Transformation*, vol. 2, 55–6.
54 Cornies to Heinrich Cornies, 4 March 1837, *Transformation*, vol. 2, 46.
55 Cornies to Wiebe, 26 July 1837, *Transformation*, vol. 2, 64–5.
56 Cornies to Fadeev, 6 August 1837, *Transformation*, vol. 2, 66–8.
57 Cornies to Doehring, 29 August 1838, *Transformation*, vol. 2, 136–8.
58 Described in Cornies to Fadeev, 12 August 1839, *Transformation*, vol. 2, 191–2.
59 Described in Cornies to Khariton Pelekh, 2 March 1836, *Transformation*, vol. 2, 4–5.
60 Cornies to Steven, 11 January 1839, *Transformation*, vol. 2, 156–8.
61 Ibid.
62 Ibid.
63 Cornies to Steven, 7 June 1840, *Transformation*, vol. 2, 253–4.
64 Peasants employed a similar tactic when selecting military conscripts. See Hartley, *Russia, 1762–1825*, 190–208.
65 Cornies to Steven, 17 June 1840, *Transformation*, vol. 2, 256–7. Moon documents similar peasant reactions to other apprenticeship programs; see *The Plough That Broke the Steppes*, 186.
66 Cornies to Steven, 12 July 1840, *Transformation*, vol. 2, 265–6.
67 Forestry Society to village offices, 16 January 1841, *Transformation*, vol. 2, 323–5.
68 Cornies to Village Offices, undated draft [probably June 1843], DAOO *f.* 89, *o.* 1, *d.* 972, l. 7.
69 See, for example, Cornies's description of Crown Prince Alexander's inspection of Akkerman; Cornies to Fadeev, 20 October 1837, *Transformation*, vol. 2, 80–2.
70 Keppen, "Mennonit Ivan Iv. Kornis i ego zavedenie," ARAN, *f.* 30, *d.* 1, *o.* 226.

71 Ibid.
72 Cornies was invited to join this committee in December 1838; see F. Dellinghausen to Cornies, 7 December 1838, *Transformation*, vol. 2, 146.
73 For Marmont's description of the Molochnaia, see *Voyage de M. Le Maréchal*, vol. 1, 356–61.
74 Cornies to Blüher, 22 June 1834, *Transformation*, vol. 21 365–7.
75 Starr, "Introduction," xiii.
76 Ibid., xiii–xv.
77 Ibid., xviii. Baron Peter von Meyendorf, Russian ambassador to Prussia, was Haxthausen's first contact; Kiselev took over once Haxthausen arrived in Russia.
78 Ibid., xlii.
79 Haxthausen, *Studien*, vol. 2, 196.
80 Ibid., 181–2.
81 Starr writes that Haxthausen received no further data from Russia after he returned to Prussia, but Keppen's and Cornies' records show that they provided him with additional information after his departure; Starr, "Introduction," xviii; Haxthausen to Cornies, 3 February 1845, DAOO *f.* 89, *o. 1, d.* 1132; Cornies to Haxthausen, 30 June 1845, DAOO *f.* 89, *o. 1, d.* 1207; Haxthausen to Keppen, 8 September 1846, ARAN *f.* 30, *o.* 3, *d.* 56, l. 2–3; Keppen to Haxthausen, n.d. [1846], ARAN *f.* 30, *o.* 3, *d.* 56, l. 6–7.
82 Fadeev to Keppen, 18 July 1843, ARAN, *f.* 30, *o.* 3, *d.* 2.
83 Kiselev to Cornies, 22 October 1841, *Transformation*, vol. 2, 404–5.
84 Cornies to Fadeev, 21 November 1841, *Transformation*, vol. 2, 413–15.
85 Cornies, "Description of the administrative and other arrangements instituted for the functioning of the Molochnaia Mennonite District in 1841," December 1841, *Transformation*, vol. 2, 427–46. For the official version distributed to ministry offices see "Po otnosheniiu Departmenta Sel'skago Khoziaistva o vvedenii u russkikh pereselentsev khoziastva i poriadka upravleniia menonitov," RGIA *f.* 383, *o.* 10, *d.* 7164.
86 Venger, *Mennonitskoe predprinimatel'stvo*, 143.
87 Fadeev to Keppen, 25 December 1840, ARAN, *f.* 30, *o.* 3, *d.* 2.
88 Keppen's letter is not extent; Cornies describes the proposal in Cornies to Keppen, 26 January 1838, *Transformation*, vol. 2, 104–6.
89 Ibid.
90 Ibid.
91 Cornies to Evgenii von Hahn, 16 March 1842, *Transformation*, vol. 2, 484–6.
92 Staples, *Cross-Cultural Encounters*, 93–105. Archbishop Innokentii and the Orthodox Church were accelerating efforts to convert Russian sectarians at this time; see Kozelsky, *Christianizing Crimea*, 27–8. Keppen played a key role in convincing Kiselev that the threat of exile would force conversion; see Kiselev to Bludov, 3 February 1838, RGIA *f.* 1284, *op.* 197, *d.* 131, *ll.* 12–13.

93 For a more detailed account, see Staples, *Cross-Cultural Encounters*, 95–102.
94 Cornies, "The Doukhobors of the Molochnaia Area," *Transformation*, vol. 1, 495–505. The report is not dated. Fadeev requested it in 1826, so it comes from after that date but before the 1834–5 investigation, which is not mentioned in Cornies's account.
95 Ibid.
96 Ibid.
97 Staples, *Cross-Cultural Encounters*, 102.
98 Cornies to Muromtsev, 22 February 1841, *Transformation*, vol. 2, 330–1.
99 Ibid. Muromtsev's initial letter to Cornies does not survive; its intent is evident in this reply from Cornies.
100 Ibid.
101 Cornies to Muromtsev, 28 February 1841, *Transformation*, vol. 2, 333–4.
102 Ibid.
103 Cornies to Muromtsev, 6 March 1841, *Transformation*, vol. 2, 336–7.
104 "Spisok dukhobortsev naznachennykh k pereselentsev v Akhaltsyskii uezd bez zhrebiiu," 26 March 1842, DAOO, *f.* 1, *op.* 151, *d.* 77, *ll.* 136–48; "Otchet o melitopol'skikh dukhobortsakh […] pereselennykh za Kavkaz," n.d., DAOO, *f.* 1, *op.* 166, *d.* 32; "Spisok dukhobortsev, prisoedinennykh k pravoslavnoi tserkvi s 27 mai 1843 goda po 7 iunia 1844," n.d., RGIA, *f.* 383, *op.* 5, *d.* 4319, *ll.* 89–91; "Spisok gosudarstvennykh krest'ian iz sekty Dukhoborcheskogo […] zhelaiushchikh obratit'sia v pravoslavie," n.d., RGIA, *f.* 383, *op.* 5, *d.* 4319, *ll.* 162–3; "Spisok prisoedinennykhsia dukhobortsev k pravoslavnoi tserkvi s 1 iiunia 1842 goda po 27 maia 1843 goda," RGIA, *f.* 383, *op.* 4, *d.* 3212, l. 70.
105 Staples, *Cross-Cultural Encounters*, 96. Vorontsov was a champion of religious toleration, leaving him at odds with Archbishop Innokentii. See Kozelsky, *Christianizing Crimea*, 27–33.
106 Ibid., 29.
107 Sunderland, *The Baron's Cloak*, 230. On the late-nineteenth-century transition, see Schorkowitz, *Imperial Formations*, 8.

8. The Warkentin Affair, 1841–1842

1 Cornies, Description of the Warkentin Affair, n.d. [between 10 September and 18 October 1842], *Transformation*, vol. 2, 555–64. In 1838 Cornies told Fadeev that the construction of the Ohrloff church from brick "makes Ohrloff village more beautiful than before"; Cornies to Fadeev, 15 August 1838, *Transformation*, vol. 2, 133–5.
2 Regarding Landskrone, see Cornies to Fadeev, 26 June 1839, *Transformation*, vol. 2, 180–3. Regarding the Ohrloff church, see Cornies to Fadeev, 28 January 1837, *Transformation*, vol. 2, 34–9.

3 Cornies to Mariupul Mennonite Gebietsamt, 28 October 1842, *Transformation*, vol. 2, 568–70. This directive was addressed to the Bergthal Mennonite settlement near Mariupol, but it referenced orders pertaining to the Molochnaia settlement.
4 Cornies to Keppen, 12 August 1839, *Transformation*, vol. 2, 193–4.
5 Cornies to David Epp, 15 July 1837, *Transformation*, vol. 2, 60–1.
6 Richmond, *The Circassian Genocide*; Kivelson and Suny, *Russia's Empires*, 172.
7 Cornies to Schlatter, 22 July 1837, *Transformation*, vol. 2, 61–2.
8 Cornies, "Description of the Warkentin Affair," n.d. [between 10 September and 18 October 1842], *Transformation*, vol. 2, 555–64.
9 DAOO 89-1-647/4v: Cornies to Johann Wiebe, 20 January 1840, *Transformation*, vol. 2, 216–8.
10 Pelekh to Gebietsamt, 23 October 1840, *Transformation*, vol. 2, 297–9.
11 Heinrich Neufeld, "The Dismissal of Aeltester Jacob Warkentin," 21. Wiens used a common alternative spelling, "Klaassen."
12 Abraham Friesen, elder of the Kleine Gemeinde, identified the issue as "the construction of Johann Epp" in Freisen to Epp, 30 July 1842, in Plett, *The Golden Years*, 283–6. All other accounts refer to Johann Klassen, so this may be an error by Freisen. In 1847 Friesen again identified building regulations as a core issue in the Warkentin Affair: Friesen, "A simple declaration with respect to the farewell-address of the former Aeltesten Heinrich Wiens of Gnadenheim," 1847, in ibid., 308–13.
13 Neufeld, "The Dismissal of Aeltester Jacob Warkentin," 21.
14 Pelekh to Gebietsamt, 23 October 1840, *Transformation*, vol. 2, 297–9.
15 Ibid.
16 Ibid.
17 Neufeld, "A Further Examination," 27.
18 Herlihy, *Odessa*, 52. On the panic in Moscow, see Blüher to Cornies, 4 April 1841, *Transformation*, vol. 2, 349–51; Blüher to Cornies, 8 May 1841, *Transformation*, vol. 2, 349–51.
19 Cornies to Steven, 5 August 1841, *Transformation*, vol. 2, 379.
20 Cornies to Fadeev, 21 November 1841, *Transformation*, vol. 2, 413–5.
21 Fadeev to Cornies, 23 December 1841, *Transformation*, vol. 2, 422–3.
22 Karev et al., *Nemtsy Rossii Entsiklopediia*, vol. 1, s.v. "Gann, Evgenii Fedorovich," (Moscow, 1999).
23 The exact date and outcome of these elections is unknown.
24 For Cornies's assessment of Toews, see Cornies to Hahn, 7 February 1842, *Transformation*, vol. 2, 470–1.
25 Neufeld claimed that Regier intended to stay in office, and this is repeated in all subsequent accounts, but Cornies's correspondence makes it clear that this was not true. Neufeld, "A Further Examination," 24.

26 Neufeld, "The Dismissal of Aeltester Jacob Warkentin," 19.
27 Cornies, "Description of the Warkentin Affair," *Transformation*, vol. 2, 555–64.
28 Ibid.
29 Neufeld's account says 400 votes; Neufeld, "A Further Examination," 24; Cornies, writing closer to the date, says 395; Cornies, "Description of the Warkentin Affair," *Transformation*, vol. 2, 555–64.
30 On the 1837 elections, see Pelekh to Guardianship Committee, n.d. [after 15 November 1838], DAOO *f.* 6, *o.* 1, *d. 4850*, l. 210–12. On the 1847 elections, see Molochnaia voting results, DAOO *f.* 6, *o.* 1, *d.* 10510.
31 Pelekh to Gebietsamt, 31 December 1841, *Transformation*, vol. 2, 426.
32 Cornies, "Description of the Warkentin Affair," *Transformation*, vol. 2, 555–64.
33 Agricultural Society to Guardianship Committee, n.d. [probably 27 January 1842], *Transformation*, vol. 2, 459–60.
34 Neufeld, "A Further Examination," 24.
35 The date of this meeting is mentioned in Cornies to Hahn, 7 February 1842, *Transformation*, vol. 2, 470–1.
36 Cornies addressed Neufeld as "brother-in-law," but the nature of the connection is not clear.
37 The date of this conference is unknown. In a letter apparently dated 28 January, Cornies said it had been held "recently"; Cornies, Gerhard Enns, and Jacob Martens to Bernhard Fast, n.d. [probably 28 January 1842], *Transformation*, vol. 2, 61). Neufeld places the meeting before 2 February; Neufeld, "A Further Examination," 24.
38 Cornies, Enns, and Martens to Bernhard Fast, n.d. [probably 28 January], *Transformation*, vol. 2, 461.
39 Ibid.
40 Neufeld, "A Further Examination," 24.
41 The letter only exists in draft, with Cornies, Enns, and Martens identified as its authors. Neufeld recorded that Cornies and "fifty-four members" of the Old Flemish Congregation signed it; ibid.
42 Cornies, Enns, and Martens to Bernhard Fast, n.d. [probably 28 January], *Transformation*, vol. 2, 461.
43 Ibid.
44 Ibid.
45 Ibid.
46 Cornies, "Description of the Warkentin Affair," *Transformation*, vol. 2, 555–64.
47 Neufeld, "A Further Examination," 25.
48 Ibid.
49 This order had not been made public in the Molochnaia when Warkentin left for Odesa on 2 February.

Notes to pages 199–204   287

50 Cornies to Hahn, 7 February 1842, *Transformation*, vol. 2, 470–1.
51 Ibid.
52 Ibid.
53 Werth, *The Tsar's Foreign Faiths*, 53.
54 Cornies to Hahn, 7 February 1842, *Transformation*, vol. 2, 470–1.
55 Regarding Regier's death and Toews's interim appointment, see Agricultural Society to Gebietsamt, 28 February 1842, *Transformation*, vol. 2, 477–8.
56 Cornies, "Description of the Warkentin Affair," *Transformation*, vol. 2, 555–64.
57 Neufeld, "A Further Examination," 23–4.
58 Ibid., 24.
59 Cornies, "Description of the Warkentin Affair," *Transformation*, vol. 2, 555–64.
60 Ibid.
61 Ibid.
62 It was after Warkentin's return to the Molochnaia from Odesa at the end of February, and before Hahn's visit to the Molochnaia at the end of April.
63 Neufeld's account says 800 votes; Cornies's account, written closer to the election, says 837 votes.
64 Cornies, Enns, and Martens to Warkentin, 27 April 1842, *Transformation*, vol. 2, 498–9.
65 Ibid.
66 Ibid.
67 Neufeld, "A Further Examination," 24.
68 Cornies, "Description of the Warkentin Affair," *Transformation*, vol. 2, 555–64.
69 Ibid.
70 Ibid.
71 Ibid.
72 Ibid.
73 Ibid.
74 Ibid.
75 Ibid.
76 Neufeld, "A Further Examination," 24.
77 Ibid.
78 Ibid.
79 Neufeld, "The Dismissal of Aeltester Jacob Warkentin," 19.
80 Ibid.
81 Cornies to Neufeld, 23 May 1842, *Transformation*, vol. 2, 501. Cornies's role in the process is detailed in a series of letters over the following months, as well as by Neufeld in "The Dismissal of Aeltester Jacob Warkentin."

288   Notes to pages 204–10

82 Cornies to Hahn, 25 May 1842, *Transformation*, vol. 2, 503–4.
83 Neufeld to Cornies, 30 May 1842, *Transformation*, vol. 2, 505.
84 Cornies to Hahn, 2 June 1842, *Transformation*, vol. 2, 506–7.
85 Neufeld to Cornies, 11 July 1842, *Transformation*, vol. 2, 514–15.
86 Neufeld, "The Dismissal of Aeltester Jacob Warkentin," 20–1.
87 Ibid., 21.
88 Ibid.
89 Cornies, "Description of the Warkentin Affair," *Transformation*, vol. 2, 555–64.
90 Neufeld, "The Dismissal of Aeltester Jacob Warkentin," 21.
91 Ibid.
92 Cornies to Neufeld, 14 September 1842, *Transformation*, vol. 2, 539–40.
93 Neufeld to Cornies, 18 September 1842, *Transformation*, vol. 2, 541.
94 Neufeld, "A Further Examination," 24.
95 Ibid., 24–5.
96 Cornies to Hahn, 14 July 1842, *Transformation*, vol. 2, 516–18; Hahn to church elders, 26 August 1842, *Transformation*, vol. 2, 530–1.
97 Schrader, *Languages of the Lash*, 8.
98 Ibid., 22.
99 Ibid., 13.
100 Agricultural Society to Hahn, 18 October 1842, *Transformation*, vol. 2.
101 Ibid.
102 Cornies to Johann Wiebe, 5 November 1847, DAOO *f.* 89, *o.* 1, *d.* 1260, p. 107.
103 Urry, *None but Saints*, 197–215.
104 Wiebe to Epp, 15 July 1843, DAOO *f.* 89, *o.* 1, *d.* 925, l. 75.
105 Epp to Cornies, 9 May 1843, DAOO *f.* 89, *o.* 1, *d.* 911, l. 91.
106 Wiebe to Epp, 15 July 1843, DAOO *f.* 89, *o.* 1, *d.* 925, l. 75.
107 Ibid.
108 Ibid.
109 Cornies to Hahn, 27 November 1844, DAOO *f.* 89, *o.* 1, *d.* 1088, l. 162.
110 Neufeld, "A Further Examination," 26; Urry, *None but Saints*, 177; P.M. Friesen, *The Mennonite Brotherhood*, 102–3.
111 Cornies to Hahn, 27 November 1844, DAOO *f.* 89, *o.* 1, *d.* 1088, l. 162.
112 Ibid.
113 For Wilhelm's relationship to Friedrich Wilhelm see Urry, *None but Saints*, 177; and PM. Friesen, *The Mennonite Brotherhood*, 102–3.
114 Cornies to Hahn, 27 November 1844, DAOO *f.* 89, *o.* 1, *d.* 1088, l. 162.
115 Hahn to Cornies, 9 December 1844, DAOO *f.* 89, *o.* 1, *d.* 889, l. 35.
116 Urry, *None but Saints*, 177, and P.M. Friesen, *The Mennonite Brotherhood*, 102–3.
117 Friedrich Wilhelm Lange to Cornies, 27 September 1843, *DAOO f.* 89, *o.* 1, *d.* 917, l. 29.

118 Friedrich Wilhelm Lange to Cornies, 13 September 1843, DAOO *f.* 89, *o.* 1, *d.* 917, l. 22; Agricultural Society to Church Elders, 15 October 1843, DAOO *f.* 89, *o.* 1, *d.* 900, l. 10.
119 For Cornies's request that the ban be enforced, see Cornies to Benjamin Ratzlaff and Peter Wedel, 22 November 1844, DAOO *f.* 89, *o.* 1, *d.* 1092, l. 2.
120 Ibid.
121 Friedrich Wilhelm Lange to Cornies, 27 September 1843, DAOO *f.* 89, *o.* 1, *d.* 917, l. 29.
122 Agricultural Society to Church Elders, 15 October 1844, DAOO *f.* 89, *o.* 1, *d.* 900, l. 10.
123 Ibid.
124 Cornies to Benjamin Ratzlaff and Peter Wedel, 22 November 1844, DAOO *f.* 89, *o.* 1, *d.* 1092, l. 2.
125 Neufeld, "A Further Examination," 26; Johann Neufeld to Cornies, n.d. [probably March 1846], DAOO *f.* 89, *o.* 1, *d.* 1229, l. 98. This letter exists only as an undated copy. From its context, it must have been written soon after the altercation.
126 Neufeld, "A Further Examination," 26.
127 Johann Neufeld to Cornies, n.d. [probably March 1846], DAOO *f.* 89, *o.* 1, *d.* 1229, l. 98.
128 Neufeld, "A Further Examination," 26.
129 Ibid.
130 Ibid.
131 Ibid.
132 Hahn to Cornies, 27 December 1846, *f.* 89, *o.* 1, *d.* 889, l. 83.
133 Regarding the Kahal, see Klier, "State Policies," 102. Regarding the Buriats, see Schorkowitz, "The Orthodox Church," 205.
134 Neufeld, "A Further Examination," 26.
135 Ibid.
136 Ibid. Neufeld's recollections are not always accurate, but the language he reproduces here is consonant with Cornies's tone in letters during the Warkentin Affair.
137 Ibid.
138 Hahn to Cornies, 27 December 1846, DAOO *f.* 89, *o.* 1, *d.* 899, p. 83.
139 Heinrich Neufeld's account suggests that Lange's letter was written in late 1846, but Cornies only requested it in early March 1847. Cornies to Lange, 10 March 1847, DAOO *f.* 89, *o.* 1, *d.* 1260, p. 30.
140 Wiens returned to the Molochnaia in the 1850s but had no further involvement in public affairs. P.M. Friesen, *The Mennonite Brotherhood*, 152.
141 Plett, *The Golden Years*, 310.
142 See, for example, Toews, *Perilous Journey*, 15–16; and Urry, *None but Saints*, 165.

9. An Agent of the State, 1842–1847

1 Hahn to Cornies, 16 June 1842, *Transformation*, vol. 2, 508.
2 Cornies to Blüher, 2 February 1844, DAOO *f.* 89, *o.* 1, *d.* 1088, l. 15.
3 Cornies to Rosen, 22 February 1843, DAOO *f.* 89, *o.* 1, *d.* 925, l. 23.
4 For Cornies's description of Ali Pasha's accomplishments, see Cornies to Rosen, 26 July 1840, *Transformation*, vol. 2, 270–2.
5 Ibid.
6 This project is described in Staples, "Iogann Kornis," 18–21.
7 "O razvedenii lesov v stepnykh uezdykh Tavricheskoi gubernii," pt. 2, 28 July 1843, RGIA *f.* 387, *op.* 1, *d.* 10408. This was part of a larger ministry project initiated in 1843. See Moon, *The Plough That Broke the Steppes*, 185.
8 See Cornies's response to Rosen's request; Cornies to Rosen, 3 April 1844, DAOO *f.* 89, *o.* 1, *d.* 1088: *l.* 51.
9 Cornies to Rosen, 15 June 1844, DAOO *f.* 89, *o.* 1, *d.* 1088: *l.* 83; Cornies to Rosen, 22 June 1844, DAOO *f.* 89, *o.* 1, *d.* 1088, l. 86; Cornies to Rosen, 7 September 1844, DAOO *f.* 89, *o.* 1, *d.* 1088, l. 126.
10 Cornies to Rosen, 12 May 1845, DAOO *f.* 89, *o.* 1, *d.* 1207, l. 156.
11 Cornies to Rosen, 29 August 1845, DAOO *f.* 89, *o.* 1, *d.* 1207, l. 240.
12 Cornies to Rosen, 30 January 1846, DAOO *f.* 89, *o.* 1, *d.* 1170, l. 15; Cornies to Rosen, 2 April 1845, DAOO *f.* 89, *o.* 1, *d.* 1170, l. 70.
13 The plan to bring the total to sixteen is described in Cornies to Rosen, 20 December 1846, DAOO *f.* 89, *o.* 1, *d.* 1170, l. 210. Various reports in the following year confirm that this occurred.
14 Cornies itemized Sudermann's bookkeeping responsibilities in Cornies to Sudermann, n.d. [1846], DAOO *f.* 89, *o.* 1, *d.* 1172. Regarding Cornies's role as paymaster, see, for example, Cornies to Sudermann, 5 December 1846, DAOO *f.* 89, *o.* 1, *d.* 1170, l. 203.
15 Cornies to Guardianship Committee, 30 March 1846, DAOO *f.* 89, *o.* 1, *d.* 1172, l. 5.
16 Cornies to Sudermann and Fast, 20 August 1847, DAOO *f.* 89, *o.* 1, *d.* 1260: l. 77.
17 Cornies to Rosen, 20 March 1841, *Transformation*, vol. 2, 341–2.
18 Ibid.
19 This was the son of Kleine Gemeinde leader Heinrich Balzer – see chapter 5. The first evidence of Balzer in this role is Cornies to Balzer, 7 May 1841, *Transformation*, vol. 2, 341.
20 Cornies to Rosen, 29 June 1841, *Transformation*, vol. 2, 373–5.
21 Ibid.
22 Cornies to Rosen, 29 December 1841, *Transformation*, vol. 2, 424–5.
23 Cornies to Rosen, 5 February 1842, *Transformation*, vol. 2, 467–9.
24 Ibid. Cornies's tone in this letter is reminiscent of his tone in his account of the Warkentin Affair: he saw opposition as rebellion.

25 Cornies to Rosen, 5 March 1842, *Transformation*, vol. 2, 480–2.
26 Cornies to Hahn, 7 July 1845, DAOO *f.* 89, *o.* 1, *d.* 1207, l. 212.
27 Cornies to Steven, 15 April 1839, *Transformation*, vol. 2, 167.
28 Steven to Cornies, 24 April 1839, *Transformation*, vol. 2, 169–70.
29 Cornies to Steven, 27 May 1839, *Transformation*, vol. 2, 175–6.
30 Cornies to Fadeev, 26 June 1839, *Transformation*, vol. 2, 180–3.
31 On New Russia's place in agricultural modernization, see Kabuzan, *Emigratsiia*, 57–8. On the Mennonites' leading role, see Venger, *Mennonitskoe predprinimatel'stvo*, 252–7, 298–307.
32 Rosen to Cornies, 10 September 1841, *Transformation*, vol. 2, 390–1.
33 Ibid.
34 Rosen to Cornies, 16 July 1842, *Transformation*, vol. 2, 518–19.
35 Cornies to Steven, 19 March 1842, *Transformation*, vol. 2, 489–91.
36 Venger, *Mennonitskoe predprinimatel'stvo*, 252–7, 298–307.
37 Hahn to Cornies, 16 June 1842, *Transformation*, vol. 2, 508.
38 On Hutterite history, see Schlachta, *From the Tyrol to North America*.
39 The first letter between the two regarding the Hutterites is Cornies to Reimer, 11 November 1832, *Transformation*, vol. 1, 289. Cornies identifies him as village secretary in Cornies to Peter Orens Draisma, *Transformation*, vol. 1, 303–4.
40 Cornies to Hahn, 3 September 1842, *Transformation*, vol. 2, 536–7.
41 Cornies to Blüher, 4 August 1843, DAOO *f.* 89, *o.* 1, *d.* 925, l. 85.
42 Fadeev to Cornies, 17 December 1835, *Transformation*, vol. 1, 430–1.
43 Cornies to Radishchev village office, 16 January 1836, *Transformation*, vol. 1, 439.
44 Reimer to Cornies, 2 April 1838, *Transformation*, vol. 2, 119.
45 Cornies to Fadeev, 2 February 1842, *Transformation*, vol. 2, 464–5.
46 Ibid.
47 Cornies to the Radishchev Village Administration, 16 February 1842, *Transformation*, vol. 2, 475.
48 Ibid.
49 Ibid.
50 Cornies to Hahn, 17 August 1842, *Transformation*, vol. 2, 527–8.
51 Ibid.
52 Ibid.
53 Cornies to Hahn, 3 September 1842, *Transformation*, vol. 2, 536–7.
54 Cornies to Hahn, 17 August 1842, *Transformation*, vol. 2, 527–8.
55 Cornies to Hahn, 3 September 1842, *Transformation*, vol. 2, 536–7. Cornies confirmed that the loan was granted in Cornies to Church Elders, 17 August 1843, *DAOO f.* 89, *o.* 1, *d.* 925, l. 93.
56 Cornies to Hahn, 3 December 1842, *Transformation*, vol. 2, 579–80.
57 Cornies to Guardianship Committee, 31 December 1842, *Transformation*, vol. 2, 586–7.

292 Notes to pages 228–31

58 Johann Cornies to Hutterthal Village Office, n.d., *Transformation*, vol. 2, 59.
59 Regarding his appointment, see Cornies to General Bradkii, 21 December 1842, *Transformation*, vol. 2, 584–5. "General Bradkii" was probably Georg von Bradke, but it is impossible to be certain.
60 Hahn to Cornies, 21 November 1845, DAOO *f.* 89, *o.* 1, *d.* 889, l. 57.
61 Ibid.
62 See Pelekh's service record, "Formuliarnyi spisok sluzhba ... Kharitona Trofimova Pelekha," 31 May 1846, DAOO *f.* 6, *o.* 1, *d.* 8924, *ll.* 5–12.
63 Cornies to Church Elders, 17 August 1843, DAOO *f.* 89, *o.* 1, *d.* 925: *l.* 93.
64 Regarding community donations, see Berhhard Fast to Cornies, 4 September 1843, DAOO *f.* 89, *o.* 1, *d.* 917, l. 13; Heinrich Toews to Cornies, 6 September 1843, DAOO *f.* 89, *o.* 1, *d.* 917, l. 13. There had already been some donations before Cornies made the formal request; see Ratzlaff to Cornies, 26 May 1843, DAOO *f.* 89, *o.* 1, *d.* 911, l. 65.
65 Schlachta, *From the Tyrol to North America*, 149–51.
66 Schlachta, "The Hutterian Brethren in The Molochna, 1842–74," *Preservings* 24 (December 2004), 39.
67 Ibid. 40.
68 Krahn, "Bergthal Mennonite Settlement." Regarding the Bergthal settlement, see Schroeder, *The Bergthal Colony*.
69 The 4 June 1842 order is not extant; Cornies refers to it in a letter to the Guardianship Committee, 4 November 1842, *Transformation*, vol. 2, 572.
70 The original lease is documented in a Guardianship Committee memo, 30 November 1829, DAOO *f.* 6, *o.* 1, *d.* 2464, l. 1. For its 1830 renewal, see ibid., 23 April 1830, l. 13–14. For the transfer of land to the Bergthal settlement, see Guardianship Committee memo, n.d. [1834], DAOO *f.* 6, *o.* 1, *d.* 3105, l. 304.
71 Cornies to Bergthal Settlement Administrators, 28 October 1842, *Transformation*, vol. 2, 568.
72 Cornies to Hahn, 4 November 1842, *Transformation*, vol. 2, 570–2.
73 Cornies to Bergthal Settlement Administrators, 28 October 1842, *Transformation*, vol. 2, 568.
74 Cornies to Hahn, 4 November 1842, *Transformation*, vol. 2, 570–2.
75 Ibid.
76 Schroeder, *The Bergthal Colony*, 9–13, 33–5.
77 The relationship between Stempel and Cornies is documented in their correspondence in DAOO, *f.* 89, *o.* 1, 1843–47. Stempel's esteem for Cornies is evident, for example, in Stempel to Cornies, 17 April 1842, DAOO *f.* 89, *o.* 1, *d.* 911, l. 37, where he promises that Cornies's report on the Molochnaia "will, from now on, serve me as a guideline."
78 Regarding the initial immigration, see Malinowski, "Passage to Russia," 27.
79 Cornies to Oppenländer, 15 November 1837, *Transformation*, vol. 2, 88.
80 Prinz to Cornies, 21 June 1843, DAOO *f.* 89, *o.* 1, *d.* 911, l. 89.

81 Hahn reported Prinz's request to resign and asked for Cornies's advice: Hahn to Cornies, 13 December 1843, DAOO *f.* 89, *o.* 1, *d.* 889, *l.* 11. For Cornies's recommendation that Hahn refuse the request, see Cornies to Hahn, 24 December 1843, *DAOO f.* 89, *o.* 1, *d.* 925, l. 152.
82 Cornies to Hahn, 14 July 1843, DAOO *f.* 89, *o.* 1, *d.* 925, l. 72.
83 Ibid.
84 Cornies to Hahn, 19 November 1844, DAOO *f.* 89, *o.* 1, *d.* 1088, l. 156.
85 Prinz to Cornies, 21 June 1843, DAOO *f.* 89, *o.* 1, *d.* 911, l. 89.
86 Cornies to Prinz, 28 August 1843, DAOO *f.* 89, *o.* 1, *d.* 925, l. 96.
87 Prinz to Cornies, 11 October 1845, DAOO *f.* 89, *o.* 1, *d.* 1132.
88 For Wüst's impact on the Mennoites, see Urry, *None but Saints*, 172–6, and Jantz, "A Pietist Pastor." For Wüst's broader impact, see Albert W. Wardin, *On the Edge: Baptists and Other Free Church Evangelicals in Tsarist Russia, 1855–1917* (Eugene: Wipf and Stock, 2013), 57–64; and Zhuk, *Russia's Lost Reformation*, 157–61.
89 Cornies to Berdiansk Gebietsamt, DAOO *f.* 89, *o.* 1, *d.* 1220, l. 73.
90 Strolle was a disciple of the controversial Catholic Pietist Ignaz Lindl. See Petri, *Ignaz Lindl*.
91 Described in Cornies to Stempel, 26 January 1846, DAOO *f.* 89, *o.* 1, *d.* 1170, l. 8.
92 Ibid.
93 Dyck, "Introduction and Analysis," 15.
94 Riediger began school in Odessa in January 1842; Riedeger to Cornies, 2 December 1841, DAOO *f.* 89, *o.* 1, *d.* 441, l. 13.
95 Plesskaia-Zebold, *Odesskie nemtsy 1803–1920*, 179–85.
96 Gebietsamt to Cornies, 12 January 1843, DAOO *f.* 89, *o.* 1, *d.* 906, l. 32.
97 Cornies, Work list, n.d. [1843], DAOO *f.* 89, *o.* 1, *d.* 906, l. 31.
98 Hahn to Agricultural Society, 10 July 1843, DAOO *f.* 89, *o.* 1, *d.* 917, l. 6.
99 On changing state policies toward education in New Russia in the 1830s and 1840s, see Cherkazianova, "Mennonite Schools," 85–109. Whittaker, *The Origins of Modern Russian Education*, 189–212.
100 Hahn to Agricultural Society, 10 July 1843, DAOO *f.* 89, *o.* 1, *d.* 917, l. 6.
101 Ibid.
102 Ibid.
103 Ibid.
104 Cornies to village offices, 6 April 1845, DAOO *f.* 89, *o.* 1, *d.* 1222, l. 1. These are reproduced in Isaac, *Die Molotschnaer Mennoniten*, 278–80, and translated in D.H. Epp, *Johann Cornies*, 60–2. Isaac and Epp dated the two documents a year later ("In the School of X" to 5 March 1846 and "In the School of A" to April 6 1846), perhaps because they were using later copies.
105 Ibid.

294   Notes to pages 236–40

106 Ibid.
107 Ibid.
108 Ibid.
109 Heafford, *Pestalozzi*, 66–9.
110 There is no extant original copy. Isaak reproduces it, identifying Cornies as the author; *Die Molotschnaer Mennoniten*, 280–9. For an English translation see D.H. Epp, *Johann Cornies*, 53–60. The document's date is unknown; it came after the creation of the school districts in January 1846 and apparently grew out of the teachers' conferences in December 1845.
111 D.H. Epp, *Johann Cornies*, 53–60.
112 Ibid.
113 Ibid.
114 Ibid.
115 Ibid.
116 Ibid.
117 Ibid.
118 Ibid.
119 Ibid.
120 Ibid.
121 Ibid.
122 Cornies to Hahn, 24 October 1845, DAOO *f.* 89, *o.* 1, *d.* 1207, l. 284. The date that Cornies took charge of the Khortitsa school system is unknown. See Cornies's undated notes regarding a memorandum from the Guardianship Committee to the Khortitsa Gebietsamt, n.d. [1846], DAOO *f.* 89, *o.* 1, *d.* 1190, l. 1. It occurred no later than August 1846, when Cornies began corresponding with Khortitsa teacher Heinrich Franz about school reforms in Khortitsa. Cornies to Franz, August 1846, DAOO *f.* 89, *o.* 1, *d.* 1229, l. 156.
123 Heese, "Autobiography," 70.
124 Jacob Neumann to Cornies, 24 April 1841, *Transformation*, vol. 2, 355.
125 Cornies to Hahn, 24 October 1845, DAOO *f.* 89, *o.* 1, *d.* 1207, l. 284.
126 Ibid.
127 Agricultural Society to Heinrich Franz, 26 April 1846, DAOO *f.* 89, *o.* 1, *d.* 872, l. 17. On Franz's distinguished career, see P.M. Friesen, *The Mennonite Brotherhood*, 709–13.
128 Cornies to Franz, August 1846, DAOO *f.* 89, *o.* 1, *d.* 1229, l. 156.
129 Ibid.
130 Ibid.
131 Johann Siemens to Cornies, 1 January 1847, DAOO *f.* 89, *o.* 1, *d.* 1271, l. 56.
132 Cornies to Hahn, 14 September 1846, DAOO *f.* 89, *o.* 1, *d.* 1170, l. 165.
133 Ibid.

134 Siemens describes Hahn's letter to Bartsch and Dyck in Siemens to Cornies, 1 January 1847, DAOO *f.* 89, *o.* 1, *d.* 1271, l. 56. On Siemens's reconciliation with Dyck, see Siemens to Cornies, 10 May 1847, DAOO *f.* 89, *o.* 1, *d.* 1271, l. 125. Siemens's reconciliation with Bartsch is apparent in correspondence between Cornies and Bartsch in 1847.
135 Slocum, "Who and When Were the Inorodtsy?," 175; Kivelson and Suny, *Russia's Empires*, 166–7.
136 Dyck, "Landlessness in the Old Colony."
137 Cornies describes the potential for Jews to become effective agriculturists in Cornies to Hahn, 6 April 1846, DAOO *f.* 89, *o.* 1, *d.* 1170, l. 74.
138 Dyck, "Landlessness in the Old Colony."
139 Hahn to Cornies, 20 March 1846, DAOO *f.* 89, *o.* 1, *d.* 889, l. 67.
140 Cornies to Hahn, 6 April 1846, DAOO *f.* 89, *o.* 1, *d.* 1170, l. 74.
141 Ibid.
142 Ibid.
143 Cornies proposed the agronomist Wilhelm Baumann, who had spent several weeks in the Molochnaia and written a complimentary article for the *Zhurnal Ministerstvo gosudarstvennykh imushchestv*: Cornies to Baumann, 25 January 1847, DAOO *f.* 89, *o.* 1, *d.* 1260, l. 14; Baumann, "Neskol'ko zemetok o khoziaistve iuzhnoi Rossii." Another friend of Cornies's, Stempel, the inspector of the Württemberg settlement, got the job.
144 Cornies to Hahn, 6 April 1846, DAOO *f.* 89, *o.* 1, *d.* 1170, l. 74.
145 Cornies to Hahn, 28 November 1845, DAOO *f.* 89, *o.* 1, *d.* 1207, l. 308.

10. Conclusion: "Something for the Future," 1847–1848

1 Cornies to Jacob Reimer, 3 December 1846, DAOO *f.* 89, *d.* 1, *o.* 1170, l. 201.
2 On his depression, see D.H. Epp, *Johann Cornies*, 128.
3 Cornies to Hahn, 9 April 1847, DAOO *f.* 89, *o.* 1, *d.* 1260, l. 42.
4 Cornies to Johann Jr., 5 April 1847, DAOO *f.* 89, *o.* 1, *d.* 1260, l. 39. This letter is also quoted in D.H. Epp, *Johann Cornies*, 129, in a different translation.
5 Cornies to Johann Jr., 5 April 1847, DAOO *f.* 89, *o.* 1, *d.* 1260, l. 39.
6 Cornies to Blüher, 29 June 1847, DAOO *f.* 89, *o.* 1, *d.* 1260, l. 67.
7 Cornies to Johann Jr., 2 March 1847, DAOO *f.* 89, *o.* 1, *d.* 1260, l. 28.
8 Cornies to Johann Jr., 5 April 1847, DAOO *f.* 89, *o.* 1, *d.* 1260, l. 11; Cornies to Johann Jr., 18 January 1848, *DAOO f.* 89, *o.* 1, *d.* 1331, l. 11.
9 Cornies to Johann Jr., 28 January 1848, DAOO *f.* 89, *o.* 1, *d.* 1331, l. 11.
10 Johann Jr.'s 21 October 1847 letter is not extant; its date and content are described in Cornies to Johann Jr., 2 November 1847, DAOO *f.* 89, *o.* 1, *d.* 1260, l. 105.

11 Johann Wiebe to Cornies, 24 October 1847, DAOO *f.* 89, *o.* 1, *d.* 1271, l. 264.
12 Cornies to Johann Jr., 2 November 1847, DAOO *f.* 89, *o.* 1, *d.* 1260, l. 105.
13 Cornies to Johann Jr., 13 December 1847, DAOO *f.* 89, *o.* 1, *d.* 1260, l. 124.
14 Cornies to Johann Jr., 28 January 1848, DAOO *f.* 89, *o.* 1, *d.* 1331, l. 11.
15 Cornies to Wiebe, 13 February 1848, DAOO *f.* 89, *o.* 1, *d.* 1331, l. 21.
16 Ibid.
17 D.H. Epp, *Johann Cornies*, 130.
18 In April David Cornies wrote Traugott Blüher that Cornies was buried on the 17th, but all other accounts say the 16th. David Cornies to Blüher, 18 April 1848, DAOO *f.* 89, *o.* 1, *d.* 1331, l. 35.
19 Wiebe to Blüher, 5 June 1848, DAOO *f.* 89, *o.* 1, *d.* 1331, l. 41.
20 Keppen's letter is not extant, but Fadeev's response implies its substance. See Fadeev to Keppen, 19 May 1848, ARAN *f.* 30, *o.* 3, *d.* 302, l. 30.
21 Steven to Keppen, 1 June 1848, ARAN *f.* 30, *o.* 3, *d.* 278, ll. 10–11. Keppen's letter is not extant – the response implies the substance.
22 For an English translation, see Gavel, "Agronomist Gavel's Biography."
23 Gavel, "Agronomist Gavel's Biography," 53.
24 Dyck provides an excellent analysis of the Gavel obituary and of the changing attitudes toward Cornies over the following 128 years in "Russian Servitor and Mennonite Hero."
25 Karev et al., *Nemtsy Rossii Entsiklopediia*, s.v. "Gann, Evgenii Fedorovich."
26 Cornies to Wilhelm Frank, 4 December 1830, *Transformation*, vol. 1, 197.
27 Forestry Society to village offices, 16 January 1842, DAOO *f.* 89, *o.* 1, *d.* 750, l. 63.
28 Cornies to Peterson, 29 November 1844, DAOO *f.* 89, *o.* 1, *d.* 1088, l. 171.
29 Venger, *Mennonitskoe predprinimatel'stvo*, 7, 88.
30 See Postnikov, *IUzhno-russkoe krest'ianskoe khoziaistvo*.
31 See Dyck, "Russian Servitor," 19.
32 Urry, *None but Saints*, 119.
33 Urry, *None but Saints*, 143.
34 Reimer, *Johann Cornies*.
35 Neufeld, "A Further Examination," 26.
36 For an introduction to the historiography, see Fox et al., "The Imperial Turn." For a recent update, see O'Neill, *Claiming Crimea*, 5–10.
37 Ibid., 10.
38 Ibid., 103.
39 I offer my abject apology to the children for my own contribution to their tedium, a brief account of the founding of the forestry. I am indebted to the organizers for inviting me to participate.

Bibliography

Allen, William. *Life of William Allen*, 3 vols. London: Charles Gilpin, 1846.
Antonov, Sergei. *Bankrupts and Usurers of Imperial Russia: Debt, Property, and the Law in the Age of Dostoevsky and Tolstoy.* Cambridge, MA: Harvard University Press, 2016.
Balzer, Heinrich. "Faith and Reason: The Principles of Mennonitism Reconsidered in a Treatise of 1833," edited and translated by Robert Friedman. *Mennonite Quarterly Review* 12 (1948): 75–93.
Barlow, Tani. "Debates over Colonial Modernity in East Asia and Another Alternative." *Culture Studies* 26, no. 5 (September 2012): 617–44.
Bartlett, Roger P. *Human Capital: The Settlement of Foreigners in Russia 1762–1804.* Cambridge: Cambridge University Press, 1979.
Bassin, Mark. "Russia between Europe and Asia: The Ideological Construction of Geographical Space." *Slavic Review* 50, no. 1 (Spring 1991): 1–17.
Batalden, Stephen. "The BFBS Petersburg Agency and Russian Biblical Translation, 1856–1875." In *Sowing the Word: The Cultural Impact of the British and Foreign Bible Society 1804–2004*, edited by Stephen Batalden, Kathleen Cann, and John Dean, 169–96. Sheffield: Sheffield Phoenix Press, 2004.
– "Musul'manskii i evreiskii voprosy v Rossii epokhi Aleksandra i glazami shotlandskogo bibleista i puteshestvennika." *Voprosy istorii* 5 (2004): 46–63.
– "Printing the Bible in the Reign of Alexander I: Toward a Reinterpretation of the Russian Bible Society." In *Church, Nation, and State in Russia and Ukraine*, edited by Geoffrey A. Hosking, 65–78. London: Macmillan, 1991.
Batalden, Stephen, Kathleen Cann, and John Dean, eds. *Sowing the Word: The Cultural Impact of the British and Foreign Bible Society 1804–2004.* Sheffield: Sheffield Phoenix Press, 2004.
Bauer, Susan. *Hypochondria: Woeful Imaginings.* Berkeley: University of California Press, 1989.
Baumann, Wilhelm Bernhard. "Nesk'olko zemetok o khoziaistve iuzhnoi Rossi." *ZhMGI* 29 (1848): 3–14.

Branca, Patricia. *Women in Europe since 1750.* New York and London: Routledge, 1978.

Brandes, Detlef. *Von den Zaren adoptiert: die deutschen Kolonisten und die Balkansiedler in Neurussland und Bessarabin 1751–1914.* Munich: R. Oldenbourg Verlag, 1993.

Braun, Abraham, and Richard D. Thiessen. "Klatt, Johann Karl (1842–1918)." *Global Anabaptist Mennonite Encyclopedia Online.* http://gameo.org/index.php?title= Klatt, Johann_Karl_(1842-1918)&oldid=88721.

Breyfogle, Nicholas B. *Heretics and Colonizers: Forging Russia's Empire in the South Caucasus.* Ithaca: Cornell University Press, 2004.

Brown, George. *British and Foreign Bible Society, from Its Institution in 1804, to the Close of Its Jubilee in 1854.* London: W.M. Watts, 1859.

Center for Volga German Studies Gazetteer, s.v. "Karass." http://cvgs.cu-portland.edu/gazetteer/other_places/karrass.cfm.

Cherkazianova, Irina. "Mennonite Schools and the Russian Empire: The Transformation of Church–State Relations in Education, 1789–1917." In *Minority Report: Mennonite Identities in Imperial Russia and Soviet Ukraine Reconsidered, 1789–1945*, edited by Leonard L. Friesen, 85–109. Toronto: University of Toronto Press, 2018.

Comaroff, John L. "Images of Empire, Contests of Conscience: Models of Colonial Domination in South Africa." In *Tensions of Empire: Colonial Cultures in a Bourgeois World.* Edited by Frederick Cooper and Ann Laura Stoler, 163–97. Berkeley: University of California Press, 1997.

Cooper, Frederick, and Ann Laura Stoler. "Between Metropole and Colony: Rethinking a Research Agenda." In *Tensions of Empire: Colonial Cultures in a Bourgeois World*, edited by Frederick Cooper and Ann Laura Stoler, 1–57. Berkeley: University of California Press, 1997.

– eds. *Tensions of Empire: Colonial Cultures in a Bourgeois World.* Berkeley: University of California Press, 1997.

De Madariaga, Isabel. *Russia in the Age of Catharine the Great.* New Haven: Yale University Press, 1981.

Depperman, Klaus. *Der hallesche Pietismus und der preussische Staat unter Friedrich III.* Göttingen: Vandenhoeck & Ruprecht, 1961.

Druzhinin, N.M. *Gosudarstvennye krest'iane i reforma P.D. Kiseleva*, 2 vols. Moscow: Izdatelstvo Akademii nauk SSSR, 1946.

Dyck, Harvey L. "Introduction and Analysis." In *A Mennonite in Russia: The Diaries of Jacob D. Epp, 1851–1880*, edited by Harvey L. Dyck. Toronto: University of Toronto Press, 1991.

– "Landlessness in the Old Colony: The Judenplan Experiment 1850–1880." In *Mennonites in Russia, 1788–1988: Essays in Honour of Gerhard Lohrenz*, edited by John Friesen, 183–202. Winnipeg: CMBC, 1989.

– "Russian Servitor and Mennonite Hero: Light and Shadow in Images of Johann Cornies." *Journal of Mennonite Studies* 2 (1984): 9–28.
Dyck, Harvey L., Ingrid I. Epp, and John R. Staples, eds. *Transformation on the South Ukrainian Steppe: Letters and Papers of Johann Cornies*, vol. 1: *1812–1835*. Translated by Ingrid I. Epp. Toronto: University of Toronto Press, 2015.
– eds. *Transformation on the South Ukrainian Steppe: Letters and Papers of Johann Cornies*, vol. 2: *1836–1842*. Translated by Ingrid I. Epp. Toronto: University of Toronto Press, 2020.
Eck, Johann. "Diarium des Johann Eck von seine u. des Br. Carl Jacob Loretz von Sarepta gemachten 7. monatlichen Reise ueber Taganrok, Odessa, Pultawa, Charkoff, Woronesch im Jahre 1806." Herrnhut, Germany. Archive of the Moravian Brethren.
Eisfeld, Alfred. "Introduction." In *Samuil Khristianovich Kontenius ob inostrannoi kolonizatsii IUzhnoi Rossii*, edited by Olga Eisfeld. Odesa: Astroprint, 2003.
Eisfeld, Olga, ed. *Samuil Khristianovich Kontenius ob inostrannoi kolonizatsii IUzhnoi Rossii*. Odesa: Astroprint, 2003.
Epp, David H. *Johann Cornies*. Translated by Peter Pauls. Winnipeg: CMCB Publications and Manitoba Mennonite Historical Society, 1995.
Epp, Jacob D. *A Mennonite in Russia: The Diaries of Jacob D. Epp, 1851–1880*, edited and translated by Harvey L. Dyck. Toronto: University of Toronto Press, 1991.
Fadeev, Andrei Mikhailovich. *Vospominaniia Andreia Mikhailovich Fadeeva 1790–1867 gg*. Odesa: Iuzhno-Russkogo Obshchestva Pechagtnogo Dela, 1897.
Foote, Paul. "Introduction." In Michael Lermontov, *A Hero of Our Time*. London: Penguin, 1966.
Fox, Michael David, Peter Holquist, and Alexander M. Martin. "The Imperial Turn." *Kritika* 7, no. 4 (Fall 2006): 705–12.
Friedmann, Robert. "Anabaptism and Pietism." *MQR* 14 (April 1940): 90–128.
– *Mennonite Piety through the Centuries: Its Genius and Its Literature*. Scottsdale: Herald Press, 1998.
Friesen, John. "Education, Pietism, and Change among Mennonites in Nineteenth-Century Prussia." *MQR* 66 (April 1982): 155–66.
– ed. *Mennonites in Russia, 1788–1988: Essays in Honour of Gerhard Lohrenz*. Winnipeg: CMBC, 1989.
Friesen, Leonard, ed. *Minority Report: Mennonite Identities in Imperial Russia and Soviet Ukraine Reconsidered, 1789–1945*. Toronto: University of Toronto Press, 2018.
Friesen, P.M. *The Mennonite Brotherhood in Russia, 1789–1910*. Translated by John B. Toews et al. Fresno: Conference of Mennonite Brethren Churches, 1980.
Fry, Gary Dean, "Doukhobors 1801–1855: The Origins of a Successful Dissident Sect." PhD diss., Washington University, 1976.

Fuchs, Rachel G. *Gender and Poverty in Nineteenth-Century Europe*. Cambridge: Cambridge University Press, 2005.

Fulbrook, Mary. *Piety and Politics: Religion and the Rise of Absolutism in England, Württemberg and Prussia*. New York: Cambridge University Press, 1983.

Gamsa, Mark. "Biography and (Global) Microhistory." *New Global Studies* 11, no. 3 (2017): 231–41.

Gavel. "Agronomist Gavel's Biography of Johann Cornies (1789–1848)." Translated by Harvey L. Dyck. *Journal of Mennonite Studies* 2 (1984): 29–41.

Gawthrop, Richard L. *Pietism and the Making of Eighteenth-Century Prussia*. Cambridge: Cambridge University Press, 1993.

Gehrmann, Rolf. "Infant Mortality in Germany in the 19th Century." *Comparative Population Studies – Zeitschrift für Bevölkerungswissenschaft* 36, no. 4 (2011): 839–68.

Geraci, Robert, and Michael Khodarkovsky, eds. *Of Religion and Empire: Missions, Conversion, and Tolerance in Tsarist Russia*. Ithaca: Cornell University Press, 2001.

Goerz, Franz. *The Molotschna Settlement*. Winnipeg: CMBC Publications, 1993.

Goossen, Benjamin W. "Mennonites in Latin America: A Review of the Literature." *Conrad Grebel Review* 34, no. 3 (Fall 2016): 236–65.

Graham, John. "Lavater's Physiognomy in England." *Journal of the History of Ideas* 22, no. 4 (October–December 1961): 561–72.

Gray, Richard T. *German Physiognomic Thought from Lavater to Auschwitz*. Detroit: Wayne State University Press, 2004.

Grellet, Stephen. *Memoirs of the Life and Gospel Labours of Stephen Grellet*, edited by Benjamin Seebohm. London: A.W. Bennett, 1862.

Haralampieva, Tsvetelina. "Scottish Missionaries in Karass and Their Role in the Russian Colonisation of the North Caucasus in the First Quarter of the XIX Century." *Via Evrasia* 2 (2013). https://www.viaevrasia.com/en/6-scottish-missionairies-in-karass-and-their-role-in-the-russian-colonization-of-the-north-caucasus-tsvetelina-haralampieva.html.

Hartley, Janet M. *Russia, 1762–1825: Military Power, the State, and the People*. Westport: Praeger, 2008.

Haxthausen, August von. *Studien über die innern Zustände, das Volksleben und insbesondere die ländlichen Einrichtungen Rußlands*, vols. 1 and 2: Hanover, 1847; vol. 3: Berlin, 1852.

– *Studies on the Interior of Russia*. Translated by L.M. Schmidt. Chicago: University of Chicago Press, 1972.

Heafford, M.R. *Pestalozzi: His Thought and Its Relevance Today*. London: Routledge, 1967.

Heese, Heinrich. "Autobiography." Translated by Cornelius Krahn. *Mennonite Life* 24, no. 2 (April 1969): 66–72.

Henderson, Ebenezer. *Biblical Researches and Travels in Russia*. London: James Nisbet, 1826.
Herlihy, Patricia. *Odessa: A History, 1794–1914*. Cambridge, MA: Harvard University Press, 1986.
Hillis, Faith. "Human Mobility, Imperial Governance, and Political Conflict in Pre-Revolutionary Kiev." In *Russia in Motion: Cultures of Human Mobility Since 1850*, edited by John Randolph and Eugene M. Avrutin, 25–42. Urbana: University of Illinois Press, 2012.
Hilton, Boyd. *The Age of Atonement: The Influence of Evangelicalism on Social and Economic Thought, 1785–1865*. Oxford: Clarendon Press, 1992.
Hinrichs, Carl. *Preussentum und Pietismus: Der Pietismus in Brandenburg-Preussen als religiös-soziale Reformbewegung*. Göttingen: Vandenhoeck & Ruprecht, 1971.
Hosking, Geoffrey A., ed. *Church, Nation and State in Russia and Ukraine*. London: Macmillan, 1991.
Huebert, Helmut T. *Molotschna Historical Atlas*. Winnipeg: Springfield, 2003.
Hughes, J. *The Excellency of the Holy Scriptures, an Argument for their more general dispersion at home and abroad*. London: Thomas Bensley, 1803.
Hutton, J.E. *History of the Moravian Church*. Whitefish: Kessinger, 2004.
Isaac, Franz. *Die Molotschnaer Mennoniten; Ein Beitrag zur Geschichte derselben. Aus Akten alterer und neuerer Zeit, wie auch auf Grund eigener Erlebnisse und Erfahrungen dargestellt*. Halbstadt: H.J. Braun, 1908.
Ivanov, Andrey V.A. *A Spiritual Revolution: The Impact of the Reformation and Enlightenment in Orthodox Russia*. Madison: University of Wisconsin Press, 2020.
Jantz, Harold. "Pietism's Gift to Russian Mennonites." *Directions* 36, no. 1 (Spring 2007): 58–73.
– "A Pietist Pastor and the Russian Mennonites: The Legacy of Eduard Wuest." *Directions* 36, no.2 (Fall 2007): 232–46.
Jantzen, Mark. *Mennonite German Soldiers: Nation, Religion, and Family in the Prussian East, 1772–1880*. Notre Dame: University of Notre Dame Press, 2010.
Janzen, Tim. "Molotschna Mennonite Settlement Census." http://www.mennonitegenealogy.com/russia/Molotschna_Mennonite_Settlement_Census_27_October_1806.pdf.
Jehle, Marianna. *Anna Schlatter-Bernet, 1773–1826: eine weltoffene St. Galler Christin*. Zürich: Theologischer Verlag Zürich, 2003.
Kabuzan,V.M. *Emigratsiia i Reemigratsiia v Rossii v XVIII-nachale XX veka*. Moscow: Nauka, 1998.
Karev, V.M., et al., eds. *Nemtsy Rossii Entsiklopediia*. Moscow, 1999–2006.
Keppen, Petr. *Deviataia reviziia: izsledovanie o chisle zhitelei v Rossii v 1851 g*. St. Petersburg: Tipografiia Imperatorskoi Akademii Nauk, 1857.

- "Spisok izvestneishim kurganam v Rossii," pt. 1, *Severnaia Pchela* (2 January 1837): 3–4; pt. 2, *Severnaia Pchela* (3 January 1837): 7–8; pt. 3, *Severnaia Pchela* (4 January 1837): 10–12.
Kivelson, Valerie, and Ronald Grigor Suny. *Russia's Empires*. Oxford: Oxford University Press, 2017.
Klassen, Peter J. "Faith and Culture in Conflict: Mennonites in the Vistula Delta." *MQR* 57 (July 1983): 194–205.
- *Mennonites in Early Modern Poland and Prussia*. Baltimore: Johns Hopkins University Press, 2009.
Klibanov, A.I. *Istoriia religioznogo sektantstva v Rossii (60-e gody XIX v.-1917 g.)*. Moscow: Nauka, 1965.
Klier, John D. "State Policies and the Conversion of Jews in Imperial Russia." In *Of Religion and Empire: Missions, Conversion, and Tolerance in Tsarist Russia*, edited by Robert P. Geraci and Michael Khodarkovsky, 92–112. Ithaca: Cornell University Press, 2001.
Konovalova, Olga., ed. *Pis'ma gertsoga Armana Emmanuila de Rishel'e Samuilu Khristianovichu Konteniusu 1803–1814*. Odesa: Institut germanskikh i vostochnoevropeiskikh issledovanii Gettingen, 1999.
Kozelsky, Mara. *Christianizing Crimea: Shaping Sacred Space in the Russian Empire and Beyond*. DeKalb: Northern Illinois University Press, 2009.
Krahn, Cornelius. "Bergthal Mennonite Settlement (Zaporizhia Oblast, Ukraine)." *Global Anabaptist Mennonite Encyclopedia Online*. 1953. http://gameo.org/index.php?title=Bergthal_Mennonite_Settlement_(Zaporizhia_Oblast,_Ukraine)&oldid=144812.
Krahn, Cornelius, and Walter W. Sawatsky. "Russia." *Global Anabaptist Mennonite Encyclopedia Online*. February 2011. http://gameo.org/index.php?title=Russia&oldid=131482.
Kumar, Deepa. *Islamophobia and the Politics of Empire*. Chicago: Haymarket Books, 2012.
Lavater, Johann Casper. *Essays on Physiognomy Designed to Promote the Knowledge and the Love of Mankind*. Translated by Thomas Holcroft. London: B. Blake, 1840.
La Vopa, Anthony J. *Grace, Talent, and Merit: Poor Students, Clerical Careers, and Professional Ideology in Eighteenth-Century Germany*. Cambridge: Cambridge University Press, 1988.
LeDonne, John P. *Forging a Unitary State: Russia's Management of the Eurasian Space, 1650–1850*. Toronto: University of Toronto Press, 2020.
Lermontov, M.Yu. *A Hero of Our Time*. Translated by Paul Foote. New York: Penguin, 1966.
Lincoln, W. Bruce. *In the Vanguard of Reform: Russia's Enlightened Bureaucrats, 1825–1861*. DeKalb: Northern Illinois University Press, 1986.

Lindgren, Hakan. "The Modernization of Swedish Credit Markets, 1840–1904: Evidence from Probate Records." *Journal of Economic History* 63, no. 3 (September 2002), 810–32.

Loewen, A., and Wesley J. Prieb. "The Abuse of Power among Mennonites in South Russia, 1789–1919." In *Power, Authority, and the Anabaptist Tradition*, edited by Benjamin W. Redekop and Calvin Redekop, 95–114. Baltimore: Johns Hopkins University Press, 2005.

Loewen, Royden. *Family, Church, and Market: A Mennonite Community in the Old and the New Worlds, 1850–1930*. Champaign: University of Illinois Press, 1993.

Lohr, Eric. *Russian Citizenship: From Empire to Soviet Union*. Cambridge, MA: Harvard University Press, 2012.

Lothe, Jean. "La 'British and Foreign Bible Society' en Russie (1812–1826)." *Revue des pays de l'est* 30, no. 2 (1989): 70–81.

Lovell, Stephen, Alena Ledeneva, and Andrei Rogachevskii, eds. *Bribery and Blat in Russia: Negotiating Reciprocity from the Middle Ages to the 1990s*. London: Macmillan, 2000.

Malinowski, Lew. "Passage to Russia." Translated by Emil Toews. *Journal of the American Society of Germans from Russia* 2 (1979): 27–9.

Marmefelt, Thomas. *The History of Money and Monetary Arrangements: Insights from the Baltic and North Seas Region*. London and New York: Routledge, 2018.

Marmont, Auguste Frédéric Louis Viesse de. *Voyage de M. Le Maréchal Duc de Raguse en Hongrie, en Transylvanie, dans la Russie Méridionale, en Crimée, et sur le Bords de la Mer d'Azoff, à Constantinople, dans quelques Parties de L'Asie-Mineure, en Syrie, en Palestine, et en Égypte*, 4 vols. Brussels: Société Typographique Belge, 1837.

Martin, Alexander M. *From the Holy Roman Empire to the Land of the Tsars: One Family's Odyssey, 1768–1870*. Oxford: Oxford University Press, 2022.

Martin, Roger H. *Evangelicals United: Ecumenical Stirrings in Pre-Victorian Britain, 1795–1830*. Metuchen and London: Scarecrow Press, 1983.

McGrew, Roderick E. *Russia and the Cholera, 1823–32*. Madison: University of Wisconsin Press, 1965.

Menger, Phillip. *Die Heilige Allianz: Religion und Politik bei Alexander I (1801–1825)*. Stuttgart: Franz Steiner Verlag, 2014.

Meshkov, D.Iu. "K istorii sukonnoi fabriki Ioganna Klassena." *Voprosy Germanskoi Istorii* (2001): 156–64.

Mikaelian, Aleksandrovich Vardges. *Istoriia Krymskikh Armian*. Erevan: Natsional'naia Akademiia Nauk Respubliki Armeniia, 2004.

Mironos, A.A. *Uchenye komitety i sovety ministerstv i vedomstv v XIX veke: zadachi, struktura, evoliutsiia*. Nizhnii Novgorod: Izdatelstvo Nizhegorodskogo Universiteta, 2000.

Molchanov, Viktor Fedorovich. *Gosudarstvennii kantsler Rossii N. P. Rumiantsev.* Moscow: Pashkov Dom, 2004.

Moon, David. "Agriculture and the Environment on the Steppes in the Nineteenth Century." In *Peopling the Russian Periphery: Borderland Colonization in Eurasian History*, edited by Nicholas B. Breyfogle, Abby Schrader, and Willard Sunderland, 81–105. London: Routledge, 2007.

– *The Plough That Broke the Steppes: Agriculture and Environment on Russia's Grasslands, 1700–1914*. Oxford: Oxford University Press, 2013.

Morgan, Benjamin D. "Topographic Transmissions and How to Talk about Them: The Case of the Southern Spa in Nineteenth Century Russian Fiction." *Modern Languages Open* 1 (2014): 1–15.

Myeshkov, Dmytro. *Die Schwarzmeerdeutschen und ihre Welten 1781–1871*. Essen: Klartext, 2008.

Neufeld, Heinrich. "The Dismissal of Aeltester Jakob Warkentin, 1842." Translated by Ben Hoeppner and Delbert Plett. *Preservings* 24 (December 2004): 19–21.

– "A Further Examination of the Molotschna Conflict." *Preservings* 24 (December 2004): 23–8.

Nikitenko, Alexander. *Up from Serfdom: My Childhood and Youth in Russia, 1804–1824*. Translated by Helen Salz Jacobson. New Haven: Yale University Press, 2002.

O'Neill, Kelly. *Claiming Crimea: A History of Catherine the Great's Southern Empire*. New Haven: Yale University Press, 2017.

"Opisanie Menonitskikh kolonii v Rossii: Proizkhozhdenie Menonistov i vodverenie ikh v Rossii." *Zhurnal Ministerstva gosudarstvennykh imushchestv*, no. 4 (1842): 1–42.

Owen, Thomas C. "A Standard Ruble of Account for Russian Business History, 1769–1914." *Journal of Economic History* 49, no. 3 (September 1989): 699–706.

Paterson, John. *The Book of Every Land: Reminiscences of Labour and Adventure in the Work of Bible Circulation in the North of Europe and in Russia*. London: John Snow, 1858.

Petri, Hans. *Ignaz Lindl und die deutsche Bauernkolonie Sarata in Bessarabien*. Munich: Oldenbourg, 1965.

Pinkerton, Robert. *Russia: Or, Miscellaneous Observations on the Past and Present State of that Country and Its Inhabitants*. London, 1833.

Pintner, Walter M. "Government and Industry during the Ministry of Count Kankrin, 1823–1844." *Slavic Review* 23, no. 1 (March 1964): 45–62.

Pipes, Richard E. "The Russian Military Colonies, 1810–1831." *Journal of Modern History* 22, no. 3 (September 1950): 205–19.

Plesskaia-Zebold, E.G. *Odesskie nemtsy 1803–1920*. Odesa: Institut germanskikh i vostochnoevropeiskikh issledovanii Gettingen, 1999.

Plett, Delbert F. *The Golden Years: The Mennonite Kleine Gemeinde in Russia, 1812–1849*. Steinbach: DFP, 1985.
Postnikov, V.E. *IUzhno-russkoe krest'ianskoe khoziaistvo*. Moscow, 1891.
Pypin, A.N. *Religiozniia dvizheniia pri Aleksandr I*. Petrograd: OGNI, 1916.
Raeff, Marc. *The Decembrist Movement*. Upper Saddle River: Prentice Hall, 1966.
– *Understanding Imperial Russia: State and Society in the Old Regime*. Translated by Arthur Goldhammer. New York: Columbia University Press, 1984.
– *The Well-Ordered Police State: Social and Institutional Change through Law in the Germanies and Russia, 1600–1900*. New Haven: Yale University Press, 1983.
Randolph, John, and Eugene M. Avrutin, eds. *Russia in Motion: Cultures of Human Mobility Since 1850*. Urbana: University of Illinois Press, 2012.
Redekop, Benjamin W., and Calvin Redekop, eds. *Power, Authority, and the Anabaptist Tradition*. Baltimore: Johns Hopkins University Press, 2005.
Redekop, Calvin, Victor A. Krahn, and Samuel J. Steiner, eds. *Anabaptist/Mennonite Faith and Economics*, Lanham: University Press of America, 1994.
Reimer, Johannes. *Johann Cornies: Der Sozialreformer aus den Steppen Südrusslands*. Nürnberg: VTR, 2015.
Reimer, Klaas. "Ein Kleines Aufsatz." In *The Golden Years: The Mennonite Kleine Gemeinde in Russia, 1812–1849*, edited and translated by Delbert F. Plett, 163–6. Steinbach: DFP, 1985.
Rempel, David G. "From Danzig to Russia: The First Mennonite Migration." *Mennonite Life* (January 1969): 8–27.
Rempel, Peter. *Mennonite Migration to Russia, 1788–1828*, rev. ed., edited by Alfred H. Redekopp and Richard D. Thiessen. Winnipeg; Manitoba Mennonite Historical Society, 2007.
Reports of the British and Foreign Bible Society: 1805–1827. London: Seeley, 1825.
Riasanovsky, Nicholas. *Nicholas I and Official Nationality, 1825–1855*. Berkeley: University of California Press, 1959.
Richmond, Walter. *The Circassian Genocide*. New Brunswick: Rutgers University Press, 2013.
Sabol, Steven. *"The Touch of Civilization": Comparing American and Russian Internal Colonization*. Boulder: University of Colorado Press, 2017.
Sawatsky, Walter William. "Prince Alexander N. Golitsyn (1773–1844): Tsarist Minister of Piety." PhD diss., University of Minnesota, 1976.
Schlachta, Astrid von. *From the Tyrol to North America: The Hutterite Story through the Centuries*. Translated by Werner Pakull and Karin Pakull. Waterloo: Pandora Press, 2008.
– "The Hutterian Brethren in The Molochna, 1842–74." *Preservings* 24 (December 2004): 39.
Schlatter, Daniel. *Bruchstücke aus einigen Reisen nach dem südlichen Russland, in den Jahren 1822–1828: mit besonderer Rücksicht auf die Nogayen-Tataren am Asowschen Meere*. St. Gallen: Huber und Comp., 1830.

- Letter. Printed in *Baptist Magazine and Literary Review* 17 (1825), 410.
- Letter to *Baptist Magazine and Literary Review* 17 (1825), 409.
- Letter to W.H. Angas, 27 April 1824, in *American Baptist Magazine* 7 (1827), 83–5.
- Letter to W.H. Angus, *Baptist Magazine and Literary Review* 16 (1824), 545.

Schlatter, Wilhelm. *Geschichte der Basler Mission 1815–1915. Mit besonderer Berücksichtigung der ungedruckten Quellen. Vol. 1 of 3. Die Heimatgeschichte der Basler Mission*. Basel: Verlag der Basler Missionsbuchhandlung, 1916.

Schmidt, Christoph von. *Genovefa*. Augsburg: Veith, 1825.

- *Rosa von Tannenburg: Die Geschichte von einem heldenhaften Ritterfräulein*. Stuttgart: Gustav Weise, 1823.

Schorkowitz, Dittmar. *Imperial Formations and Ethnic Diversity: Institutions, Practices, and Longue Duree Illustrated by the Example of Russia*. Halle: Max Planck Institute for Social Anthropology, 2015.

- "The Orthodox Church, Lamaism, and Shamanism among the Buriats and Kalmyks, 1825–1925." In *Shifting Forms of Continental Colonialism: Unfinished Struggles and Tensions*, edited by Dittmar Schorkowitz, John R. Chávez, and Ingo W. Schröder, 201–26. Singapore: Palgrave Macmillan, 2019.
- "The Shifting Forms of Continental Colonialism: An Introduction." In *Shifting Forms of Continental Colonialism: Unfinished Struggles and Tensions*, edited by Dittmar Schorkowitz, John R. Chávez, and Ingo W. Schröder, 23–68. Singapore: Palgrave Macmillan, 2019.
- "Was Russia a Colonial Empire?" In *Shifting Forms of Continental Colonialism: Unfinished Struggles and Tensions*, edited by Dittmar Schorkowitz, John R. Chávez, and Ingo W. Schröder, 117–47. Singapore: Palgrave Macmillan, 2019.

Schorkowitz, Dittmar, John R. Chávez, and Ingo W. Schröder. *Shifting Forms of Continental Colonialism: Unfinished Struggles and Tensions*. Singapore: Palgrave Macmillan, 2019.

Schrader, Abby M. *Languages of the Lash: Corporal Punishment and Identity in Imperial Russia*. Dekalb: Northern Illinois University Press, 2002.

Schroeder, William. *The Bergthal Colony*, rev. ed. Winnipeg: CMBC, 1986.

- *Mennonite Historical Atlas*. Winnipeg: Kindred Productions, 1996.

Scott, James C. *Seeing Like a State: How Certain Schemes to Improve the Human Condition Have Failed*. New Haven: Yale University Press, 1998.

Seegel, Steven. *Mapping Europe's Borderlands: Russian Cartography in the Age of Empire*. Chicago: University of Chicago Press, 2012.

Shepelev, L.E. *Chinovnyi mir Rossii XVII-nachalo XX v.* St. Petersburg: Iskusstvo-SPB, 1999.

Skinner, Barbara. *The Western Front of the Eastern Church: Uniate and Orthodox Conflict in 18th-Century Poland, Ukraine, Belarus, and Russia*. DeKalb: Northern Illinois University Press, 2009.

Slocum, John W. "Who and When Were the Inorodtsy? The Evolution of the Category of 'Aliens' in Imperial Russia." *Russian Review* 57 (1998): 173–90.
Smith, Alison K. *Recipes for Russia: Food and Nationhood under the Tsars*. DeKalb: Northern Illinois University Press, 2008.
Smith-Peter, Susan. *Imagining Russian Regions: Subnational Identity and Civil Society in Nineteenth-Century Russia*. Leiden: Brill, 2018.
Sprunger, Mary S. "Dutch Mennonites and the Golden Age Economy: The Problem of Social Disparity in the Church." In *Anabaptist/Mennonite Faith and Economics*, edited by Calvin Redekop, Victor A, Krahn, and Samuel J. Steiner, 19–40. Lanham: University Press of America, 1994.
Stanley, Brian. "Christian Missions and the Enlightenment." *Christian Missions and the Enlightenment*, edited by Brian Stanley, 1–21. Grand Rapids: W.B. Eerdmans, 2001.
– ed. *Christian Missions and the Enlightenment*. Grand Rapids: W.B. Eerdmans, 2001.
Staples, John R. *Cross-Cultural Encounters on the Ukrainian Steppe: Settling the Molochna Basin, 1783–1861*. Toronto: University of Toronto Press, 2003.
– "Iogann Kornis i osnovanie Berdianskogo Lesnichestvo." *Voprosy Germanskoi Istorii* (2017): 18–21.
– "Johann Cornies, Money-Lending, and Modernization in the Molochna Mennonite Settlement, 1820s–1840s." *Journal of Mennonite Studies* 27 (2009): 109–27.
– "The Mennonite Commonwealth Paradigm and the Dnepropetrovsk School of Ukrainian Mennonite Historiography." *Voprosy Germanskoi Istorii* (2007): 58–68.
– "'On Civilizing the Nogais': Mennonite–Nogai Economic Relations, 1825–1860." *Mennonite Quarterly Review* 74, no. 2 (2000): 229–56.
– "Religion, Politics, and the Mennonite Privilegium: Reconsidering the Warkentin Affair." *Journal of Mennonite Studies* 21 (2003): 71–88.
– "Romance, Marriage, Sex, and the Status of Women in Nineteenth-Century Tsarist Russian Mennonite Society." In *Sisters: Myth and Reality of Anabaptist, Mennonite, and Doopsgezinde Women, ca 1525–1900*, edited by Mirjam van Veen et al., 302–18. Leiden: Brill, 2014.
Starr, S. Frederick. "Introduction." In *August von Haxthausen, Studies on the Interior of Russia*. Transated by L.M. Schmidt. Chicago: University of Chicago Press, 1972.
Steinwedel, Charles. *Threads of Empire: Loyalty and Tsarist Authority in Bashkiria, 1552–1917*. Bloomington: Indiana University Press, 2016.
Stephenson, Barry. *Veneration and Revolt: Hermann Hesse and Swabian Pietism*. Waterloo: Wilfrid Laurier University Press, 2009.
Sunderland, Willard. *The Baron's Cloak: A History of the Russian Empire in War and Revolution*. Ithaca: Cornell University Press, 2014.

- "The Ministry of Asiatic Russia: The Colonial Office That Never Was but Might Have Been." *Slavic Review* 69, no. 1 (Summer 2010): 120–50.
- *Taming the Wild Field: Colonization and Empire on the Russian Steppe*. Ithaca: Cornell University Press, 2004.

Tempest, Richard. "Madman or Criminal: Government Attitudes to Petr Chaadaev in 1836." *Slavic Review* 43, no. 2 (Summer 1984): 281–7.

Toews, John B. *Czars, Soviets, and Mennonites*. Harrisonburg: Faith and Life Press, 1981.

- *Perilous Journey: The Mennonite Brethren in Russia 1860–1910*. Winnipeg: Kindred Press, 1988.

Treitschke, Heinrich von. *Historische und politische Aufsatze*, 4 vols. Leipzig, 1896.

Unruh, Benjamin Heinrich. *Die niederländisch-niederdeutschen Hintergründe der mennonitischen Ostwanderungen im 16., 18. und 19. Jahrhundert*. Karlsruhe: Selbstverlag, 1955.

Urry, James. "The Mennonite Commonwealth Revisited." *Mennonite Quarterly Review* 84, no. 2 (April 2010): 229–47.

- *Mennonites, Politics, and Peoplehood: Europe–Russia–Canada 1525–1980*. Winnipeg: University of Manitoba Press, 2006.
- *None but Saints: The Transformation of Mennonite Life in Russia 1789–1889*. Winnipeg: Hyperion Press, 1990.
- "Ohm Heinrich Balzer 1800–46, Tiege." *Preservings* 24 (December 2004): 12–15.
- "'Servants from Far': Mennonites and the Pan-Evangelical Impulse in Early Nineteenth Century Russia." *Mennonite Quarterly Review* 61, no. 2 (1987): 213–27.

Valladeres, Jaime Prieto. *Mission and Migration (Global Mennonite History: Latin America)*. Translated and edited by C. Arnold Syder. Intercourse: Good Books, 2010.

Veen, Mirjam van, et al., eds. *Sisters: Myth and Reality of Anabaptist, Mennonite, and Doopsgezinde Women, ca 1525–1900*. Leiden: Brill, 2014.

Venger, N.V. *Mennonitskoe predprinimatel'stvo v usloviiakh modernizatsii iuga Rossii: Mezhdu kongregatsiei, klanom i rossiiskim obshchestvom (1789–1920)*. Dnipro: Dnipropetrovsk National University, 2009.

Vishlenkova, Elena. *Zabotias' o dushakh poddannykh: religioznaia politika v Rossii pervoi chetverti XIX veka*. Saratov: Izdatel'stvo Saratovskogo Universiteta, 2002.

Visvanathan, Shiv. *A Carnival for Science: Essays on Science, Technology, and Development*. Delhi: Oxford University Press, 1997.

Ward, W.R. *The Protestant Evangelical Awakening*. Cambridge: Cambridge University Press, 1994.

Wardin, Albert W. *On the Edge: Baptists and Other Free Church Evangelicals in Tsarist Russia, 1855–1917*. Eugene: Wipf and Stock, 2013.

Werth, Paul. *The Tsar's Foreign Faiths: Toleration and the Fate of Religious Freedom in Imperial Russia*. Oxford: Oxford University Press, 2014.

Whittaker, Cynthia H. *The Origins of Modern Russian Education: An Intellectual Biography of Count Sergei Uvarov, 1786–1855*. Dekalb: Northern Illinois University Press, 1985.

Woodcock, George, and Ivan Avakumovic. *The Doukhobors*. London: Faber and Faber, 1968.

Woods, Robert. *Children Remembered: Responses to Untimely Death in the Past*. Liverpool: Liverpool University Press, 2007.

Young, Robert J.C. *Empire, Colony, Post-Colony*. New York: John Wiley and Sons, 2015.

Zacek, Judith Cohen. "The Russian Bible Society, 1812–1826." PhD diss., Columbia University, 1964.

– "The Russian Bible Society and the Catholic Church." *Canadian Slavic Studies* 5, no. 1 (Spring 1971): 51–69.

– "The Russian Bible Society and the Orthodox Church." *Church History* 4 (December 1966): 411–47.

Zhuk, Sergei I. *Russia's Lost Reformation: Peasants, Millennialism, and Radical Sects in Southern Russia and Ukraine*. Baltimore: Johns Hopkins University Press, 2004.

Zorin, Andrei, and Andreas Schönle. *On the Periphery of Europe 1762–1825: The Self-Invention of the Russian Elite*. DeKalb: Northern Illinois University Press, 2018.

Index

The initials "J.C." refer to Johann Cornies.

administrative system: bureaucratic lack in, 16, 65, 69, 95, 159; Catherine the Great and, 12–13; congregational, 15; co-option in, 69; district (*volost*) system, 15; era of small reforms and, 137; *Gebiet* system, 15; individual role in, 87; individualism vs., 93; landed nobility in, 69–70; military colonies, 49; model paradigm and, 6; and peasantry, 137–8; recruitment from Europe, 70; responsibilities of officials, 15; Russian Bible Society and, 56; Vistula Mennonite, 15. *See also* cameralism; colonial policy/policies
afforestation, 125–6, 147–8; Alexander I and, 123–4, 249; Bergthal Mennonite settlement and, 230; Forestry Society bulletins on, 128; Forestry Society inspections, 146; fruit trees/orchards, 44, 125–6, 134, 147, 167, 219, 230; and fullholding sales, 146; on Iushanle estate, 177–8; Nicholas I and, 124; Nogais and, 218–19; plantations, 125, 126; rebellion against, 147, 190; shade trees, 125; targets, 133–5; tree lots, 26, 230; tree nurseries, 125, 177, 218; village compliance, 128. *See also* forestry
agents of state: J.C. as, 52, 65, 105, 136, 163–4, 186, 215–16, 217; Molochnaia Mennonites as, 65, 67–8; Russian Mennonites as, 7
agricultural modernization, 167–76, 224–5; Agricultural Society and, 198; Contenius and, 66; Great Drought and, 145; religious freedom and, 153; as worldliness, 72
Agricultural Society: about, 138; and brick and tile building style, 188, 190; creation of, 138, 149–51, 182, 215, 216, 252; defiance in records of, 190; and education, 234; and election of 1842, 198; Fadeev and, 137, 149–51; Forestry Society compared, 149, 151; and four-field crop rotation, 170; *Gebietsamt* and, 137, 155, 156, 182, 199; and grain-growing, 170; and Guardianship Committee, 182; and Hutterite–Russian dispute, 212; J.C. Jr. and, 165; and J.C.'s letter to B. Fast, 196–7; in Khortitsa, 194,

312   Index

Agricultural Society (*cont.*)
239, 240; Klassen and, 190–2; and land transfers, 167; and Lange family, 211; and Large Flemish Congregation, 187, 205–6; J. Martens in, 165; W. Martens in, 165; and Mennonites as model for peasants, 172; and modernization, 182, 217; punishment by, 198; and reforms, 198, 249; Regier and, 156; resistance to, 155–6, 187; and schools, 235; waning of, 187; Warkentin and, 155, 187, 191, 198; P. Wiebe as chair, 248; A. Wiebe in, 171

Agricultural Society, J.C. and, 137, 149–51; blurring of authority in relationship, 224–5; creation of society, 216; J.C. on purpose of, 199; in J.C.'s administrative study, 182; J.C.'s death and waning of, 187; and Klassen's cloth factory, 117; members in Cornies Party, 153; and reform, 224–5

agriculture, 222–3; Allen and, 74; crisis of 1824–5, 105; didactic model vs. colonies as laboratory in, 34; environmental constraints on, 139–40; equipment manufacture, 168; fullholding division and, 145; Hahn and, 217; and immigration, 6; Jewish people and, 241; mixed, 67; Molochnaia Mennonite settlement's achievements in, 250; in New Russia, 12; Nogais and, 154–5; of peasantry, 159; in Poland, 9; productivity improvement, 152–3; separation from secular world and, 17–18; in state–Mennonite relationship, 98; winter of 1824–5 and, 169; Württemberg settlement and, 232. *See also* agriculture, J.C. and

agriculture, J.C. and: and Agricultural Society, 137, 149–51; and agriculture, 169–70; crop cultivation/experimentation, 140, 222; and crop rotation, 170; and environmental constraints on agriculture, 139–40; and Forestry Society, 107, 123, 126–7, 130, 133–5, 147–8; grain growing, 34; livestock numbers, 42; markets, 34; and Mennonite machinery, 222–3; and modern farming methods, 145; as peasant, 20; on peasants, 159; and potatoes, 171, 172, 175, 220–2; and reform(s), 145, 249; as sheep buyer, 94; sheep raising, 34, 42, 67, 169, 174–5; and sheep vs. grain growing, 34

Akkerman, 154–5; J.C.'s negative assessment of, 221; Keppen and, 158, 178; as model village, 177, 218; mosque in, 176; visits to, 177, 178, 222

Alexander, crown prince, 3; Akkerman visit, 154–5; visit to Molochnaia, 154–5, 164–5, 177, 178

Alexander I, tsar, 3, 4; administration of empire, 110; attitude toward Mennonites, 107; and cameralism, 64; death, 77, 108, 109; and Doukhobors, 26, 46; and forestry, 123–4, 125, 249; and military colonies, 49; and mysticism, 45, 54, 55, 77; and Privilegium, 50–1; and Prussian Mennonites, 49, 50; and Quaker visit, 58–9; and Russia as land of opportunity, 111; and Russian Bible Society, 55, 58; transformation from liberal to reactionary, 45; visits to Molochnaia, 48–9, 65, 77, 78, 109

Alexanderwohl, 53, 143, 148–9, 197
Allen, William, 44–5, 58–9, 61, 62, 65, 74

Anabaptist faith, 6, 41, 225
Angas, W.H., 91
Anna, tsarina, 70
Antonov, Sergeii, 114
apprenticeship program, 175–6, 219–20
artisanship/crafts: and agricultural economy, 169; J.C. and, 168, 169; and *Judenplan* villages, 241; landlessness and, 163, 168, 223; Mennonites and, 18, 223; Neu-Halbstadt crafts village, 168, 223
Aul, 221–2
Avakumovic, Ivan, 45
Azov, 12, 25; Sea of, 25

Baerg, Jacob, 148
Balzer, Heinrich, 51, 122, 221, 237; "Faith and Reason," 118, 120–2, 131–3; and J.C., 120–2, 131, 132–3
banditry, 83–4
banning, 10–11, 39–40, 41, 147, 210. *See also* punishment(s)
Baptist Missionary Society, 91, 92
Bartlett, Roger, 13
Bartsch, Jacob, 239–40
Bärwalde, 5
Basel Institute for the Education of Young People in Missionary Work, 91, 92
Bassin, Mark, 85
Belinsky, Vissarion, 173
Berdiansk: grain merchants in, 171; model plantation in, 219–20; port, 116, 167, 169; Staro-Berdiansk forest plantation, 253–4
Bergthal Mennonite settlement, 229–31, 244; J.C. and, 230–1, 244
Berlin Missionary Institution, 91
Bernet-Schlatter, Anna, 59–60, 89
Bessarabia settlement, 103, 112, 184; J.C. and, 111–12
Biron, Ernst Johann von, count, 70

Blüher, Joseph, 74
Blüher, Traugott: A. Cornies and, 166; J.C. Jr. and, 75, 139, 140; J.C.'s first meeting with, 74–5; Tsaritsyn as home town, 174. *See also* Blüher, Traugott, J.C. and
Blüher, Traugott, J.C. and: about relationship, 83; and cholera, 130; and drought/famine, 80, 119, 131; first meeting in St. Petersburg, 74–5; friendship, 74–5; and J.C. Jr. staying with Blüher in Moscow, 140–1; and moneylending, 115; and wool trade, 83
Boldt, Dirk, 148
Bol'shoi Tokmak, 129, 164
books: Balzer on, 132; J.C. buying, 120–1
Boos, Martin, 89
Bradke, Georg von, 172
Brallovskii, Jankel, 83
brandy distilling/distillery, 6, 29, 43, 113–14, 136, 153
Brenkenhofswalde, 142, 143
brick and tile building style, 188–9, 190
British and Foreign Bible Society (BFBS), 54–5, 57, 58, 61, 103. *See also* Russian Bible Society
Brüdergemeinde Colony, 231
Bruderschaft (Brotherhood), 39
Bukhbinder, Gershka, 83
burial mounds, 156, 157–9
butter, 27, 30

cameralism, 6, 49–50, 64–5, 68, 69–70, 73
Catherine the Great, empress, 12–13; and administrative system, 69–70; and cameralism, 64; land grants to nobility, 69–70; and model colonists, 34; and Privilegium, 17; terms of immigration, 36

Catholic Church: Orthodoxy vs., 110; persecution of Mennonites, 7
Catholic immigrants, 15, 26
Central Directorate for the Spiritual Affairs of Foreign Confessions, 54
Chaadaev, Petr, "Philosophical Letter," 85
Chancellery for the Guardianship of Foreigners, 12–13
Chercheuslidsov, Sakhar, prince, 129
Chernigovka, 176
cholera, 121, 128–30, 135; J.C. and, 129–30
Christian School Society: and Cornies–Warkentin dispute, 153; Enns and, 116; J. Fast and, 61; Flemish congregation and, 61; founding of, 60; J.C. and, 60, 88, 116, 122; Voth and, 60, 92; Warkentin and, 63, 72
Circassians, 188
"civilization": European vs. "other" in J.C.'s Nogai study, 84; of Molochnaia Mennonites, 85, 89; Nogais and, 85–6, 88, 106, 154–5, 158, 163, 178, 182; Pietism and, 57; state and, 84
cloth factory, 38, 116–17, 118, 168–9, 188
colonial policy/policies: as contingent, 3–4; Inspector of Colonies, 44–5; J.C.'s records and, 4; Mennonites and, 50–1; and Mennonites as laboratory of modernity, 4; Molochnaia religious issues and, 64; and national vision, 4; policing of frontiers, 83–4; standardization in, 95, 186, 235; subsidies to, 28. *See also* administrative system; state–Mennonite relationship
Contenius, Samuel: about, 66, 70–1; administrative style, 87; and Alexander's visit, 48, 49; and cameralism, 68; death, 66, 70, 124, 135; and Fadeev, 70, 135; focus on Mennonites, 49; and Forestry Society, 151; and Grellet and Allen's visit, 44; Grellet on, 46; and Guardianship Committee, 65, 66, 68; and J.C., 65–6, 68, 96; loyalty to tsar, 70–1; and patronage, 71; retirement, 66; Russian Bible Society and, 56; and Saxony sheep-buying trip, 82, 83, 97–8, 99, 100–1, 106; and sheep raising, 67–8, 97; and wool improvement societies, 66–8, 150–1
Cornies, Aganetha (née Klassen): death, 33, 245–6; health, 33; illness, 164, 192; infant deaths, 32; and J.C. Jr.'s depression, 245; marriage to J.C., 31–3
Cornies, Agatha (née Klassen), 32
Cornies, Agnes (later Wiebe): birth, 32; care of young Johann, 245; education, 166; in Ekaterinoslav, 166; illness, 192; in Iushanle, 166; and J.C. Jr.'s remarriage, 246–7; as J.C.'s assistant, 31, 166; and J.C.'s death, 247; lack of correspondence with J.C. Sr., 165–6; marriage, 33, 167, 246; in Moscow visiting Blüher, 166; in Sarepta, 166, 174
Cornies, David: birth, 5; farm work, 31; gravestone, 27f; J.C. and, 31; management of J.C.'s landholdings, 31; remaining at family fullholding after J.C. Sr.'s death, 42
Cornies, Heinrich: birth, 5, 24; A. Cornies and, 166; J.C. and, 31; with J.C. Jr. in Prussia, 245; management of J.C.'s landholdings, 31; remaining at family fullholding after J.C. Sr.'s

death, 42; and sheep farming in Sarepta, 174; wife, 32
Cornies, Helena (née Klassen), 42
Cornies, Johann (J.C.), 23, 216; on administrative system of Mennonites, 181–2, 193; as arbitrator/mediator/negotiator, 21, 120, 209–10, 214; and artisanship, 169; assistance to neighbours/community, 79–80, 105, 133, 208; baptism, 23; birth, 5; book buying, 120–1; characteristics, 7, 21–2, 30–1; convalescence after Saxony trip, 78; Cornies Party, 153, 156, 171, 207–8; crisis of 1824–5 and, 78; death, 3, 187, 247–8; documents/materials left by, 20; and elections of 1845, 207–8; friends, 3; horse theft accusations against, 94–5, 96–7, 98; illness, 104–5, 106, 107, 247; influence/power, 3, 38, 94, 187, 216; and land transfers, 146; monument to, 253–4; obituary, 248; as outlier, 20, 21; personality, 21, 80–1, 133, 144, 147–8, 153, 172; reading, 42; success, 30–1, 80; talents, 80; trades/commerce promotion, 168; and treatment of women, 166, 210. *See also entries below*

Cornies, Johann, business activities/entrepreneurship, 30; and apprenticeship program, 175–6; bookkeeping, 42, 43, 113; brandy distribution, 113–14, 153; establishment of, 41–3; for father, 29–30; as flour mill apprentice, 30; fullholding purchase, 30, 42; Iushanle estate, 33–4, 35; and Klassen's cloth factory, 116–17, 153, 168–9; as land surveyor, 38, 51, 52–3, 64, 68, 89, 94, 95, 139–40; moneylending, 114–20, 121–2, 127, 168–9, 192; spirits selling business with Martens, 43; as trader, 30; wealth, 20, 29, 41–3, 73, 79–80, 105, 113, 133

Cornies, Johann, and family: and Aganetha, 31–3, 164, 245–6; children, 32; and David, 31; and Heinrich, 31; infant deaths, 32; inheritance from father, 30, 42; and J.C. Jr., 31, 123, 138–9, 140–2, 165, 245–7; and Johann, son of J.C. Jr., 246; and Peter, 31, 78, 207; relationship with father, 31; relationship with parents, 31

Cornies, Johann, religious beliefs, 80; on agricultural crises, 197; attitude toward crises, 121–2; on Balzer's preaching, 131; on cholera epidemic, 130; on community service, 104–5; divine right of kings, 109; on drought and famine as divine guidance, 131; and drought as test, 80; duty/assistance to community, 79–80; ecumenism, 91; on engagement with world, 75–6; on evangelicalism, 75–6; on Great Drought, 135; illness and, 104–5, 106; influences on, 78; on Islam, 86, 88; Lavater's ideas and, 90, 91; in letters to J.C. Jr., 141–2; and love, 104–5; as member of Flemish congregation, 93; on Muslim apprentices, 175–6; on Orthodox apprentices, 175–6; personal calling, 91; personal wealth and individual responsibility, 80; on predestination, 86; on reforms as God's vs. secular will, 136, 198; and Russian Bible Society, 60, 63; Schlatter and, 91; on Warkentin's beliefs, 197; on wealth and responsibility, 119. *See also* Pietism, J.C. and

316   Index

Cornies, Johann, and state: as agent of state, 52, 65, 105, 136, 163–4, 186, 215–16, 217; ambiguity in relationship, 52; assertion in Russian affairs, 172; and cameralism, 49–50; delegation of supervision in, 220–1, 222; on differences between Molochnaia and Prussia, 90; investigation of Romny murders, 83; land surveying, and engagement with, 64; Ministry of State Domains and, 217; on state and colonial peoples, 90–1; state demands on, 49, 163–4, 182–3; and state–Mennonite relationship, 21, 49, 90; trip to St. Petersburg and J.C.'s perception of Russian administration, 71

Cornies, Johann, travel: to Astrakhan *guberniia*, 172; in Caucasus, 172, 173–4, 188–9; on Circassians, 188; with Fadeev, 172–5; to Kalmyk Horde, 172; to Moravian Brethren at Sarepta, 172; in Sarepta, 174–5; to Saxony, 23, 82–3, 97–104, 111; to St. Petersburg, 71–5, 78

Cornies, Johann, world view: changes in approach to public life, 111; and corporal punishment, 238; dissension among Prussian Mennonites and, 111–12; engagement with secular world, 38, 104–5; on Europeans vs. "other," 84–5; on individual freedoms vs. state interests, 87; and individualism, 93; interpretation of drought/famine, 131; leadership and supervision in, 242; on love, 104–5; on marriage, 32–3; on Mennonites as role models, 177; and modernization, 217, 250; on Molochnaia vs. West, 23; on New Russia as land of opportunity, 23, 47; on order/beauty and morality, 188–9; political views, 20; and role of wealth in Mennonite society, 118; sense of mission, 105, 106, 189

Cornies, Johann (son of J.C. Jr.), 165, 245, 246, 247

Cornies, Johann Jr.: and Agricultural Society, 165; and art, 139; birth, 32; and Blüher, 75; education, 123, 138–9, 140–1, 166; in Ekaterinoslav, 138–9, 141; and Fadeev, 141, 165; and Guardianship Committee, 141; J.C.'s precepts to guide travels, 141–2; J.C.'s relationship with, 31, 120–1; Justina's death and, 245–6; and land surveying, 139, 140; management of J.C.'s landholdings, 31; marriage, 33; and Moravian Brethren, 165; in Moscow with Blüher, 140–2; remarriage, 33, 246–7; in Sarepta, 166, 174; in Tashchenak, 166; travel to Prussia, 245–7. *See also under* Cornies, Johann, and family.

Cornies, Johann Sr.: about, 5–6; age at arrival in Molochnaia, 29; characteristics, 30; as community doctor, 29; death, 30, 31, 42; distilling business, 6, 29–30; engagement with other groups, 38; J.C.'s relationship with, 31; legacy, 42; marriage, 5

Cornies, Johanna (formerly Willms, wife of J.C. Jr.), 165, 192, 245

Cornies, Justina (daughter of J.C. Jr. and Johanna), 165, 245

Cornies, Katharina, 5, 29

Cornies, Margaretha (née Klassen), 32

Cornies, Maria (née Klassen): about, 5; age at arrival in Molochnaia, 29; death, 31; J.C. Sr.'s death and, 42; marriage, 5; work of, 29, 31

Cornies, Peter: about, 31; assuming J.C.'s business affairs, 78; birth, 5; death, 31, 207, 245; election candidate, 207; farm work, 31; fullholding purchase, 42; inheritance from J.C. Sr., 42; J.C.'s relationship with, 31, 207; wife, 32
Cornies, Therese (formerly Thiessen), 246–7
Cornies family: and economic opportunities, 18; emigration, 3, 5, 24, 25; finances, 28; fullholders among, 42; hearth site, 26; inheritance from J.C. Sr., 42; in Khortitsa, 24, 25; livestock, 42; location of fullholding, 26; and Ohrloff village establishment, 25; poverty, 29
crafts. *See* artisanship/crafts
credit. *See* moneylending
Crimean Khanate, 12
crises: agricultural, 105, 197; blizzards, 16; and Forestry Society, 128; J.C. and, 121; and modernization/reforms, 121, 197
crisis of 1824–5: blizzards, 78, 79; drought, 80; *Gebietsamt* and, 81–2; and German colonists, 82; Guardianship Committee and, 81; hurricane, 78, 79; J.C.'s relationship to community during, 79–80, 82; livestock losses, 82; and Nogai Tatars, 82; recovery from, 107; and religious tensions, 105; and Slavic villages, 82; and starvation, 82; summer 1824, 78–9; and winter 1825–6, 107
crop agriculture, 164, 169, 222; distance of ports and, 16; employment in, 169–70; experimentation at Iushanle estate, 140, 171, 172; field rotation in, 170; as interference in fullholders' affairs, 170; Nogais as haulers, 171; ploughing and, 170; precipitation and, 16, 25, 28; rotation systems, 140; sheep raising vs., 169–70, 192; soil and, 16, 25. *See also* grain

Dahlke (householder in Alexanderwohl), 148–9
Danzig, 7, 103
daughter settlements, 103, 227
Decembrist Revolt (1825), 77–8, 108, 109, 111, 197
Department of the Imperial Economy, 72, 74
Doehring, Daniel, 174–5
Dohna, count, 102
Dolgorukaia, Elena Pavlovna, princess. *See* Fadeev, Elena Pavlovna, princess (née Dolgorukaia)
Doukhobors: about, 26; border dispute with, 51; Christian School Society and, 122; conversion to Orthodoxy, 185, 214; crisis of 1835–6, 184–6; exile, 185–6, 251; J.C. and, 51, 84, 163, 184–6, 214; Orthodox Church and, 46; pacifism of, 26, 45; religious beliefs, 26, 184; state and, 45–6
Driedger (senior deputy mayor), 160
drought(s), 25, 28; and cloth factory, 117; of 1833–4, 117, 121; Forestry Society and, 147; as God's judgment, 119; mixed agriculture and, 67; summer of 1824, 78; as test, 80; and tree planting, 147. *See also* crises; Great Drought
Dyck, Harvey, 248
Dyck, Jacob, 189, 194, 240
Dyck, Klaas, 98
Dzialynskaia, countess, 71

Eck, Johann, 30, 44
ecumenism, 54, 55, 56–7, 89, 91, 93, 142
education: apprentices and, 175; Balzer on, 121, 132–3; and cameralism, 69; of forestry apprentices, 220; Gnadenfeld congregation and, 143–4; of J.C. Jr., 121, 138–9, 140–1; and land surveying, 234; Large Flemish Congregation and, 237; Lavater on, 90; and modernization, 234; moral function of, 234; and Nogais, 86, 88, 90; Official Nationality and, 110; Pietism and, 11, 59, 238; primary, 59; professionalization of, 233–8; Prussian-Mennonite emigrants and, 53; quality of teaching, 234; Russian language, 138, 141, 143; and Russification of minorities, 235; secondary, 142; state–Mennonite relationship and, 59. *See also* education, J.C. and; schools
education, J.C. and, 42; and apprentices, 175, 220; Balzer and, 132, 133; and Christian School Association, 60, 63; and educational innovations, 132; and future of Mennonites, 123; "General Rules on the Instruction and Treatment of School Children," 236–8, 240; Gnadenfeld School Society and, 144; and improvement of schools, 143; and J.C. Jr.'s education, 123, 140–2; J.C.'s own education, 21, 42, 53, 60; Khortitsa Central School, 239; and Nogais, 86; Ohrloff school, 60, 122–3, 234, 236; as passion for J.C., 233, 234; and professionalization, 233–8, 243; school reform, 235–8; and secondary school, 122–3, 144; secular education, 88, 133; and teachers, 143, 144; and teaching quality, 235–8

Efimenko, Stepan, 176

Ekaterinoslav: A. Cornies in, 166; Guardianship Committee in, 16, 54, 65, 66, 73, 81, 97; *Judenplan* village in, 241; Russian Bible Society in, 55–6

elders, 37; about, 15; as court of last resort, 198; Forestry Society and, 127–8; *Gebietsamt* and, 128; and Ohrloff school curriculum, 88; ordination of, 61–2; reforms vs. authority of, 162; and religious education, 59; Wiens's dismissal, 214

elections, 36; 1826, 101; 1832, 136; 1838, 160–1, 162; 1841, 193–6; 1842, 198–200, 201, 206; 1845, 207–8; fullholders' voting rights, 42

elites. *See* nobility/elites

engagement with secular world: evangelicalism and, 75–6; J.C. and, 105; Moravian Brethren and, 74, 75, 103; Pietism and, 11; practical need for, 18–19. *See also* separation from secular world

Engbrecht (Wernersdorf), 148

Enlightenment, 12, 17, 57, 85, 90, 189

Enns, Gerhard, 116, 126–7, 128, 197, 201–2

Enns, Jakob, 36–7

Ennz, Klaas, 148

epidemics: cholera, 121, 128–30, 135; of 1841, 192

Epp (member of Khortitsa Agricultural Society), 240

Epp, David: and Bessarabia settlement, 103, 112; and British and Foreign Bible Society, 103; on Cornies family, 29–30; J.C. and, 42, 61, 90, 103, 247; on J.C. Sr., 5; and Lange, 143; and Pietism, 61; and Prussian Mennonite

Church, 61, 111–12; and Regier's letters regarding Warkentin's removal, 208–9
Epp, Jacob, 115
Essays on Physiognomy (Lavater), 89–90
evangelicalism/evangelism: and "city upon a hill," 58; Molochnaia Mennonites and, 57; Moravian Brethren and, 74, 103; of Nogai, 58; Pietism and, 11; Russian Bible Society and, 57, 59; and secular engagement, 75–6; separation from secular world vs., 11; and Tatars, 57

Fadeev, Andrei: about, 66, 71; as administrator, 87, 124; and Agricultural Society, 137; and burial mounds, 157; on colonist experiment, 124; Contenius and, 70, 135; on didactic models as failure, 182; on Ekaterinoslav, 73; as "father" to Mennonites, 238; and Forestry Society, 125, 126, 127–8, 151, 249; on frontier bureaucracy, 65; and *Gebietsamt* control over brandy distribution, 136; as Guardian of Kalmyk Tatars, 138, 149; on Guardianship Committee's survival, 193; on Haxthausen's visit, 181; on the immigration of 1818–22, 54; J.C. Jr. and, 141, 165; Keppen and, 156; and land transfers, 146; and Martens, 164; and Mennonite privileges, 126; and Mennonites, 124; on Mennonites as model, 182, 183–4; Molochnaia success, and career of, 178; and Moravian Brethren, 172; and patronage, 71; personality, 124; Russian Bible Society and, 56; transfer to Odesa, 138; and wool improvement societies, 66. *See also* Fadeev, Andrei, J.C. and
Fadeev, Andrei, J.C. and: about relationship, 66; and Agricultural Society, 149–51; and crisis of 1824–5, 81; departure of Fadeev and, 138; Fadeev's departure and weakening of J.C.'s power, 153; friendship between, 124; and *Gebietsamt* 1838 elections, 160; on *Gebietsamt* and brandy distribution business, 114; impact of relationship, 65–6; on interpretation of drought/famine, 131; and J.C. on community responsibilities vs. Guardianship Committee, 118–19; and J.C.'s children's marriages, 33; and J.C.'s death, 248; and J.C.'s leadership role in colonial mission, 78; and J.C.'s travel to St. Petersburg, 73; letter on duty to community, 79–80; letter regarding 1824–5 crisis, 81–2; moneylending, 116, 119–20, 150; patronage and friendship in, 135–6; power in relationship, 149; and Saxony sheep-buying trip, 82, 83; and tree planting, 134
Fadeev, Elena Pavlovna, princess (née Dolgorukaia), 66, 70, 71
"Faith and Reason" (Balzer), 118, 120–2, 131–3
Fast, Bernhard, 40, 61–2, 154, 155–6, 196–8, 204, 214
Fast, Jacob, 61
Fast, Peter, 219, 220
Fifth Department of Tsar's Own Chancellery, 151, 161, 215. *See also* Ministry of State Domains
Filaret, archbishop, 55
Flemish congregation: and ban, 10–11; breakaway to form *Kleine Gemeinde*, 38; Frisian immigrants

Flemish congregation (*cont.*) and, 61–3; merger with Frisian congregation, 37; and Moritz's visit, 62; and Pietism, 11, 54, 61; Prussian Mennonites and, 54; reputation/ characteristics, 38; of Vistula Mennonites, 9–10. *See also* Large Flemish Congregation; Old Flemish Congregation
Fletnitzer, Karl Friedrich Wilhelm, 234, 236
forestry: Alexander I and, 125; apprenticeship program in, 219–20; creation of societies, 249; and modernization, 125; Nicholas I and, 123, 125, 249; plantations as symbolic of Mennonite role, 254; state peasants and, 219; supervision of, 242. *See also* afforestation
Forestry Society: about, 107, 125; Agricultural Society compared, 149, 151; and artisans' cottages, 168; and Bergthal Mennonite settlement, 230; charter, 125, 127; confiscations and reallotments of land, 135; Contenius and, 151; crises and, 128; expansion of authority, 147; Fadeev and, 125, 126, 127–8, 151, 249; founding of, 123, 128, 215, 252; and fullholding disrepair, 148–9; and *Gebietsamt*, 126, 127–8, 136, 149, 156; and Great Drought, 135, 144–5; and Guardianship Committee, 126; and laboratory of modernization, 125, 136; and land transfers, 146–7, 149; members as elite, 127; as new vision for administration, 137; on problems with fullholding ownership, 145; and tree planting, 147–8; tsarist policy and, 136; Württemberg settlement and, 232. *See also* Forestry Society, J.C. and

Forestry Society, J.C. and, 107, 126–7, 130, 144–5, 147–8; and afforestation, 147–8, 249; and agricultural reform, 144–5; J.C. as representative of reform agenda, 135–6; members in Cornies Party, 153; tree-planting targets, 133–5
Francke, August Hermann, 58
Frank, Wilhelm, 98, 99, 100, 102
Franz, Heinrich, 236, 239
Frederick the Great, 11
French Revolution, 17, 70, 71
Friedmann, Robert, 56–7
Friedrich Wilhelm II, king of Prussia, 11, 179
Friedrich Wilhelm III, king of Prussia, 142–3
Friedrichstal, 229
Friesen, Abraham, 40, 160, 203, 214–15
Friesen, David, 194, 195, 207, 208, 248
Friesen, P.M., 4, 147, 160
Frisian congregation: Balzer as member, 131; and ban, 10–11; and J.C., 63; J.C. and, 60–1, 63; merger with Flemish congregation, 37; and Pietism, 11, 63; Prussian Mennonite migrants from, 53–4; and Prussian Mennonites, 63; Prussian-Mennonite emigrants of 1818–22 in, 53–4; and Western innovation, 63
Frisian immigrants (1818–22): and election of 1845, 208; and Ohrloff school, 60; and Pietism, 208; relationship with Flemish congregation, 61–3; support for J.C., 60–1
Froebel, Friedrich, 236

Gavel (writer of J.C.'s obituary), 248
Gebietsamt: about, 15; Agricultural Society and, 137, 155, 156, 182, 199;

and brandy distribution business, 136; and cholera, 129; and congregational elders, 128; and crisis of 1824–5, 81–2; elections, 36; elections of 1832, 136; elections of 1838, 159–61, 162; elections of 1841, 187, 193–6; elections of 1842, 198–200, 204, 206; elections of 1845, 207–8; Forestry Society and, 126, 127–8, 136, 149, 156; and Guardianship Committee, 105, 126; and Hutterite relocation, 227; and Hutterite–Russian dispute, 212; and J. Klassen (mayor of Münsterberg), 190, 191; J. Klassen (Warkentin's brother-in-law) as mayor, 95, 101; and Klassen cloth factory, 169; and land transfers, 146; and Large Flemish Congregation, 152, 205–6; Privilegium and, 36; Reimer on, 41; and religious controversy, 37; and Thiessen rape, 40; Warkentin/Warkentin Party and, 95, 101, 114, 156. See also *Gebietsamt*, J.C. and

Gebietsamt, J.C. and: appointment of J.C. as land surveyor, 51; brandy distribution business and, 113–14; and definition of scope of J.C.'s activities, 123; and education, 235; and elections of 1841, 194–6; horse theft accusations, 94, 96–7, 105; and J.C.'s community influence, 94; J.C.'s resignation from duties, 94, 95, 96, 97; and J.C.'s sense of mission, 106; and letter to Fadeev re 1824–5 crisis, 81–2; Saxony sheep-buying trip, 97–101

"General Rules on the Instruction and Treatment of School Children: A Manual for Teachers in Molochnaia School Districts," 236–8, 240

Gessner, Georg, 89
Giesbrecht (householder in Wernersdorf), 148
Gnadenfeld: church, 144; and election of 1845, 208; Lange family of, 209–12; school, 143, 144, 234
Gnadenfeld congregation: Epp and, 61; immigration of 1834, 142; J.C. and, 142, 143, 211; J.C.'s accusations against, 197; and Mennonite Brethren, 215; and Pietism, 61, 142–3, 215
Goerz, Franz, 53, 62, 63
Goerz, Heinrich, 147
Golitsyn, Aleksandr, 54, 55, 56, 58, 66, 77, 179
Gomol'skii, Gigal, 83
Gorchakov, general, 48
grain, 34, 169, 170; Berdiansk port and, 116, 167; moneylending and, 115, 116. See also crop agriculture
Granobarskii (nobleman), 70
Gray, Richard, 90
Great Drought, 128, 130–1, 135; and agricultural diversification, 171; and agricultural modernization/reform, 137, 145, 153; and cloth factory, 168; Forestry Society orders during, 144–5; and livestock, 169; and sheep, 168
Great Reforms of 1860s, 3, 16, 186, 193
Grellet, Stephen, 44–5, 46, 58–9, 61, 62, 65, 70, 89
Grodno, 24, 28
Guardianship Committee, 3; about, 15–16, 28–9, 68; as agent of change, 105; Agricultural Society and, 182; authority moving to Ministry of State Domains, 192–3; bureau moved from Ekaterinoslav to Odesa, 120; and cameralism, 64; Contenius and, 65, 66, 68; and crisis

Guardianship Committee (*cont.*) of 1824–5 relief, 81; decline of, 158; as division of Department of State Domains, 137–8; and economic reforms, 249; Ekaterinoslav bureau, 65–6, 138; and election of 1841, 187; and election of 1842 (results), 200–1; and empire-wide policies, 173; Fadeev and, 65, 217; and flogging of Thun, 225; Forestry Society and, 126; *Gebietsamt* and, 105, 126; Hahn and, 193, 248; and Hutterite relocation, 226, 227, 228, 229; in Kinishev, 66; and land transfers, 145–7; and Large Flemish Congregation, 187, 204; Mennonite Settlement Commission and, 51; Ministry of State Domains as eclipsing, 171, 217; and minorities, 84; on moving families to Bessarabia, 184; and Nogais study, 84; in Odesa, 138; and Penner, 195; and Privilegium, 192; recordkeeping, 109; reorganization, 125, 215; and sheep raising, 34; state contemplating closing, 192–3; and P. Toews, 195, 200–1; and Warkentin, 187; weaknesses of, 68, 224; and wool improvement societies, 66, 67. *See also* Guardianship Committee, J.C. and

Guardianship Committee, J.C. and: about, 65; alliance as God's will, 105; brandy distribution business and, 113; Contenius and, 65–6, 96; and crisis of 1824–5, 81, 118–19; and Doukhobors, 51; Hahn and, 224; and horse theft accusations, 96–7; and immigration of 1818–22, 51–3; and J.C. Jr. in Ekaterinoslav, 141; J.C.'s influence with, and within community, 94, 99, 101; and J.C.'s land lease, 35; and J.C.'s status, 94; and J.C.'s time/energy, 217; and liaison between Committee and settlement, 96; as Mennonite representative, 72, 105; Ministry of State Domains vs., 171; and Nogais study, 84; as *Oberschulz*, 51, 65; reorganization and, 138; Saxony sheep-buying trip, 98–9, 105–6; as settlement liaison, 96; and sheep-buying trip to St. Petersburg, 72–3; stationery buying for, 72–3; Warkentin vs., 64, 65; and wealth vs. community responsibilities, 118–19

Hahn, Evgenii von, 207; about, 193; and agriculture, 217; and Bergthal Mennonite settlement, 229–30; as Deputy Chief Guardian, 215; as Director of First Department of Ministry of State Domains, 248; and education, 234, 235, 239; and elections of 1841/1842, 198–9, 200, 201, 204; and Great Reforms of 1860s, 193; and Guardianship Committee, 193, 217, 248; and Hutterites, 226; and intra-congregational disputes, 212; and *Judenplan* villages, 241–2; and Lange family of Gnadenfeld, 209, 210, 211, 212; and Large Flemish Congregation disbandment, 204–6; and move of Mennonite communities to Bessarabia, 184; and Pelekh, 228; and privilege of Mennonites, 216; and punishment of Hutterite, 213–14; and Thun, 225, 251; and A. Toews, 204; and Warkentin, 196, 198–200, 201, 203–4, 224; and Wiens, 251; and Württemberg settlement, 231. *See also* Hahn, Evgenii von, J.C. and

Hahn, Evgenii von, J.C. and, 198–200, 203, 207, 214, 217, 224; agricultural knowledge and, 217; and dismissal of Wiens, 214; as Hahn's agent, 216; Hahn's dependence on J.C., 224; Hahn's support of J.C., 207, 214; J.C. as agent of, 216; and Lange family affair, 209, 210; as partnership, 217; in Warkentin Affair, 198–200, 203, 207, 224
Halbstadt: as administrative/economic centre, 126; brewery, 196; cloth factory, 38, 116–17, 118, 168–9, 188; crafts village, 163, 168; distillery, 43; Keppen in, 178; Neufeld as mayor, 196; school, 143
Hansen, Georg, 9–10
Hausknecht, Adrian, 119, 122, 236
Haxthausen, August von, 3, 179–81, 184; on J.C., 180–1; *Studies on the Interior of Russia*, 179–81
Heese, Heinrich, 122, 123, 143, 239
Hekel (Württemberg minister), 231, 232
Henderson, Ebenezer, 57, 59–60, 61, 92
Herrnhut, 74, 102–3, 143, 174
Heubuden, 103, 229
Hiebert, Agatha, 48, 50
Hiebert, David, 48, 49
Holy Alliance, 77
horses: Cornies family holdings, 42; at Iushanle, 42; Nogais and, 25, 35; theft accusations, 94, 96–7, 98, 105
Horwitz, Theodor, 103–4
Huebert, Abraham, 221, 222
Huebert, Johann, 37
Hutter, Jakob, 225
Hutterites: punishment of, 212–15; relocation of, 225–9. *See also* Hutterites, J.C. and

Hutterites, J.C. and: attitude toward, 225–6; effect of J.C.'s policies on Hutterites, 229; punishment of Hutterite, 212–15; and relocation of Hutterites, 225–9
Hutterthal, 208, 228

identity: crop agriculture and, 170; European vs. Asian Russia in, 85; modernization and, 252; Nicholas I and Russian identity, 157; of Russia, 85; state–Mennonite relationship and, 19, 252. *See also* Official Nationality
Imperial Geographical Society, 156
Inspector of Colonies, 44–5
Inzov, I.M., 55, 150, 151, 156, 160, 193, 198, 226
Iov, archbishop, 55–6
Islam, 86, 88, 175–6
isolationism. *See* separation from secular world
Iushanle: agricultural experimentation at, 177–8; Agricultural Society headquarters located at, 172; Alexander's visit to, 154; apprentices at, 219–20; brick and tile building style, 188; Agnes Cornies in, 166; crop agriculture at, 163; crop experimentation at, 171; as experimental farm, 172; Forestry Society headquarters on, 126; full ownership of, 82; as headquarters of J.C.'s activities, 166; housebarn, 41–2; J.C.'s acquisition of, 33–4, 35; and J.C.'s new villages locations, 53; Keppen and, 158; and laboratory of modernity, 177–8; as model, 154, 178; official visits to, 177–8; origins, 34; sheep raising, 42; shepherds at, 42; trees on, 126, 177–8
Iushanle River, 25, 26

Jantzen, Mark, 10
Janzen, Cornelius, 39–40
Jewish people: and agriculture, 241; identified as Romny bandits, 83, 84; and *Judenplan*, 240–3; Kahal, 213; Nicholas I and, 213; state policies regarding, 110
Johann Cornies: Der Sozialreformer aus den Steppen Südrusslands (Reimer), 250
John III Sobieski, king, 9
Judenplan, 240–3; J.C. and, 241–2
Jung-Stilling, Johann Heinrich, 89

Kaethler (Wernersdorf), 148
Kakbas, 129
Kalenitchenko, Pavel, 221–2
Kalmyk Tatars: Fadeev and, 138, 149, 172; J.C. and, 172, 174, 188–9; reform of, 163; and sheep raising, 174
Kalmykov, Ilarion, 185
Kapustin, Savelii, 46
Karass, 174
Kazan University, 110
Keppen, Petr: about, 156; and Akkerman, 218; and burial mounds, 156, 157–9; and crafts village, 168; and Crimean settlers as models to Tatar populations, 183; and Haxthausen, 180, 181; on Iushanle, 178; and J.C., 158, 217; J.C. and, 156, 157–9, 168, 183, 217; and J.C.'s death, 248; and Ministry of State Domains, 156; and model paradigm, 183; and Official Nationality, 156–7; official visit to Molochnaia, 177, 178; peasant surveys, 193; and Württemberg settlement, 231
Kherson, *Judenplan* village in, 241, 242, 243
Khortitsa Central School, 239

Khortitsa settlement: about, 24; Agricultural Society, 194, 239, 240; Cornies family in, 24–5; establishment of, 14, 24; Hutterites in, 225, 227; J.C. and, 239–40, 244; J.C. Jr. in, 141; Molochnaia compared to, 189; sheep-buying for, 102; Vistula Mennonites in, 14
Kirilovsky (J.C. Jr's tutor), 138–9
Kiselev, Pavel D.: commissioning of J.C.'s administrative study, 181, 193; and crafts village, 168; creation of Ministry of State Domains under, 138; and Haxthausen, 179; and Hutterite relocation, 226; and *Judenplan* villages, 241; in Khortitsa, 239; relationship with J.C., 3; support for J.C., 196; visit to Molochnaia, 193, 223
Kishinev, Guardianship Committee in, 16, 66
Klassen, Aganetha. *See* Cornies, Aganetha (née Klassen)
Klassen, Agatha. *See* Cornies, Agatha (née Klassen)
Klassen, Cornelius, 31
Klassen, Helena. *See* Cornies, Helena (née Klassen)
Klassen, Johann (Halbstadt), 38; cloth factory, 116–17, 118, 168–9, 188; in Cornies Party, 153
Klassen, Johann (Warkentin's brother-in-law): and *Gebietsamt*, 190, 191; as *Gebietsamt* mayor, 95, 101, 114, 190; Regier succeeding as mayor, 136; son as adjunct to, 204
Klassen, Johann (Warkentin's nephew and mayor of Münsterberg): disappearance from view, 204; disobedience of Agricultural Society, 190; Hahn's audience with, 196; J.C. and, 190,

191, 203; punishment of, 190–2, 194, 203; tour of 1842 attacking J.C. and A. Toews, 200
Klassen, Margaretha. *See* Cornies, Margaretha (née Klassen)
Kleine Gemeinde (Small Congregation), 54; Balzer as member, 131; emergence of, 41; formation of, 38; Friesen as elder of, 203, 214–15; J.C. and, 63, 132; Reimer as leader of, 41
Kochubei, Viktor P., 55, 82
Konstantin Nikolaevich, prince, 12, 55, 108, 222
Kozelsky, Mara, 186
Krahn, Cornelius, 38
Kurakin, Aleksei, 34
Kurushan River, 25, 26

laboratory of modernization: agricultural machinery and, 224; Akkerman as, 155; Forestry Society and, 125, 136; Iushanle estate as, 177–8; J.C.'s study of Mennonite administrative system and, 181; and *Judenplan*, 241; Mennonite settlements as, 4, 14, 151, 178; New Russia as, 13–14; in state–Mennonite relationship, 35, 107, 161; and Warkentin Affair, 187. *See also* modernization
Ladekopp, 135
land: confiscation/reallotment, 135; Forestry Society and, 145–7; fullholdings, 26, 145–6, 148–9, 167, 168; grants to nobility, 69–70; halfholdings, 167; Mennonite tradition, 146; and military service, 8, 11–12; ownership rights, 145–7; pacifism and, 8; Privilegium and, 17; Slavic peasants and, 146; transfers, 145–7, 167

land surveying, 38, 51–3, 68, 89; education and, 234; J.C. Jr. and, 139, 140; and land allocation, 140
landlessness, 167–8; and artisanship, 223; and Bergthal Mennonite settlement, 229; crisis of 1860s, 208; and daughter settlements, 174; and diversification of economy, 164, 168; and election of 1845, 208; and employment in cloth factory, 169; increase in, 145
Landskrone: brick and tile building style, 188; and election of 1845, 208
Lang, Jakob, 174
Lange, Friedrich Wilhelm, 144, 209–10, 214, 236
Lange, Henriette, 209–10
Lange, Wilhelm (Friedrich Wilhelm's cousin), 210–11
Lange, Wilhelm (Gnadenfeld elder), 142, 143, 144, 154, 155; death of, 209; Warkentin and, 156, 196
Lange family (Gnadenfeld), 209–12; J.C. and, 211–12
Langeron, count, 55, 70
Large Flemish Congregation: and Agricultural Society, 187; disbandment of, 187, 204, 251; division of, 187, 204–6, 208; dominance of, 215; and education, 237; formation of, 62, 72; and *Gebietsamt*, 152; Guardianship Committee and, 187; J.C. and, 94; Klassen as member of, 190; membership of, 114; Ministry of Internal Affairs' recognition of, 95–6; J. Neufeld as member, 196; numbers of families as members, 208; as obstacle to change, 215; opposition to outside interference in settlement, 98; and Pietism, 63; punishment of 70 members, 206; quietism of,

Large Flemish Congregation (*cont.*) 63; and state, 213; state approval, 112; and state interference, 63; state recognition of, 107; and state–Mennonite relationship, 63; students at school from, 122; Warkentin and, 62–3, 152, 204
Lavater, Johann Kaspar, 89, 91, 188; *Essays on Physiognomy*, 89–90
LeDonne, John, 14
Lemberg, 102
Lermontov, Mikhail, 173
Liberum Veto, 9
Lichtenau congregation, 197, 206
Lincoln, W. Bruce, 151
livestock, 28, 42, 78, 121, 130–1, 169. *See also* horses; sheep
Lizovzov, Mikhail, 119
Lutheran Church, Württembergers and, 231
Lutheran immigrants, 26; and church–state relationship, 15; students at Ohrloff school, 122

Magnitskii, M.L., 110
Maison, comte de, 70, 86–7, 218–19
Margenau: congregation, 205; Warkentin's conference in, 196–7
Mariupol: apprentices from, 175; for Bessarabia settlement, 112; J.C. leasing land in, 79, 112; livestock wintering in, 79
Marmont, Auguste de, 30, 179; and J.C., 179
Martens, Jacob, 165, 197, 201–2
Martens, Wilhelm: brandy distribution business, 43, 113–14, 153; in Cornies Party, 153; and Crown Prince Alexander's visit, 164–5; and Forestry Society, 127; and *Gebietsamt* monetary shortfall, 200; illness, 164–5; iron mill, 164; J.C. and, 43, 153, 164–5; J.C. on Moravian Brethren and, 102–3; J.C.'s friendship with, 23, 43; loan to Fadeev, 120; at Piatigorsk, 164–5; and sheep-buying in Saxony, 98; suicide, 165, 245; water mill, 164; wealth, 29, 43, 78
Melitopol, 14, 219, 253–4
Mennonite Brethren, 142, 187, 215, 233
Mennonite Commonwealth, 47
Mennonite Settlement Commission, 49, 51, 52, 60, 63, 65, 79, 131; J.C. and, 49, 52, 60, 63, 65, 79
Mennonite settlements: Guardianship Committee and, 15–16; as laboratories of modernity, 14; secular administrative structure, 35–6; secular vs. congregational administrative structures, 35. *See also* Molochnaia settlement
Mennonites: credit, and economic success, 114–15; Fadeev on, 124; idiosyncratic practices of, 37; and imperialism, 19; J.C.'s study of administrative system, 181–2; legacy of, 253–4; as model colonists, 13; Nicholas I and, 107; in Poland, 9–10; Russian recruitment of, 12–13. *See also* Flemish congregation; Frisian congregation; Mennonite Brethren; Molochnaia Mennonites; Prussian Mennonites; Vistula Mennonites
Mikhail Pavlovich, prince, 193
military service, 8, 11–12, 17
Miliutin, Nikolai, 3
Ministry of Education, 235
Ministry of Internal Affairs: Guardianship Committee and, 15, 137–8; and Large Flemish Congregation, 95; and Nogais, 129, 219; recordkeeping, 109–10; and Saxony sheep-buying trip, 95–6, 97

Ministry of Religious Affairs and Public Instruction (Dual Ministry), 54
Ministry of State Domains, 3; apprenticeship program, 175–6; attention to Mennonites, 21; creation of, 138, 182; and economic reforms, 138, 249; Fifth Department as, 151; Guardianship Committee and, 15–16, 171, 192–3, 217; Guardianship Committee as division of, 137–8; Hahn as Director of First Department, 248; and J.C., 158, 172, 217, 218; Keppen in, 156; Learned Committee, 156, 158, 172, 178, 252; and model forestry plantation, 219; and modernization, 182; and moving of Mennonite families to serve as local models, 186; and peasantry, 138, 218; and potato growing, 220–1. *See also* Fifth Department of Tsar's Own Chancellery
Mitskevich (Russian official), 221
model colonists/colony: in administrative system, 6; in agricultural modernization, 153; and Akkerman as model peasant village, 155, 218; and cameralism, 64–5; and change, 177; as "city upon a hill," 57–8; and "civilization" of Nogais, 85; cloth factory in, 168–9; and conflict among Mennonites, 41; crop experimentation and, 172; didactic model, 13, 34, 182–3, 218, 219; direct service vs., 242–3; and Fadeev/Cornies survey of peasant conditions, 173; failure of paradigm, 182–3; failure with Doukhobors, 184–6; as function of leadership vs. inherent industry, 183–4; German peasants as, 13; Haxthausen's study, 181; J.C. and, 215; J.C.'s insistence on Mennonites as, 177; and *Judenplan*, 241, 242; leadership vs. supervision in, 184; Mennonites as, 13, 178; and modernization, 161, 186; Molochnaia Mennonite settlement as, 50; and move of families to serve as models, 183, 186; Nogai Tatars and, 252–3; Privilegium and, 17, 41, 49, 95, 154, 177; Prussian Mennonites as, 6–7; and punishment, 206; and reforms, 154, 197; Saxony sheep-buying trip and, 97, 100; sheep raising and, 67–8; Slavic peasants and, 13, 252–3; state–Mennonite relationship and, 64, 177; as static vs. laboratory of modernity, 253; supervision vs. modelling in, 242; supervisory role vs., 244; and Tatar populations, 13, 183; Warkentin and, 189. *See also* privileges/Privilegium; state–Mennonite relationship
"Model of Christian Charity, A" (Winthrop), 57–8
modernization: Agricultural Society and, 182, 217; of agriculture, 167–76; crises and, 121; education and, 234; Enlightenment and, 57; forestry and, 125; and identity, 252; J.C. and, 217, 250; Mennonite immigrants and, 17; Ministry of State Domains and, 182; model paradigm and, 161, 186; Molochnaia Mennonite settlement's accomplishments in, 250; moneylending and, 114, 119, 122; Moravian Brethren and, 74; Nicholas I and, 107, 251; of peasantry, 181; Privilegium and, 18, 74; and Prussian-Mennonite

modernization (*cont.*)
emigrants, 53; religion/religious beliefs and, 250–1, 253; secularizing effect of, 250–1; separation from secular world and, 18, 19; state–Mennonite relationship and, 19, 74, 251. *See also* agricultural modernization; laboratory of modernization; reform(s)

Molochnaia Mennonites: as agents of state, 67–8; challenges of region to, 27–8; conservatism vs. liberalism of, 38; contributions to government during Napoleonic Wars, 38; and crisis of 1833, 121–2; and ecumenism, 56–7; engagement with local world, 38–9; and evangelism/evangelicalism, 57; as Flemish congregation members, 37; as laboratory of modernization, 4, 151; lack of unity among, 41; prosperity, 29; and quietism, 61; religious practices, 37, 142; Russian Bible Society and, 56–7; Schlatter on, 93; and secular punishments, 38; separation from world, 56–7, 61; split in church, 95–6; subsidies, 28; tax exemptions and, 28

Molochnaia River, 14, 25

Molochnaia settlement: agricultural accomplishments, 250; Alexander I's visit, 77, 78; Alexander's visit to, 48–9; Balzer on, 120; brick and tile building style in, 188–9; conditions facing immigrants, 16–17; congregational administrative structure, 39–41; Crimean Tatars compared, 252; differing religious expectations among, 37; fissures within, 47; freedom/independence of, 44–5, 46–7; Hutterite relationship with, 228; individual conscience and self-regulation system, 40–1; infighting in Ohrloff, 37; land grant, 25; Ministry of State Domains attention to, 21; Moravian Brethren compared to, 102–3; Moravian Brethren missionaries on, 26–7; as oasis, 43; as outlier, 21; prosperity/success of, 24, 43–4, 47, 50; Quaker visitors, 44; size of land grants, 50; three congregations in, 54; trees in, 134; and tsarist economic development, 250; village placement in, 52–3; Vladimir *guberniia* compared, 252. *See also* privileges/Privilegium

Molochnaia Society to Improve the School System, 239

Molokans, 26, 84

moneylending, 114–20, 127

Moravian Brethren: about, 74; Allen and, 74; Blüher and, 74; engagement with secular world, 75, 103; and evangelism, 103; Fadeev and, 172; Gnadenfeld Mennonites and, 143; in Herrnhut, 102–3; J.C. and, 75, 102–3, 143, 163, 173, 174–5; J.C. Jr. and, 165; missionaries in Molochnaia, 26–7; and modernization, 75; and Pietism, 75–6; Waldner and, 225

Moritz, Johann, 62

Mühlhausen, 5, 29

Muromtsev, M.M., 119, 179, 184–5

Napoleonic Wars, 24, 29, 38, 41, 44, 45, 50, 71

Neufeld, Heinrich: account of Warkentin Affair, 190–2, 195–6, 198, 202, 204; and division of Large Flemish Congregation, 205; as J.C.'s liaison with Large Flemish Congregation, 204–5; on punishment of Hutterite, 212,

213; on size of Large Flemish Congregation, 208
Neufeld, Johann (brandy distribution business manager), 114, 153
Neufeld, Johann (Halbstadt), mayoral candidate in 1845, 207–8
Neufeld, Johann (Heinrich's brother): Hahn–Warkentin meeting at home of, 203–4; as interim deputy mayor, 200; and Large Flemish Congregation, 205; Warkentin and, 196
Neu-Halbstadt craft village, 168, 223
Neumann, Jacob, 239
New Russia, 12; about, 6; agriculture in, 12; cameralism and, 64; ethnic diversity, 42; German peasant settlements in, 13; as laboratory of modernity, 13–14; location, 12; military colonies in, 49; population growth in, 169
newspapers, 121, 132, 133
Nicholas I, tsar, 3, 4, 14; accession to throne, 108; and afforestation, 124; and agriculture, 152–3; attitude toward Mennonites, 107; and cholera, 129; control of population, 136; Decembrists and, 77–8, 108; and European revolutions, 110; and Fifth Department of Tsar's Own Chancellery, 151; and forestry, 123, 125, 249; and German state, 14; Haxthausen and, 179, 180; and J.C., 111, 154; J.C. and, 111; and *Judenplan*, 240; on Kiselev, 181; and liberalism, 14, 108–9; Mennonite attitudes toward, 109; and Mennonites, 110; and modernization, 107; and nobility, 108–9, 110; and Official Nationality, 110–11, 136; and Orthodox Church, 110, 186, 213; and peasantry, 186; and penal code, 206; policies, and J.C.'s approach to public life, 111; and potato growing, 171; pressure on non-Slavic/non-Orthodox, 213; and Privilegiuim, 154; as reactionary conservative, 108; and reform, 136, 159, 251; reorganization of peasant administration, 137–8; and Russian Bible Society, 55; and Russianness, 157; single, unifying policy, 159, 240; travel to Crimea, 154; and Western industrial model, 152
Nickel, Jacob, 149
nobility/elites, 69–70; and Catholic Church, 110; co-option of, 4; Decembrist Revolt, 108; era of small reforms and, 137; moneylending to, 114; monopoly on state power, 20; Nicholas I and, 108–9, 110; in Poland, 9
Nogai Tatars: about, 25–6; and afforestation, 218–19; and agriculture, 154–5; Akkerman as model village, 177; at Aul, 221–2; cholera among, 129, 130; "civilization" of, 85–6, 88, 106, 154–5, 158, 163, 178, 182; crisis of 1824–5 and, 82; and didactic model, 218, 219; drought, and starvation among, 130–1; education of, 86, 90; evangelization of, 58, 60, 92–3; fatalism, 130; as grain haulers, 171; Guardian of, 86–7; Haxthausen on, 180; and horses, 35, 94–5; individual freedom among, 87; and J.C. Sr. as doctor, 29; and *Judenplan*, 241; Maison and, 70, 86–7; malleability of, 88; marriage customs, 33; and Mennonite-built wagons/carriages, 223; Ministry of Internal Affairs and,

Nogai Tatars (*cont.*)
129, 219; model paradigm and, 252–3; nomadism of, 88; and potato growing, 175, 221–2; Russian Bible Society and, 58; Schlatter and, 92–3; and sheep, 35, 155; treatment of women, 33, 166; and violence, 30. *See also* Nogai Tatars, J.C. and

Nogai Tatars, J.C. and: and afforestation, 218–19; Akkerman and laboratory of modernization, 155; and Akkerman as model village, 218, 221; and civilization of Nogais, 106, 154–5, 163, 218, 222; Epp on, 30; J.C.'s disengagement from, 218; J.C.'s study regarding, 84–9, 90; Lavater's views on education and, 90; on Maison as Guardian, 86–7; marriage customs, 33; Mennonite lack of impact on, 241; Pietism and, 106; and potato growing, 175; sheep raising, 218; study of, 84–9, 90, 91, 106; treatment of women, 166

None but Saints (Urry), 250

Odesa: Fadeev in, 120, 138, 149; Fletnitzer in, 234, 236; Guardianship Committee in, 16, 120, 149, 226; Hahn in, 193, 196; Ministry of Internal Affairs in, 96; Pelekh in, 228; Russian Bible Society in, 55, 70; Warkentin meeting with Hahn in, 196; wool market, 192

Official Nationality, 55, 110–11, 136, 156–7, 161, 179, 186, 252

Ohrloff: agricultural land, 26; church, 36, 188, 189; Cornies family and, 20; establishment of, 20, 25; founding of, 3; fullholdings in, 26; location of, 25; religious vs. security authority conflict in, 36–7; setting of, 26

Ohrloff school, 143; apprentices and, 175; A. Cornies in, 166; curriculum, 88; Frisian immigrants and, 60; Heese teaching at, 122, 123, 143, 239; J.C. and, 60, 234, 236; J.C. Jr. in, 123, 138, 166; Large Flemish Congregation and, 237; mission prayer meetings at, 63; Riediger teaching at, 234; T. Voth teaching at, 60, 63, 92, 122–3

Old Flemish Congregation, 63, 131, 142, 197; J.C. and, 63

O'Neill, Kelly, 14, 252, 253

Oppenländer (district mayor), 231

Orphan's Fund (*Waisenamt*), 115

Orthodox Church: apprentices from, 175–6; Catherine the Great and, 12; Catholicism vs., 110; dominance over religious life, 77; and Doukhobors, 46, 185; Golitsyn and, 54; Mennonites and, 111; Nicholas I and, 110, 186; Official Nationality and, 110–11; and Pietism, 77; power over religious attitudes, 56; Procurator of the Holy Synod, 54; and Russian Bible Society, 55; and Russian identity, 157

Ottoman Empire, 6, 12, 112

pacifism: Doukhobors and, 26; and land, 8; Mennonite, 37, 39; military service vs., 8, 11–12; Prussia and, 11; and punishment for crime, 84; Vistula Mennonites and, 10

Pale of Settlement, 240, 241

Pasha, Ali, 218–19

pasturage, 26

Paterson, John, 54–5, 59

patronage, 68–9, 71, 73, 82, 120, 135–6, 138, 158–9

Patterson, Alexander, 174

Paul I, tsar, 15, 17

peasantry: administrative reorganization regarding, 137–8; and agricultural machinery, 224; agriculture, 159; apprenticeship program for, 175–6; Bible distribution to, 59; cholera among, 129; crisis of 1824–25 and, 82; drought, and starvation among, 130; Fifth Department and, 151, 161; and forestry, 219; from German states, 13; Great Reforms of 1860s and, 186; J.C. on, 159; J.C.'s study of Mennonite administrative system as model for, 181–2; lack of leadership among, 159; and land, 146; laws of 1797 regarding, 51; Mennonite lack of impact on, 241; military colonies and, 6; Ministry of State Domains and, 138; model colonies for, 13, 252–3; modernization of, 181; potato growing, 171, 175, 221; reform of, 53, 151, 152, 161; and serfdom, 69; settlement of New Russia, 12; subsidies to Ukrainian, 28; surveys of, 151, 172–5, 193; as wards of state, 69

Pelekh, Khariton: and elections of 1841–2, 201; Guardianship Committee district inspector, 192; Hahn and, 228; and Hutterite relocation, 227, 228; and Klassen's punishment, 191; reassignment to Odesa, 228; and Warkentin Affair, 195, 196, 198; and Württemberg settlement, 232

Penal Code (1845), 206

Penner, Jacob, 102, 194, 196, 200; J.C. and, 194, 195, 200

Penner, Wilhelm, 230

Pestalozzi, Johann Heinrich, 236

Peter the Great, 64, 69, 70

Petershagen, 36

"Philosophical Letter" (Chaadaev), 85

Piatigorsk, 164–5, 173

Pietism, 11, 17; among Russian Mennonites, 4; and art, 139; as balance between belief and imperial ambition, 76; Balzer and, 132; and civilization, 57; congregational dispute over, 105; Contenius and, 46; and ecumenism, 89; and education, 11, 59, 238; and engagement with larger world, 11; Enlightenment and, 189; Epp and, 61; and evangelism, 11, 38, 57; Flemish congregation and, 11, 54, 61; Frisian congregation and, 11, 63; Gnadenfeld community and, 61, 142–3, 144; Gnadenfeld congregation and, 215; Golitsyn and, 54; Large Flemish Congregation and, 63; and Mennonite Brethren, 187, 215; and modernization, 189; Moravian Brethren and, 74, 75–6; Old Flemish Congregation and, 63; and ordering of nature, 189; Orthodox Church and, 77; in Prussia, 11; of Prussian Mennonites, 53–4; Prussian-Mennonite emigrants of 1818–22 and, 54; quietism vs., 250–1; Schlatter and, 89; in Switzerland, 89; of T. Voth, 122–3; Warkentin Affair and, 187; Warkentin and, 63; Württemberg settlement and, 231, 232, 233. *See also* Pietism, J.C. and

Pietism, J.C. and, 250–1; and changes in Mennonite religious life, 249; cholera epidemic and, 130; and civilization of Nogais, 106; compared to J.C.'s engagement with state, 64; D. Epp and, 61, 103; "General Rules" and, 238; illness and, 104; in letter to J.C. Jr., 141–2;

Pietism, J.C. and (*cont.*)
meaning for J.C., 61; Moravian Brethren and, 75–6, 103; Prussian Mennonite disunity and, 112; Schlatter and, 93; Smissen and, 103; and Voth, 63
Polish Mennonites, 37
Polish Rebellion (1830), 197
Pordenau congregation, 206
potato growing: machinery for, 223–4; Ministry of State Domains and, 171–2, 220–1; Nicholas I and, 171; in Nogai villages, 221–2; in peasant villages, 175, 221; supervision of, 242
Prinz, Friedrich, 231–2, 233
privileges/Privilegium: about, 17; Alexander and, 50–1; centrality to politics, 159; confirmation of, 95; Contenius and, 46; and Cornies–Warkentin dispute, 154; and corporal punishment order, 213–14; and engagement with society, 19; Fadeev and, 126; *Gebietsamt* and, 36; Guardianship Committee and, 125, 192; Hahn and, 216; and immigration of 1818–22, 50–1; and independence, 44–5; and individualism vs. community as single unit, 41; J.C. and, 215; and land grants, 17; loss of, 71, 127–8; and Mennonite way of life, 152; military service exemption in, 17, 36; and modernization, 18, 74; Nicholas I and, 154; and punishment, 194, 206; and religious beliefs/practices, 17; rights and obligations in, 36; single corporate identity in, 95; state official control over, 177; and state service, 51; supervisory role and, 244; of Vistula Mennonites, 9–10; Warkentin and, 75, 100;
Warkentin Party and, 152, 159; withdrawal from world and, 18. *See also* model colonists/colony; state–Mennonite relationship
Protestant Bible Society, 56, 234
Prussian Mennonite Church: controversy, 103–4, 111–12; Epp and, 61, 111–12; J.C. and, 112; Schlatter on, 93; state intrusion into affairs, 104; worldliness of, 41
Prussian Mennonites: Alexander and, 49, 50; Balzer and, 121; emigration to Russia, 49; and Flemish congregation, 54; and Frisian congregation, 53–4, 63; J.C. and, 112; letters to, denouncing J.C., 208–9; as model colonists, 6–7; Napoleonic Wars and, 50; Pietism of, 53–4; and Warkentin Affair, 208–9
Prussian-Mennonite immigrants (1818–22): about, 53–4; J.C. and, 51–3; Pietism of, 54; and Privilegium, 50–1; and reform, 53, 54; and Russian Bible Society, 58; state–Mennonite relationship and, 49, 50–3
punishment(s): agricultural crisis as God's, 105; congregational discipline vs., 210–11; congregational vs. secular authority for, 191–2, 194, 196, 198; corporal, 10, 39, 160, 202, 206, 212–13, 238; crises as, 121; of Hutterite, 212–15; individual conscience/self-regulation system of, 40–1; J.C. and, 238; of Klassen, 190–1, 194, 202; of Large Flemish Congregation members, 206; model colonists and, 206; privileges and, 206; for rebellion, 197; secular, 38; state vs. congregational, 40–1; of Thun, 202, 206, 213; of Warkentin, 201. *See also* banning
Puritans, 58

Quakerism, 44, 45, 58–9
quietism, 38, 61, 62–3, 135, 215, 250–1
Quiring, Heinrich, 117, 149

Radishchev, 225, 227, 229
Raeff, Marc, 64
Ratzlaff, Benjamin, 155, 211, 214
Razumovskii, A.K., 55
reform(s): aesthetic, 188; agricultural crises and, 197; Cornies Party and, 127; elder authority vs., 162; era of small, 137, 187, 251, 252, 253; as God's vs. secular will, 136, 198; Great Drought and, 145; Great Reforms of 1860s, 151, 156; Guardianship Committee and, 249; J.C. and Forestry Society and, 144–5; lack of bureaucracy and, 65, 159; mayors and, 159–60; Mennonites as models for, 154; Ministry of State Domains and, 138, 249; model colony and, 197; Molochnaia Mennonites as showcase for, 151; moneylending and, 121–2; peasants and, 53, 151, 161; Prussian-Mennonite immigrants of 1818–22 and, 53, 54; state–Mennonite relationship and, 135; Warkentin and, 62, 192. *See also* modernization
Regier, Abraham, 208–9
Regier, Johann, 114, 129, 136, 156, 160, 163, 194, 195, 200
Reimer, David, 219
Reimer, Johannes, *Johann Cornies: Der Sozialreformer aus den Steppen Südrusslands*, 250
Reimer, Klaas, 37, 38, 39–40, 41
Reimer, Peter, 225
religious beliefs/practices: adult baptism, 8, 61, 91; and agricultural crisis as God's punishment, 105; agricultural modernization as worldliness, 72; apprentices and, 175–6; on cholera epidemic, 135; differing religious expectations and, 37; of Doukhobors, 26, 45, 184; economic activities as reflection of, 153; of Frisian vs. Flemish congregations, 10–11; on Great Drought, 135; imitation of early Christian communities, 161–2; life modelled on biblical precepts, 90; marriage, 31–3; in Molochnaia settlement, 37, 142; non-violence, 213; on ostentation, 189; patriarchal, 40; personal wealth and community responsibility, 79–80; Polish Mennonites and, 37; Privilegium and, 17; on punishment, 191, 213; self-discipline, 8; separation from secular world, 11
"Reorganisation of the Administration of the Colonists," 136, 182
Richelieu, duc de, 13, 70
Riediger, Martin, 234
Ritterakademie, Halle, 11
Romny, 83–4
Rosen (Ministry of State Domains), 193, 217, 219, 221
Rudnerweide congregation, 197
Russian Bible Society: about, 54; Alexander I and, 55; branches, 55–6; closure, 56; and conservative Mennonites, 61; and Cornies–Warkentin dispute, 153; and ecumenism, 55, 56; and evangelicalism/evangelism, 57, 59; founding of, 54, 55; and frontier administration, 56; Golitsyn and, 54, 56; Heese as member, 122; J.C. and, 60, 63; Kochubei and, 82; Langeron

Russian Bible Society (*cont.*)
and, 70; Magnitskii and, 110; Molochnaia chapter, 59–60; Orthodox Church and, 56; Prussian-Mennonite immigrants of 1818–22 and, 58; and Quaker visitors, 58–9; Schlatter and, 92; Warkentin and, 72. *See also* British and Foreign Bible Society (BFBS)

Russian Mennonites, 4, 6–7

Russian–Ottoman Empire war, 112

Russification: accommodation with diversity vs., 243; education and, 235; Mennonites and, 252

Russo-Turkish wars, 12

Sailer, Johann Michael, 89

Sarepta: as beachhead for missionary work, 74; A. Cornies in, 166; J.C. in, 173, 174–5; J.C. Jr. in, 166; Moravian Brethren at, 74, 164, 173; sheep raising in, 173, 174–5

Saxony, sheep buying in, 82–3, 97–104, 105–6

Schellenberg (buyer of Martens's water mill), 164

Schlachta, Astrid von, 229

Schlatter, Daniel: about, 89, 91; and adult baptism, 91; arrival in Molochnaia, 89; on August 1824 storm, 79; criticism of Mennonite society, 93; and Dohna and Moravian Brethren, 102; and ecumenism, 91, 142; evangelization of Nogais, 92–3; financial donations to, 91; on Flemish congregation, 38; Heese and, 122; Horwitz and, 103–4; illness and convalescence, 104; individualism of philosophy, 93; and J.C., 89, 93, 106; J.C. and, 89, 91, 92–3, 106; Lavater and, 89–90; as missionary, 91, 92; and Molochnaia Mennonites, 92–3; Moravian Brethren compared to, 103; and Pietism, 89, 142; as secondary school teacher, 59–60

Schlatter, Kasper, 60

Schleiermacher, Friedrich, 89

Schmidt, Peter, 116

schools: Agricultural Society and, 235; elementary, 143; funding, 60; Gnadenfeld congregation, and teachers, 143; J.C., and quality of teaching, 235–8; Mennonite conservatives and, 59; as model for other foreign settlers, 235; Nogai, 86; Quaker visitors and, 59; secondary, 59, 122, 143–4; secular, 88; teachers training, 143, 144; Teaching Service (*Lehrdienst*), 15. *See also* education; Ohrloff school

Schrader, Abby, 206

Scott, James C., 125

Scottish Missionary Society, 174

Second Great Awakening, 4, 54

Secret or Unofficial Committee, 55

Sect of Nazareth, 233

Seegel, Steve, 52

Sejm, 9

separation from secular world, 153; and agriculture, 17–18; and community identity, 16–17; evangelism vs., 11; modernization vs., 18, 19; Molochnaia Mennonites and, 56–7, 61; and state–Mennonite relationship, 18, 64; Warkentin and, 62–3. *See also* engagement with secular world

Serebrennikov, Amvrosii, 45

sheep: barn-feeding, 165; blizzards and, 79; buying in Saxony, 82–3, 97–104, 105–6; buying in St. Petersburg, 71–5; Contenius and, 97; Cornies family holdings, 42; crop agriculture vs., 169–70, 192; Great

Drought and, 168; Guardianship Committee and, 34; herd growth, 116; improvement program, 34–5; at Iushanle, 42; J.C. and, 34, 42, 67; kurdiuch, 34–5, 67; Martens and, 98; merino, 34–5, 67; and model colony, 67–8; Moravian Brethren and, 173, 174–5; Nogais and, 25, 35, 155, 218; raising, vs. grain growing, 34; and state–Mennonite relationship, 67–8. *See also* wool

Sheep Society, 252
Siemens, Johann, 239, 240
silk manufacture, 171
Simons, Menno, 4, 6, 7
Slavic peasantry. *See* peasantry
Small Congregation (*Kleine Gemeinde*). See *Kleine Gemeinde* (Small Congregation)
Smissen, Jacob van der, 103
Smith, Alison, 171
Smith-Peter, Susan, 137, 252
Sparrau house fires, 188
Spener, Philipp Jakob, 11
Speranskii, Mikhail, 55
Spittler, Christian Friedrich, 89
St. Petersburg, J.C.'s travel to, 71–5, 78
Starr, S. Frederick, 180
state peasants. *See* peasantry
state–Mennonite relationship: adult baptism in, 8; and agricultural reform, 72; agriculture in, 98; and congregational administrative structure, 35; congregational split and, 95–6; congregational vs. secular authority for punishment in, 198; Contenius/Fadeev on J.C.'s leadership role in, 78; control in, 109–10, 136, 137; cooperation vs. co-option in, 164; creative engagement in, 75; and cultural practices, 253; and divisions among Mennonites, 199; education and, 59; end of Napoleonic Wars and, 46; and failure of didactic model, 182–3; Forestry Society in, 128; fullholdings in, 145–6; and identity, 252; independence in, 251; intra-congregational disputes in, 211–12, 214; J.C. as agent within, 52; and *Judenplan* villages, 243; and laboratory of modernization, 107, 161; and land transfers, 147; Large Flemish Congregation and, 63, 107; mayors in, 159; and Mennonite identity, 19; and Mennonite secular administrative structure, 36; and Mennonite settlements as laboratories of modernity, 14; Mennonite supervisors as state employees, 242; and Mennonites as agents of state, 65, 67–8; Mennonites as initiators in, 44–5; Ministry of State Domains vs. Guardianship Committee in, 192–3; and modernization/reforms, 19, 74, 135, 251; Official Nationality and, 110–11; Pietism and, 105; in Prussia, 104; and Prussian-Mennonite emigration of 1818–22, 49, 50–3; punishment in, 191–2, 213; recordkeeping and, 109–10; religion vs. economy in, 152; and religious beliefs, 253; self-discipline and, 8; separation from world and, 18, 64; and service to tsar, 75; sheep raising and, 67–8; single corporate identity within, 95; state-defined policies in, 243; subsidies and, 28; Warkentin and, 72, 152, 161–2, 187, 213. *See also* laboratory of modernization; model colonists/colony; privileges/Privilegium; separation from secular world

Steinbach school, 143, 144, 234
Stempel, Carl, 230, 231, 232, 233
Steven, Christian: and crop agriculture, 171, 222; J.C. and, 217; and J.C.'s death, 248; J.C.'s growing assertiveness toward, 172; Keppen and, 156; and Mennonite-built equipment, 222–3, 224
Stoler, Ann Laura, 13
Strolle, Johan, 233
Studies on the Interior of Russia (Haxthausen), 179–81
Sudermann, Hermann, 219, 220
Sunderland, Willard, 14, 186

Tashchenak: brick and tile building style, 188; brickworks, 229; Hutterites and, 226, 227; J.C. Jr. at, 165, 166
Tatar populations: Crimean settlers as models to, 183; evangelism among, 57; model colonies and, 13; Molochnaia Mennonites compared to Crimean, 252
Tavria State Agrotechnical University, 254
Tavrida, *Judenplan* village in, 241
teachers. *See* schools
Teleskop, 85
Thiessen, Anna, 40, 41
Thiessen, Franz, 40, 41
Thiessen, Therese. *See* Cornies, Therese (formerly Thiessen)
Third Department of Tsar's Own Chancery, 109
Thun, Dirk: flogging of, 206, 213, 225, 251; keeping to home, 207; and Large Flemish Congregation disbandment, 205; tree planting, 147, 148, 190; Warkentin and, 194, 200, 203

Toews, Abraham, 195, 200, 204, 206
Toews, Abram, 156, 160
Toews, Heinrich, 206
Toews, Peter, 194–6, 198, 200–1, 204, 205, 206, 207
Tokmak River, 25
tree planting. *See* afforestation
Tsaritsyn, 174
Tsarskoe Selo, 72, 74; Lycée, 193

Unterhaltungsblatt für deutsche Ansiedler im südlichen Rußland, 248
Urry, James, *None but Saints*, 250
Uvarov, Sergei, 55, 110, 156

Venger, Natalia, 125, 250
Vishlenkova, Elena, 55
Vistula Mennonites, 111; about, 7–8; congregational administrative system, 15; Cornies family as, 3; divisions among, 10; Flemish congregation, 9–11; integration into Prussian secular life, 111; Khortitsa settlement, 14; and market economy, 18; in Molochnaia, 14; pacifism, 10; privileges, 9–10; under Prussian rule, 10, 11–12; in Russia compared to Poland, 10
Visvanathan, Shiv, 14
Vladimir *guberniia*, 252
Voht, Franz, 148
Vorontsov, general, 179, 186
Voth, David and Mrs. David, 117
Voth, Tobias, 60, 63, 92, 122–3, 143–4; J.C. and, 60, 63, 122–3, 144

Waldheim: and election of 1845, 208; Lange family and congregation in, 210–11, 212
Waldner, Johannes, 225
Walther, Jacob, 225

Warkentin, Diedrich, 119
Warkentin, Dierk, 127
Warkentin, Dirk, 206
Warkentin, Jacob: about, 62–3; Agricultural Society and, 155–6, 187, 198; approved in position, 112; and brick and tile construction, 189; and Christian School Association, 63; conservatism of, 152; disappearance from public life, 204, 206–7; and J. Dyck, 194; and education, 144; on elders vs. secular authority, 198; and elections of 1838, 159–61; and elections of 1841, 194–6; and *Gebietsamt*, 95, 114; Guardianship Committee and, 187; Hahn and, 196, 198, 200, 201, 203–4, 224; and Inzov, 160; and J. Klassen, 95, 101, 190, 205; and Large Flemish Congregation, 62, 152; and Margenau meeting, 196–7; and Mennonite punishment, 192; and model colony concept, 65; and official recognition of Large Flemish Congregation, 96; opposition to outside interference in settlement, 98; and Pietism, 63; and Privilegium, 75; punishment of, 192, 201; quietism of, 62–3; and reforms, 192; Regier on removal of, 208–9; and religious vs. secular authority, 198; and state–Mennonite relationship, 64, 161–2; success/popularity of, 62; and Thun, 194; and P. Toews, 194, 195, 196; and worldliness, 72. *See also* Warkentin, Jacob, J.C. and

Warkentin, Jacob, J.C. and: antipathy of J.C., 128; brandy distribution business and, 114; brick and tile construction and, 189; and Fast letter regarding Margenau Conference, 196–8; history of dispute, 153–4; and J.C.'s resignation from *Gebietsamt* duties, 97; J.C.'s service leading to conflict with Warkentin, 94; leadership contest between, 151; letter of apology from J.C. to Warkentin, 201–2; and Margenau conference, 196–7; meetings, 202–3; Privilegium as central to dispute between, 154; and punishment of J. Klassen, 194; on Regier's letters regarding Warkentin's removal, 208–9; and split of Large Flemish Congregation, 205; stolen horse accusations, 97; as threatening J.C.'s influence, 94; Warkentin as foil to J.C., 62; Warkentin on J.C.'s activities, 63; and Warkentin's beliefs, 197

Warkentin Affair, 163, 215; bitterness remaining, 207; and dismissal of Warkentin, 204; elections of 1841–2, 193–5, 198–200, 201, 206; end of, 206–7; Enns and, 201–2; Fast and, 196–7, 200, 201–2; D. Friesen and, 194, 195; Hahn and, 198–200, 201, 207, 209; J.C. and, 195–6, 197–200, 206, 207, 209, 215–16; laboratory of modernization and, 187; and Large Flemish Congregation disbandment, 204; Margenau conference and, 196–7; J. Martens and, 201–2; and Mennonite Brethren, 187; H. Neufeld and, 196, 200; J. Neufeld and, 196, 200, 203–4; Pelekh and, 196, 198, 201; Penner and, 194, 195, 200; and Pietism, 187; Prussian Mennonites and, 208–9; punishment of

Warkentin Affair (*cont.*)
　Klassen and, 190–1, 194, 202, 238;
　Thun and, 190, 206, 251; A. Toews
　and, 195, 200, 204, 206; P. Toews
　and, 194, 195–6, 198, 200–1, 204,
　205, 206, 207; Wiens and, 205–6,
　209, 212, 214–15, 251
Warkentin Party: about, 152; and
　Agricultural Society, 191; and
　brick and tile building style, 188;
　conservatism of, 152; and economic
　activities as religious beliefs, 153;
　and *Gebietsamt*, 156; and Mennonite
　punishment, 191; and Privilegium,
　152, 159; return to power, 248; and
　separation from world, 153; and
　state intervention, 152
Wedel, Peter, 54, 155, 196, 211
Wernersdorf, 148
Wieb, Abram, 116, 127
Wiebe, Abram, 171
Wiebe, Dirk, 212
Wiebe, Johann, 130, 131, 246
Wiebe, Philipp, 166–7, 209, 246–8;
　J.C. and, 166–7
Wiens, Heinrich, 205–6, 209, 212,
　214–15, 251; J.C. and, 212–16
Wiens, Klaas, 36
Willms, Johanna. *See* Cornies,
　Johanna (formerly Willms)
Winthrop, John, "A Model of
　Christian Charity," 57–8

withdrawal. *See* separation from
　secular world
women: inheritance, 210; J.C.
　and treatment of, 33, 166, 210;
　lack of knowledge regarding
　contributions of, 5; marriage
　customs and, 31–3; workload, 29
Woodcock, George, 45
wool, 167; banditry on way to markets,
　83–4; Blüher and, 83; Great Drought
　and shortages in, 168; improvement
　societies, 66; J.C. and Martens
　marketing, 43; local vs. Moscow
　sales, 115–16; moneylending for
　trade, 115–16; prices, 67, 167, 192,
　218; quality improvement, 67–8;
　selling in regional markets vs.
　Moscow, 83–4; sheep, 34, 35; shift
　from wool to grain economy, 116;
　tariffs, 192. *See also* sheep
Wool Improvement Society (Sheep
　Society), 66–7, 68, 71, 72, 79, 116,
　123, 150–1
Württemberg, Henriette, duchess
　of, 89
Württemberg settlement, 231–3; J.C.
　and, 231–2
Wüst, Eduard Hugo Otto,
　144, 233

Zaporizhzhe, 14
Zhikharev, Fatei, 185

TSARIST AND SOVIET MENNONITE STUDIES

General Editor: Harvey L. Dyck, Department of History, University of Toronto

A Mennonite in Russia: The Diaries of Jacob D. Epp, 1851–1880. Edited and translated by Harvey L. Dyck.

Ingrid I. Epp and Harvey L. Dyck, *The Peter J. Braun Russian Mennonite Archive, 1803–1920: A Research Guide.*

David G. Rempel with Cornelia Rempel Carlson, *A Mennonite Family in Tsarist Russia and the Soviet Union, 1789–1923.*

John R. Staples, *Cross-Cultural Encounters on the Ukrainian Steppe: Settling the Molochna Basin, 1783–1861.*

Anne Konrad, *Red Quarter Moon: A Search for Family in the Shadow of Stalin.*

Jacob A. Neufeld, *Path of Thorns: Soviet Mennonite Life under Communist and Nazi Rule.* Edited, with an introduction and analysis, by Harvey L. Dyck. Translated from the German by Harvey L. Dyck and Sarah Dyck.

Transformation on the Southern Ukrainian Steppe: Letters and Papers of Johann Cornies, Volume 1: 1812–1835. Translated by Ingrid I. Epp and edited by Harvey L. Dyck, Ingrid I. Epp, and John R. Staples.

Minority Report: Mennonite Identities in Imperial Russia and Soviet Ukraine Reconsidered, 1789–1945. Edited by Leonard G. Friesen.

Transformation on the Southern Ukrainian Steppe: Letters and Papers of Johann Cornies, Volume 2: 1836–1842. Translated by Ingrid I. Epp and edited by Harvey L. Dyck, Ingrid I. Epp, and John R. Staples.

Leonard G. Friesen, *Mennonites in the Russian Empire and the Soviet Union: Through Much Tribulation.*

John R. Staples, *Johann Cornies, the Mennonites, and Russian Colonialism in Southern Ukraine.*

www.ingramcontent.com/pod-product-compliance
Ingram Content Group UK Ltd.
Pitfield, Milton Keynes, MK11 3LW, UK
UKHW042030130825
461675UK00016B/88/J